PRAISE FOR

Retelling Sacred Stories

Our Journeys to a Shared Sacred Story

EXCERPTED FROM REVIEWS OF INDIVIDUAL STORIES*

A Telling of a Shared Sacred Story
Journeys to the Sacred

"This strikingly beautiful story resonates powerfully with my Christian experience of God's Love, which grounds me in solidarity for the shared sacred flourishing of all." **—H.E. Cardinal John Onaiyekan**

"A masterpiece in which almost each sentence stands as an epigram, an aphorism, capable of touching one's heart. . . . It can (re)ignite spiritual longing in every person who reads it." —**Diwakar Ancharya**, Professor, All Souls College, Oxford University

"In my language, this story is *mashkiki*—the medicine of the spirit. It comes at just the right time." **—Elder Dominique (T8aminik) Rankin (Kapiteotak)**, Anishinabe Hereditary Chief, Canada

"Meets very successfully the challenge of being shareable as a sacred story for any spiritual . . . faith." **—Robert A. F. Thurman**, Jey Tsongkhapa Professor Emeritus, Columbia University

"A cornucopia of wisdom." **—Cyprian Consiglio, OSB**, Secretary General, Monastic Interreligious Dialogue

"I'm grateful . . . to those around the globe who embody . . . this sacred story." **—Tessa Bielecki**, Co-Director, The Desert Foundation

"Profound and . . . compelling . . . speaking meaningfully to the present." **—Sharon A. Suh**, Professor of Buddhism, Seattle University

*Full reviews can be found at www.fetzer.org.

"A fascinating story open to science, about the really important questions beyond it." —**Denis Alexander**, Emeritus Director, The Faraday Institute for Science and Religion

"The harmony of science and religion is . . . here brought to life." —**Iain McGilchrist**, Quondam Fellow of All Souls College, University of Oxford

"A true insight on the *ordo armoris*." —**Jonathan Lewis-Jong**, Editor, *Cambridge Elements in Psychology of Religion*

"Sacred traditions and . . . scientific inquiry . . . spring . . . from the same awareness." —**Mark Vernon**, Psychotherapist and Writer

"Our challenge . . . is to harmonize deep exploration of nature . . . with a spiritual orientation to life." —**Philip Goyal**, Theoretical Physicist, University at Albany, SUNY

"Offers a course of spiritual exercise for people from all walks of life." —**Erin M. Cline**, Distinguished Professor, Georgetown University

"I have not encountered a short work of fiction . . . better suited to helping us confront . . . our current dilemmas." —**Matthew T. Lee**, Professor of the Social Sciences and Humanities, Baylor University

"This penetrating story reminds us, and we forget it at a great cost, that love is the gateway to the transcendent for which we exist." —**Nick Spencer**, Senior Fellow, Theos

"Invites the reader into a contemplative space where life, consciousness, and cosmos can be unified in one sacred story." —**Nidhal Guessoum**, Astrophysicist, American University of Sharjah, UAE

"A hopeful vision of being human in a scientific age." —**Pui Him Ip**, The Faraday Institute for Science and Religion

"Movingly and bravely conveys humankind's fundamental mutuality." —**Salley Vickers**, Prize-winning Author

A Retelling of the Buddhist Sacred Story
Kisa Gotami

"Beautiful . . . profound insight into Buddhist teachings . . . I cannot wait to share this story with my students!" —**Sharon A. Suh**, Professor of Buddhism, Seattle University

"Rarely have I seen such a clear and concise introduction to the essence of Buddhism." —**Thupten Jinpa**, Principal Translator for H.H. Dalai Lama XIV

"Captures the essence of Buddhism—our deep interconnectedness and shared well-being." —**Rev. Kosho Niwano**, President Designate, Rissho Kosei-kai

"A vivid portrayal of the Buddha's compassionate engagement with ordinary people." —**Venerable Gijun Sugitani**, Chief Priest of Myoho-in Temple, Tendai Tradition

A Retelling of the Christian Sacred Story
Dialog in a Desert Place

"This bold, ecumenically sensitive, and biblically rooted fictional story points all readers to the living experience of Christ's Love behind the Church's mission of Love."
—**H.E. Metropolitan Emmanuel Chalcedon**

"We discover Jesus . . . with a boundless salvation of compassion, forgiveness, and hope." —**Christine MacMillan**, Senior Advisor, World Evangelical Alliance

"This timeless story remains relevant, and its power to transform lives is matchless." —**Sheran Harper**, Worldwide President, Mothers' Union, Anglican Communion

A Retelling of the Confucian Sacred Story
When the Fire Came

"The perfect way to show Confucianism in its best light."
—**Daniel A. Bell**, Professor of Political Theory, University of Hong Kong

"An inspiring, creative presentation of the Confucian tradition and its rich resources for... realizing our common humanity." —**Erin M. Cline**, Distinguished Professor, Georgetown University

"It invites us all to become more caring, responsible, and respectful global citizens." —**Ann Pang-White**, Professor of Philosophy, University of Scranton

"A moving experience of the Confucian tradition... that will inspire further exploration." —**P. J. Ivanhoe**, Professor, East Asian Languages and Cultures, Georgetown University

A Retelling of the Hindu Sacred Story
Maitreyi's Quest

"Gives the seeker a taste of the many paths that lead to self-realization."
—**Acharya Shrivatsa Goswami**, Sri Radharamana Mandir, Director of the Vraja Prakalpa

"This retelling... is needed for the survival of humanity and Mother Earth."
—**His Holiness Sri Sri Sugunendra Theertha Swamiji**, Abbot, Sri Puthige Matha

"Creatively conceptualized and elegantly written." —**Vasudha Narayanan**, Professor, Department of Religion, University of Florida

"A profound range of Hindu concepts and practices."
—**Swami Atmapriyananda**, Pro-Chancellor and Secretary, Ramakrishna Mission Vivekananda Educational and Research Institute

"The creative tension between the immanent and the transcendental... is the crest-jewel of the story." —**Swamini Svatmavidyananda Saraswati**

A Retelling of Indigenous Sacred Stories
Kindred Spirits

"Delightful… spiritually profound and humorous."
—Sakej Youngblood Henderson, Fellow, Royal Society of Canada

A Telling of an Interspiritual Sacred Story
Season of Remembrance

"This gorgeous narrative points us to the sacred stream."
—Cyprian Consilgio, OSB, Secretary General, Monastic Interreligious Dialogue

"Reading it opened my heart and evoked tears of remembering, recognition, and insight." **—Rabbi Tirzah Firestone**, Rabbi Emerita of Congregation Nevei Kodesh

"This story of shared experiences kindles the flame of the human heart."
—Venerable Pannavati Maha-Theri, founder of Heartwood Refuge

A Retelling of the Sacred Story of Islam
Surrendering to the Merciful Will of God

"A good introduction to some of Islam's most profound meanings and teachings, particularly those related to spiritual elevation, facing life with love and patience, and reliance on God. . . . It also portrays Muslims in their true image." **—H.E. Shaykh Abdalla bin Bayyah**, President of the United Arab Emirates Fatwa Council and the Abu Dhabi Forum for Peace

"This is the message that the world needs today."
—H.E. Shawki Ibrahim Abdel-Karim Allam, Former Grand Mufti of Egypt

"Demonstrates that . . . what is best for us may be hidden somewhere we least expect." **—H.E. Raja Naji Makawi**, Morocco's Ambassador to the Holy See

"A magnificent narrative and a profound vision that deeply moves the heart."
—Noor-ul-Haq Qadri, Former Pakistan Minister of Religious Affairs and Interfaith Harmony

A Retelling of the Jewish Sacred Story
A Saga of Life and Faith

"Very fine and original. . . . The continuity of both faith and tradition, from Abraham to the Holocaust and beyond."
—Rabbi Arthur Green, Hebrew College, Newton, MA

"Wonderful. . . . Between the lines we receive an inkling of the mysterious ways of God, ultimately leading to salvation, affirmed for all humanity."
—Rabbi Daniel Sperber, Professor of Talmud, Bar Ilan University, Israel

"Invites us to reconnect with a commitment to faith and the dignity of life that illuminates the darkest realities." **—Rabbi Silvina Chemen**, Marshall T. Meyer Latin American Rabbinical Seminary

"The protagonists guide the reader to . . . Judaism's sense of the Divine presence and purpose." **—Rabbi Julie Schonfeld**, CEO Emerita of The Rabbinical Assembly

"The sacredness of the human condition is evident when the choice is made to protect and save the lives of others." **—Rabbi David Saperstein**, Director Emeritus, Religious Action Center of Reform Judaism

A Retelling of Sikh Sacred Wisdom
The House by the Sea

"By gently illuminating the rich legacy of the Sikh Gurus, this story reattunes us to timeless virtues." **—Bhai Sahib, Bhai Mohinder Singh**, Chair, Guru Nanak Nishkam Sewak Jatha

"Divinely portrays the virtues of the Preserver, Liberator, Benevolent and Boundless." **—Neelam Kaur**, Advisor, The Kalgidhar Trust

Retelling Sacred Stories

Retelling Sacred Stories

OUR JOURNEYS TO A SHARED SACRED STORY

The Fetzer Institute

ORBIS BOOKS
Maryknoll, New York 10545

Founded in 1970, Orbis Books endeavors to publish works that enlighten the mind, nourish the spirit, and challenge the conscience. The publishing arm of the Maryknoll Fathers and Brothers, Orbis seeks to explore the global dimensions of the Christian faith and mission, to invite dialogue with diverse cultures and religious traditions, and to serve the cause of reconciliation and peace. The books published reflect the views of their authors and do not represent the official position of the Maryknoll Society. To learn more about Maryknoll and Orbis Books, please visit our website at www.orbisbooks.com.

Published by Orbis Books, Box 302, Maryknoll, NY 10545-0302.

Manufactured in the United States of America

Library of Congress Cataloging-in-Publication Data

Names: Fetzer Institute author
Title: Retelling sacred stories : our journey to a shared sacred story / The Fetzer Institute.
Description: Maryknoll, NY : Orbis Books, [2025] | Summary: "Scholars and spiritual leaders from all the major religious traditions each compose a fictional "story" that conveys the essential message of their tradition"— Provided by publisher.
Identifiers: LCCN 2025010771 (print) | LCCN 2025010772 (ebook) | ISBN 9781626986039 hardcover | ISBN 9798888660584 epub
Subjects: LCSH: Religion—Fiction | Spirituality—Fiction | Religious fiction | LCGFT: Fiction
Classification: LCC PN6120.95.R4 F48 2025 (print) | LCC PN6120.95.R4 (ebook)
LC record available at https://lccn.loc.gov/2025010771
LC ebook record available at https://lccn.loc.gov/2025010772

CONTENTS

PREFACE

This book comes to you as a gift from the world's religious and spiritual traditions. It is their shared witness to the sacredness of reality, the centrality of Love, and the possibility of profound spiritual liberation and transformation. As its title suggests, it is an openhearted effort to give voice to the Shared Sacred Story of the human family.

This gift comes at a moment of great peril. Over the past several centuries, our science and technology have made us prodigiously more powerful over each other and the natural world, power we can use for good or for ill. But our spiritual and moral development has not kept pace; indeed, in important respects we have lost ground. Materialist science has denied the Sacred, cutting us off from meaning, value, and sacred connection. And exclusivist religion has tried to constrict access to the Sacred, closing minds and hardening hearts. Both forms of ridged exclusivism pull strongly toward arrogance, conflict, fear, and despair, making it ever more likely that we will use our ever-greater power to destroy life rather than to sustain it.

But this is also a moment of great promise and possibility. Powerful forces within both the religious and spiritual traditions and science are pushing back on these narrow exclusive forms and pulling toward a sacred worldview solidly grounded in both the spiritual and scientific ways of knowing.

On the spiritual side, as our world grows smaller, open-hearted persons within all traditions are seeing ever more clearly that we are a single human family engaged in a common quest to understand and come into right relationship with a single Sacred Mystery. This, in turn, is helping us see that our traditions converge on two shared affirmations of monumental importance. First, all affirm that there is a non-material dimension of reality, both within and beyond the material world, that infuses meaning, purpose, and objective value into the very fabric of reality and that, in an ineffable but profound way, holds us in Love, calls us to love, and empowers us to love. And second, they affirm that while we can discern deep truths about this non-material reality and come into life-affirming relationship with it, we can never know it fully. These two shared affirmations interact in a powerful way; the profound spiritual and epistemological humility called forth by the second creates the space for the shared affirmation and celebration of the first.

And within science, beginning a century ago with the revolution in quantum physics, multiplying streams of scientific inquiry are demonstrating the fundamental inadequacy of a strictly materialist understanding of reality and creating increasing openness to the possibility that consciousness, not matter, is foundational. This radical shift opens the ontological space for the Sacred as the ultimate ground of being, and with it the epistemological space for a mutually enriching dialogue between the scientific and spiritual ways of knowing.

It was our own experience of the transformative power of this shared sacred worldview that inspired the Fetzer Institute to initiate the project that resulted in this book. My colleague William Vendley has provided superlative leadership, and he offers a beautiful description of the project in the following introduction. This project is part of the Institute's broader efforts to help build the spiritual foundation for a loving world. To learn more about our community and our work, you can visit Fetzer.org.

So please accept this precious gift from the world's religious and spiritual traditions in the spirit in which it is offered. They offer it not to replace the richer, deeper sacred stories that each tells, and to which many of us remain deeply committed, but rather as a spiritual meeting place—a spiritual common ground on which we as a human family can come together to build a world in which all persons and the entire community of life can flourish.

Bob Boisture
President
The Fetzer Institute

INTRODUCTION

An Invitation to Love

The ten stories in this volume are invitations into the Love that lies at the heart of the Sacred. These sacred stories don't so much "teach" about this Love as invite you to taste it. They call upon the luminous depths of your own experience to find within yourself the space to contain the experiences of Love opened by the stories. They also welcome you to discern for yourself their relevance to the truthfulness and goodness of your sacred tradition's or your personal experiences of the Sacred.[1]

Followers of a particular religious tradition are warmly invited to read the stories from the perspective of their tradition's sacred story. You will find differences from your tradition's story but also surprising resonances that may align with your tradition and find a home in your heart's depth of care. This invitation is extended to all persons, regardless of religious heritage.

Sacred Story and the Paradox of Being a Person

Our voyage through the mystery of existence is told in a story. We wonder, feel, perceive, learn, remember, doubt, anticipate, plan, revise, believe, hope, despair, awaken, and love in story.[2] Our buzzing blizzard

1. Whenever the term "Sacred Love" is used, readers are invited to substitute their tradition's resonant symbol. Unconditioned Compassion and Infinite Mercy are such terms that have an especially venerable tradition.

2. See Barbara Hardy, quoted in Brian Wicker, *The Story-shaped World: Fiction and Metaphysics: Some Variations on a Theme* (Notre Dame, IN: University of Notre Dame Press, 1975), 4.

of experience coheres in a story. We come to ourselves and share ourselves within our own stories. We are—so to speak—"story-bound," always telling our stories to live within them.

Lurking within our storytelling lies the paradox of who we are as storytellers. We find ourselves already plunged into existence, yet wondering from where we have come and whither we go; in the thrall of the "givenness" of our existence, yet anxious for survival; in time, yet oddly somehow already beyond it; in the "light" of knowing, yet endlessly questioning in the dark; summoned to forms of love and mercy, yet conflicted over doing what is truly worthwhile; already wounded and oppressed, yet yearning for awakening, healing, and fulfillment.

If our storytelling makes clear that we are "story-bound," it also discloses that we are simultaneously "story-beyond"—somehow perpetually outside, beyond, or above our story. Events of all kinds can awaken new levels of awareness that alter our cares and shift our understandings. Then, we see our past, dwell in our present, and anticipate our future differently. Sub-stories can compete within us and our collective groups. We can feel challenged to unfold, deepen, revise, and even change our stories. This capacity to deepen into or change our stories is a clue that we are somehow also beyond or outside of our story as the possibility of telling it in the first place. We are both in our story and stand outside it to tell it. In our storytelling, we dramatically live out a fundamental paradox: Perpetually "story-bound," we tell ourselves stories by—oddly—telling them from "beyond" our story. The key to this paradox is "transcendence," our openness to the endless depth of reality. Sacred stories hold the root paradox of our being open to the Sacred, even as we inhabit the worldly particulars of our stories.

Historic Sacred Stories and Sacred Worldviews

Humanity's living sacred stories offer worldviews that tell us of an original *wholeness*. In them, the Sacred, Heaven and Earth, heart and mind, the human family, and the natural world coexist together. This community of all that exists is experienced as a mysterious "whole" grounded in the Sacred: alive, beautiful, fecund, and multi-hued.

Humans are open to the mysterious presence of the Sacred, to the vital play of energies animating all things, to harmonies now hidden.

The stories tell us of awe of the Sacred and that people can live in contact with the sacred grounding of the other members of the community of life. They tell us that spontaneity, light, and even bliss are features of our original participation in the wholeness of reality rooted in the Sacred.

The stories also tell of *wholeness lost,* of losing our relationship with the Sacred and the community of life linked to it. The primordial light dancing across the Cosmos seems to dim; ignorance envelops us; the world's music becomes overbearing; easy work becomes bitter toil. What is more, our very nature, once luminous, is darkened. We become ignorant of the Sacred and reality's ultimate grounding in it. We become a contradiction to ourselves and alien to each other. We become aggressive, selfish, greedy, and violent. We neglect our communities and desecrate the Earth.

These same sacred stories point us back to restoring our living link with the Sacred. They tell us that the Sacred, however transcendent, is also imminent in human hearts. They tell us that surrendering our whole hearts to the Sacred is the way to union with it so that true fulfillment is conceived as a union with, or dissolution into, the Sacred that also re-establishes kinship with all that is grounded in it.

So it is that our human family's historic sacred stories position us in a sacred worldview. They invite us to awaken to the goodness and wholeness of the community of life rooted in the Sacred, warn us about the grave distortion of turning away from it, and point us toward a healed and awakened relationship with the Sacred and all held by it.

Retelling Sacred Stories in Our Time

Most of the human family's sacred stories were first told millennia or centuries ago.

Life's circumstances change: historical movement is relentless. So, these ancient sacred stories must be faithfully retold again and again to honor their profound original disclosures of the Sacred. At the same time, they must be creatively retold across the changing vicissitudes of time so that their original disclosures of the Sacred can illumine those ever-changing circumstances. This retelling of sacred stories is not about watering them down but showing the relevance of their enduring truths in an ever-changing world.

Over the last few centuries, our view of ourselves has rapidly and radically altered. A marking point is December 7, 1972, when the crew of the Apollo 17 spacecraft took the Blue Marble photo of the Earth, one of the most reproduced images in history. The photo showed us a single Earth, allowing each viewer to grasp the whole Earth, even as their eyes searched for the rough location of their small home. Continents, large islands, and countries could be seen, and the position of smaller sites guessed, but everything was different. Each place's relationship to the whole stood out in a new way.

Something similar has been afoot in our understanding of our human family's past. We rightly study specific areas of history, including the histories of religions. Today, we can increasingly see the religions we study in relation to our total history as a human family. This widening of our awareness does not change each religion's core truths. Rather it casts new light on how each religion might understand and share these truths to benefit us all. For today, we know we are a single human family on a single Earth, with a single history writ large, facing common challenges and promises.

The retold sacred stories in this volume, and the shared sacred story, are positive responses to the following questions, which are directly linked to our deepening awareness that we are a single family on a single Earth sharing in a single history and facing common perils and promises:

1. Could the believers of diverse historical sacred stories faithfully retell their respective tradition's sacred story to the entire human family in a way that makes clear how their tradition's experience of the Sacred calls them to support all of us and the goodness and beauty of our shared Earth?

2. Could the beauty and power of the scientific mode of inquiry be understood as complementary to the more ancient spiritual mode of inquiry?

3. Could positive answers to the above two questions provide preconditions for an honest shared sacred story, one we need to live together as a single human family today, and one that can live side-by-side with historic sacred stories?

Brilliant, deeply committed, and highly competent religious scholars, scientists, and historians and philosophers of science collaborated to produce these retold stories and the shared sacred story as affirmative answers to the above three questions.

How Religious Scholars Collaborated to Retell Their Stories

Scholar-practitioner teams

The project commissioned "scholar-practitioner" teams for eight historical world religions (Indigenous [limited to North American], Hinduism, Buddhism, Confucianism, Sikhism, Judaism, Christianity, and Islam)[3] to retell their respective sacred stories. The term "scholar-practitioner" is important: the project sought out mature, practicing followers of these eight religions who have spent years cultivating their hearts to open to the experiences of the Sacred known by their respective traditions. In addition, these same religious seekers were also distinguished scholars of their respective traditions, as well as keen students of the modern world.

Each team comprised approximately six scholars representing diverse sub-streams of their respective sacred traditions. Gender balance was sought, and beyond the diversity within the respective teams, up to nine additional scholars from each tradition reviewed and contributed to the retelling of the stories. Finally, each retold story was reviewed by senior religious figures from that respective tradition. Participants on these extended teams came from around the world, including many with living links to the geographical origins of their respective religious traditions.

---

3. Only practical considerations limited the project to these sacred traditions. Fetzer honors other sacred traditions not yet included in this project and hopes over time to engage them.

A ninth inter-spiritual team was charged with telling the story of how believers positively identify with and draw resources from more than one tradition in varying ways. These range from those who remain rooted in a primary tradition and welcome the good in other sacred traditions to a smaller group claiming multiple traditions as their core identity.

Mandate

Each team was to faithfully retell its tradition's sacred story. Crucially, this retelling wasn't simply to be recounted as a catalog of doctrines or beliefs. Instead, the teams were invited to offer a literary "experience" of the awakening, changing, and surrendering of the heart evoked by the Sacred in their tradition. This mandate did not require the teams to set their respective stories in the present, though some did. It did invite them, however, to retell their stories so that you might experience their community's solidarity in relationship to our shared flourishing in our time.

Science and the Sacred

The intellectual beauty of modern science, its stunning contributions to our understanding of reality, and its technological fruits have radically transformed our world. Given its massive impact on our world, science must be involved in retelling historical sacred stories and a shared sacred story.

Today, we stand at the end of a process that has been in motion for more than four centuries, which has given science not only a special kind of autonomy from other realms of social activity—such as practices related to the Sacred, the arts, politics, philosophy, and so forth—but also a position of cultural preeminence. Up until recently, modern natural science was dominated by a powerful yet reductionistic account of nature closed off from the Sacred. The model that quickly came to define the new methods of the sciences—especially physics, often regarded as the "ideal'"science—was that of nature conceived as a great machine.

This reductive materialistic story remains the dominant *de facto* public shared story. It is the omni-pervasive "background" story told by international organizations like the United Nations, most governments, and other public institutions, including our premier universities and public schools.

As this story tells it, matter is dead, and the mind is essentially an emergent physical property of a purposeless universe. People are often modeled as non-relational, isolated, and increasingly "machine-like." At the same time, the world and its web of life are made to appear less and less as our home, where it is possible to draw near to and respond to its sacred foundations with awe and reverence. Instead, we increasingly experience the world as a mirror of our arbitrary power and a resource to be exploited. Not only are we spiritually impoverished by this reductive story, but in living out its truncated notion of flourishing, we are also rapidly murdering our world and destroying ourselves.

As it turns out, this reductive materialistic *interpretation* of science is not scientific. Alert to the profound shifts under way in science over the last one hundred years, Fetzer took three steps in this project to advance the complementarity of the scientific and spiritual modes of inquiry and understanding.

First, it convened a team of eminent physicists, biologists, philosophers, and historians of science to examine the profound stirrings under way within physics for more than one hundred years, which are now also taking place in the biological and other sciences. This team's work clarifies that the questions and data of today's sciences do not fit within a mechanistic, materialistic model of reality. Modern science is disclosing reality to be endlessly more open, dynamic, complex, and interactive than the machine model championed by mechanistic determinism.[4]

A second probe focused on the extraordinarily rich hemisphere theory linked to the bipartite structure of our brains. The key lies in each hemisphere's mode of attention. The left hemisphere's world

---

4. See the fine paper "Science and Religion," co-authored by Celia E. Deane-Drummond, David Bentley Hart, Iain McGilchrist, Philip Goyal, Nick Spencer, and Pui Him Ip, published by Fetzer Institute and available at www.Fetzer.org.

comprises comparatively familiar things, including all the objects we can grasp with our hands or tools. These objects are seen as isolated and explicit. The left hemisphere's stance is detached, its understanding is limited, and its vision is a representation, like a map, and its practical utility is great.

By contrast, the right hemisphere's world has the quality of a presence rather than a representation; it preserves the complexity and beauty of the world that the left hemisphere has simplified. The right hemisphere's world is relational, marked by open, flowing, and animate webs of relationships. Its strength is an apprehension of reality as a relational whole, open to the Sacred.

While both hemispheres are engaged in concert, their distinctive modes of attention can become personally and even culturally unbalanced. This key insight provides the basis for a remarkably fertile hypothesis that an accessible foundation for the "complementarity" of the scientific and spiritual modes of attention and inquiry may be rooted in our single but bipartite brains.[5]

A third social science team inventoried the burgeoning research that provides the ever-growing social science evidence that openness to Sacred Love (Compassion, Mercy) fosters vital dimensions of personal flourishing and can unite diverse groups into a beloved community committed to the common good.[6]

These three probes provided remarkable insight into the complementarity of the spiritual and scientific modes of inquiry. Combined, they led us to the conviction that what draws both spiritual and scientific modes of questioning onward is nothing other than the original experience of the mystery of existence that first awakens wonder and the desire for truth. Both the scientific and spiritual modes of inquiry venture all their energies upon the wager that the structure of reality and consciousness are at some level not merely compatible but identical and, therefore, genuinely transparent, one to the other. This is why

---

5. See the published works of Iain McGilchrist, a co-chair of the Fetzer Science and Religion Working Group, for seminal work on this hypothesis.

6. See Dr. Matthew T. Lee, "Love and Human Flourishing: A Converging Synthetic Evidentiary Summary and Directions for Strategic Growth," published by Fetzer Institute and available at www.Fetzer.org.

the scientific and spiritual modes of inquiry undertake their perpetual journeys toward an end that, perhaps, they can never fully reach. Both pursuits set out upon their different paths from the same innocent instant of *amazement.* They seek to end their journeys at a place where description fails but where that primordial wonder finds its final consummation in the light of a knowing union with Sacred Love.

The discovery of this deep consonance between the scientific and spiritual modes of knowing is the seed for a future science that will grow to be a foundational pillar for a shared sacred worldview. It underlies all the retold sacred stories and comes explicitly to the fore in the shared sacred story.

A Shared Sacred Story

Retelling historical sacred stories and advancing the complementarity of the scientific and spiritual modes of inquiry were recognized as essential pre-conditions for telling a shared sacred story.

Mandate. The mandate was to prepare a shared sacred story set in our time, marked by today's perils and promises, and open to both the spiritual and scientific modes of questioning. Like the retold stories, the shared sacred story is a dramatic evocation of the *experience* of Sacred Love (Mercy or Compassion) that can ground us in a Sacred Love–based solidarity with one another and our shared Earth. The story's protagonists represent all of us in our time; their nationalities and religious backgrounds are intentionally not identified.

The shared sacred story is offered to all—those following a particular religious tradition and those not. It is offered as—to borrow a musical metaphor—a "polyphonic" story, one with multifaceted dramatic characters who can evoke a variety of resonant notes in each reader's heart, whether or not a particular religious legacy shapes their sacred quest.

The shared sacred story is not a replacement for historical sacred stories.[7] The project appreciates that for many, it will modestly co-exist side-by-side with their respective historical sacred story, with the advantage of providing a shared sacred worldview in seed. The expectation

7. Fetzer respects individual conscience in all such matters.

is that you, the reader, will read the story through your heart as shaped by your religious heritage and/or your personal quest for and experience of the Sacred.

The Writers

Writing the story involved the leaders of the nine teams and the review of those involved in the work on science. From this remarkable group, a smaller writing committee was assembled to produce a draft to be extensively reviewed by all involved in the project. The draft was then further reviewed by many religious scholars and senior religious figures.

Mutuality

Writing the story was daunting; the project was fully committed to honoring the enduring integrity of historical sacred traditions. These traditions have symbols intimately linked to their experiences of the Sacred that can be adequately interpreted only in their respective religious contexts. The project participants knew they couldn't write a shared sacred story based on one tradition's religious "grammar." Everyone understood that the impact of each of our teams being "story-bound" included their primary allegiance to the nest of symbols of their respective traditions. So, how could we proceed?

Generously, all agreed to make soft compromises based on trust and goodwill. For example, we agreed to use the word "Sacred" but understood that each tradition has its way of experiencing and inflecting its meaning. We also used the phrase "Sacred Love." Still, we agreed to invite each other and you, the reader, to freely substitute words like "Compassion" or "Mercy" if they are more natural for your sacred tradition or personal experience. Beyond these generous compromises, however, we searched for a genuine foundation for a shared sacred story.

We knew that while we are all "story-bound," we also somehow tell our stories from "beyond" our stories. Being "story-beyond" is another way of expressing our respective experiences of transcendence, of always standing out beyond our diverse stories before or with the Sacred as the necessary condition for telling them.

Helpfully, each team member had their own experiences of meeting deeply spiritually awakened people from diverse sacred traditions and feeling a joyful sense of mutual recognition despite their sacred stories' differences. As a group, we could understand this epiphany of mutual awareness as a disclosure of transcendence (or interbeing, as some Buddhists say). We could understand that the most unconditioned dimension of "persons" can, in their transcendent mutuality (or interbeing), be an opening to a genuine form of community.

Not surprisingly, this transcendent mutuality has been deeply plumbed by our forebears. Indigenous Peoples continue to experience profound and living forms of mutuality with all of nature. Hindus speak of *darshan*, the awakening to the sacred openness of the other, known and loved in the bottomless depths of God. Buddhists show us that the awakened wordlessly know the awakened, and this knowing occurs in unconditional Mercy. St. Paul speaks of the Holy Spirit flooding our innermost hearts as the ground of our loving God and all others in God's Love. Muslims teach us that the All-Merciful Allah created us as different, as separate tribes, precisely so that we might know one another before our common Creator.

As leaders of diverse religious teams, we found that we could connect spiritually with one another across all the religious language barriers that separated us. This is not surprising, for, after all, tiny babies do not need to be able to speak for communication to occur. Before exchanging words, a recognition of the other breaks through in the radiance of the baby's smile, and this mutual recognition is the basis for future shared words.

Nevertheless, we knew we needed to cultivate this transcendent mutuality if it was to serve as the foundation for telling a shared sacred story. So, we shared our hearts, which included meditating and praying regularly in each other's presence, often in silence. Over time, this allowed us to know one another on a pre-verbal level and brought interior smiles of mutual recognition not unlike the ones we all experienced as infants. This also unleashed the silent flood of tender affection that mutual Love (Compassion, Mercy) sets loose.

In this honest sharing of ourselves, we opened ourselves to an ever-deeper connection that could allow us to bond as a new form of multi-religious community that could hold our respective commitments to our sacred traditions. This equipped our hearts—on a far more fundamental level than our collective scholarship—to try to write a shared sacred story. In short, we tried to live a shared sacred story as we did our best to write one.

A Shared Sacred Story as the "Seed" of a Shared Sacred Worldview

Every sacred story is the seed of a sacred worldview, a total vision of reality grounded in the Sacred.

The project participants believe that there is an honest form of a shared sacred story that respects religious diversity and honors the beauties of science. An early expression of such a shared story, titled "Journeys to the Sacred: A Telling of a Shared Sacred Story," is presented as the first story in this collection.[8] It is not offered as a replacement for today's historical stories; instead, it is a story that can stand beside them as a modest companion, a story we need to tell ourselves as a single human family today.[9] Like every sacred story, it will need to be retold again and again over time.

Importantly, a shared sacred story has a companion shared sacred worldview. The lack of a shared sacred worldview and the widespread embrace of a materialist story that excludes the Sacred is a fundamental problem behind today's myriad, seemingly disconnected problems. The elimination of the Sacred severely distorts the human family's chances for shared flourishing. A shared sacred worldview welcomes that possibility; it is a call to community instead of isolation, to care for and ultimately love one another. Our shared sacred story embodies a shared sacred worldview in seed, inviting all to co-build societies that serve the common good aligned with justice, harmony, and healing, and are attuned to the vital beauty and promise of the Earth.

Such a shared sacred worldview is a kind of "solution" behind the myriads of particular solutions we must labor for together.

---

8. The retold stories are then offered in alphabetical order.

9. Each reader's conscience is respected in this regard.

We believe that the shared sacred story can be unfolded and lived as a shared sacred worldview and that doing so is our duty and destiny.[10]

A First Word of Thanks

At the end of the book, you will find an expression of heartfelt appreciation for all who have worked on this project with such care, talent, and generosity of spirit.

Allow me to mention briefly the pivotal role of the Fetzer Board. It began contemplating this project a full five years before it was initiated. Its foresight, courage, and commitment to advancing the project created the conditions essential to bringing it forth. Each Board member played a vital role, and they—speaking for all of us—gratefully singled out President Bob Boisture's visionary contribution.

Finally, serving this project has been the privilege of my life. Before joining Fetzer, I was the director of the world's largest multi-religious organization for twenty-seven years, working globally on deeply challenging problems. I can now see those years of earnest multi-religious cooperation engaging so many beautiful people on all continents as an expression of our human family's search for our shared sacred story—one that can hold our differences while inviting us to open ourselves in solidarity in Sacred Love for our shared flourishing.

William Vendley
Vice President for World Religions and Spirituality
The Fetzer Institute

10. See the Fetzer paper by William Vendley, "A Shared Sacred Worldview: A Framework for Shared Sacred Flourishing," available at www.Fetzer.org. It provides an initial framework for unfolding the shared sacred worldview embodied in "A Telling of a Shared Sacred Story."

Journeys to the Sacred

A TELLING OF A SHARED SACRED STORY

Journeys to the Sacred

A time in the indeterminately but not vastly distant future—

PART ONE

A Mother's Letter to Her Son

Since you ask, my dear,

I suppose it was the way the old man died that made me want to understand how he had lived. He had a gift for taking me by surprise, right up to the end. He said more than once that he had spent much of his life preparing to die well, but the remark had seemed meaningless. Nothing was more obvious to me in those years than that death comes when it will, and it doesn't matter whether we try to prepare for it or not; it takes what it wants without asking and leaves nothing behind that it will not soon take away.

On that last day, however, he left me no choice but to surrender my cynicism—and the comfort it gave me. He was in the most miserable setting, attended by strangers, and devoured by cancer, and yet he somehow turned his death into a—well, "triumph" is not the right word, but I'm at a loss for a good alternative. All I can say is that his death had a strange, radiant beauty, one that was peaceful—even joyful—to those of us present.

You were only four when we arrived at the camp and seven when we left. There were things I could not explain to you, and perhaps have failed to say since. The day of his passing, fourteen years ago, marks the moment at which I crossed an emotional and spiritual frontier, one dividing despair from hope, though at the time I didn't grasp what had happened to me. Its consequences would have to unfold in my heart. I doubt that you and I would have survived those years if I had not been at his bedside that day. My need to protect you gave me the will to persist, but not the strength to live; his way of dying somehow gave me that strength.

He always insisted that I was stronger than I thought I was, but I never believed him.

Anyway, this is why I can't reproach you for your choice to live for now as a kind of "spiritual vagabond" (as you put it). I should, I suppose. If nothing else, I should at least ask you to finish your studies. Perhaps in time I will regret it. But, when you tell me that you want to follow a course so much like the one he pursued, which was what gave him the power to rescue me from the hell of my despair, I don't know how to object. Candidly, I doubt you will be the sort of permanent wanderer he was, because that's not your temperament. But, for now, I'm even a little proud that you want to live as you describe, defying practicality, exploring different religious traditions, traveling near and far to the world's holy places, seeking to understand the mysteries of existence.

My only bit of maternal advice is to keep your mind and heart open: avoid, I mean, any path that asks you to disdain all other paths—avoid any supposed way to ultimate truth that refuses to acknowledge that truth is infinitely rich. That infinite richness is the true measure of all paths, not the reverse.

But here we are again. In my typical fashion, I've already strayed from the topic. I'm not answering the questions you actually asked.

∞

So, how did he come to ask me to take charge of his "literary" remains? There was no other candidate for the job. As you know, his whole "estate" amounted to a slim notebook, but even that was a burden to take on. At that point, I was all but shattered, and it was only for your sake that I resisted disintegration. But how could I refuse his request? I had to agree, for the reason that he had no one else. I had no interest in the notebook, related to what he called a telling of "the human family's shared sacred story." To be honest, I doubt I would have opened it had his death not affected me so deeply.

I hope this doesn't make me sound callous. I know you had little sense of the constant fear and mourning that was in the air. Of course, that was a favorite observation of his. "Children bring their paradise into the world with them," he liked to say, "and the world only gradually drives it out of them." That may or may not be true, but children have a mysterious ability to create the happiness that the world refuses to grant them. They can make toys out of sticks, craft games out of pebbles, raise enchanted kingdoms out of the dust; the medium doesn't matter, because their joy is infinitely artful. For the adults, though, it was a time of crushing despair.

Since those days, I suppose, humanity has grown somewhat better at dealing with the catastrophes we have brought upon ourselves; some semblance of stability has been restored in desperate parts of the globe, at least for now. Back then, though, that seemed impossible. No one in the developed or developing worlds had been prepared for how rapidly things fell apart, and when the great ruin came we were all too tormented by a sense of approaching doom to imagine that things might ever get better again.

How could we, after all? In many regions of the earth, environmental collapse had led to economic and then political collapse, and the worst repercussions were suffered by countries too small and too pressed for resources to accommodate or resist the flow of refugees. The refugee encampments were overseen by fragile local governments and survived principally on international aid; that aid was barely sufficient, since its principal purpose seemed to be to allow benefactor nations to refuse to open their borders while still giving the appearance—and even convincing their own consciences—that they were doing all they could. Again, you know all this.

You know also that I had lost everything except you; but for you I had no reason to carry on. You may remember how anxious I became when I was apart from you for any length of time, even when I had entrusted you to someone in whom I had full confidence—though, I suppose, you probably found it all quite natural, since you had never really known an ordinary childhood. What I've never told you—and perhaps should not tell you now—is that I had resolved that, if I should lose you, I would take my own life. I know this doesn't sound like the woman I am now, but I am not exaggerating, and I am not distorting my own memories. My despair was total. Your father and sister were gone already and I could not even visit their graves again; everything had collapsed at home and the civil conflict had driven us away from what had once been our island—that little emerald lost in a sea of sapphire, as my father liked to call it. Even the possibility of return was inconceivable. We had no place in the world, you and I, and you were (and are still, of course) everything to me.

I did not lose you, however, and so I had to go on.

∞

Obviously, there was no child care anywhere in that place, and so I had to have you with me; but I would not have been able to have been parted from you in any event. You may recall the sad shadow of a school that was run for a few hours every day out of two tents and an old trailer. It had few resources and no distinct grades, but many parents sent their children to it in the hope of establishing something like a normal life for them. I, however, was conscious only of its futility. You were too young for school for most of our time there, anyway, and you never seemed too bored when playing in the clinic or accompanying me on my rounds.

The old man spoke as if those rounds were a mission on my part, or some kind of spiritual vocation. He told me that I loved my patients—all of them—and if I protested that I did not he would correct me, as if he knew me better than I knew myself. I explained to him that I had agreed to act as head of the camp's clinic only because it allowed me to keep you safer and nearer at hand than I could otherwise have done. I wasn't even a proper physician then; I had my pre-med training and some familiarity with medical procedures, skills that no one else in the camp possessed, and this allowed me to keep the small room for us in the army-surplus Quonset hut that also housed the "pharmacy" (such as it was); at least it was protected, and sheltered us at night. Most of the camp's population had to sleep in rows of cots in tents or below tarpaulins tied to the warped trees along the edges of the compound; because there weren't enough cots to go around, people had to sleep in shifts or find a corner in which to collapse. Oh, and there were the structures some of the refugees built out of wooden crates. Everything there was a reminder that we were the forgotten—the suppressed conscience of the world—and so I cherished our little retreat from it all.

Anyway, I told him I needed to keep you close by and away from strangers, somewhere where I could safely fall asleep. The world was dissolving around us, I told him, and I had lost so many of those I loved already, and I feared—even expected—that what little I had would also be taken away. And that was my entire reason for agreeing to act as the camp physician. He acknowledged my words, graciously, but then insisted that, no, even so, I loved the patients under my care. "You simply don't realize it yet," he said. He claimed that neither personal need alone nor conscience would have driven me to look after them so tirelessly. "You love them, and there's no use denying it," he would say, turning on his side and pretending to fall asleep.

He could be so very infuriating at times.

∞

Actually, there was no safety in sleep for me. I was tormented by recurring dreams that combined all the horrors we had already suffered with all the others I dreaded might come. There was one dream in particular that repeatedly brought me to the unmarked graves where your father and little sister lay, which in reality I had barely glimpsed before we had had to flee the island. I had never found the time or the emotional energy properly to mourn the two of them. The physical details felt real and familiar—the rattling sigh of the palms in the breeze, the sharp taste of the salt wind, the dark green of the undergrowth below the trees and brilliant white of the sand along the shore; but always also, in the distance, the strange red glow of great fires seemed to rise and swell above the palms' crowns. Sometimes, I would look down at my own empty hands, surprised to find that I had no flowers with me and trying to recall how I had misplaced them.

In another dream, which was even worse, I had somehow lost you and was desperately seeking you everywhere in the camp. Other refugees kept telling me they had seen you here or there, but the more

I looked the more I realized that no one knew where you were, and that I would never find you again. The feeling of desolation was so deep that I almost wept for joy every time I woke and found you still there nearby. But I would also remember the reality into which I had woken, and the joy would subside. We were still in a world of squalor enclosed within coldly guarded boundaries—a world that in my memory seems to me wholly devoid of colors, other than gray and khaki, tin and rust. Whenever I try to recall it now, even the sky there comes back to me as always colorless, though I know that could not really have been the case.

Near the end, when he and I had become one another's confidantes, I told him about the dreams of the gravesides and the missing flowers. He remarked that mourning was essential to everything, that mourning rituals were part of the foundations of most early religious cults; this veered into a reflection on how those had become rites for the ancestors, and then those liturgies for gods and spirits which in time… well, I listened to him for a few minutes, not because I was in the mood for abstract pedantries about the anthropology of religion, but because I was amazed that my story about my nightly ordeals, which were so painful to me, had seemed to send his thoughts off on some excursion into the old books on religion he had absorbed on his spiritual adventures. Later, though, after his death, I came to think that he had been attempting to tell me something important about myself, and about the necessity of overcoming my despair. And maybe how to do it.

I doubt I would have been interested in what he was saying even if I had not been in so miserable and bitter a state of mind. Our island was small and poor, and such places tend to abound in faith and piety. But I had grown up largely untouched by all of that. Your grandparents were not militantly secular, but neither were they devout. It was more or less taken for granted in our household that religion is a matter of cultural identity, and that none of it should be believed except perhaps as a collection of charming tales, interesting symbols, wholesome moral principles, and excuses for celebration. The spiritual traditions of the people around us were, as far as my family was concerned, aspects of the local atmosphere, akin to our cuisine, our music, clothes or architecture or gardens. My family remained casually observant of traditional feasts and holidays, but as no one instilled any real religious beliefs in me I entered adulthood indifferent to questions of faith or things supernatural.

I was also blissfully insulated from many of the ordinary pains of existence. I was able to study to become a scientist. I fell in love with molecular and cell biology early on, and so I abandoned my medical practice before it really commenced. Soon, I had absorbed the culture of the sciences as I understood it. By the time I had completed my formal education, my indifference to religion had become something more like a mild hostility, colored by disdain. I abandoned even my parents' casual observance of the sacred calendar.

Oh, you already know all this. I suppose I miss you. Still, how strange it is to remember that side of my youth now. It makes me realize how deeply my friendship with him shaped who I have since become.

∞

I would not have come to know him at all, of course, had there been a properly qualified cancer-specialist anywhere in the camp. Certainly, I had no practical experience in the field; what I knew of oncology I had acquired through my research work, but that was enough to get me conscripted into the role of principal physician for those in the camp who were in various stages of the disease. His case was the most advanced, and the prognosis grim. My first impression of him when I entered his little room at the back of the clinic—quite a luxury, accorded to him because he required more help and privacy than any of the other patients who were ill enough to earn a cot in the infirmary—was that he was unlikely to live many more days. He was a mere wisp of a man; he was so emaciated. He told me later that he had always been a bit "on the skeletal side." There was a graceful delicacy in his wrists and hands, but it was also apparent that he was withering away.

One uncanny moment in that first encounter comes back to me now. The first time I entered his room, it happened to be early in the evening; the curtain of the small window above his head was drawn, and there was only an electric lamp burning overhead—just a lightbulb in a yellowed paper globe—and when he turned to me his eyes seemed to shine with a soft golden luster that looked so unnatural that I couldn't help but gasp. Idiotic of me. It was the jaundice, of course; it had turned the whites around his irises yellow; and, while the light in the room was weak, it was just strong enough to cast his upturned eyes into relief against the darkness. But for that moment, I felt as if I was seeing something miraculous.

As much as that moment had caught me off-guard, the surprise was brief. I was far more taken aback moments later by how mild and cheerful he was. My expectations of the state of a man in his condition were various—resentment, anger, fear, and so on—but nowhere among them was gentle contentment. In time I would get used to his...what?...his effervescence, I suppose; but just then his behavior seemed so out of place that I found it offensive. I spoke to him in a curt voicc—thc onc I uscd with paticnts, thinking that it convcycd a reassuring tone of authority—but he insisted on replying in a disarming manner, answering my questions with questions of his own: my name, where I came from, whether I was well myself, whether I still had family in the world, whether I was a believer of any variety, and so on. Every time he did this, I made an effort to re-establish formality. I consulted his "chart" and asked if he had been taking his medications. He told me he had and then immediately asked after my family history and my childhood.

As I say, I slowly became used to his geniality even on days when he was in considerable pain, and his voice had grown thin and frail. Even then—after we had become friends—there were days when it all roused indignation in me. Part of me wanted him to resent his situation far more than he evidently did, if only because I could not imagine being able to maintain anything like his equanimity. What right did he have not to be as angry as I thought he should be—and as I was myself?

I was fortunate, I suppose, in having ways of taking my mind off that anger: caring for and worrying over you, chiefly, but also trying to administer the clinic as best I could. My entire staff consisted of one registered nurse who spoke none of the languages in which I had any real competency, one hospice-care nurse, one young pharmacist, one former accountant with a knack for inventories and requisitions, one janitor, and two large brothers who served as security-guards and stretcher-bearers (incidentally, the old man not only knew the whole staff by name, but also the names of their parents and siblings). I rarely had any prolonged period in which to dwell on my memories, my despair, or my quiet rage. I performed my medical duties as best I could and, apart from a sporadic impulse of hopelessness, I did so in a state close to emotional paralysis.

He liked talking to anyone he could, but it was clear to me he also wanted to draw me out of myself. I think he knew that, left to my own thoughts, I was capable only of torturing myself. So, he kept trying to engage me in conversation whenever I visited his bedside. I found this a nuisance at first, until a day came when I discovered myself asking him questions about his life in turn. I told myself for a while that I was doing this simply to distract him from his illness. Apart from prescribing what palliative medications we had, there was little I could do. But soon I had to admit to myself that I truly wanted to know the answers to my queries. I discovered that there was something about him that was comforting to me, and that his company made the days easier to endure. So, we became friends, mostly because we each needed someone to talk to—he because he soon must die, I because I must not.

∞

He too had lost everything. Certain details of his upbringing I never learned, because they were so unimportant to him. All I knew then, or know now, is that he had spent most of his life as a religious seeker. He was mostly self-taught, acquiring the better part of his learning on his feet. And, while he was broadly read and widely traveled, he had had to earn his way. "Oh," he once said to me, "I've lived everywhere at one time or another; but I've never really had a home anywhere—at least, not for long."

One thing I could never tell was whether his quest had led him to settle into any single tradition. Instead, his talk ranged freely over all the world's religious and spiritual traditions, with a richness of detail that seemed to me as astonishing as it did pointless.

His driving curiosity was to understand the "one great story" told by the religious and philosophical traditions of the world. "Is there only one?" I asked him the first time he told me this. He tilted his head, then smiled in that charming way he had and said, "Yes, but it's told in countless different forms." When I protested that this sounded as if there were simply countless different stories, he nodded and said, "Yes, that too."

I found solace in his friendship, but it did little to lighten the general atmosphere in which all of us lived. Everyone above a certain age needed to believe that he or she would be delivered from it any day now and was bleakly certain that that day would never come. The life of refugees is a kind of hell, which is something you and I have a real duty to remember. There is a cruel irony in the very term "refugee," since the one thing we were consistently denied was any sense of refuge. We were all on our own. There was little distinction between the alleged purpose of affording shelter and its effective function as a place of internment. We had security personnel from various nations there, meant to serve as a kind of police force and emergency service, but they often behaved more like prison guards; and there was little question that, in reality, we were in a detention camp. We could not leave at will; and even the rare excursions some of us could make to aid facilities or shops in the nearest town had to be undertaken in the custody of armed men from the military, or the United Nations.

Even those who died in the camp remained prisoners of its rules. Their bodies had to be taken away to a crematorium, whether their families or friends wanted this or not, and no one was allowed to accompany them. All that came back were ashes in black plastic boxes, each with an attached slip of paper identifying the remains (one simply had to hope that the identification was correct).

Every condition of life there was miserable.

For one thing, the climate oscillated between extremes, as had been the case for so many decades, and we were largely unprotected from it. Nature was suffering, and we suffered along with her. The heat was oppressive; the cold no less so; days of drought; rains, when they came, turned everything into a mire, and it was impossible to get clothes dry except by wearing them.

And then, too, each day brought disease, hunger, and death. Even that old man, despite his unnatural spiritual buoyancy, confronted me physically every day with the horror of the place. I can't imagine what it must have been like for him to be dying of cancer in a refugee camp. I remember the kindness of his words, his bravery and good humor, the wisdom he had to offer, the graciousness with which he invited us into his heart; but I also remember how often he was overcome by exhaustion or pain, or how his voice would suddenly fail and his breathing become labored; how he often had to rely on our physical assistance in ways that must have been humiliating, how he sometimes had to be spoon-fed mashed rice and applesauce—and so many other aspects of his sufferings that I prefer not to talk about.

Anyway, I still don't really know what you do and do not remember. I sometimes think you pretend to have forgotten it all just to ease my mind.

As for the old man himself—well, he tried to convince me more than once that our plight, as terrible as it was, was simply a more acute version of what everyone suffers, and that we must not lose hope. His words struck me almost as mockery. By seeing our situation as part of our universal condition, I thought he was trivializing it. I even lost my temper with him one day and had to apologize several hours later.

∞

He was in many ways more typical of the camp's population in this regard than I was. Having been raised to think of religion as little more than local color, I found it mystifying that so many refugees continued to cling to their faiths. I also kept asking myself why they did not feel more betrayed by the powers or principles they revered. Almost everything essential was in short supply in that place—warmth, sanitation, adequate medicine, sufficient food, water clean enough to drink or hot enough for the showers—but what the camp had in abundance was religious devotion. Naturally, I mostly wrote it off as just an emotional sedative, consoling in the way a teddy bear might be for a frightened child. And yet even I could see that to those who were capable of it, faith endowed strength; even I could tell that, for many of those displaced souls, attending prayer services under tattered canvas canopies, or finding a few candles to light before an image torn from a magazine or a calendar, or chanting, or telling beads between stained fingers beside the palettes or cots of dying relatives, or whatever else they did to wring sacred comfort out of their situation, somehow sustained them in a way that surpassed any ordinary emotional resources.

This provoked a deep indignation in me. In my heart, I wanted everyone there to be as incapable of belief or religious trust as I was; I wanted them to feel as I did the meaninglessness of our lives and the indifference of the universe. Odd as this may sound, the sight I found most appalling was the sight of children at play. I should have been able to delight in it, but all it signified to me was the disillusionment that would one day destroy that happiness. Their innocence seemed to me tragic; the knowledge that it would be brutally stolen from them, and that they wouldn't understand why until it was too late, made me hate everything around me.

He was completely different. He professed to find peace in that place, and all his behavior seemed to confirm his words. He was delighted by the birds when the small window in his room was open, even though sometimes he could express it only in a voice full of physical pain. And the sound of children playing, far from oppressing him, could render him rapturous. The babble that sounded to me like tragic ignorance of the world was to his ears the music of the "wisdom of innocence." He liked to go on so, about children bringing paradise with them into the world.

Having by that time had to pronounce a certain number of the camp's children dead, sometimes after they had endured agonizing illnesses, I found it difficult to share his enchantment.

This is not to say I was entirely unaware of moments of beauty in those days. Sometimes, against my will, I could suddenly be aware of, say, a vivid twilight rising from the western horizon. I remember one in particular submerging the camp in violet shadows and in that unearthly light one sometimes sees as evening is falling, with a color that seems to shift from silver-blue to pale purple to faint scarlet without actually appearing to change; gazing at it, I became so spellbound that my anxiety and anger seemed momentarily to melt away. I also remember on another occasion finding myself staring peacefully at a rambling cluster of small blue wildflowers that had defied the camp's boundaries by spilling in through the chain-link fence from the other side.

And I remember that one afternoon, about a week before his death, the old man called my attention to the sound of a bird somewhere beyond his window, and I allowed myself to be captivated by the loveliness of its song. Afterward, I let the sweetness of the experience stay with me. I even felt a little grateful for it, I think. By that time, I suppose, he had begun to have more of an effect on me than I realized.

For most of the time we knew each other, though, our attitudes toward our situation were starkly at odds. I once asked him in exasperation how he could claim to be at peace in this place. That very morning, I told him—a bit spitefully, I'm ashamed to say—that a little girl had died in the clinic from meningitis while we were waiting for an ambulance to come and take her to a hospital. And, I added, three days earlier a small boy had nearly died from septicemia contracted from a deep cut on his ankle. And the week before that, a sixteen-year-old girl had died from eclampsia while giving birth, leaving a newborn orphan behind.

He grew grave. I could see that the stories genuinely moved him; the look in his eyes grew kinder even as it grew sadder. He told me that he was hardly unaware of human suffering and was acutely conscious of the suffering all around us in the camp; and yet, still—I think I remember what he said more or less exactly—"When one sees all things with the will to love—with the will toward compassion and kindness and sympathy for all others—it alters things radically."

I'm fairly sure I had never heard anyone speak of love as something one wills to do. I think I smirked at him, or worse, and replied that loving everyone is impossible. Loving one person, or two or three or a few more than that is already a labor at the best of times and a torment at the worst, yet at least it can be done. But to speak of love for everyone is nonsense.

That was one of the occasions, of course, when he told me I loved my patients, which prompted yet another smirk from me. "Of course," he told me, "it's true that love's usually particular, but it can also become universal by way of the particular." I sighed impatiently. "You love your son," he went on, "but I believe you can also move outward from that love, in ever-expanding circles of affection and concern . . . right up until you've taken in the whole world. From loving one person, you can come to love everything. You can love universally by loving everything in particular."

I told him that paradoxes are not compelling arguments, and that I thought he was talking mystical gibberish.

At this, he smiled with that infuriating kindness of his and said, "Seeking to love others does put you a bit at their mercy. I admit that. But, then again, if you love for the sake of that love, selflessly—truly selflessly—requiring nothing in return except the peace that the love gives you, then you can't be disappointed no matter what happens."

I'm reconstructing his words from memory, but I think I have them more or less right. They fixed themselves in me somehow, even though I supposed they were merely washing over me. I suspect I was drawing sustenance from them, the way a plant draws sustenance from thc sunlight.

"You want to know why I'm content to live here?" he asked. "And, for that matter, to die here? I'm at peace because we're mostly at peace with one another in this place, even when we don't wish to be... even if that peace is fragile." Perversely, that was his surest conviction about our situation. We were, whether we chose to be or not, a community, united to one another by need but also by compassion. We were all equal in our hope and in our despair—in having lost everything and in needing to believe life was still worth living. So, we cared for one another, not perfectly but in a thousand unanticipated and necessary ways. "Look about you," he said, "especially when you're out on your rounds. It's terrible, it's monstrous—it's also beautiful. There really are the seeds of a good society, even in all this misery—the seeds of a community that's genuinely held together by love rather than sunk in greed or violence. So, yes, whether it makes sense to you or not, I can find happiness here. There's a real happiness to be had in being made transparent to one another—stripped of pretensions and advantages—forced to rely on our spirits because the body has lost its power...."

It went something like that, but, as he was speaking, he was also falling asleep. Even a few minutes of prolonged talking exhausted what little strength he still had in his ravaged body.

∞

Sooner or later, almost all our conversations came around to the same small assortment of topics: my "rationalist" view of the world, his spiritual convictions, his contention that there was spiritual longing in me that I refused to acknowledge. He had a genius for getting me to speak about myself, and was relentless when interrogating me about what had inspired my love of the sciences as a young woman, and whether my research had ever moved me to a sense of awe. ("Occasionally," I usually told him, chiefly to curtail further discussion.) I see now that he had recognized that this was his best angle of attack—past my defenses—because it really was the case that my early studies of the life-sciences were filled with countless moments of grateful astonishment. There is bliss to be found in scientific exploration and discovery, and the fascinating mysteries of life provided me with what, if I had been another person, more like the person I am now, I might have called an experience of transcendence: the sudden awareness of something real that was also in excess of all I could imagine, and of a richer mystery that seemed always to have more to disclose.

It is so absurd, he would tell me, that so much of modern culture treats the sciences as requiring religious disenchantment, a hostility to spiritual longing, when there is already a deep spiritual longing for truth at their very heart. There are different kinds of truths, I would sometimes say. Or I would point out that much of the antagonism between science and spirituality came from the side of religion (I had met more than a few rigid religious exclusivists of one kind or another on our little island). But he was never deterred. Religious exclusivists and strict "rationalists" were just reverse images of one another, he said, committed to the same false divisions and fragmentations of our knowledge of reality: "That's why, when they argue with one another, they so often just harden one another into even more rigid intolerance."

"What could be worse," he liked to lament, "than to mistake living beings for mechanisms—for technology? Wasn't that the horrible delusion of the last century—thinking of human nature as some kind of technology, genetic or racial or economic or social or political or what have you? Something to be corrected and altered and controlled? Isn't it the same madness that makes us see nature as part of a great machine of production and consumption—something we can exploit and plunder for the sake of convenience and possessions and power? Isn't that what's brought all these disasters on the world?"

You have heard me say similar things often enough. I got those views from him. Back then, though, I would just let him go on one of his tangents unaccompanied. But, of course, he was planting seeds in my mind that would sooner or later take root and grow into opinions of my own. That was another of his annoying gifts.

His ability to make me speak of my youth was testament to how thoroughly he had won my trust by the end. It was that same trust that made me willing to leave you with him in that back room at the clinic to play with the one or two toys we had there while I went on my rounds. He obviously enjoyed watching you and you seemed to take to him from the first, at least after your initial fear at the sight of his illness—it was that kind smile and that gentle voice, I imagine. I always worried when you were out of my sight; but I was able to entrust you to him and the two nurses without rendering myself useless for my duties. It also gave him the opportunity for his most effective answer to one of my challenges to him: "What makes you think life is good?" I asked him. He pointed at you, seated contentedly on the floor and absorbed in making a tower of wooden blocks, and said, "Him."

I realized that I had become patient with him because I was truly fond of him, even though I thought I had lost the capacity to care about anyone other than you; and I began quietly to dread his nearing death.

It was not long in coming. During his last days, as the poor medications I could give him ceased to have any discernible effect, my company became ever more precious to him, and his to me, and I made an effort to give him as much as I could of my time. It was only a few days before his death, when I was about to leave after a visit of nearly an hour, that he asked me to take care of his notebook on the "sacred story shared by the human family." (He could utter phrases like that without making them seem trite.) He made the request, I realized immediately, because he knew that the end would soon come.

∞

I want to say something to you that I really do not have words for. It is always impossible to describe another soul—or to describe one's own, for that matter. I keep wanting you to see him in your mind's eye as I see him in mine, but I have to trust you, my love, to remember him as best you can, for his gentleness, his unpretentious humor... again, perhaps, for his soft voice.

There are no words for the experience of his death. I'm not even sure how it was that those of us who spent time with him in his last hours—myself, the two nurses, the young pharmacist, the janitor, those two guards and stretcher-bearers—all shared in it together; but we manifestly did. There were no miracles, no supernatural signs, no hints of unseen presences. There was only the light—and the lightness, for want of a better word—that seemed to break through his pain and his weakness: a radiance, even joy at times on his face, and a peacefulness that he emanated. We all had a sense of it, and talked about it afterward, and concluded together that in his fading moments he was reconciled with everything, and that what he saw—in us, in the world, even maybe in his death—was something real to him, even if it was invisible to us. Certainly the love he felt—for us, for everyone, for everything—was suddenly palpable in the room, as if it were pouring out toward us in waves.

Even before his heart and breathing had stopped, I thought how odd it was that I felt so dead in the midst of life while he seemed to overflow with life in the midst of his own dying. I think that was when I began to waken from my emotional numbness, a little reluctantly perhaps—despair, after all, can be a safe and restful condition. In the days that followed, as I continued to awaken more fully, the effects of the experience began to show themselves. About four days after his death, something broke through all my defenses.

It was in the afternoon, not long before twilight. You were inside the clinic taking a nap under the watchful eyes of the practical nurse. I had stepped outside as a break from the day's routine in the infirmary. There were children playing not far away. I found myself staring at them in fascination, and realized that what I found entrancing about them was not their horribly ephemeral happiness and innocence, as had been the case before, but instead their beauty. One child in particular caught my attention—a little girl, perhaps six or seven years old—surrounded by barren earth and weathered canvas tents and heaps of debris and rubbish, dressed in rags, but with her arms outspread, a look of delight on her face, dancing, turning around and around.

To me it was a heartbreaking sight, of course, but also not heartbreaking at all. Just then, I was seeing precisely what he had told me I should see. Her dance was glorious: the ecstasy of innocence, the happiness of a child who can exult amid despair and desolation because her joy came with her into the world and demanded of her that she dance as if she were in the midst of paradise. And all at once, I knew that I loved her. I even realized I loved her with the love I felt for you—not, I mean, with a love equivalent to what I felt for you, but instead—just as the infuriating old man had told me—with the love that you drew out of me, now somehow mysteriously continuing to extend beyond the two of us to enfold that little girl into its embrace. And for just a moment, I had an overwhelming sense of the real possibility of—the real experience of—being seized by love for everyone and everything—of loving everything by loving in particular.

I know, of course, that momentary states of euphoria can come to any of us at one time or another, and can be induced just as easily by either extreme joy or extreme sorrow. I know also that they are almost always fleeting. But what I was feeling then was not some merely emotional moment of exuberance. I am sure of it: it was not psychological neediness on my part, or possessive desire. I don't know quite how to explain it: not a surge of sentimentality, definitely not a possessive clasping and clinging to anything. I want to say it was impersonal, but that is not right either, as it was as deeply personal an experience as I had ever felt. Call it dispassionate love, lovingkindness, compassion—call it whatever you like—but it was also something very like joy.

In the next few days, I tried to psychologize away the experience. What had I actually felt, after all? Was it a gift or just a discharge of pent-up emotions? Was it sorrow on account of the old man's death, maybe mixed with relief that his ordeal was over at last? Or was it exhaustion and grief releasing a flood of serotonin through my brain? But it was no good; I remembered what I had felt—and seen—even if it remains ineffable to this day. The best I can say is that it had been a kind of light, momentarily and mysteriously permeating everything. I had seen what he had been trying to tell me.

This place—this little hell on the margins of life—was also a good place. We were a family. We were inextricably involved in one another whether we had chosen to be or not. Watching those children, watching that little girl turning in circles, I had been flooded with a certainty that the isolated self is an illusion—or, at least, is as nothing compared to the self that is open to all others—though I would not have been able to say so as it was happening. It was almost too much: an overwhelming sense of beauty and truth and goodness, in a tide so vast I thought it might drown me. The tide soon receded, and for some time thereafter I was able to recapture only a trace of that feeling, in passing moments of beauty—the songs of birds, or shafts of late afternoon sunlight turning a cloud of dust into a haze of gold—but I never wholly forgot how it had felt when it had descended upon me in its full force. As I sat watching those children, I began to weep, quietly but convulsively. It had been so long since I had shed tears that I felt as if I might never be able to stop.

In the days that followed, I realized that what I had experienced was something more durable than a passing private mood. There are moments of clarity (though I suppose some would think them moments of delirium), which come very rarely; but, when they do come, all at once everything is changed without having changed at all. But I could not help wondering, as the days continued to pass, what it would be like to sustain that clarity indefinitely, to see the world like this at all times and in all places, without tiring and turning away. I began to think that perhaps it was possible to know the world as I had glimpsed it in that moment. I began even to think that for once I had seen the world as it truly is, and that I had discovered that all other persons were my family, my brothers and sisters, my children and parents, and that all things living were kindred to me. Maybe, I began to believe, behind the surface of reality as I thought I knew it there was a realm of invisible connections, within whose weave all life and all consciousness move and exist; and perhaps this was the deepest truth in everything. If nothing else, I could see how someone who has known that love even for only a moment—that love without clinging, without ego, without desperation—might spend the rest of his or her life seeking to recapture the experience, if not to fathom it.

In any event, my dear one, I wept again, now gratefully, a few nights later when I was holding you before your bedtime, and then of course had to explain to you that I was not crying because I had hurt myself. Moreover, my dreams gradually ceased to torment me quite so relentlessly—or, in time, at all. In fact, the recurring dream of my visit to the graves of your father and sister at some point changed—now I had flowers with me, like the blue wildflowers which had given me a fleeting glimpse of joy—before it vanished altogether. And my dream of looking for you and not being able to find you disappeared overnight.

I will not lie, though. I didn't suddenly start living every hour as if I were in a state of grace. I had long been sustained by a strong, joyless, desperate will to live, for your sake, and the habit reasserted itself in me for some time to come. And yet, I recovered more than a mere will to persist: the desire to live fully in the world, without holding fast to everything I feared I might lose, but instead joyously. I knew now that this was something I truly wanted. And since then, in my best moments, I have been able to feel it all again as immediately as I did when watching that little girl's dance. I love you first and best, I admit—I am a mother, after all—but sometimes everyone and everything else shines in the light of my love for you.

It would be still another two years and more, of course, before you and I finally found a way to leave the camp.

Anyway, what a roundabout reply this has been. Ask a simple question from a doting mother, get a vastly involved answer. Ask two questions, and the answer becomes interminable. The long and the short of the matter is that this is how I became the curator of the old man's notebook, and that you have my blessing on your adventures as a "spiritual vagabond," so long as they sustain you. I know too that your quest will not be a selfish one—a search for mere private certainty or ease of mind—but will always also be a search for newer (or perhaps much older) ways to live into the mystery of things. I know that what moves you is a real spiritual love and compassion for others—for the whole of the suffering world of nature and humankind. I know you too well to imagine anything else.

As you requested, I attach our old friend's letter and his notes on a "shared sacred story," though I would have thought that you had it committed to memory by now. Maybe it will be a good guide along the way for you. Or maybe you will improve upon it. Whatever the case, I send it along.

And, of course, as ever and always, I send all my love as well.

PART TWO

The Old Man's Letter

My Dear,

You just left the room as I began to write this letter, but your presence remains. You eased my pain and comforted me more than you know. Despite the depravations of our camp life, there is still such grace. Even dying can be stretched out to seem like living, and it's possible to feel so achingly alive.

You left with my notebook in hand, lifting that burden. You already know that I spent much of my life studying on my own and moving from one place to another, drawing close to communities with different living experiences of the Sacred. That slim notebook contains my reflections on those years. It's my contribution to what I like to call the human family's Shared Sacred Story. I am grateful that you now hold it.

You're already familiar with its contents because they have been the background of our conversations. Other hearts open to the Sacred also know its contours. Many people may find the notebook unhelpful and feel no need to read it; indeed, the contents fall short of the living reality they refer to. Still, perhaps some people will find it useful, and with luck, more than a few will be inspired to improve it, for it will always remain unfinished.

There is a story from my earlier life that I don't want to miss sharing with you, an experience that changed me and focused my life on the purpose of the notebook.

When I was in my twenties, I lived for a while in a region wracked by religious strife and violence; along with a small cadre of aid volunteers, I was kidnapped and held hostage by one of the conflicting groups. The sounds and smells of that place were not so different from those in our encampment, and the seasick feeling of being suspended in time was oddly similar, too. My captivity was short-lived, as I was rescued along with my group after several weeks.

Being freed was a shock, and we were soon led past our incarcerated captors, who were as hungry and filthy as we were. In the harsh light, my eye was suddenly caught by the sight of one of them leaning exhausted against a wall, and in the way of intense experience, time stopped, while silence enveloped every sound. It's difficult to speak of this in a way that conveys its proper weight: fear and anguish fell away in that suspended moment as compassion, suffused with light and love more interior than I knew myself to be, overcame us both. We shared the experience of the other as the Sacred flooded our encounter. Your more reserved side might feel my experience overwrought, but its truth staggered me and altered my course.

From that day onward, I began practicing being present to the people around me, attentive to an invisible awareness imbuing each word, gesture, and facial expression. I learned to do this as a matter of course and extended my practice to the natural world, welcoming its endless grades of presence in silence.

I found these experiences of presence uncanny, while still ordinary, in the sense that they are offered to us always. We generally pay little attention, though almost anyone who has held a baby knows the recognition that breaks forth in the radiance of the baby's smile.

I gradually understood that this epiphany of mutual awareness, which you and I are unfolding in our friendship, is a disclosure of transcendence (or "interbeing" as some Buddhists like to say). Then, the more I looked, the more I discovered that each religion had its way of experiencing our sacred-rooted connection with one another, which—as in our infancy—is present before our first words and opens the space for them.

As I entered more deeply into the mystery of shared awareness, I realized that my childhood religious training had equipped me in some ways for my encounter with my captor, but in other ways, it had not. Too much of what I'd been taught about Sacred Mercy and Love had been domesticated, narrowed, or even turned against others. Yet, my silent connection with my former captor allowed me to see better the original radiance of my birth tradition, and soon I began to recognize forms of sacred mutuality everywhere.

During my travels and encounters with other people, I also became aware that their stories expressed the paradox of being seized by the Sacred and journeying in time toward it. Yet each story opened a particular doorway that I had not perceived as existing, and yet a doorway that, in some sense, I could eventually recognize within myself. My release from captivity became a metaphor for venturing further into the sacred wilderness. This wilderness is known by all sacred traditions, each in its own way, as most interior and intimate, yet beyond full comprehension.

Throughout history, for a great many people, the way to live a shared sacred story is to live their own tradition's story. But today it's possible to live our respective stories open to the echoes and insights we find among the other traditions. This is so despite earnestly held differences, which we rightly hold as dear to our hearts. Let each follow their conscience in this regard. As for me, encountering goodness and truth in other traditions led me to recover what lay hidden from me in my own.

Like everyone, I am telling my story in the way I try to live. The notebook is different. It asks no one to give up their story. It doesn't pretend to surmount the diversity of traditions or to homogenize their symbols, but it does attempt to explore the insight that we are and have always been a single family on a shared journey, returning to a sacred origin that is our true home.

Perhaps the notebook can help others more capable of composing a shared sacred tale than I could ever be.

Finally, my Dear, you've said I appear to have no secrets, but I have one to confess. Despite any appearances to the contrary, I haven't been a stranger to loneliness. I've found it crushing at times. Some of my loneliness arose from estrangement from the Sacred. Only slowly could I discern another kind of aloneness—solitude—as a friend who guided my passage into ever deeper ranges of connection. Some people may find it strange that I've found that solitude and deeper connection go hand in hand. You, I feel sure, know this in your way.

I'm sharing this because I recognize a struggle within you between suffering and love. I can see that the first threatens to overtake you, though you work hard to hide it. The sources of your suffering are various, of course, and though you rarely mention them, I know they lurk at the edges of every room you enter. I don't imagine you'll welcome advice, but since it comes from someone who won't be lying in this bed soon, I offer this: sometimes, invite your suffering in; let your heart befriend it as you can. Suffering and love can draw close.

You love more than you know. I have received that love. My love gladly meets yours.

You have my blessing to use the notebook as you deem wise.

Adieu, dear Friend.

PART THREE

Notes for a Shared Sacred Story
from the "Old Man's Notebook"

There is an ancient sacred story…

There is an ancient sacred story that has been told in every land and in every age of human history, but told always differently. Yet all peoples recall it, almost as though remembering a dream we shared in some earlier, forgotten time, but cannot grasp except through the words our various traditions have given us. It is not, I hasten to say, an inner secret teaching within our traditions, known only to a few special initiates; it is there to be heard by all who listen. Neither is it a tale forcibly composed or distilled from some artificial blending of our faiths into some featureless and anonymous "wisdom." Instead, for those with ears to hear, it rings out and echoes within all our sacred stories, emerges from both their harmonies and their dissonances, and is all the more audible the more those stories express their origins. This may be what is most beautifully strange about the tale: that it is one and many simultaneously. Perhaps this sounds foolish. Differences are real and rightly resist being glossed. At the same time, every hearer can listen with generosity rooted in their experience of the Sacred for the ring of truth in different tellings. I know that I have heard the tale told countless times and recognized it as echoing the same story on each occasion, yet I have never heard it told in the same way twice. And I know also that, while it is timeless, it must be retold anew in every generation according to the language and circumstances of the day. I myself have been trying to give it expression for many years now, as I am convinced that it must be told and retold by everyone who has heard and known it. After all, it is the true story of the world.

I have to admit, though, that I find it difficult to know quite how to begin, because in our time, especially in the wealthiest and most "modern" quarters of the earth, the task has become perhaps uniquely hard. For one thing, in previous ages it would have been easy to tell the tale as one about "religion," in the singular, since religion would for most have been regarded as a single thing: a universal virtue to be cultivated in each individual soul, a concern common to all peoples, an encompassing reality in which all of humankind participates in numberless ways, a single realm of human longing, always embraced within one and the same sacred reality. That is not really how, as a rule, we think today. We have learned instead to speak of many separate "religions," which we think of not as expressing a common human experience of reality, but as sealed systems of propositions and concepts, each isolated within itself and at odds with every other. If one religion is true, we tend to think, all others must simply be false. This is something new in the human understanding of the Sacred. Yes, of course, in every age, believers have been prone to see their own traditions as superior to all others, and even as uniquely correct; yet no one seems to have doubted that all of humankind, in its prayers and devotions and spiritual explorations, was responding to the Sacred that calls out to each of us in every moment.

So, needless to say, the tale would be much easier to tell now if—even as we embrace our particular tradition—we could also recover that older sense of the profound unity of our spiritual longing. Then, we could cease to think of our traditions as solely rival systems and see instead something far richer: different responses to the one great mystery in which we are immersed in every moment. This might free us to try to see how each sacred tradition illuminates aspects of the Sacred with particular clarity while also making space for what is true and good in other traditions. But, whether we can easily acquire the habit of thinking that way or not, still the tale must be told—and we can begin only from where we are.

It would be easier, perhaps, if we all still understood not only that the sacred realm is not the property solely of one creed, but also that—as the peoples of previous ages most certainly did understand—it is not something belonging only to "religion" in the impoverished sense of a special sphere detached from ordinary getting and giving. Not only does the mystery lie open to all of us, whether we are believers, non-believers, or—as is perhaps the case for some—neither precisely one nor the other; it addresses us all in every aspect of our existence, in even the most mundane aspects of our lives.

We all really know this, if we let ourselves. We may experience the call of the Sacred most purely and immediately when we are still children, in instants of wonder at the being of the world, when our minds are not as yet burdened by narrow certitudes or personal ambitions. But even when that innocent astonishment has faded from our lives, or we have had it drummed out of us and fixed our attention on only our daily concerns, there come moments in later life, however brief, when the extraordinary strangeness of existence breaks through the frozen surface of our conventional habits of thought, and we are seized once again by the wonderful "thereness" of the world, and by the abiding riddle of our place within it. It is this experience of amazement, surely, that inspires in any of us the consuming desire to understand our world; and it is to this desire that the sacred story, in all its variants, speaks.

And if we are properly attentive to those moments of wonder, we find that the dimension of the Sacred calls to us not only from without, but from within ourselves, speaking to us from our own depths. The marvel of the world is not purely its being, but also our consciousness of it. That immense inner capacity by which our minds receive reality into themselves is also somehow one and the same with the vast spiritual abundance of reality beyond our minds, out of which the world comes to us to be known. How very beautiful and imponderable is this depth calling out to depth. Mind and world are open to one another from the very first, each illuminating and disclosing the other as no merely material realities could. We are not machines simply recording interactions with an environment. Instead we are life and thought and awareness, actively taking all things into ourselves, joining ourselves to everything in our act of judgment and will, bringing all into a unity in consciousness, holding past, present, and future together in each instant. We are present to ourselves, abiding in ourselves precisely by letting the world make itself present within us. Every moment of experience is imbued with this mystery, and it is maybe the strangest superstition of the modern age that it can be explained away in the language of mechanism and mindless physical forces.

Here too, I think it fair to say, the call of the Sacred is especially unrelenting, and we should be especially willing to listen to it. We all desire to understand who and what we are. What is the self? What is consciousness? No question compels and troubles us more profoundly than that of whether there is some deeper or more elusive truth about each of us than our ordinary states of mind can comprehend. All of our sacred traditions tell us that there is a fuller tale, that we can know our own truest nature only if we understand that what we mistake for our isolated selves is inseparably related to others and to the whole of the living world by ties that are as incomprehensible as they are unbreakable.

Within all our natural desires to know the world and the self, we desire happiness: not, that is, mere pleasure or distraction, and not the transient, ultimately empty satisfactions we gain from material acquisitions, power over others, jealously guarded privileges, or self-aggrandizement. Rather, we yearn for a happiness that abides, that nourishes our most insatiable spiritual hunger, that brings us peace even amid our sufferings, that does not wax and wane according to fortune, and that grants us harmony both with our own deepest nature and with the world. Our shared sacred story reveals to us all the ways in which we have become estranged from the true sources of that happiness and teaches us how to find our way back to a shared flourishing of all that lives.

That way is hard to find. All the ways lie open, but are narrow for us in our present state. All of us sooner or later become insensible to the Sacred, or at least unresponsive to its call. We have all known what it is to become disenchanted: with the world, with our neighbors, most deeply with ourselves. Though it is true that our first experience of the Sacred declares itself in all things before we could possibly possess any way of naming it, and though we are provided with sacred traditions to help us find the language we lack, we often resist both that amazement and those traditions. Maybe we become fatigued by wonder. Maybe we flee from it, fearing we might be trapped forever in infancy. Whatever the case, most of us cannot sustain that innocent experience. Sooner or later, even when we hear our sacred stories told, we convert them to those systems of propositions which—though they have legitimate functions can inadvertently close us off from the Sacred. For, then, we run the danger of employing our several systems not to penetrate the mystery of our existence but instead to explain that mystery away so that it can no longer divert us from worldly pursuits.

Still, though, the memory of wonder lingers in the depths of our minds, if often at levels within ourselves of which we are scarcely aware. And we can never be wholly satisfied so long as we refuse to respond to it.

Disenchantment occurs in many ways. Probably before all others, there is the disenchantment that arises from the purely personal experience of losing our capacity for innocent surrender before the world's openness to the Sacred. The very first summons of the Sacred is much the same for all of us, as are the first stirrings of our response to it. But that initial innocence passes, habits of thought and the choices we make conspire to render that first experience of the Sacred ever more difficult to recollect, material fixations engross us, and at the last we somehow lose sight of whatever it was that evoked our original astonishment amid the tangles of our preoccupations and our prejudices. This is sad but, for most persons, inevitable. Then too, of course, there are the deeper disenchantments that come in time to most of us, bred in us by the pains, misfortunes, injustices, and illnesses we suffer, either in private or in company with others. And over almost all our lives the knowledge of our own mortality casts an ever deepening shadow, which we try to ignore but which ever and again forces itself upon us, often in our idlest moments. But, however far away from that first awakening we may wander, the desire to know that enigma more fully persists no matter how hard we struggle to force it down below the threshold of consciousness.

It is not only as individuals that we suffer this loss; a people, a culture, even an age can become disenchanted in its own, very distinctive ways. In our time, in fact, especially in the most materially secure societies, we have discovered a new, particularly destructive kind of disenchantment, one that has tragically alienated us from the natural order, one another, and ourselves. For four centuries now, we have been taught to think that we inhabit a world in which the Sacred has no place because, quite simply, there is no mystery to be found in the being of things—or in life, or in mind, or in any dimension of reality before which we might naturally stand amazed—but only a certain amount of factual information yet to be obtained and a certain degree of material mastery yet to be exercised. Above all, we have been taught to think that matter is something essentially dead, that nature is only a machine made up of lifeless parts, and that the mind is either an anomaly within or an accidental physical biproduct of an intrinsically spiritless universe. The world appears to us less and less as the home in which we dwell, inviting us to draw near and respond to the mystery at its center, and more and more as the mirror of our own power and the object of our avarice.

There is a genuine horror in this view of things. We have progressively transformed our home into a heartless engine of ceaseless material production and consumption, and reduced everything natural to either a resource to be exploited or an obstacle to be surmounted. Not only are we spiritually impoverished as a result; we are rapidly murdering the earth and destroying ourselves. If only we were still better able to experience the Sacred spontaneously, and to recall—as all the great traditions would have us do—our profound spiritual connection to all things living, perhaps we would be less able to violate, despoil, pollute, and destroy the world with quite the abandon that we do.

This is insanity. It is a way of living that withers our own nature even as it destroys the natural order about us. It makes a necessary virtue of greed but a mere dispensable luxury of moral community. In place of all those shared human needs and desires that naturally bind us together as a family—those healthy needs that must be filled for us to flourish—it gives us only an unending succession of ever newer and more trivial material appetites. It empties social life of the very grounds of human flourishing—of association and affinity and common purposes—and destroys the natural ecology of community. And, without those grounds and that ecology, we cannot learn how to expand our intimate loves and local sympathies into something more universal, able to include the whole of humanity and of the natural world into its embrace. We become imprisoned in our little selves—while all around us the true world falls into ruin. What a strange age ours is: on the one hand, an age of a homogenizing global culture of consumerism and jealous individualism; on the other, an age of tribalism, fear of the unfamiliar, and ethnic and nationalist resentment. It makes us strangers in the world that was once our home.

We cannot continue along such a path; it can lead only to ever greater fragmentation and catastrophe. This, above all, is why the need to explore our shared sacred story is especially acute at this moment, and why it is particularly necessary to tell it in a way that loudly affirms at once both the diversity of our traditions and the spiritual oneness of our humanity—both the endlessly various ways in which we respond to the Sacred and the universality of its claim. Such a story has the power to meet the urgency of this moment. And perhaps, too, this telling of the tale is possible now as it never was before; perhaps the crisis of our time is also an opportunity for moving toward a new stage in our spiritual history. If nothing else, ours is a time of truly global communication with one another. For all the threats peculiar to our age, a broad avenue has also opened up for knowing and learning from one another's cultures and religions in a depth our ancestors could scarcely have imagined.

Still, though, the impediments are formidable. To tell the story, we must first "untell" the story that has replaced it, and we should be honest about how we have come to be where we are. It is specifically Western modern culture, in its militantly secularized and materialist expressions, that has in many respects thrown up the greatest obstacles to a recovery of a sense of the Sacred, and none more insurmountable than the modern prejudice that some essential antagonism exists between religious yearning and scientific inquiry. This is the result of a very particular intellectual history, which—because of a certain intellectual parochialism among prosperous nations—has often been promoted throughout the world as the highest achievement of reason. And yet, this is all little more than an accident of history.

We should recall that the fruitfulness of modern science was achieved by a severe narrowing of focus. The first principle of the new method of seventeenth-century natural philosophy was a negative one: it excluded not only any notion of essence or purpose—what the classical philosophers called formal and final causes—but also the exclusion of any distinct principle of life beyond mere mechanical forces. At first, of course, most early modern thinkers were content simply to draw brackets around physical nature and to study it in isolation from spiritual or metaphysical questions. Most even held onto some notion of God and the soul. But they often tended to think of both as realities merely set alongside a natural order composed of nothing but machine processes, and for just this reason it became ever more common for the culture at large to think of the world as a machine and of everything sacred or spiritual or divine as belonging to some ghostly realm wholly outside the fabric and structure of nature. It was inevitable, then, that one side of this absolute division would come to devour the other. For the culture of the sciences, ultimately this meant that the realm of spirit had to be made subject to the logic of the machine. For a scientific view of reality, it came to be believed, everything—even consciousness—had to be reducible to mindless physical forces. The brackets that had once isolated the physical from the spiritual merely as a matter of scientific method increasingly came to be mistaken for the shape of reality itself.

As I say—an accident of history. And yet, even so, in only a handful of centuries the sciences have radically reshaped both our concept of reality and the material conditions of the world around us, and it would be impossible now credibly to tell our sacred story without acknowledging this. Nor should we wish to do so, since the achievements of modern science, both in granting us knowledge and in revealing new aspects of reality that were once closed to us, demand our reverence and our gratitude. Again, we enjoy insights into the deep structures of the cosmos, and these add whole new dimensions to our story: new magnitudes of wonder, new amplitudes of light, new paths by which to seek the truth of things. But this also makes it all the more vital that the fiction of an irreconcilable difference between sacred and scientific ways of knowing be defeated.

We might be tempted to do this by building a wall between the sciences and religious seeking since they explore different questions and spheres of inquiry. Proper distinctions must always be drawn. Nonetheless, religious seeking and scientific research are both driven by the same longing to know the truth of things in its fullness, the same hunger for ever fuller explanation, the same need to understand the world not simply in its discrete aspects but in its ultimate foundations. And it is simply false that either, in pursuing its own path, cannot be nourished or chastened by the other. It would be absurd to suggest, for instance, that modern discoveries in the sciences—in say, animal cognition, cosmology, molecular biology, physics, and so forth—should not have profound implications for the way religious seekers understand the nature of the cosmos, of consciousness, of our relations to one another, to animal creation, to the natural world, and even to the Sacred. But the reverse is true as well: the culture of the sciences could learn much from the long metaphysical, logical, and even spiritual traditions of the world's faiths: about, say, the limits of what the scientific method can address—such as the sheer existence of anything at all—or about not presuming a reductive physical explanation of every aspect of human experience, or about realms of mental life that escape convincing quantitative calculation.

The picture of physical reality produced by the modern sciences is astonishing and beautiful; but, when mistaken for the complete picture of all that is and all that may be truly affirmed, it is not only radically incomplete but distorted, because by itself it simply does not have the power to encompass vast ranges of the human experience. Having rendered the world mute—or, at least, having willfully deafened ourselves to its entreaties and admonitions—we today for the most part have no compunction about forcing it to serve the ends we will for it. No vision of things could be less conducive to an awareness of the Sacred.

But again, I have to say—have to remind myself, at least, if no one else—that ours is also perhaps a hopeful moment. The times not only cry out for a new telling of our sacred story; in many ways, they invite it and are even hospitable to it. As much as we must recover and newly express ancient wisdoms, we need not—we must not—lose sight of the genuine spiritual riches of the present. It is true that no sacred tradition's understanding of reality can accept the mechanistic metaphysics that lingers on tacitly in much of the culture of the sciences today. But there is no need to wrestle with ghosts. Both rigid religious and materialist exclusivism can be shed. The sciences themselves, in any number of recent advances, already point us beyond mechanistic metaphysics. At the same time, the truest forms of our own religious traditions, if properly recovered from the forgetfulness into which they have so often fallen in our time, are the most powerful enemies of exclusivist narrowness. And, after all, both religious and scientific cultures, in differing ways, have all too often subordinated the cosmos as a whole to purely human interests and ends. Perhaps then, having arrived together at this perilous moment, they should find ways of chastening one another, and of encouraging one another to revise their most stubbornly narrow habits of thought.

The ancient sacred story is our own story...

The ancient sacred story is our own story, of course, inasmuch as it is the story of everything. The first question we tend to ask when seized by wonder before the mystery of being, is the question of being itself: Why is there anything rather than nothing? How is it that anything in this world of constant change and ceaseless transience has any reality to begin with? And this question touches upon a more original, more perplexing enigma than that of the causal history of the cosmos or of how the present physical state of things may have arisen from earlier physical states. It is the question not merely of how the world came to be, but why. More than that, it is the question of the very possibility of a world composed entirely of contingent things—finite things, things composed of other things, things that come to be and waver for a while in existence and then pass away. Every particular reality we experience through our senses is dependent upon and conditioned by other realities, and belongs to endless chains of cause and effect, and nowhere do we find any unmoving ground that we can isolate as a distinct object of experience. We rarely think about this, of course, but when we do, in those moments when the strangeness of the world takes us out of our normal habits, we almost inevitably find ourselves wondering as well whether all the dependent realities we can perceive rest upon some absolute reality we cannot.

Our ancient sacred story and all our sacred traditions tell us that this mystery cannot be reduced simply to physical forces, or to the flow of material causes, or indeed to anything conditional, dependent, or essentially impermanent. Beyond the flow of transient forms that surrounds us, there is an eternally abiding reality, at once manifest and hidden in all that is. Our traditions understand and speak of this reality—this source or ground or origin or ultimate truth—in various ways: as a more original dimension of spiritual reality, as the transcendent God from whom all things come forth and to whom all things return, as infinite mind pervading all things, as a divine unity that resonates throughout the whole, as infinite spirit, as the Way of Heaven, as an absolute oneness or luminous emptiness, or simply as that which is inconceivably unconditioned and "awake." Whatever they call it, however, they all agree that its nature surpasses our ability to grasp it, that what we know of it is only a partial glimpse of its limitless nature, and that it is futile therefore to try to reduce it to a single concept or principle. At the same time, however, they also tell us that, so long as we are incurious or unaware of it, we risk condemning ourselves to a kind of spiritual restlessness and dissatisfaction, even a kind of homelessness, adrift in a world in which can find no sure refuge. The desire for truth and the desire for an abiding happiness both find their proper object in apprehending—though not necessarily comprehending—this mystery. To be conscious of it is to know our unity with one another and with all things, and to know that our existence touches upon an eternal truth.

This is because this transcendent reality—the One, luminous emptiness, God, Ik Onkar, Brahman, Wakan Tanka, or however we speak of it—is not merely the world's highest truth, but also the deepest truth within each of us. We cannot rightly know ourselves apart from or in separation from that reality. We cannot find the fulfillment we seek—the deepest happiness for which our nature longs—except through a union of knowledge and love with this transcendent origin and end. We cannot reach our final and most enduring rest except by finding refuge from the conditioned in the unconditioned, and by obtaining release from the terror of transience in the peace of what abides.

When we see clearly that this absolute reality is the Sacred upon which everything—the entire cosmos, in all its infinite variety and vastness—depends, we are set free. We are liberated from that most destructive of delusions, the fantasy of self-sufficiency. We come to see that we are never the source or the foundation of our own being, that we are never complete in ourselves alone, that we cannot find our own highest fulfillment in separation from one another. Yes, that ultimate truth is the transcendent horizon of our world, beyond everything finite and impermanent, but it is also an immanent depth within each of us, more original than our isolated selves, always there already, underlying and sustaining our small, individual, private egos. And, since this reality is one and the same truth for all of us, at once within all things and beyond all things, it binds the whole of existence together in a community of being from the very first. The world about us in its every natural dimension is to be cherished and protected by us, pitied and revered, feared and loved, but also recognized as a greater reality to which we always already belong, in which we always must participate, and for which we are always morally responsible. So long as we do not recognize this—do not recognize how essentially we belong to one another and to the whole of life—we cut ourselves off from the transcendent wellspring of reality, and do so even right within ourselves.

This means, of course, that all of humanity is joined from the first and forever in a living solidarity that none of the divisions we create among ourselves can abolish. Our dependence upon that sole ultimate truth is also our dependence upon one another, and our need for one another. We are, whether we wish to see it or not, a family, a single household. And, of course, that unity does not end at the boundaries of the merely human. All life is kith and kin to us; humanity belongs to a still greater household; the whole of the cosmos gives us life and shelter and companionship, and we are called as spiritual beings to sustain and cherish it in return. Only in spiritual communion with the whole of nature are we who and what we are. That which is within each of us is also that which lives in all things, giving them life. It is called by many names—*ase*, *chi*, *wakan*, *pneuma*, *neshamah*, *ruh*, *ātman*, the light of consciousness, Buddha nature, wakened mind, and so forth—but, none of these names can fully define or exhaust its mystery. What we can know, though, even as our words fail us, is that all that lives is one community grounded in the Sacred.

Hence, and inevitably, we are social creatures—not simply out of practical necessity, but in our very essence. We are responsible for one another, reliant upon one another, bound to one another by ties of morality and fellow feeling and common needs, but also ideally by bonds of love; and we can flourish fully only in and through and with one another. Thus the Sacred shows itself to us with particular urgency and immediacy in the faces of those around us, and tells us—even when we try to silence the voices of our consciences—that the wisdom and happiness we seek are never truly possible unless we also desire and seek them for all others. That ultimate reality is the sacred horizon of our deepest rational desires—the source of goodness, truth, and beauty, of peace and refuge, of love and eternity—and therefore the true happiness for which we ceaselessly long. And yet, even so, its transcendence is available to us firstly through those who are close at hand, in the concrete reality of our everyday lives. Happiness for ourselves, it seems, is paradoxically found in desiring it for others first.

Supreme, then, among the powers that unite us to the transcendent source and to one another, and that unite that source to us, is love, in all its forms: the serene love of compassion or charity, the deep self-renouncing love that seeks the welfare of all, the tender love of a parent for a child, the love of siblings one for another, nuptial love, protective love, the passionate abandon of the soul's ecstatic devotion to God, the love of beauty, the hunger for justice, care for nature (and on and on). Love—not appetent clinging, not jealous possessiveness, but real love in all its selfless generosity—is a "sure path" that leads us toward the highest truth.

For the most part, though, the truth of things is near to us at all times. It is everywhere and in all things, and yet it is also beyond our reach. Our daily existence is as a rule one of alienation from the transcendent, separation from the absolute, loss of our true selves, estrangement from our neighbors and from nature. Both as individuals and as communities, we regularly find ourselves living lives of struggle, suffering, violence, ignorance, fear, and death, without even remembering having chosen to do so. Hate all too often triumphs over love, falsehood over truth, conflict over peace, selfishness over community, avarice over generosity, sorrow over joy—and death over life. Even those traditions that have best preserved a sense of how to remain at peace with the natural world and to preserve community are still keenly aware that there are countless ways in which we fail to live as we should. This world is our home, and yet we dwell in it as if in exile.

Why is this so? Words here once again prove inadequate, though also once again necessary. Whatever it is that has made us strangers in the world has arisen from causes that we cannot wholly comprehend and is perpetuated by forces we can only rarely and feebly resist. We speak of it as the forfeit of an original innocence, as a broken communion with God, as captivity in illusion, as departure from our true estate, as bondage in a chain of causes without any known beginning or end, or in countless other ways, and we describe ourselves as a result as wandering in ignorance, or as languishing in sin, or as being borne along in a stream of ceaseless becoming, or as being entangled in a web of unending birth and death and rebirth, or as suffering in obliviousness of our true nature, or what have you. Whatever words we use, the experience we share is one of fragmentation, alienation, oppression, and loss.

We are also, however, beset on all sides by inimical forces. A great many are entirely impersonal, "natural ills" such as suffering, disease, bereavement, old age, poverty, and death, to which all living things are subject and from which they must be delivered. True happiness or spiritual freedom, obviously, is impossible so long as these ills wield unopposed power over our minds and bodies, or over the minds and bodies of our families, loved ones, neighbors, and fellow creatures. But our traditions tell us too that we contend in this life with moral evils—with human malice and with social structures of cruelty and injustice—from which we must also be delivered; and, to achieve this deliverance, we must struggle with forces beyond and within ourselves. Each of these moral "adversaries" is terrible in its own way, and each can be defeated only by its spiritual contrary. Hatred can be overcome only by charity, suffering only by care, violence only by peacefulness, transgression only by forgiveness, injustice only by equity, malice only by benevolence. To be free from this dimension of evil's power, we must seek reconciliation both with those we harm and with those who harm us; to change the hearts of others, we must be willing to change our own hearts first. Even then, moral evil—cruelty, violence, deceit, exploitation, greed, and every other willful or callous violation of the well-being of others and of the world—must remain something of an enigma. It emanates from human freedom, and its seeds are found in all of us, but something about it always eludes our understanding, and in fact should do so, because it is alien to what we most truly are. There is an emptiness at its heart—an absence—which cannot be grasped, but only refused and, when possible, healed.

Then too—or so our story usually tells us—there are perhaps malign spiritual agencies arrayed against us, intentional accomplices of ignorance and strife, resourceful forces of anger and enmity, cunning powers of darkness. We may not be able to understand them precisely, or even to say to what degree they have their reality in the world or in our minds or in both at once, but nevertheless they actively strive to keep us bound in ignorance, fear, and misery. These too, whatever they are, as they invade from without or emanate from within, can be resisted and defeated only by the same refusal of violence, the same longing for wisdom, and the same life of love by which we resist more mundane spiritual adversities.

Whatever the nature of the evils that confront us, though, we must not imagine that they can be overcome solely at the level of our immediate personal relations. The forces that oppose the Sacred are far more ingenious and formidable than that. Moral evil, for instance, works its harm not merely in individual acts of malice and selfishness, but also in enduring structures of social and political inequity. Such structures are entwined with the corrupt desires and ambitions of human hearts; but over time they grow into oppressive powers in their own right, preserving and extending themselves in an impersonal way, and often escaping anyone's immediate control. We live lives encompassed within countless social customs, traditions, institutions, and fixed orders of privilege that not only create, but strive to perpetuate economic and political injustice, the oppression of the weak, the neglect of the sick and the suffering, and the cruel exploitation of our fellow human beings and of the natural realm. These too are spiritual malignities, spiritual antagonists, states of spiritual bondage from which we and the world must be set free.

Happily, we are not alone in our struggles against the powers that hold us in thrall. We do not have to rely entirely upon our own exertions to find release from the evils that oppress us, our neighbors, or our world. Few among us have the resources, wholly unaided, to find spiritual truth and freedom. Others come to assist us. There are, all the traditions seem to agree, persons or communities with special gifts for helping us along the path: prophets, hidden prophets, sages, gurus, teachers, monks and nuns, contemplatives, and countless other spiritual guides among our fellow human beings who can offer us wisdom, enlightenment, counsel, spiritual instruction, even—for some—flashes of revelation. But many of our traditions tell us too that our condition requires a remedy more radical than counsel or spiritual guidance alone.

They say that it is beyond our native powers to free ourselves unassisted from bondage to ignorance, sin, mortality, and all else that separates us from our true end, and that therefore we are in desperate need of rescue: the conquest of death's dominion, the raft of *dharma* that conveys us across to the other side of the sea of suffering and illusion, the bridge of souls that delivers us beyond the cycle of becoming, or perhaps even the interventions of the Sacred who takes human form in our midst. These traditions assure us that there are figures of far greater power and capacity than the merely natural, who come not only to our assistance, but in order to act on our behalf, and to deliver us from the alienations and afflictions of this life in ways that far exceed anything we in our present state could accomplish. They bring us not only wisdom, but also grace or merit or supernatural power, and they dedicate themselves to the liberation of all who suffer and who despair of ever finding release: divinely inspired prophets, *tzadikim*, *bodhisattva*s, gods, angels, spirit-guides, saints—or even avatars of God, or God's Logos incarnate, the Seal of the Prophets, or emanations of the primordial Buddha.

What, though, is it to be saved or set free entirely from all that holds us captive? Words fail yet again. What we can perhaps say is it is to be raised into a new, and scarcely imaginable, reality. We can, as well, point toward it as the ultimate horizon of all our hope and longing, using the various symbols and images and concepts our traditions give us to do so. We can try to conjure up pictures of it that fall within the scope of history, or that belong entirely to eternity, or that have dimensions proper to both: universal reconciliation, the eschatological reign of cosmic peace, cosmic restoration, the kingdom of love and knowledge, Ramrajya, the Buddha field, deification, union with God, the final *parinirvāṇa*, ascent to a higher plane, release from birth and death, return into the primordial timeless time, and so on. Still, all that we say about it is far surpassed by what cannot be said.

What we can certainly know, however, is that to be joined to that end in this life is also to be reconciled with our true selves: our inmost or most original nature, the Sacred within us, that which is deeper, truer, and more real than the fleeting, dim, and fluctuating psychological ego. It is to be cleansed of sin, roused from forgetfulness, delivered from ignorance, fully awakened, restored to innocence, made whole, blessed with the highest happiness. It is a state in which the self has become perfectly transparent before the divine, or the absolute, or the unconditioned ground within. And it is to be set free to receive and to give the fullness of love, which is the highest freedom of all, because it joins us to everything we otherwise have lost: the absolute or the One or God; our world, our neighbors; our fellow beings; ourselves.

Still, at the last, we must admit that nothing we can conceive is wholly sufficient to that final dimension of the Sacred.

We are called to live within this story...

We are called to live within this story and cannot hear it if we are not willing to attempt to do so. All its various tellings, in all our traditions, provide us not merely with stories to enjoy but with forms of life to inhabit. True, they are tales told about God, the gods, the Buddha nature, the absolute, the unconditioned, and so forth, but they are also the retelling of who and what we ourselves can be. Through them, we enter into the mystery of the Sacred ever more deeply and in countless ways—by prayer, common worship, sacraments, pilgrimage, adoration, contemplation, ecstatic devotion, spiritual surrender, reading and interpretation of scripture, *śrāddha*, feasts and fasts, as well as in many ways so deeply instilled in us that we do not even think of them as religious. These tellings of the story do not merely give us information about the transcendent truth of things: they show us paths to illumination that others have walked before us and teach us how to follow. They make that ultimate truth present to our spiritual eyes. They instruct us in moral and spiritual virtues and arts that bring us nearer the transcendent source and that therefore, as our paths converge upon it, bring us nearer to one another, and allow us to flourish together.

All these many tellings of the story are also the retelling of the world. They show our true relationship to the world to be one of care, reverence, and adoration of the sacred reality hidden and upholding all things. They grant us a vision of a world freed from ruthless exploitation, domination, and consumption, returned to its original innocence, transfigured once more into our common home. In part, they do this by transforming the world into a mystical geography, marked out by holy places, paths of pilgrimage, sacred landscapes, "thin places," consecrated grounds, clearings in the forest where the transcendent is present with a special immediacy. They not only make us aware of a cosmos charged with numinous power, mystery, and sanctity, they open real avenues of entry into it. They are not just stories about the true way; they offer expressions of it, as it is found in innumerable different places, among all peoples.

The story's tellings are also the retelling of time, disclosing its inmost essence, its primal purity, its openness to paths of reconciliation, and its final peace. Our shared sacred story is a kind of secret history within the history we know, both cosmic and human. It offers not a rival account of past events or an alternative to scientific and historical scholarship but instead touches upon a foundational narrative—a more original dimension of reality. It grants us glimpses of a universal spiritual history within which our local cultures and particular histories are always already embraced. It calls us to the world that lies veiled behind the flow of passing events. To know it is to be set free from the illusion that we are fated to the violent and oppressive chronicles of division and cruelty in which we find ourselves confined. But, again, of necessity, it is told in the language of revelation, myths, symbols, dream images, and parables.

And yet, it must be told in a way that calls attention not only to the incidental similarities between differing traditions but to the deepest harmonies that unite them. This way of telling the shared tale can be especially helpful in a global age. Essential differences among traditions can and should be honored, but I sincerely doubt that in our time we can preserve what is truest within our particular tradition unless we are willing to recognize what is resonant in other traditions and that we can learn from them.

Ours is a time of crisis. To remedy the ills affecting the earth and heal our fractured society requires committed spiritual solidarity. All the old passions that divide us and impoverish our moral imaginations must be healed in our cultures, minds, and hearts. Only in the light of our shared sacred story does humanity have any real chance of overcoming the most devastating evils incubated by the modern world.

I fervently hope that this is what the future holds for us. Given the challenges that now stand before us, a dedication to our shared sacred story has become a task we must not evade. The reasons for embracing it are of the greatest imaginable urgency. In this age, as in every age, we need to tell it—and always to tell it better and more fully—so that it might instruct us in the supreme virtue and highest freedom: love, in its every true expression, in all and for all.

Kisa Gotami

A RETELLING OF THE BUDDHIST SACRED STORY

Kisa Gotami

The tale of Kisa Gotami has been told for more than two thousand years. It is relevant now. It tells of a young woman who escaped the misery of poverty and social bias when she married into a rich family, believing that her happiness was assured. When her only child died, she was overwhelmed with suffering. Her tale is a story of recovery and awakening, even in the worst of times. It is about the transformation of grief into wisdom and compassion. The story lies at the heart of the multi-faceted family of traditions that we call Buddhism.

In Madhyapur, a village in ancient India, it was the custom for villagers to gather around a fire in the evenings when the weaving, farming, and labors of the day were done. It was a time for rest and for stories. This particular evening was special: a greatly revered nun from the nearby temple had been invited. She sat silent near the fire, somewhat apart from the others. A village elder welcomed her and said, "Sister Kisa Gotami, thank you for agreeing to spend a few evenings with us in the village. We are grateful. Will you tell us your story?" The old woman looked up slowly and nodded. "It is time," she said. Kisa Gotami wrapped the simple cotton robes she wore around her shoulders. She took the seat of honor by the fire, and a young girl brought her a tumbler of fresh water. A young man placed more wood on the fire. An expectant quiet came over the gathering. Everyone, including children and even animals, leaned forward to listen.

My name is Kisa Gotami. I was always called the Thin One as I was growing up in this village. Gotami is my family name. It reminds me of my teacher, Gotama Buddha, and my dear family.

I have walked here from my temple this evening to be with you. I remember many of you and am grateful for the food you offer the nuns of my community. The sounds of the birds, the winds, and the humming of wheels spinning cotton are familiar music. They remind me of growing up in this village, full of happiness and tenderness.

As far back as I can remember, I worked in the fields with my younger sister and brother, side by side with others picking cotton for the spinners, pricking my fingers on the needle-like thorns, and bagging the soft balls of fluff. My family was allowed gleanings when a day's work was done. We took them home to my father, who was a cotton weaver, and my mother, who mended clothing for those with means. I had already found out that survival governed everything. My wages brought home yogurt curd and a few coins for my family. I was content.

Then, one evening, I learned another truth about being a young woman. While picking cotton carefully from the bolls, my back bent, I heard a young man, not much older than myself, shouting: "Hey, Scrawny. How are you doing!" No one ever called me scrawny. It was demeaning.

I ignored him, but the boy continued, "I know you love me, Kisa." I did not love him or any of the village rowdies who often watched me work as they drank village hooch in the late afternoon. For some reason, that day I stood tall. I said boldly, "I don't think so." But I could not afford to be rude. The cotton and linen clothes they were wearing would no doubt be in my mother's mending basket soon.

As I walked toward the village, I noticed another young man. He saw me as well. He was wearing a linen tunic of very fine blue weave not made in this village. The boys continued to call out to me, but the stranger simply approached me. Awkwardly, he said, "I don't think you are scrawny." I heard him clearly but pretended not to have heard him and kept walking.

Everyone knew everyone else in the village. Merchants and storekeepers greeted me. The dairy man who knew how poor we were slipped an extra pot of curd into my basket. He winked at me—something he had never done before. I took the curd.

As a child, I had not realized we were poor or that boys could speak to me as if they knew me well. My parents, trying to protect me, had always made sure my bowl was filled. All that changed one day as I went with my mother to buy lentils. I noticed that she looked worried. When it came time to pay for the lentils, I realized that the merchant seemed angry and condescending as she was counting out the coins. There weren't enough. We returned home with half a bag of lentils. This is how I learned that my parents could barely manage. And it was obvious that we were not the only ones. Times were hard, and I saw others around us who were like us. My heart went out to them. At about that time, things gradually grew worse. The terrible claw of poverty gripped many of us. My parents always managed to get enough to fill the rice jar and find some vegetables, so we were not starving. But I never left a meal feeling full.

Even as a young girl I contemplated my lot. I wondered if there might be another way, a way that was not bound by poverty and worries about survival, or by wealth, station, and gender, by gain and loss. In the midst of happiness, there always seemed to be suffering and insecurity. Surely there could be a way of freedom, a way that was not dependent on life's circumstances? I could taste the flame of my own spiritual yearning.

One evening, after returning home from the fields, I sat down by my mother. Hunger gnawed at my stomach and I tried not to complain. I helped her card and prepare the cotton—combing out the tough seeds and vegetable matter so it could be made into soft *puni* rolls for the frames outside. The cleaned cotton was washed by dew at night and dried in the sun before my mother and I spun it into thread. At the other end of our hut, my father was always working the loom. He made a very simple weave.

My mother handed me a special bright skirt and blouse from a chest. I sensed what was coming. She said, "It's your father's cousin's family. They've come back! They earned much money in the hills, where the cotton is finer. But they have returned to Madhyapur and bought some land. They have only daughters and one son." I held my breath. "They are looking for a wife from a family in this village." She was speaking quickly. "They would like their son to marry a nice, sensible local girl. I am sure it will be fine." My mother paused and added, almost pleadingly, "We will never get an opportunity like this again." She herself had come from the lowest caste and grasped at this chance.

A young girl who had offered drinks earlier blurted out, "What happened?" Sister Kisa smiled remembering the curiosity she had felt as a young woman.

I bowed to my mother. I looked to my father. His eyes were downcast. I could see he was worried that I would feel out of place amidst the wealth. But the luxury of choice was not an option for me. The marriage would help everyone. I said, "I will do this. It will be fine. I will have a son!" I was seventeen.

When I was introduced formally to the young man, I discovered that he was the same young man who had spoken to me, the boy in the blue linen shirt whose voice and eyes had heartened me. I cheered up and my parents were delighted at my happiness. I would have security and even help my family.

In the early days of my marriage I was filled with joy. The smell of jasmine and mountain flowers pervaded my husband Raja's beautiful family home. It was located on a steep hillside above the fields, shaded from harsh sunlight by tangles of trees and shrubs. Every day I chose new clothes—red silk, with a burnished copper shawl, or a sober grey fine muslin with silver stitching. Scarves trailed from my shoulders like mountain waterfalls. My husband and mother-in-law gave me bangles and strings of jewels. I believed that this happiness would endure. Food was plentiful. I never worried about the next meal. My parents' lives were improved as well.

But even blissful realms contain the seeds of discontent. I soon began to experience discomfort and difficulties. In subtle ways, my in-laws let me know that I was fortunate to have married into their family. They commented on the darkness of my skin, on my lower station in the village, on my unpolished ways. I did everything I could to please them, but I was always afraid. I realized that the only way to really prove my worth was to have a son.

I had found wealth and fine clothes, but I was no longer content. My siblings and childhood friends did not come to see me. Although I was still in the same village, it was as if I were living in a world apart. I was used to being busy and needed. On seeing the girls I knew picking and carding cotton and spinning together in the distance I would feel lonely. I yearned for joy and companionship. When I shyly asked my husband if he could speak to his parents, he replied, "You have to understand, they are doing their best." He could not see the problem.

I longed to spend time with my parents, but my sister and brother, who lived nearby, felt they were the ones who should be caring for the aging couple and seeing to their needs. My sister seized the cooking pan from my hands when I tried to cook rice for them: "No no no! Your shawl will get dirty!" No one in the village was ever rude—I almost wished they had been. Money and fine clothes seemed to have created barriers. The dairy man and people in the houses bowed as I passed, but they gossiped behind my back. This was very different from the offerings and respect that a nun receives. Today when I come here, you offer donations for us nuns and our temple. This shows genuine devotion and respect for our way of life, rather than disregard, or derision, or contempt.

The storytelling continued. Sister Kisa was careful to tell the truth but not to blame anyone for what had happened in the village. It was as if with great kindness she was holding a mirror up to us. The fire was flickering, and Sister Kisa smiled as a child placed wood on the coals.

If I could just have a son, everything would be all right, I thought. I saw my husband's disappointment when nothing happened. I heard the housemaids chatting as they clattered plates after meals. I overheard one say, "What do you think they'll do if she does not get pregnant? They need sons. Will they find him another wife or send her back?"

One morning, I went for a walk in the garden at dawn and suddenly felt sick. A washerwoman saw me as she walked by with clean sheets to hang on the line. By breakfast, every woman in the house knew even before I did. They asked, "Is madame alright sitting there?" "Does madame need a fan?" "Dear Kisa, please sit here and make yourself comfortable. Have some rice-gruel!" All the unhappiness and doubts of the previous months dissolved. I started to cry and laugh at the same time. I was expecting a child.

"It is time to return to the temple," said Sister Kisa, leaving everyone anxious to hear what had happened next. Even if some of them already knew, they all wanted to hear more of the story. The next evening, she began again, smiling:

I was pregnant. My stomach grew like a ripening mango. But I wanted a boy so much that I had terrible nightmares about giving birth to a girl. After two weeks of fear, I decided to take things into my own hands. I decided that my child must be a boy like his father, not a girl with all the troubles of being a woman like me. Secretly I made a pact with the gods to make it so. I was consumed with prayers and wishes. I slept on the floor so that I would not disturb my husband. What if I did not have a boy? I felt indebted to Raja for having lifted me out of poverty. I was pleased I had left the servant caste. I valued my new status and did not want to lose it. One thought led to another, and in no time at all I began to hate everything about being a female. My mother had told me that when I was born, she cried for months and mourned. She explained that when a boy comes first, everyone rejoices.

The day came when I felt the first pangs of childbirth. The household women surrounded me, but my desire for a boy kept me tight and anxious. While giving birth I experienced the most excruciating pain I had ever felt. I pleaded with the gods, "Grant me a son!" I even bargained with them, promising that if they granted me a son, I would do everything in my power to repay the blessing with my life—if I survived. The pain of birth was terrible, but when I thought of the possibility that I might give birth to a girl, the fear was even more agonizing. My emotions were raging inside me, like an inferno with flames fueled by a fire-breathing monster! If anyone had asked me whether I wanted to die a premature death from childbirth or a premature death by giving birth to a girl, I would have chosen death by childbirth.

Sister Kisa felt the pain of all those like her, born as women, who suffered in this way. Recognizing that she was sharing a harsh truth with the villagers, the old nun sat tall and softened her voice so that the sting was felt, but the love of the old woman was stronger.

When my time came, I began shouting out the names of boys, believing that if the gods heard me, I would have a son. Immediately after I heard the infant cry, it was brought to me. I held up the baby and screamed in delight, showing him to the women around me. "It is a boy!" They cheered.

The listening villagers all laughed and cheered as well. Many had not known that the nun Kisa had had a child so many years ago. "A lucky woman," they murmured in appreciation. Sister Kisa understood and waited until they grew silent again.

As I cried for joy, my tears were like streams flowing into the Ganges River. I named my baby boy Anupam, "the precious one," as I thanked the gods. But the true gift was the overwhelming love that arose in me. Nothing was more important to me than this child.

Anupam was a plump, healthy baby who happened to be a boy. While I was relieved, I was also fearful because, like all mothers, I wanted nothing to happen to my child. During his first year I watched his every move. There was never a time when he wasn't with me. He slept with me and my husband. Once Anupam turned two, I relaxed. I felt he was in less danger now that he had survived thus far.

One day, when Anupam was three years old, I took him by the hand and we went outside for walk. I was not concerned because the monsoon rains were not due for at least a week. But suddenly, without warning, rain started to fall in a deluge. It was as if the Ganges

River had risen up to the heavens and then turned upside down. The teeming rain rapidly carved deep gullies around our house. Torrents of water streaming in waves down the steep hillside flooded the village. I had trouble seeing, because the rain created an opaque wall, nearly blinding me to everything. The raindrops fell so hard they felt like pebbles pelting down from the clouds. Within a few seconds, I was knee-deep in the rising flood. The force of the water stunned me, and suddenly Anupam was swept from my hand. Drenched with the pounding drops, I frantically reached into the torrent, stumbling forward to rescue him. I kept screaming, hoping he would hear me. Then I fell, my arms flailing wildly in desperation. My hand hit something. I grabbed hold of whatever it was in an attempt to get on my feet. To my great relief, it was Anupam. I pulled him into my arms and stood up. I was so happy to have found him! He was quiet, and his body was soaked. I hurried home, dried him, and placed him on blankets and cushions.

I sang lullabies and I held him close. His body remained limp as if asleep. I took him in my arms and rocked him gently. He did not wake up. Time passed and I panicked. The servants said they thought the child was no longer alive, but I believed they were wrong. I wrapped him in a shawl and ran through fields filled with bushes and shrubs to the village in search of help. There were voices I thought I heard, gods and goddesses speaking to me, "Kisa, we'll bring him back to life, just as we brought him to life in the first place."

Villagers attempted to help, but I was mad with fear and grief, insisting that I needed a doctor. I searched all night. As the sun rose, I came across Kalyana, the grain merchant's wife, as she was leaving the park nearby. She had offered a meal to the Buddha, her teacher. Now, because the monsoons were arriving early, she needed to get home. It was a dangerous time, and she had to protect her stores.

When she noticed me, Kalyana did not at first want to stop or get involved. But compassion can come to us unexpectedly, and Kalyana could clearly see what had happened. Her voice reached me through the chaos of my mind. She looked at me and said, "Kisa Gotami, look at me for one moment. I will help you." I knew she could help. I wept, pleading, "I need a doctor. My child is ill. I must make him better." Kalyana touched my shoulder, saying, "I know a doctor who can heal this sickness. He is in a park nearby. He will give you the medicine you need."

How her words calmed me was a mystery at the time. Seeing that I was exhausted, Kalyana gently took Anupam in her arms. I followed Kalyana, certain that my child would be cured. At the entrance to the park, I grabbed Anupam from Kalyana and said, "The doctor must see me holding him. Otherwise, he'll think I did it!" I remember that moments of lucidity sometimes broke through my delusion. Then we walked into the verdant grove, where there was still a large crowd. The air was cool, and everyone was quiet and attentive. We stopped at the edge of the gathering where the Buddha was teaching.

It was growing very dark. The fire had almost turned to ash. Sister Kisa smiled softly, and the tremendous sadness that had come over the village settled. "Tomorrow, I will tell you how the Buddha healed us." She chanted blessings. Young girls helped her stand. As Sister Kisa departed, she stopped and nodded to another aged woman who was bending down, paying homage to the storyteller. It was Kalyana. She smiled and Kisa tenderly touched her arm. The girls and Kalyana walked with Kisa along the river back to the temple.

The next evening Sister Kisa returned to her seat by the fire, and everyone settled in to hear more.

It is not often that people who can really help us come into the world, but such a person was my teacher Gautama, the Buddha Shakyamuni, the Great Healer. I'd like to tell you something about him, as so much here—our community, our well-being, our good fortune—can be traced back to him. Our monks and nuns are preserving his teachings to be passed on to others. But some events in his life are being forgotten or have become hearsay. Many of you, new to the village, have come from regions far away to find work with our looms. Some of you have had different teachers, with different customs. If you have not heard anything of the Buddha, I would like you to know that his teaching is open to anyone who wants it. Here is his story.

The Buddha was not born, as I was, to poverty and hardship. He was a prince, Siddhartha, who grew up shielded from experiences of death, grief, and loss. His parents surrounded him with beauty, entertainment, health, and wealth, intent on shielding him from worry and suffering. As a result, of course, he grew curious about the world beyond the palace walls—how everyday people lived, worked, and socialized in the capital city. Early in his twenties the young prince and his groom, Channa, began taking carriage rides outside the walls of the palace into the capital city. There for the first time, he saw a hunched, white-haired man, aged and infirm, stumbling along the streets, leaning heavily on a cane, unable to see. The next day he saw a man who was desperately ill, wasted, feverish, and vomiting on the street, covered in own filth. The following day he witnessed a funeral procession with the shrouded corpse of a loved one being carried along, followed by weeping family members. Finally, he saw a solitary ascetic, untroubled and walking free.

Unlike us, who are familiar with sights like these, Siddhartha had never seen such things. The impact of these four visions penetrated his young heart. What could he do? At first, he simply continued indulging his desires. But unrest kept at nudging him, so he chose to abandon his comfortable life of privilege altogether, even going so far as to leave his family—his beautiful wife Princess Yashodhara and their baby son Rahula—to seek the path to freedom. Channa agreed to take him far away and, after having done so, he tearfully left his master to pursue his quest. The prince wandered as an ascetic for six years, seeking the guidance of various renowned gurus and yogis, mastering many forms of meditation, learning to withstand exposure to the elements, and going without food, sleep, fine clothing, sex, even shelter. Although he attained moments of calm and clarity, anxious thoughts would always return and with them unsettled waves of emotions. He stayed with five other renunciants who were also following a hard and rigorous path. But he did not find wisdom or peace.

Finally, emaciated and on the verge of death, he realized that the path he had been taking was fruitless. What if the way to wisdom did not involve deliberate deprivation? He remembered the great happiness of meditations he had tried as a child on his own. They arose from a sense of contentment and joy, not suffering. He decided he would accept food. A laywoman named Sujata brought him a bowl of *kheera*—milk pudding—and he ate it. Sujata was the first person he encountered who made no judgment, who expected nothing, and who offered him something—a simple bowl of rice pudding—out of the purity of her own heart. He, too, had approached her expecting nothing, having exhausted every possible method or idea to relieve his torment. He accepted her gift, his hands open to receive the bowl from her. In that moment, his mind and heart also opened, letting go of any need to attain something.

Having eaten, he found shelter under a small *pipal* tree on the banks of the river, its canopy no more than twenty feet wide. He sat in the lotus position with his legs folded under him and entered into a meditation deeper than any he had previously experienced. Buoyed by deep inner peace he saw through his attachment to pleasures of the senses, and he was no longer held in their sway. He saw his own pasts and those of others, stretching back through many lives and eons. He felt no ill-will, only equanimity and compassion, for this endless rise and fall of beings.

At one point, threatened by Siddhartha's wisdom and resolve, Mara the Tempter with his terrifying armies appeared to him in a vision. Mara sent three daughters—Craving, Discontent, and Delight—to entice Siddhartha to leave his seat and give up his quest for enlightenment. Siddhartha remained unmoved. Then Mara sent showers of rain, rocks, ashes, and all kinds of debris and covered the area with darkness. He challenged Siddhartha's authority to seek enlightenment. In response, Siddhartha touched the ground, calling upon the earth for support. The goddess of the earth let down her hair, releasing all the water that had accompanied Siddhartha's countless acts of generosity in past lives. She had seen them all. Mara and his terrifying armies were routed.

Siddhartha went deeper into the silence, and arrived at stages of absorption beyond description, feeling inimitable bliss. He explored even more deeply letting go of attachment to that bliss. Finally, he found peace. There was no longer any restlessness in his heart. He was home. He was free. Hours later, after the darkest watch of the night, he emerged from silent depths and opened his eyes under rays emanating from the morning star. The coming dawn dispelled all shadows. He was now the awakened one, the Buddha.

At first, he planned to remain silent and live out his days in peace, immersed in the deep tranquility of nirvana. But the gods implored him to not remain silent. They entreated him to go forth and teach others the path to peace, for there were so many who were suffering. He told them that if he tried to teach others, he doubted they could ever understand. They might listen to his words, but they would fail to grasp their meaning, which ultimately arose from the depths of a silence beyond words. A few might understand, some others might glean some insights, but many would confuse the surface meaning of words for the depths of inconceivable liberation.

Finally, however, he relented, understanding that he could not refuse the mandate of compassion. He stood up from his seat and returned to the world to help others see the path of freedom and inner peace if they wished to do so. The Buddha found the five renunciants who previously had been his companions. When he taught them this path of contemplation, they too gained insight and peace, becoming his first followers. Then he went back to his hometown and many family members became awakened too: his wife, and his son, and many relatives. Thenceforth he taught wherever he was invited. He always traveled on foot. As his reputation grew, so did the demand for his liberating presence: he made his way across northern India, moving from east to west and back again. And so it was that now he had come to share his teachings in a grove in the town of Shravasti, near Kisa Gotami's village of Madhyapur.

Everyone sat rapt, listening; a few even remembered this great man. Sister Kisa paused. The same man who had asked Kisa to tell her story asked simply, "So what happened when you met the Buddha?" Everyone leaned forward to hear. Logs were added to the fire.

Among the assembly of those gathered in the verdant grove there were monks, nuns, merchants, farmers, craftspeople, women, men, and children. Even animals seemed to have stopped their comings and goings to join the people there: goats, monkeys, peacocks, dogs and cats, a few elephants, and cows. The Buddha sat under the spreading branches of the huge banyan tree at the center of the grove, responding to questions. He radiated calm and deep understanding, and his skin glowed with a golden light. Kalyana and I found ourselves just outside the circle of the assembly. I heard some people talking: they were marveling at how the Buddha seemed to receive questions right into the heart of his awareness, holding them and the questioner in the depth of his great compassion.

I could not take it in. I sensed a pool of stillness there, but I felt afraid and distressed as I held Anupam close. I hardly heard a word the Buddha uttered. When he had finished, the crowd began to disperse. They looked happy and inspired. Even the elephants moved away with quiet dignity. Monkeys chattered and chased one another's tails as they bounded up into the trees.

The Buddha would have normally left now, but when he saw his follower Kalyana with me, holding my child, he paused. He beckoned us forward and Kalyana spoke quietly with him about my son. But it must have been clear to him why I was so was deeply troubled. The scent coming from the baby blanket was not of new life but of death. The Buddha's very presence resonated with me, and I trusted him.

"My child is very ill," I said. "Please help him." I saw a softening in his eyes.

"Thank you for coming. Let me take a look. What is your name?"

"Kisa Gotami. I am from Madhyapur village," I added, choking back my tears.

As he spoke, he gazed into my eyes, bringing me out of distraction. The clarity of his awareness and the expansiveness of his heart were holding me. I felt protected. He addressed me calmly. "Yes, I can help you, Kisa Gotami. This is a very serious situation, but I can offer some special medicine. Because the circumstances are so grave, the medicine must be potent, made from the purest of ingredients. . . ."

He told me to go to every house in the nearby town of Shravasti and gather a yellow mustard seed from each home that had never known death; then I was to return to him.

I was so happy that the Buddha had promised to help me! He had promised to make a medicine. The town of Shravasti was large and prosperous. There were certain to be many who could give me a yellow mustard seed.

Early the next morning I set out with joy, urgency, and determination. Still carrying my poor son, I hurried to the first hut in the village. A young mother met me at the door. I asked, "Have you ever known death?" Her eyes brimming with tears, she answered, "Yes. Last spring my five-year-old son died of a terrible chill that refused to loosen its grip." When our eyes met, I knew she understood the depth of my pain, but I hurried on.

At the next simple hut, a man bent with age sat in the sun near his doorway. "Old father, has your household ever known death?" His rheumy eyes welled up with tears. "Last year my wife died of a wasting disease following a long illness. After her cremation, we scattered her ashes in the sacred river." When he turned away, I saw his shoulders shake with sobs.

At the next hut there was a young man. His sister and her baby had died in childbirth the month before, and the family was still engaged in the rituals of mourning.

One whole neighborhood reported losing multiple family members when fevers had swept the town five years earlier. At one prosperous home, a matron said her healthy husband had been killed when the well he was digging collapsed. These householders could hardly speak. I felt tears springing up in my own eyes. My heart hurt for them.

Everywhere I went, the litany was the same. Death from fever and stomach ailments, from heart attacks, from accidents, as well as mysterious unattended deaths. The people in each household, whether rich or poor, had known death. I began to see my own face in each of theirs.

It was a dawning realization. Perhaps what Raja and my family had told me was true. Perhaps my son was not merely sick. Perhaps he had already died? I looked more closely at his little body in my arms. Perhaps he was dead. His skin was pallid, turning blue. His body was stiff. Perhaps it was too late. Could he not be saved?

But underneath all of these questions was the realization that I was not alone. I had not been singled out for cruel suffering nor isolated from others' lack of understanding. There was no evil spirit torturing me or bad luck that happened to find me. Still, I continued my search, not knowing what else to do. With tears streaming down my face, I nursed a last shred of hope.

The final house I visited was at the edge of town, occupied by an ancient woman named Sita with gnarled hands and a serene and compassionate face. She was wearing a simple white, coarse cotton garment. When I asked whether she and her household had known death, she responded, "It is the nature of life to end. All of us will die someday. I am a widow." She said this with calmness and clarity, with no tragedy or drama. Smiling gently, she reached out to touch my hand and caressed my son's forehead. I knew in that moment what was true. Everyone who lives dies. My son had died. I will die. This old lady will die.

The tranquility of Sister Kisa's acceptance stilled the crowd, creating a moment of silence amongst the villagers, though some sighed. But then a child spoke up, asking, "What did you do then?"

Heartbroken, I set off to find the Buddha, still carrying the body of my son. Not a single home could offer me a mustard seed. Every home had known death. I was now ready to accept this truth. But something new had awakened in me. I wished that one day I would have the calm and serenity of this ancient woman.

I returned to the Buddha early the next day, still carrying the body of Anupam. I placed him gently on the grass and bowed deeply before the Buddha, touching my head respectfully to his feet. "There was not a single home that had not known death." I could not stop my tears from falling. "My son is gone."

The Buddha smiled gently and spoke. "The mustard seed is small and its taste is exceedingly sharp. It is also common to every household. Now you have received the medicine that I promised."

He reassured me, saying that I could come back to him. I returned home, cradling Anupam's now discolored body. My entire family was in deep mourning. They sat with their faces reddened by weeping, unadorned and wearing simple white cotton skirts, shawls, and *dhoti* pants. We put the body of my son in his bed. Together, Raja and I washed his body in saffron water and massaged it with sandal paste. We wrapped Anupam in clean lengths of white cotton cloth. The priests placed his body on a bier decorated with marigolds. As was the custom, our little boy was carried to the cremation grounds on a bamboo stretcher, while our entire family followed behind. Raja presided sadly over the customary rituals chanted by priests, circumambulating the pyre and lighting the cremation fire.

Sister Kisa paused, knowing that each and every individual in her audience had witnessed the cremation of a loved one, a friend, or an acquaintance. She picked up the story, her brown eyes wide and tender, speaking as if addressing each person individually.

I stood watching my darling Anupam burn in the cremation fire. I witnessed the fragility of his body and life consumed by flames. I remembered suckling and bathing that dear boy, rocking him to sleep at night, dressing him in the morning. Now his body was being consumed. Our family stood watching, sobs giving way to silence. The only sounds were the sonorous hymns chanted by our family priests accompanied by the crackle of flames near the constant flow of the wide sacred river nearby. Only then did I realize that I was emerging from a nightmare—my ordeal of denying death. This right now was the truth of things. Everything became vivid, tender, and very sad. I felt completely present and awake.

There were three other cremation fires burning nearby. Each was ringed by grieving family members, supported by chanting priests. Every mourner had lost a loved one, like I had. For a moment, time and space expanded and I found myself in a vast throng of people from many cultures, times, and places, each of us grieving loss together. Family members wearing the mourning garb of their cultures and regions all joined in heartfelt sadness. There were robed monks, nuns, and priests from many cultures, some chanting, some meditating, some comforting the bereaved. Interspersed in the throng were long-haired *yogis* and *yoginis*, simply dressed, serenely sitting among the ashes of extinguished fires, counting their mantras on bone rosaries in meditations that embraced grief as the portal to transcendent wisdom. Wandering among the pyres were nonchalant dogs, cows, and birds poking among the detritus of many past fires, still smoldering despite recent rains. The entire scene was enveloped by the vastness of space and time brought down to the immediacy of the present moment. I could feel the blessings of spirits, near and far. A kind of radiance glowed from everyone present.

The sense of tenderness that filled me was different from the madness I had experienced. I felt a greater clarity than I ever had before. An upwelling of yearning arose: a desire to do whatever was necessary to understand and embody everything I was witnessing in that moment. Some of my relatives had said, "You can always have another child." But I was beginning to know that that was not my path. In fact, I held Anupam closer than ever to my heart. The child I thought I knew was limited by my fevered imagination: a strong, wise, kind boy who would grow up to protect his mother and make her proud. The true Anupam, even as my heart felt the grievous pain of loss, was showing me the impermanence of life that connects all of us in suffering, and more importantly, in compassion. Some silent illumination was dawning in the darkness of my grief. There was a new path ahead. It would be challenging, but I would follow it.

We all watched as the fire turned to embers, the chants continued, and the priests gathered Anupam's ashes and then scattered them on the surface of the river. In the fading light of the late afternoon, they were washed downstream. My fledgling bird had flown. His body, the little dwelling he had lived in for too short a while, was now gone.

Raja and I both wept, sharing the most tender time of our lives as we mourned. I described the quest for mustard seeds. It was then that I told Raja that I wanted to return to the Buddha. He nodded in understanding. He said that, from the very first time we met, he had recognized in me a yearning for freedom. I asked for his blessings and sadly, but willingly, he agreed to let me go.

I remained with my family for thirteen days of mourning, completing my preparations and making my farewells to everyone there. Then I set off to find the Buddha. When I arrived, I bowed, touched his feet with respect, and asked to leave the household life and become his follower as a nun. He looked into my eyes and readily accepted me.

This story of Kisa Gotami and the Buddha's medicine has been told many times. The traditional story ends when she became a nun. But that was only the beginning. The next evening, she told the story of how she recovered and of her eventual awakening. She returned to the village fire with several nuns. Food was offered to all those who were present. Accustomed to the rhythms of the storytelling, the villagers enjoyed the offerings in silence. They watched their children chatting amongst themselves until Sister Kisa began to speak.

The night I arrived at the temple door, the nuns offered me steaming rice-gruel. Then they showed me my bed, with a rug and humble clothes laid out on it. I slept soundly, untroubled, lulled by the pattering of rain until the peacocks' cry at dawn. I was offered warmth and simple, good nourishment by my new companions, just as you are being offered rice cakes and sweets now. Sharing food, kindness, and friendship is where my healing and recovery began.

In the first months of my training, I thought often about the moment when the Buddha accepted me into the nuns' community. He gave me a verse to contemplate, and it has stayed with me all these years.

It is better to have one day knowing the deathless
Rather than a hundred years not knowing the deathless.

From the moment I heard this verse, I recalled my early spiritual yearnings—knowing deep in my bones that there was a deathless awareness at the heart of all my travails. I never stopped thinking about my son. I missed him so much. What did my journey now hold?

I felt drawn to return to the cremation ground. There, I remembered a wish, a passing thought that I had as a child, perhaps from another life, to become a nun, one who wore rough, coarse robes, a sign of embracing simplicity. Some Buddhist monks and nuns even fashioned robes made of cloth discarded at cremation grounds. I would join them. I wouldn't "own" things, outside or inside. Plain cotton from discarded funeral shrouds would remind me, with truthful comfort, of where I came from and what I was.

One day, I asked Kalyana to come with me to the cemetery. She steered me through mud, ashes, and broken bodies. Decaying flowers had been squashed under foot. I felt protective spirits guiding our steps. Those once rich had been cremated and were now ashes. The bodies of the poor were left on nearby ground uncremated, some discarded, some eaten by birds and animals. Wild creatures had torn all coverings away. I remembered that the silks I had worn before had always felt borrowed. Now I would choose only the simplest scraps of cloth, strewn around from the poverty-stricken and the renunciants, the criminals and the untouchables, cast away both in life and death. These were my people. I would help others like them.

Kalyana and I collected a bag of cloth in the charnel ground. As we threw it down on the ground by the temple, I felt I was throwing down the weight of victimhood. The pile stank, and flies came to settle on it. Some nuns approached. "Ugh. Kisa!" they laughed, "You could have much nicer robes. Kalyana always gives us beautiful cloth! But we will help you." The nuns all pretended to retch but helped Kalyana and me throw the bag of cloth into the freshwater bathing pond. At first, a dark pool of stinking mud burbled up, as if the pool were choking on the filth—but it was gradually washed away by the underground spring feeding the pond. The waters filled with dirt again and again: the encrustations of many discarded lives. We rinsed and washed, re-rinsed and scrubbed. Gradually the stains and marks dissolved, like stains and marks on the mind. The cloths became clean and we laid them out to dry under the now-hot sun.

But it was the gentle teasing, the laughter and my new companions' love that was really rinsing and rooting out victimhood and unhappiness from me. I was doing something rare—not many nuns used discarded graveyard clothes, though it was encouraged. The sunshine of my sisters' jokes was making me forget my troubles. I even relaxed sometimes, and I caught myself smiling. We all together dyed the strips and left them to dry again. Later we sat in the shade of a big mango tree and pieced them together the traditional way. As you can see from my robe, the criss-cross template of nuns' robes is patchwork, with the hems of each piece fitting the complex design. My mother had always done the sewing in our home, and I felt her guiding and helping my hands. The needle's even pace on the simple cloths felt like meditation. When we worked together, all our stitches seemed to even out, each sewn with ever steadier hands and greater confidence. We shared the enveloping companionship of silence.

And then the robes were done, a refuge crafted with our own hands.

On the appointed night my head was shaved. I watched it fall, shedding memories of my son clutching it while nursing and my husband and family caressing it. The community of monks and nuns entered, and I chanted the sacred vows in their presence. All those in the circle smiled at me in encouragement. I felt such relief and happiness: I was wearing the same robes as they were, the same robes worn by the Buddha. I was now ordained. I was now Sister Kisa.

The way of life was arduous but I adapted to the simple routines of a nun. Every day we all gathered offerings in the village. There were rituals, sermons, walks, and visits from laypeople. I learned to love chanting, where our minds settled and our voices felt as one. My teacher was Sister Patacara, a senior nun. She too had experienced the great loss of both her children and her entire family. I often went to talk with her. Just being in her personal presence made me feel safe and valued. Sister Patacara taught me to be aware of the body at all times. She suggested I do some sewing and mending for the community, as she had seen how much it had helped me. I even started to laugh with other nuns, now friends, going to dharma talks and contemplating the new teachings we heard each day. Kalyana came regularly to visit. Her cheerful words helped me keep my feet on the ground.

Each morning in the hall there was a meditation session. Sister Patacara suggested I try it when I felt ready. I had never thought women could meditate. Words like “mindfulness” and “calm” were for other people. But most nuns meditated, and many laypeople too, like the wise widow Sita. I will tell you about this tomorrow.

As Sister Kisa left that evening, she was offered donations for the temple. She accepted graciously, on behalf of her community, and she chanted blessings for people’s happiness. The next day, she smiled as people joined her around the evening fire.

Many of you are asking about meditation. I will tell you about my first session—it was very memorable for me. I sat and looked and listened; now it felt natural to be in this hall with other people supporting me with their presence. There were others who felt as I did, who had suffered and were suffering. So many of my insecurities about being with people had slipped away. We waited expectantly. The temple, as you know, is a center for our village and so many people I knew were there. I saw dear Sita at the back, and the mother of the five-year old child who had died. Sister Patacara gave the talk.

She spoke about the body and being aware of its presence: "Just watch your breath: just feel it, get to know it, and appreciate it for being always there. It is your life. Know when it is long and know when it is short." I closed my eyes and took a deep breath and watched and listened. I saw what my breath was doing. All sorts of thoughts came up and I shifted my body often. She told us not to worry if the mind wandered: just come back to a new breath. She called it a fresh start, moment to moment. I tried another breath, and then another. But still a mild buzz of jumbled thoughts circled, like bees around a cotton plant. There were always turbulent feelings about Anupam, my family, and my old life. They arose with force. And when I came to the breath, it was like always finding tough seeds during the carding. But these obstructions sometimes eased and there was a feeling of flow: I started to enjoy the breath, like fingering a *puni* of softened cotton fleece. And then the bees settled on the flower, finding nectar.

We were being taught to let the breath quiet on the inbreath and the outbreath: "Mindfully breathe in, mindfully breathe out." Now, with less effort, the softness of the breath guided me. Its touch found me, and I felt it in my whole body. It became a friend, supporting me. It reassured, encouraged, spreading calm where it was needed, nourishing the mind, easing tensions in the legs, supporting the back. The breath was pouring balm on pain—if I could let it do what it does best, in its own time. I found how to observe it, ever more gently, and to discover it as something to trust. I started to enjoy the breath and found stillness.

When the first meditation session was finished, we chanted blessings for teachers, family, those alive and those dead, the people there around us and nearby, the spirits of trees and rivers, the monkeys and the animals. Trees and birds murmured answering notes in return. Then a dog howled piteously, and another dog barked back. Maybe they didn't get it. Everyone started to laugh. I felt tears streaming down my cheeks and was not sure if I was laughing or crying. I did both.

That session was a turning point. Meditation stopped being something other people did. I learned to walk mindfully. The scent of jasmine and frangipani and the smells of the woodland became more vivid. The forest was alive with change. The Kisa now was not the same as the Kisa who arrived this morning. This Kisa could notice and enjoy again: as she walked, she felt and heard rustling leaves underfoot and could smell their dank richness. The woods around breathed and crackled with life.

There is always the present moment, the breath, the body. Anytime. That was my first lesson in meditation. This new Kisa practiced, and the rhythms of her life rested her mind: she walked, she ate, she chanted. The stillness of meditation and the friendships she made allowed her to be attentive to others and to find peace. Sometimes meditation seemed not to go well. The mind wandered all over the place! But sometimes it wanted quiet. The softness of the breath became my reassuring home. I became aware of others, as my body and my heart were restored. I realized that I could perform any action, however small or inconsequential, with care and presence.

In this way Sister Kisa shared with the villagers her experiences of meditation. Kisa paused and sat back to sip some water. One woman, sitting on the blanket at the back, began to sing ballads. Others joined her, and the children lay down on the parents' knees and drowsed. Some people asked about meditation and Kisa promised to sit with them during the day, by the river, and teach them the basic stages. Tomorrow, said Kisa, I will tell you about my forest retreat.

The Buddha recommended I enter retreat in the forest to deepen my spiritual journey. I knew of a beautiful glen, with a stream running through it. There were towering trees and a soft forest floor, and nearby there was a small hermitage where I could take rest. On the banks of the stream there was a large tree with spreading branches providing shelter. I settled at the base of the tree and began my meditation.

As thoughts and emotions fell away into the rhythmic flow of breath, my mind quieted; my body relaxed. I found simplicity in the present moment. The morning passed and the warmth of the afternoon caressed my skin. I could not forget my visits to the huts in the village in search of a single mustard seed. Yes, everything that lives dies. When I first heard these words, I felt only sadness. Now I knew them in my bones. My mind traced the life of my son back to my own life, and I could feel the truth—I will die. My husband will die, and his parents and siblings will also die. My mother and father will die, their parents before them have died, everyone I have ever met will die. My child has died. All life is impermanent.

I looked at the stream, seeing its currents constantly changing. I watched the tiny seeds and twigs flowing down the stream, bobbing here, sinking there. I saw that they were breaking down, becoming fragments, pummeled by the stream. Everything changes, just as afternoon was giving way to evening, tiny buds were sprouting leaves, and shadows were moving and deepening.

Then words of the Buddha came to me. To the builder of the house of life, he taught,

> *O house-builder, you are seen!*
> *You will not build this house again.*
> *For all your rafters are broken and your ridgepole shattered.*
> *My mind has reached the Unconditioned:*
> *I have attained the destruction of cravings.*
>
> —Dhammapada 11:154

With fresh inspiration, I resolved to continue my retreat.

Over the days that followed, I continued to return to this spot. I realized I could not separate the currents of the stream from the whole. The currents constantly move and change, rising and falling. Each current has currents behind it, propelled by forces I cannot see. And each current turns into another current and cannot be separated from it. There is no way to isolate one as it flows from and into other currents. Nothing stands on its own, all things arise from causes and conditions and then cause other things. Eventually I realized that the flow of cause and effect in the stream—and in the world—is powerful and unstoppable.

I came to know that there are many causes and many effects, flowing like the stream before my meditation seat. I came to understand my son's drowning in this way. It happened from going for a walk with him at a certain time and under certain conditions, so many circumstances coming together. My son's life came from his father and me, our lives from our parents' and so on. There is no solid, independent anything that does not depend on other events and everything else. I began to experience a network of events and beings tied together through causes and patterns all flowing together so inextricably I could not isolate and see any one of them apart from the others. We are all deeply connected throughout time and space. Our thoughts and emotions flow, come and go; our bodies grow, change, and shift. As the shadows lengthened, the air cooled, and dusk descended. With gratitude, I retired again to my hut.

The following morning, the trees outside my window seemed fresher and greener than I remembered, and I couldn't wait to return to my practice. We belong to one another. My suffering is connected to all other suffering and my joy and clarity are connected to the vastness of the universe beyond all space and time. Each and every thing that exists in the universe is intimately connected to who I am, and I am intimately connected to each and everything in the universe!

Seen from this vantage point, there is no self that is separate from everything else, since we, everything, and everyone in this entire universe are made up of one another. "Kisa," "Kalyana," "Patacara," "Siddhartha"—you, me, everyone, everything—we are all mere impermanent conglomerations of this all-embracing whole that cannot be grasped conceptually! Unless we see this truth behind all constituent elements of existence, we will forever be trapped in a web of suffering caused by our own ego-delusions. But once we free ourselves of this deluded state of mind and see things just as they are, radiantly interconnected, then our sufferings cease, and we enter into a blissful state of freedom.

As Sister Kisa, sitting very erect, was speaking, those gathered saw her change before their eyes. Her face opened and softened, and her wrinkled skin glowed with inner youth and radiance, almost gold in hue. Her presence and quiet charisma touched the villagers deeply, as they fell into silence. They sat together in the flickering light of the fire, joined together in the power of Kisa's discovery. After some time, Sister Kisa bowed and quietly departed for her temple, escorted by a few village leaders.

When Sister Kisa returned the following evening, a larger crowd of villagers was waiting expectantly. Word of Kisa's teachings had spread, and all those gathered sat in rapt attention wanting to hear every word. As she took the seat of honor, a shy teenaged boy asked, "Please tell us what happened next."

Thank you for inviting me to continue my story. But first I would like to ask someone here who knows this journey to speak first. My dear friend and companion Kalyana, please come and sit by me. Tell people your experience and understanding, as we have discussed this.

Nuns were highly revered, and Kalyana was reluctant at first. But when Kisa insisted, Kalyana laughingly agreed to approach and sit near her.

I have often discussed this with my friend, Sister Kisa. There is a story about Indra, King of the Gods, protector of the natural world and its life force. It is said that at the beginning of time he created a vast magical net above the roof of his palace on Mount Meru, revealing the true nature of the world. Mount Meru is considered the very center of the world itself, sustaining all life and experience. This golden net is woven with radiant, many-colored jewels at each knot and each jewel reflects every other jewel. The net extends in all directions throughout the entire universe, connecting everything. Indra proclaimed that we are each like the luminous gems of Indra's net, reflecting one another, connecting to one another, each containing all the wisdom of the world within ourselves and reflecting that wisdom to everyone else. Although we think we are separate, we are part of everything that exists.

I am a laywoman, but the power of Indra's net sustains my life. It is not my path to be a nun. I live with a husband, in-laws, children, grandchildren, relatives. They show me that we are connected and our care for others arises spontaneously. My actions affect others, and we share the happiness. Any action, anywhere, is connected to other things: when I receive my neighbor's food, or sell good grain, I am helping others, being happy doing what I do. The Buddha and his teaching have given me so much. I hope that what I do affects others in large or small ways.

Kisa thanked her old friend and continued her story:

During the forest retreat, following Sister Patacara's guidance, I contemplated all the causes and effects working in our lives. As I contemplated, a vision arose in my mind's eye. I saw a huge golden net-like canopy with sparkling threads vibrating their connection through the entire universe. It was just as Kalyana described. As the day wore on, the net constantly changed and moved, dynamic and luminous, and I was integral to the net. The day passed quickly and slowly at the same time, and the sense of vastness expanded. I returned to my hermitage and my sleep was deep and dreamless.

The next morning, I had urgent questions: Does this sense of connection with all beings and all events mean this is all there is? Do these realizations erase my personal experiences of despair and joy? Am I trapped by circumstances? Does suffering have meaning? I could feel the pregnancy of the moment, and in it a question that opened the space of the mind further: "How do my own realization, experience, and action relate to the network of all things?" The stream sparkled, carrying all my questions like an echo.

Early in the morning, at the base of the tree, a knowing opened like a spark and I experienced clearly my connection with all beings. My life, my journey, my experience, with all its joys and sorrows, opened me to the experiences of all other beings. This time, the vision of the golden net included jewels at all the intersecting strands of the web. It was like a fisherman's net. Each crystal-clear jewel radiated tiny beams of reflected light, every one unique but mirroring the radiance of each and all the other jewels. Everything I was experiencing reflected in some way in the experiences of others, from the tiniest insect to the regal elephants. Each and every thing I see around me is like a jewel, each one reflected in every other: trees, pebbles, clouds, moon, cats, dogs, and people I meet along the way. Nothing and no one excepted. Each and every one, each and every thing, is kin to me. They are me, and I am them! The Buddha taught this as "dependent arising." Bliss pervaded my body as I could feel the tendrils of the net coursing through my torso, arms, and legs. I could feel the connection with all of life, and life streaming through me as well. I was one jewel among all the jewels in the universe. A new sense of clarity emerged from deep within.

As shadows deepened in the late afternoon, I realized my own journey shone in the radiance of all other jewels, and my choices and actions could shape and support others as well. We were not trapped by fate, but connected and supported by the wisdom of change, the knowledge of vastness in which change occurs, the heart of compassion, and the dedication to helping one another. I felt I was sitting at the heart of the universe. This was a freedom unlimited by past, present, or future. I remembered the verse the Buddha had given me:

It is better to have one day knowing the deathless
Rather than a hundred years not knowing the deathless.

Beginning with the mustard seed that had taught me that death is pervasive, I had undergone a journey. Now I had tasted the deathless as he predicted, and my life could now have new purpose and freedom. In this moment of clear awareness, death and deathless, impermanence and eternity all came together in the tranquil depths of my mind.

I remembered that my teacher Sister Patacara had lost her children and all her family. Her wisdom and kindness amid loss inspired me and many others. My fellow nuns and friends who helped me had all experienced losses, and their dedication supported me. My heart was deeply touched by this suffering and the many others continuing to suffer, and I felt a tender but powerful desire to be of service. This was my life's purpose. By mid-afternoon, I was suffused with gratitude, appreciating all life and connection. I still had much work to do, but I could feel the beginnings of genuine compassion and where it might lead me.

I returned to Sister Patacara, eager to share my experience. When she heard of my retreat she was deeply touched by my awakening to Indra's net and urgent desire to care for others. She offered me an opportunity to make a formal vow based on these invaluable insights. We entered the shrine hall the next evening and I bowed before her, my preceptor and spiritual friend, taking the compassionate vow of the *bodhisattva*, one who dedicates one's whole life and future lives to the welfare of others. This meant striving to drive away the sorrows of the world, committing to the happiness of all beings as well as myself.

With this dedication I was like a blind person finding a precious jewel lost in a heap of dust, and I was suffused with joy. I knew at that moment that I had committed to all beings in mutual love for the shared flourishing of all.

Again, a silence fell over the assembly around the fire as the villagers absorbed the enormity of Sister Kisa's commitment. Her description explained the intangible warmth and power of her presence with them that evening, and they realized the subtle skill she had brought to her teaching all these weeks. She was surfacing the palpable presence of the interconnectedness of them all and modeling how to serve and strengthen their community. They knew they could turn to her for guidance, kindness, and wisdom no matter what they faced. After some time, Sister Kisa quietly withdrew into the evening and returned to her temple. The next evening she continued her story:

You may think my journey was over, but I can tell you I still had much to learn. As time went on, I was learning to accept the universe as it was and could see that compassion was the only natural response. Evil surfaced in the form of extreme emotions, cruelty, impulsiveness, callousness, greed. The seeds of these emotions were in me. I remembered one day on a walk I came across a group of children playing. Some kids were egging a shy boy to jump across a dangerous crevasse, and when he cried they bullied him. I felt a flash of anger and wanted to strike them, but instead I stopped them with a few words. Still, I was shaking when I came back to the temple to sit in meditation. It took an hour for the shaking to stop. The children had needed telling off. But who was the bully in my body and mind? Later I felt calm again. I found the ringleader and saw he had his troubles too. We talked about how to work with hurt without causing harm to others. As we talked, I could feel his demeanor soften as he let me into his heart.

Experiences like these were profound. It was not all perfect, I can tell you. I still had so much to learn. I kept doing stupid things, forgetting where I had put my sandals, and slipping into inexplicable annoyance or jealousy. My dharma sisters occasionally annoyed me, and at times I felt lonely. I woke sometimes at night with a hollow feeling inside, just yearning for companionship. But underneath the passing storm clouds, I felt an unshakeable peace. I had found a way of life.

My vision of the net of Indra was not merely a mystical vision, but a transformation of the way I experience things. I now know that moments of personal anger or fear are temporary blemishes on a vast radiance of mutual human goodness finding itself. I know that our deepest human yearnings are for harmonious and rewarding lives devoted to helping others in a flourishing community and a culture of beauty and joy. Underneath everything, each of us longs to contribute to that flourishing. The greatest joy comes from giving to and supporting others. In love we find our greatest humanity.

When I was a young woman spinning cotton, I had glimpses of that vision. But I became ensnared in self-concern and a spiral of attachment and loss that made me forget. From the moment I began searching for a mustard seed until now, I have awakened to the powerful potential of clarity and great love and compassion to transform the way we can all live together.

My karma is to help as a monastic. Kalyana helps as a laywoman and businesswoman. Raja and his family help through developing a textile cooperative. You each can find a way to help in your own lives, a way to contribute to our shared flourishing and fulfill your deepest longing. Together we can create communities of caring and connection.

For many years after this, Sister Kisa was sought out for advice and support by those in her monastic community and in her village. Everyone who heard her story was moved by it. So it was that parents who had lost children came to her. The dying, the anxious, the troubled felt nurtured by her compassionate listening and wise counsel. Those who had lost children knew they would be understood. Kisa also took a special interest in orphaned children who were cared for by the temple. Those who were angry and caught in seemingly irreconcilable conflicts approached her to find resolution. Sister Kisa listened patiently and provided comfort for hours.

One evening, the village once again invited Sister Kisa to return to the evening fire. Moved by her compassion, a villager asked how she had navigated intense emotions in her tumultuous journey. The old nun had not spoken at the fire for a long time, but she was touched by the request. "Through stilling the mind we become aware of the way strong emotions can liberate us or enslave us. There is so much unnecessary suffering in our lives." It was then that Kisa related her personal experience of a practice for working with the six realms of existence.

Even after many years of meditation, emotions and reactions do not disappear. However, my relationship to the arising of powerful states of mind has changed. Years ago I too asked how I could work with the force of feelings that overtook me like storms, like swirling currents.

Sister Patacara saw my struggle. She taught me to befriend every single mind state I had ever known. She assured me that if I could learn a practice for working with my own thoughts and emotions, I could loosen the habits that bound my mind and be of service to others. It did not take me long to realize that indulging in preoccupations without compassion and without understanding their nature had brought every suffering into my life. There was no need to banish the emotions or thoughts. Through the practice she showed me, I could explore the nature of the energy of emotions without judging them, and therefore uncover how in each powerful arising, natural compassion, space, and intelligence could be found.

Sister Patacara was an excellent guide. She asked me to spend several days devoted to this practice. First, she had me call to mind the most painful time in my life. A visceral recollection arose immediately of the torture I had undergone with my son's death and my refusal to acknowledge it. I sank into the agonizing abyss of what she called the Hell Realm, the first of the six realms of existence. The anger and fear I felt were like white-hot needles puncturing every pore of my skin. There was no relief. I was instructed to simply sit with the strong emotion and not try to dispel or suppress it. The more I let myself feel the agony, the more I was seared with pain. I was on fire. My mind overflowed with rage and fear. I wanted to escape, but instead, as instructed, I remained where I was, in silence. Quieting my mind while feeling the piercing torment helped it to open. It was as if in the oven of preoccupation there was a cool stream. I opened into equanimity. There, within and beyond the storm, was an abiding sense of calm.

This deep sense of calm opened my heart further, and I could envision all beings throughout the universe still struggling in their multifaceted and many-layered kinds of suffering brought about by their grasping and fixation, stuck on their attachment to this main delusion of the egoic self. My heart went out to them with an embrace of compassion, wishing them all to be relieved of their suffering. A warm sense of kindness flowed from my heart to each and every one of them, wishing them well, wishing that they might attain the utmost well-being for themselves. "May all beings be happy," came the spontaneous prayer from my lips, from my heart, followed by the compassionate prayer, "May they be free from suffering." As I saw other beings experiencing liberation, as I saw them beginning to find some joy in their lives as they let go of their delusive ego, I could not but likewise feel a sympathetic joy with them. With this I returned to calm openness to everything and everyone.

Suddenly I began to remember the obsessive searching that compelled me senselessly when I had tried to find a way of healing the small corpse I carried in my arms. Seated in the meditation hall, I felt as if I were parched and starving with need. I could not find relief. I was, as my guide explained, in the Realm of the Hungry Ghosts. Truly I felt like a bloated creature with a small head and a ceaseless compulsion. Again I resisted the temptation to escape from this feeling. I allowed it to pervade me without judgment. Gradually, sadness and tenderness dawned in my heart, replacing the hunger. Desperation was replaced with a vast expanse of acceptance. But in remembering my child's death, I recalled too what had happened at the time of my son's cremation.

That time had been the closest I had come to being in the Animal Realm. Survival pervaded my days. I had accepted that my son was dead, but my senses were dulled. I could not connect with anyone. My eyes were cast down, and I went through the days as if in a dream. I realized that I was trying to hide from my pain. But in recalling, in reliving the mechanical actions and the strange lack of feeling, I now sat in the gloom and tasted it fully. While I fully felt the pain of numbness, tenderness began to dawn while my mind eased. From this dark shadow of eating and sleeping like a wounded animal, a sense of spaciousness arose. Like the sun, it dawned from the dark and I breathed and felt what I had lost.

It was then that I re-discovered the Human Realm, the place where we feel and embrace both joy and sorrow. I acknowledged human relationship again. Memories arose of neighbors who supported me when I sought a mustard seed from a home that did not know death. The kindness of my companions came to mind, the empathy of my dharma sisters I have come to trust and love in the monastery. I felt filled with affection. I had forgotten the power of love in my life, and now remembered my parents, Raja, and the precious time I had with my son Anupam. But when I recalled the hurt, attachment, and loss of those relationships, the contentment vanished. As always, I wished to eliminate the sorrow and have only the happiness. As I sat in meditation, both states of mind fought for my attention. Sister Patacara's instructions reminded me to let both joys and sorrows coexist in my heart. Instead of seeing misery as an enemy, or happiness as the only worthy state of mind, what arose was compassion for both extremes. The warmth in my heart increased.

That was not all that occurred in those days. Jealousy, acrid and hateful, sharp as a knife, penetrated my relaxation. I recalled how it pierced me when I saw neighborhood children playing with their mothers. I resented the mothers and wanted to take the children as my own. Harboring these thoughts of envy and resentment, I was like an *asura*, a jealous spirit with a grudge against everyone. I stayed still, allowing myself to feel the jealousy without bias, and I recognized that it was part of me as well. I let the energy of jealousy congeal. Sister Patacara had said this was the Realm of the Jealous Gods. As I breathed slowly in and out, the seemingly solid ball of jealousy began to untangle naturally. I discovered beneath it a true generosity of heart that opened up like a snake uncoiling and slipping into the grass. Without escaping the pain, I relaxed.

I thought that perhaps now I would no longer experience pain even in the practice. I found myself dwelling in what was described as the Heavenly Realm. It was what happened to me when I first married and thought my life would no longer be miserable. I had escaped poverty. I would be different from those I had left behind in the fields. At first it was pleasing, even to remember it. But it was also a state of great suffering, because I had been blind to the certainty of change and the fragility of life. All beings, including the wealthy or the monastics, experience pain. Through the meditation practice of staying with what was arising, I felt its power and I also became aware of its limits. My heart melted. What arose was deep care and openness. This too was me.

When I returned from the retreat, I knew I wanted to live in the temple near this village so that I could share what I had learned with all of you. All these emotions are part of our humanity. While everyday shifting thoughts and emotions remained on the surface, like waves on the ocean, the center of awareness was gradually deepened. I knew the still water below pervaded every surface wave and whitecap.

Kisa was steady as she described the practice that had led her to new insight. The villagers listened. For some it was like finding a long-lost spring of fresh water. One person asked, "Can people get over their unhappiness and put it behind them?" Kisa paused for a while, then said,

Sorrow is sorrow. It is part of life. But it too can change, if we let it move us. When we truly understand the causes of our unhappiness there is peace.

At that moment, a flying insect bit a child who started screeching. Her mother apologized, "I will take her away." Kisa reassured her and everyone gathered there by the fire.

The world is always sending us bites and scratches, things that make us cry. Wars, conflicts, and injustices arise because we resist this truth and react. The Buddha taught, "Everything will end. When we understand this, all quarrels fade away." Within painful experiences are wisdom, compassion, and love that restore us. Everything is included in our lives. If we see the universe in this way, we realize it is through these difficult experiences that our minds and hearts find more joy. Our minds can know the entire universe. There are endless galaxies within us and outside of us. There are trillions of stars, and as many heavens as anyone can count. It goes on infinitely in all directions. Universes arise and pass way. Whole world systems are created and dissolve. Once we know that, our hearts have no limit.

The sky was growing dark, and the villagers had remained much longer than usual. Nanda thanked her for the teaching on behalf of the whole village and asked her for a blessing, which she chanted for them. Many people started gathering their children and quickly left. Some, however, stayed, sitting quietly where they were. They wanted Sister Kisa to tell them more about her experience.

On a night like this, a long time ago. I did not feel like sleeping either. We had had a busy day, chanting, talking, and receiving lay people. Everyone else went to bed.

I walked to the meditation hall, easing my way through the darkness and pushing aside branches with my hands. Before, I had ignored things around me, but now I noticed and listened: to the clicking of the cicadas, the swish of leafed branches, and the pervasive silence. Fireflies, tiny, solitary evanescent lights, swam in seas of darkness. I stepped into the coolness of the shrine hall and slipped off my sandals.

My feet felt steady on the floor. The hall felt still after an evening of blessings. An oil lamp—the only one still lit from the evening meditation—flickered in the corner. The lamp provided light in the darkness for me to find my place. I sat down, legs folded; spine stretched tall, upright but tension-free; shoulders at ease, even and balanced; arms, jaw, and fingers relaxed, with palms resting on my lap. I became aware of the space around me and the weight of my body on the ground. A whole universe in one body.

I gazed again at the steadiness of the lamp and its single flame. My mind settled in meditation, and I sat throughout much of the night.

When I surfaced, the flame of the lamp had started to hiss and splutter, unsteady as the oil was giving out, just as the fire is now. In the flickering light I sat and observed the world around the space where I was sitting.

I noticed that the trembling was not just in the lamp. Around us, and inside us, there is a fine, ever-moving, flickering inherent in the solidity of the physical world. A burning and dancing hold all physical objects together as they rise and fall. All events in the body and mind burn. Just knowing this was the greatest happiness. I realized that this is what the Buddha had called "knowing the deathless" so many years ago, and yes, this experience brought clarity and contentment.

I understood what remained. So many beings were stuck in their states of greed, ill-will, and delusion. Again I vowed to return my attention to the world of sentient beings, to help them find their way to liberation. I knew my purpose was to be of service to others, to comfort the bereaved, to soothe the angry, to accompany the lonely. I now wished for the happiness of others, consoling them in their need, rejoicing in their virtues, and resting in boundless equanimity. This was the human purpose I had sought my entire life, and I blessed my good fortune. The universe seemed latently awake, everywhere, in the moment before dawn. The dying sputter of the lamp fizzled out.

Tears of relief and gratitude filled my eyes and flooded my mind, while devotion held me firm and calmly seated. I paid homage to my teacher, the teaching, and my community. When I left the shrine room the sun was beginning to rise. The skies were streaked with the glorious reds, blues, golds, purples, and greens of dawn while we got on, as usual, with the alms round.

But our fire is now down to embers here too. Let's make our way back to our homes.

The small group of people walked along the river with Kisa back to her temple.

For the last part of her life, Kisa taught quietly. Her husband's family —now becoming even more powerful in the neighborhood— invited her to meals and to give dharma talks. Kisa saw their familiar faces soften and felt compassion for the fear that had been behind their coldness. Through her teachings, they learned how to practice loving kindness for themselves and then extend it outward to others, so that they could benefit too. They looked out for the villagers and saw them differently.

Raja remarried and had many children. He and his family established a village textile cooperative that pooled resources for the benefit of all. Farmers shared the arduous cotton harvest along with the cleaning, carding, spinning, and weaving of cotton cloth. Many new workers had come to Madhyapur. Some were from the lowest castes or were outside caste. Now several of these had responsibilities leading teams and bringing new expertise to the work. All worked together, laughing and gossiping. Raja's family learned more about the cares and troubles as well as the joys of the entire village.

Sister Kisa's home was with her sister nuns at the temple at the edge of the village. Each year during the three-month rainy season she spent time in retreat with them, deepening her meditations to rest in the mind, refreshing herself and finding new inspiration.

Together the sisters chanted, sat, walked, and discussed the practice and teachings. Meditation and chant replenished her wellsprings, giving her peace so she could help others.

At the end of one rainy season retreat, Raja and other members of the textile collective came to the temple for the annual offering of new robes for the monastics. They proudly presented their freshly hand-loomed cloth. Sister Patacara and the senior nuns received these offerings graciously. The gift came from the labors of the entire village. The cotton was simple, but Sister Kisa could feel the weave of the threads. When she fingered the fabric, she could detect the warp and the weft, with an occasional bump and imperfection. It was like the village now, monastics and lay people living closely together, a single human community. Kisa blessed those gathered around:

The path is like a loom, weaving discoveries from the warp and woof of our lives. Warp threads from our ancient pasts meet cross-threads from the new, creating intricate patterns that mix confusion, wisdom, and all our actions. Fine weave is mixed with bumps and textures, but wisdom is continuous throughout. Each length of cloth is unique and beautiful. Knowing this, may you all be well and happy.

As years passed, respect for Kisa grew in her village and its surroundings. Everyone found in her care, her joy, and her presence a refuge and support. Whenever she sat under a tree near the temple, villagers would gather to ask for advice and succor. As she grew older, she taught through silent presence. People came to sit with her. While Kisa had become a legend, her actual story was known to only a few who had heard her talk years ago by the fire.

For Kisa Gotami's seventy-fifth birthday, the village wished to honor her. At first, she refused celebrations as unsuitable for a nun. But the villagers persisted. Offerings were made to the temple. The poor were fed and given baskets of cotton and rice. The textile collective gave fine cloth to everyone. Those who received became generous too. Kisa's story gradually spread throughout many regions and among many people. She was one woman. But there were many people then, as there are now, who find stillness and peace in a life of service. Their names are unknown, but their influence spreads far.

Now, when once again our world is awash with great suffering, pestilence, and loss, we leave this story with you in hopes that it will uplift your heart and bring peace into our world. The greatest gift Kisa could have received was knowing that her story continued to release others from their suffering and became a source of joy.

Dialogue in a Desert Place

A RETELLING OF THE CHRISTIAN SACRED STORY

Dialogue in a Desert Place

The story unfolds as an ancient dialog enabling the contemporary reader to listen in on the final lessons passed between a master and student on "The Way" of early Christian discipleship. The characters address one another in in familial language that indicates the depth of their spiritual bond. The term "story" here is multivalent, signifying not just a basic narrative but also an exploration of how what is discussed in the dialog might also be viewed from an eternal, timeless perspective. In this telling, the questions of a former lowly slave girl can help the reader discover our human place within the story and how we might each begin to approach "mysteries that surpass the powers of our imagination" (in the words of St. Makrina).

PERSONS IN THE DIALOGUE

Makrina *(St. Makrina the Younger, c. 327–379 CE): a nun, daughter of a prestigious Christian family in Cappadocia, sister of St. Basil of Caesarea (330–379 CE) and St. Gregory of Nyssa (c. 335–c. 395 CE).*

Kallista*: a young nun, formerly a slave in the household of Makrina's family, but emancipated along with her fellow slaves by Makrina's mother Emmelia (d. 375 CE), and now a member of the monastic community that the family founded some years earlier. Kallista is Makrina's best student.*

SETTING

Early in July 379 CE, beginning in the late afternoon and concluding near dusk. Makrina is in her cell at a convent in what had been one of her family's remote estates in the lower elevations of the mountains of

Pontus, not far from the shores of the Black Sea. She is on her deathbed, which in her case is a plain pallet made from rushes and laid directly on the floor, with only a folded blanket to support her head. A single lamp burns in a niche in the wall near the doorway.

PART ONE

The Image of God in Us

[*Kallista enters the cell, carrying a clay pitcher of water and a cup, both of which she sets on the floor. She then kneels beside the pallet and briefly places a hand upon Makrina's brow. Satisfied that there is no sign of fever, she draws back her hand and begins to rise.*]

Makrina: No, please, stay with me a little while, my dear Sister.

Kallista: Mother, I don't wish to disturb you. I don't expect a lesson today, although you know how much I cherish them.

Makrina: Disturb me? Hardly. [*Reaching out a hand lightly and laying it on Kallista's wrist*] I want to talk. I'm not tired, and your company is always a joy to me. Your heart is deep, and you're a very gifted student.

Oh, and tell me, has any word reached us from my brother yet?

Kallista: Yes. A messenger arrived from Bishop Gregory's traveling party just this morning. He said that Bishop Gregory should arrive within two days, attended by two deacons, and asked that beds be prepared for them.

Makrina: That's good to hear. I'm afraid my time is growing short, and I would like to see his face one more time before departing the world.

Kallista: [*After a pause of several seconds*] That's why he's making such haste to get here. But I'm still praying that God will restore you to health.

Makrina: [*Gently*] Well, that's as God wills. I would like to spare him further grief, so soon after our brother Basil's death especially. But we're both accustomed to loss. You know, we had another brother who died more than a quarter century ago. And, of course, our parents have both left this world. And my brother Gregory, as you know, is a widower. [*More gently still*] Life here, as you know, is fleeting. But, whatever God allows at this moment, we'll all be reunited in the age to come... and we'll shine with God's glory like stars in the heavens. [*Laying a hand softly on Kallista's wrist again*] Don't grieve overly much, dear Daughter, whatever should happen.

Kallista: [*Lowering her eyes*] I'll grieve greatly indeed if you don't recover.

Makrina: [*Softly, with tender laughter*] Then you have more need for my prayers than I have for yours. Anyway, have you any further news?

Kallista: Only that the messenger also delivered the book of your brother's sermons for this past Great Lent and Easter, celebrating the death and resurrection of Jesus, as you requested.

Makrina: Have they been read out to the sisters?

Kallista: Only one so far, after noonday prayer, by Sister Evdokia.

Makrina: And was it... edifying?

Kallista: [*Slightly wrinkling her brow*] Yes, I suppose... though it was also very... very unusual.

Makrina: How so? I know my brother can be obscure sometimes...

Kallista: Oh, that he certainly wasn't. He was very clear. The homily was on a verse from: "I got me male and female slaves and also had slaves who were born into my household" (Eccl 2:7). Naturally, when I heard the reading, I was sure I knew that your brother was going to make the usual recommendation that slaveholders should consider setting some of their slaves free... maybe as many as could be provided for without damaging the household. I thought he would tell them what a fine penitential preparation it would be for the Easter feast.

Makrina: But he didn't?

Kallista: Well, yes, dear Mother, he *did*... but he didn't leave the matter there.

Makrina: What did my brother say, then?

Kallista: He said things I've never heard anyone say before and never with so much... *indignation*.

Makrina: Oh, now I must know what he said.

Kallista: Well, you see, he didn't just rebuke those who own too many slaves or tell them they should temper their desires by setting their unneeded slaves free. It was more... provocative than that...

[*With an expression of uncertainty on her face*]... He said that owning any slaves at all is a wicked thing... a sin against the image of God. It all seemed very fierce. He said that for anyone to presume mastery over another is sheer arrogance and a challenge to God... a robbery of God, to whom alone we all belong. He said divine law gives us no rights over one another, and that all the money in the world isn't enough to purchase such a right. He even... I mean, he upbraided his listeners for even daring to *imagine* that they could possibly buy a creature made in the image of God. And that was only the beginning.

Makrina: Well, go on, then.

Kallista: And he said—I'm not exaggerating—that not even God has the power to enslave human beings.

Makrina: That sounds like my brother. What was his argument there?

Kallista: That divine gifts can't be taken back, and God's greatest gift to us is the liberty restored to us in the salvation of the world in Jesus Christ.

Makrina: I see.

Kallista: And he pointed out that when a slave is bought, so are that slave's possessions, but God has made every human being a steward of the whole world, which no one can buy. The exchange of money and written receipts, he said, may make a master think he's superior to other persons, but all of us are equals, prey to the same frailties, capable of the same joys, beneficiaries of the same salvation, and subject to the same judgment. And yet—and these are his very words, as I recall them—"You have divided human nature between slavery and mastery and have made it at once slave and master over itself." And . . . well, I don't recall any more than that.

Makrina: But does it truly surprise you, Daughter? You must know that my mother believed that and that I do, too. Hence, dear Daughter, your own release from slavery.

Kallista: Mother, my heart leapt when your brother spoke with such boldness and passion. I also know that slavery is a consequence of the first sin. My heart hasn't stopped pondering his claim that God's greatest gift to us—to all of us—is the restoration of our liberty.

But, strangely perhaps, my head also felt confused. I found myself wondering how any household could function without slaves? How can fields bear a harvest without slaves to sow and reap?

Makrina: Dear Daughter, your heart is already growing wise beyond your years; it knows more than it can understand. Let's consider the matter to see if we can bring heart and mind closer together.

Didn't the church of the apostles in Jerusalem hold all things in common and serve one another, out of love?

Kallista: Yes, but didn't the Apostle instruct slaves not to be rebellious against their masters?

Makrina: Yes, but did he instruct the masters to keep slaves? Didn't he ask Philemon to receive his slave Onesimus as a slave no longer, but as a beloved brother instead (Philem 1:16)? Didn't he tell slaves to become free if the opportunity arose and not to become slaves of any man (1 Cor 7:21–23)?

Surely you remember my brother saying that the Son of God came in the "form of a slave" (Phil 2:7), not like an actor playing a part, but to abolish slavery—along with every other ill—from our one shared human nature? That, in the life to come, there'll be neither sickness nor curse nor sin nor death nor slavery? Christ himself tells his disciples, "I call you no longer slaves, but friends" (Jn 15:15).

Kallista: Yes, dear Mother, of course, in the Age to Come... when the Kingdom arrives, and all things are restored, and the Ruler of this world is overthrown, and we're all made co-heirs of the Father...

Makrina: Yes, very good, dear Daughter. But there is more to it. Our Lord tells us to ask our Father each day for the bread sufficient to the day, and to imitate the freedom of the birds of the air and the idleness of the lilies (Mt 6:11, 25–32). And doesn't scripture repeatedly command us to serve one another (Gal 5:13; 1 Pet 4:10) and even to wash one another's feet (Jn 13:14)? Doesn't the Apostle tell us that in Christ there can be no division between the enslaved and the free (Gal 3:28)? Yes, of course, slavery will be utterly abolished when the Kingdom comes. But that future is already present with us now, isn't it, my daughter?

Kallista: [*Smiling*] You always say that, Mother.

PART TWO
God's Eternal Counsels

Makrina: [*Smiling in return*] But it's true, dear Daughter. Doesn't the Lord himself say that the ruler of the world has already been cast out (Jn 12:31) and that the Kingdom has already come in our hearts (Lk 17:21)? You speak as if the final things are merely a story yet to be told; but the way you lovingly serve others shows me that you also know that what shall be already also *is*... that all that is promised has also already come to pass in Christ.

Your actions express that presence and why we live as we do in this place. We must live in the Kingdom even now, even though it is invisible to most eyes, including often ours. For we've already died with Christ and so died to the age that's passing away. As we are to be raised with him, we must live already in the new life he has given us (Rom 6:1–5). Indeed, not only have we died with him, we've even already been raised with him and ascended along with him into the heavenly places and been seated alongside him on God's throne (Eph 1:20–23; 2:6; Col 1:12–14; 2:12; 3:1–2; 4:1; Heb 9:28; 10:37).

[*Softly but firmly*] Daughter, the signs of your embracing the Kingdom are plain for those with eyes to see: your kindness, your modesty, your willingness to walk the extra mile, and your faith bravely seeking understanding. You know that I love your courage in trying to understand as best we can our faith.

Kallista: Mother, you always encourage my heart. Still, I can understand clearly only one way of telling the story of our faith, beginning at the beginning and ending at the end.

Makrina: And how would you tell our story?

Kallista: [*With a hapless shrug*] As I've always heard it told. At one time, we dwelled in peace with God and with creation but fell through disobedience and became slaves of the devil in the household of death. And creation, too, was made subject to death, and to evil powers.

But God loved us and refused to abandon us to death, and so sent his Son to become a man to pay the price to free us from slavery in death's household and to overthrow the realm of death's kingdom and all the hostile spiritual rulers of the cosmos.

Then, at the end of time, having re-ordered all of creation under himself, and having joined us to himself, the Son will hand over all things to the Father, and God shall be all in all (1 Cor 15:22–28). That story I understand. I can follow it from beginning to end.

Makrina: Good, dear Daughter, you tell it well.

But let's ponder further: It's also true that that final reality has been prepared for us from everlasting. That's the mystery hidden in God from the world's foundations (Eph 3:9). God didn't just begin the world at some point in the past and then wait to see what would happen, only redeeming it when things went amiss. God made the world for the ends he intended and made each of us within those ends.

God redeemed the world in the divine eternity *before* ever bringing it into existence; God joined humanity to the divine glory in that eternity *before* making the human race from the dust of the earth (Eph 1–4).

Kallista: Mother, your words tug at my heart beyond the reach of my understanding. I've heard you say this before, but even so, all I can clearly understand now is that we've fallen and that we'll be raised up again; I don't see yet how the latter comes before the former.

Makrina: Well, your heart already knows about all this in its own way, and that's what is most important.

Kallista: Even so, I can't yet grasp it clearly, even though I want to!

Makrina: Some water, Daughter, please. [*After drinking*] You may think my brother was being *extreme* when he reproached slaveholders for having divided the human race against itself. But what does he mean? In the world we know, human beings have always been divided against one another.

Kallista: Yes, that seems so.

Makrina: My brother would tell you—and this is important—that the truest way to see the world is to see it the way God wills it from all eternity. So, when scripture tells us that God created humankind as male and female in the divine image and likeness (Gen 1:27), it is speaking of God's act of creating the whole human family as one in eternity, with its single human nature.

It is speaking of the one humanity that God first willed in fashioning a creature in the divine image, and it points to the heavenly eternity of the one ideal human being who dwells eternally in the wisdom and foresight of the Father, who alone is truly that God-like thing in whom God has reached down in love to impress the divine likeness. And it is here, in the one eternal human being, that each of us has his or her truest existence. This passage in scripture asks us to see ourselves as God has called us into being.

Kallista: So, Mother, when later scripture speaks of the creation of Adam from the dust of the earth, and of God breathing his Spirit into Adam to make him a living soul (Gen 2:7), is it referring to something else—not so much to the making of that eternal humanity "according to the image"? Is it, rather, speaking of the making of individual men and women, and specifically of our father and mother here below?

Makrina: Oh, very good, Kallista! Your mind is catching up to your heart. Scripture asks us to see ourselves as God created us in eternity. It also asks us to see ourselves on our passage on earth as toward the communion God originally created us for.

Kallista: I am beginning to see it, Mother, although it still comes in and out of focus for me. Apart from sin, our human family is to make its way on earth as part of the pure and glorious body of Christ in surrender to the Father so that God will be fully revealed in creatures.

Makrina: Yes, dear. Our human family is called into the body of Christ from eternity.

Kallista: Ahhh. . . . So, it is the body of Christ that the slaveholder violates and disfigures by dividing humanity against itself. I can see that now. And we know this, because to know what is to come is also to know how God sees all things in eternity and would have us see them now.

Makrina: Amen, dear Sister, amen. You bring my old heart joy. So tell me, what difference does this make in our lives?

PART THREE

The Lord Who Comes in a Slave's Form

Kallista: [*Drawing in her breath pensively*] Well, Mother, I am sure it must make all the difference in the world. It makes me think of how often we exalt what God disdains and disdain what God exalts.

Makrina: Good, Daughter. We can consider how the Lord showed himself to us: not as a prince upon the earth, or a mighty warrior honored for his conquests, and certainly not in the form of a god, but in the form of a slave (Phil 2:6–7). Someone like what you once were, my sister.

Kallista: [*Smiling*] Yes, but Mother, perhaps he did that to remain hidden from the eyes of men and the demonic Powers who govern the cosmos. Even a king must hide his majesty in the midst of his enemies.

Makrina: [*Pausing, then softly*] Oh . . . really? . . . I don't think so. He had no need to hide. He may not have revealed that he was the Christ until the appointed time, but before men and the cosmic Powers he never ceased to proclaim the One from whom he came. No, he wore the form of the slave—the form in which you yourself were born—because in the eyes of his Father the slave is more illustrious, more splendid, more truly human than the master is . . . more radiant with the beauty of the divine image . . . more glorious in dignity. Had he come as an earthly king, *that* would have hidden his true nature. Let's ponder, little sister, what John the Evangelist tells us by depicting our Lord when he was brought before Pilate.

Kallista: Do you mean the scene that shows us how God's truth differs from this world's truth?

Makrina: Yes, dear, that one. Tell me what you see in that scene.

Kallista: Mother, on one side stands a man so far removed from my life. He's powerful, a noble, invested with the full authority of the Roman Empire. On the other stands a working man, a poor man of humble origins who, when asked if he is "King of the Jews," replies that his "Kingdom is not of this world" and speaks about a "truth" to which he is called to bear witness.

Makrina: [*Very quietly*] Yes, exactly. In this world, Pilate could scarcely hold a more exalted place. Our Lord, by contrast, could scarcely be of less significance in worldly terms: a rustic, from the household of a mere artisan, his mother a humble girl from the provinces, so poor she had to bear him in a stable among animals. In the eyes of this world, he has no natural claim whatsoever upon Pilate's mercy nor any legal rights; like a slave, he has no status at all before the law. He is no one. Pilate has perfect sway over life and death, while our Lord no longer even belongs to himself.

Kallista: Pilate seems to wear the form of a god, and seems to be the one whom the gods favor and appoint as their earthly representative.

Makrina: Yes. And Pilate asks, "What is truth?"—while the one real truth is this very man standing there in the humblest and most abject of human forms: he, the slave, is the glory of God, the eternal image of the Father.

Kallista: [*Hushed*] Oh, mother, you make me want to weep. I carry the story in my heart. No, the story carries my heart.... I know the Lord is then brought before Pilate for the second time (Jn 19:1–11), having been scourged, wrapped in a soldier's cloak, crowned with thorns.

And then Pilate's question: "Where do you come from?" Is he reminding the Lord that, compared to himself, the Lord is no one at all? He says: "I have the power to crucify you." That's his proof of worldly authority.

Makrina: [*Quietly and firmly*] Yes, Kallista. But this is not the way of our God is it? We see in Christ that God doesn't make the powerful or the violent representatives of his will, but rather the lowly whom the powerful and violent oppress. The Gospel overturns the order of the ages... all the wisdom of empires and kingdoms. The one who is of no account—the slave condemned by the gods of the nations, the crucified one who has no earthly power or preeminence—*he* is the very form of God in our midst.

Kallista: Mother, when I open my heart to this truth, it seems that the pillars of the world are shaken.

Makrina: Yes, utterly shaken. If we teach ourselves to see the glory of God in a crucified slave, then we must see *all* the forsaken of the earth as the children of heaven. It's the Father—not Pilate—who pronounces the true verdict upon our Lord, by raising him from the dead in the power of the Holy Spirit. It is the crucified one who is the true Lord of all things.

Nothing can hide this beauty from our hearts once we've seen it. Those who reviled the Lord tried to conceal it under a crown of thorns, a reed scepter, and a soldier's cloak, but they couldn't. We who know the risen Lord can see that the mockery is only cast back upon the kings and rulers of the world. In the light of the resurrection, we see that all their finery and symbols of privilege are but rags and brambles compared to the true radiance of God's Son.

Pathetic and ridiculous are those emblems of earthly authority that have been draped over his shoulders and pressed into his scalp. In his radiance, we see now the vanity of empires and kingdoms, the absurdity of men who wrap themselves in silks and satins, promote themselves with preposterous titles, claim the right to rule over others, and prove their "right" by killing.

Kallista: Mother, all the powerful of the earth together can't begin to surpass the beauty of the God who makes even the dust seem radiant, But [*lowering her eyes*] our Lord wasn't simply any slave like me.

Makrina: Yes, in a way you are right. But I know you can also see how every person, however powerless, grows in dignity when seen in the light of the truth of the Lord. The way you live and the joy you have in serving others shows me that you recognize the beauty of the human countenance shining out in each person made in the Father's eternal counsels. This can help us also see that when the eternal Son came in the form of a slave, he wasn't hiding the divine beauty from our eyes but revealing it. And it also shows us the divine beauty that lies within every soul . . . no matter how lowly or despised. Daughter, I could glimpse this radiance in you even before you were freed, and I have never been able to see anyone otherwise since then. Does *this* make my brother's words any clearer to you?

Kallista: Thank you, mother. Yes, it helps. And yet—forgive me—I remain uncertain as to why this tells us not only how it shall be in the Kingdom but how it should be now. I am, I know, stubborn, but your kind patience allows me to say . . . [*lifting her eyes again*] there are still slaves and masters in this world . . . and our holy Emperor yet reigns . . . and . . . [*she falls silent with another slight shrug*].

Makrina: [*Now closing her eyes, her voice becoming very quiet*] Well . . . as my brother has also often said, the Lord came to purge such things from our shared humanity. This is a hard, but liberating truth.

Kallista: We shouldn't speak of such things, Mother. Forgive me.

Makrina: We can speak freely. If you were my own child, I couldn't love you more . . . [*she pauses, and Kallista holds the cup to her lips again*]. Thank you. All I can say is that we *should* live as if the Kingdom has already come, because its life is already ours, as we've already died and been raised with the Lord. The Kingdom we await is already within us. . . . We're already its citizens and its heirs.

And, because our Lord has made his Father our Father too, we're already one family in the God for whom all the families of heaven and earth are named (Eph 3:15). Perhaps if I were to tell you the story as I see it—as I understand what's been revealed—you would find my brother's claims in that sermon nothing more than... obvious.

Kallista: Perhaps, Mother.

Makrina: [*Opening her eyes again and looking into Kallista's*] Shall I do so?

Kallista: Now? Sister... dear Mother, you're too weak. It would be dangerous.

Makrina: Oh, nonsense. I wish to talk, Daughter; it makes me feel better. If you're willing, that is. Are you?

Kallista: I am, of course. Very much so. But...

Makrina: Very well, then. If you'd just be so good as to pour me some more water, permit me to speak to you as long as God gives me the strength.

[*After Makrina has raised her head and drunk from the cup, with Kallista's assistance, she lies back again, composes herself, and resumes speaking.*]

PART FOUR
The End for Which the World Was Made

Makrina: Are you ready, Sister?

Kallista: I am, Mother.

Makrina: Very well. But, you know, the beginnings of stories are always difficult—some much more than others, of course, and none more than in this case. Actually, one might say the story our faith tells has two beginnings... and maybe two endings, now that I come to think of it.

Kallista: [*Smiling and sighing affectionately, clearly well accustomed to Makrina's ways*] Doesn't that mean that there are two stories?

Makrina: No, only the one—the one story of all stories—but there are very different ways of telling the tale. One can tell it as beginning in eternity or as beginning in time. In both versions, of course, neither beginning nor ending has an exact date or place. Both lie outside our ordinary experience. Even scripture wouldn't be able to enlighten us; if we weren't instructed by the Spirit in our reading, all we would see would look like trivial myths.

Kallista: Just as I've also heard your brother say. Will you begin our tale from our earthly perspective or from the heavenly perspective, Mother?

Makrina: [*Her brow furrowing*] Oh, it's hard to choose. [*Now laughing softly at herself*] Let's say we tell it from our earthly vantage. First, God's making of the world wasn't simply a particular event that came and went at a moment in the past. Creation is always happening, in every moment.

God is always drawing all things into being out of nothingness, into union with the divine—with the infinite ocean of existence that is the divine nature.

Or maybe one might say that creation is the journey of all things being created by God and returning to God. In being made, creatures are receiving all they are from God alone, and yet they're also becoming all they may ever be by entering more deeply into communion with God. God is himself the infinite, uncreated, flowing fountain of beauty and love from which we yearn to drink.

Kallista: And in drinking freely we become more truly ourselves?

Makrina: Exactly so. We become more what God has created us to be, more the divine image and likeness.

But this means also that creation, as God intends it from the first, won't have truly come to pass until the consummation of all things when "God shall be all in all" (1 Cor 15:28).

Kallista: This much I think I already know: As in the beginning, so in the end.

Makrina: There's more to say, though.

[*Kallista nods, inviting Makrina to continue.*]

Makrina:: The Age to Come isn't simply something that will one day occur in the far future, when history has been exhausted. The creation of the world and its perfection are also real now, in the present.

As the Lord has said, "Now is the judgment on this world" (Jn 12:31). The light of the Father's truth falls across the entirety of time, separating love and justice from hatred and injustice.

And the final judgment on creation is the one pronounced at the very beginning: "It is good" (Gen 1:31). For us, this will be fully revealed only at the consummation of all things. True. But scripture also tells us that "the Kingdom does not come as something one observes, for look: the Kingdom of God is inside of you" (Lk 17:20–21).

Kallista: Our first beginning is in our last end, and our last end is even now present in the Spirit. And yet we're still in transit, aren't we, Mother? For us now, the Kingdom lies ahead.

Makrina: Yes, but we are also already in our Father's house.

Kallista: In promise, yes, but in reality?

Makrina: Yes, Sister. If we tell the tale only from our earthly perspective, then of course we look to the future for the Kingdom's coming. But the story has two beginnings. If we choose to tell it from its eternal beginning and in light of its eternal end, we find that, in a profound manner, the beginning and the end of the story are each present in the other.

In God's eternity, the world is created already in its final state. But in God's eternity, there's no before and after; there's only the one act of creation. What for us is an end to be achieved is for God the beginning of all things.

The Apostle tells us that all creation shall at the end "gladly praise" Jesus as Lord (Rom 14:11; Phil 2:11), but in eternity that has always already occurred. That final state is the one eternal moment when creation comes into being. It's true that we can glimpse that end only as in a mirror darkly, and only in part; but we know it's already accomplished in God, through our Lord, and know too that we shall see it to be so, when we see God's glory face to face and shall know even as God knows us (1 Cor 13:12). "What we shall be has not yet become manifest. But we know that when he appears we shall be like him, because we shall see him as he is" (1 Jn 3:2). Only then shall we know ourselves as truly created in God's image.

Kallista: Yes, Mother. But from my earthly perspective, it feels like these are only promises and not descriptions of what is . . . or should be.

Makrina: [*Smiling warmly*] Daughter, your brilliant mind still finds it hard to catch up to your deep heart. These are not promises such as we human beings make, which may or may not be fulfilled. We know—insofar as we know the Lord is risen—that those promises were fulfilled even before we ever heard them . . .that the end they promise is eternally real.

Kallista: [*Pausing*] I do know that God is steadfast . . . that God's promises are certain.

Makrina: Well, perhaps that's all we need say. And it's enough to make my brother's words comprehensible, isn't it? Only God's way of seeing things is absolutely true. How God looks upon his creatures is how they are in their truest essences. Ordinary history as we know it is fallen; all it tells us are tales of violence and tyranny, delusion and cruelty. But in our Lord, we see the true story of who we are.

For now, I admit, from the perspective of time, that truth is something we can only glimpse as we make our way through a world that is both a shining reflection and a shadowy remnant of the true story. But, we've also experienced within time the truth that is from the beginning—we've heard it, we've seen it with our eyes, it's something we've gazed upon and touched with our hands (1 Jn 1:1).

Now, since we've spent much time together, and I have seen how keen your mind is and how it struggles to serve your living faith, I know you already know this, don't you?... That the whole mystery of our faith lies in this paradox: that in Christ Jesus, time and eternity meet.

In him, both ways of telling the story of all things come together. For "all things were created through him and for him, and he is before all things and all things hold together in him" (Col 1:16–17). And yet "he pitched a tent among us, and we saw his glory, glory as of the Father's only-begotten, full of grace and truth" (Jn 1:14). He restores all things to their true—their eternal—reality.

Kallista: I know that time was severed from its eternal truth when creation fell. Our existence became a kind of prism in which the light of God and its reflection in the beauty of creation were distorted and scattered. The light of God was lost to our eyes. I have felt this, too, Mother.

Makrina: Yes, we all have. But then the eternal Son bent down to us, came among us, brought that light back into our darkness as one among us. Christ is the perfect mirror in which that scattered light of glory is gathered up again and restored to unity, so that the divine and the created both shine forth again in their fullness.

The truth revealed in the earthly life of this man, Jesus of Nazareth, really is the truth of God that should shine out in all of nature and all of history.

Are you following me, Sister?

Kallista: I believe so, yes—though I'm not entirely clear where we're heading.

Makrina: That's my fault. I have complicated the tale. So let me start yet again.

Kallista: I would be grateful if you would.

Makrina: Again, though, where to begin?

Kallista: Well, Mother, perhaps it's best to begin with God in his eternity. Surely that comes before all else.

PART FIVE

God as Our Father

Makrina: Very well.

Ours is a tale that perhaps can't be told like a normal story, because God isn't a changing, finite thing like you or I who have a past and a future. He's simply the One "I am that I am" (Ex 3:14) who is beyond all becoming: that One who exceeds all concepts and language, the transcendent source and end of all that is.

Even here, however, we must distinguish the various ways we speak of God in eternity.

We must always speak first, it seems obvious, of the One God (Dt 6:4), the creator of heaven and earth (Gen 1:1), the one who is (Ex 3:14), beyond all shadow of turning (Jas 1:17), the first and the last (Is 44:6), the beginning and the end (Rev 22:13), who is above all and through all and in all (Eph 4:6), who alone has immortality, who dwells in light inaccessible, whom no one has ever seen or can see (1 Tim 1:17, 6:16), who was and who is and who is to come, the Ruler of All (Rev 1:8), the perfect Spirit who must be worshiped in spirit and truth (Mt 5:48;

Jn 4:24), the infinitely good Father in whom there is no darkness at all (1 Jn 1:5).

The divine reality known to all persons and peoples throughout the world (Rom 1:19–20) is at once hidden and revealed in all things. The divine reality is so pervasive in its mysterious transcendence that even the wise can fail to grasp it, but so splendid in its immediacy that even children can see it (Mt 11:25, 18:3; Lk 10:21).

Kallista: So, the Christian story begins in sheer wonder before the infinite mystery of Being. We all know that wonder, although we often forget it.

Makrina: Exactly so, Daughter. It reveals itself in the endless variety of created things; the mystery of God is revealed in all times and places.

Kallista: I both glimpse the greatness and mystery of God and find it impossible to grasp. But to be honest, Mother, it sometimes causes me more fear than anything else.

Makrina: Fear?

Kallista: Well, sometimes prayer brings me peace beyond all understanding. Other times, I don't know how I can dare to approach such a God.

Makrina: [*Nodding and then taking a deep breath*] Well, scripture does say that fear is the beginning of wisdom (Prov 9:10), so I would never reproach you for that. But it's only the beginning. Yes, if we knew God only as an unfathomable mystery, as the hidden transcendent source of all things, then we'd be able to adore and fear God, but I doubt we'd be eager to call upon God or imagine that such a God would hear us.

But, my dear, this is why we must remember that the Lord tells us not to fear. God isn't only our God, but also our loving Father, and we may call upon him as Father. And who has the authority to grant us that license if not the eternal Son? You, I feel certain, know this in your heart.

We know God not simply as "God," but as the one Jesus of Nazareth called his Father (Jn 2:16) and addressed as "Abba" (Mk 14:36) and told us to address as Father as well (Mt 6:9; Lk 11:2), assured of God's parental love for us (Mt 7:9–11; Lk 11:11–13).

Of course, even here we must not think only in a worldly manner, as if God the Father were like a human father. God is neither male nor female, but is at once both Father and Mother to us. We see this clearly in the first account of creation in Genesis, where we're told that we're all created according to the image and likeness of God, male and female, together and alike (Gen 1:26–27).

God is our Father, but God also gives us life, calls us into being, nurtures and cares for us like a mother who conceives, bears, suckles, and comforts her children (Num 11:2; Deut 32:11, 18; Is 49:15; 66:13). So too the eternal Son is held in the "bosom" or "womb" of the Father (Jn 1:18). Our Lord even compares himself to a mother hen who gathers the children of Jerusalem under her wings (Lk 13:34). God our Father is the One in whom all persons and all of creation have their common source and eternal home (Jn 14:23).

So yes, Daughter, even if you might fear to call upon the God of all things, you can't fear to call upon your Father. You are your heavenly Father's daughter and beloved child.

Kallista: [*Returning her gaze at last to Makrina*] No, mother, my heart knows I can't.

Makrina: Mind you, if we're to begin our tale with God in eternity, we can't simply speak of God as Father—at least, not if we're to give voice to the deepest mystery of our faith. For, as I say, that name—"Father"—is the name also of an eternal relation.

PART SIX

God as Trinity

Kallista: [*Lifting the cup to Makrina's lips*] Take some more water, Mother.

Makrina: [*Having taken several sips from the cup*] Thank you, my dear Sister.

Kallista: Will you continue? You were saying that, according to our faith, we use the name "Father" in two ways.

Makrina: Indeed. Sometimes, especially in prayer and worship, we use it to mean the one God of all Creation. Other times, though, when using it to indicate the eternal nature of God, we are speaking of the mystery of the one God as Trinity—Father, Son, and Spirit. And this, too, is revealed by our Lord, when he both calls upon his Father and proclaims that he and the Father are one (Jn 10:30). Again, the Lord tells us (Jn 16:13) that he will send us the Spirit who proceeds from the Father.

Yet we know we're speaking here not of three gods, but of the one God known in three persons. This one God is the Father, the hidden infinite fountainhead of deity and being. This one God is also the Father's radiantly perfect "express image" (Heb 1:3), the divine Logos or Son. And this one God, too, is the endless flooding of the Father's Love of the Son and the Son's Love of the Father. This proceeding Love is also God, whom we call the Holy Spirit. It is the Spirit of Light, Love, Bliss, and Glory.

Kallista: This I've never pretended to understand, even to myself.

Makrina: And you're wise not to. No one could fully understand it.

Kallista: But what about that most essential thing, Mother? I'm thinking of love.

Makrina: [*Smiling*] Your question is no surprise to me, Daughter. I've seen the love radiant in all you do, and it is the divine thread running through our lives. [*She pauses and briefly closes her eyes.*] We can know that our true love of one another has its source in God as Trinity. The Son is the eternal image of the Father's beauty, by which the Father looks upon and loves the divine essence. The Only Begotten, who dwells in the Father, sees the Father in himself, and loves that limitless beauty. The Father's Love of the Son and the Son's Love of the Father is the endlessly proceeding Love of the Holy Spirit that embraces all life. This communion of Love in God invites and empowers us both to be open to receiving love and to love others freely.

But we know all of this not because we've reasoned our way to it. Yes, the philosopher may deduce that God is the transcendent divine mystery, the manifest divine image, and the eternal divine life, but that's not yet to know the one God as Father, Son, and Spirit. That mystery is known to us because it pitched its tent and dwelt among us.

God has poured divinity into creation and history, revealing to us within time the foundations of eternity.

Kallista: [*Holding back tears and speaking slowly*] I know somehow you are pointing us to the most profound truth of all.

Makrina: We can see the marvelous truth unveiled for us. It means that, even in the perfect oneness of God, there's also already—however inconceivable to us—relation, perfect community in love, knowledge, and delight in otherness; God is by nature a self-outpouring love: the Father loves totally, holding nothing back, the Son returns the Father's Love totally—holding nothing back, and their mutual Love proceeds as the endless flooding of the Holy Spirit. The most profound truth scripture tells us about our God is…

Kallista: "God is love" (1 Jn 4:8), Mother. No part of scripture pierces my heart more deeply.

Makrina: None could be more glorious. More and more, I see you trying to embody this love in all you do; in this way, your knowing sometimes surpasses mine. You are nursing me, but if I could, I would get up and wash your feet as our Lord did for his disciples.

Kallista: [*Lowering her eyes*] Mother, this can't be, but thank you; I'm trying be to return the love you have always extended to me. [*Hesitantly*] There is something that I sometimes wonder about... [*She falls silent.*]

Makrina: [*After several moments*] Yes...?

PART SEVEN

Creation and Our Role within It

Kallista: [*Choosing her words with care*] The story you tell...the story our faith tells us about God's life as Father, Son, and Spirit is beautiful beyond words. But then, I can't help but wonder what need God had to create. If he always already possessed the fullness of love and communion in his eternal nature, why would he need to create us for fellowship and union with himself?

Makrina: It's a good question, a philosophical one, on the surface. It's a matter not of need, but of the nature of who God is. Love doesn't withhold itself.

Love gives itself away, and in the case of God's Love, even gives itself to those who in themselves are nothing. But it's good you turn our attention in that direction—to the story told not from the point of view of eternity, but from that of time.

When we tell it that way, it begins with the making of the world, the cosmos, and all that's been drawn from absolute nothingness, receiving its existence from God. From the first, we're not our own; we're not the source of our existence; instead, we're entirely dependent upon the One. We belong to God, but also to the mystery of creation. We weren't created only for ourselves but to be the caretakers of the garden of God in this world (Gen 2:4–9).

Kallista: I know this, Mother.

Makrina: Indeed. According to our faith, the Father creates all things, both hidden and manifest (Wis 7:22). It tells us that creation isn't merely an external work of God, detached from divine life; it occurs within divine life itself.

Christ is himself the image of the invisible God, the first-born of all creation, in and through and for whom all things were created, in heaven and on earth, visible and invisible. He is before all things; in him, all things hold together.

Moreover, the Spirit shapes and animates all things, giving them life and making them shine as signs of God. Creation itself is already divine revelation, given freely to all people, and a gift of grace made to all and everyone (Sir 24:19–21). All creation is grace, and anything real is also part of God's good ends.

Humanity is fashioned in the image of God, after the pattern of the one who is the eternal image of the Father (Heb 1:2–3; Wis 7:25–26). "We are his workmanship, created in Christ Jesus for good works" (Eph 2:10). And for this reason, when the Son is made manifest as a man, he comes into his own (Jn 1:9); he is not just one particular human being among other human beings; he is the truest image and archetype of humanity as well. In this sense, he is the truest human being of all, just as he is the very form of God among us.

Kallista: [*Lifting her hand momentarily from her lap and holding it out toward Makrina*] Yes, now that you say it, I recognize that I've had something like that thought before. It's astonishing... our Lord is both the true image of the Father and the true image of humanity. Humanity is created in the image of God because it's created in the likeness of the Son. What we are at bottom... what we are called to be... which is nothing but a manifestation of what he is... what he is eternally.

Makrina: [*Her voice, despite its weakness, becoming more animated*] Yes, yes, it's wonderful to contemplate. This tells us what the true purpose of creation is. Not only does creation come forth from God, but all things are called to greater unity with the God from whom they come.

God dwells in creation so that creation may come to dwell in God.

And the destiny of spiritual creatures is to fulfill their high vocation within creation. All creatures possess a natural desire for God, because we exist for no other reason than that we might be "deified" or "glorified" in God. Humankind too, has a special and priestly role to play in this great harmony of all things. God chose us in Christ before the foundation of the world and marked us out to be conformed to the image of the Son—to be sons and daughters according to the divine purpose, to unite all things in heaven and on earth in Christ (Rom 8:29; Eph 1:3–4, 9–10). And the proper end of all persons is to have life more abundantly (Jn 10:10), to become partakers of the divine nature (2 Pet 1:4), to be transformed into the selfsame image of God (2 Cor 3:17–18), to be glorified with the divine glory that Christ brought into the world (Jn 17:24), and to be made God in God (Jn 10:33–36; Ps 82:6). And this cosmic destiny... this only true human destiny ... unites all the dimensions of created existence—the Sacred, the natural, the social, and the personal—in the one story that all of us share.

Are you scowling, Sister?

Kallista: I'm sorry, Mother. If I look displeased, I assure you I'm not. I'm merely... puzzled.

Makrina: At what?

PART EIGHT

The Origin of Evil

Kallista: At evil, Mother. At sin. All that you've said stirs my heart and soul. That God is love, that God pours that love forth in creatures, that we are called from eternity to union with God, that our hearts are consumed with a natural yearning for God—all this is beautiful.

But, if this is so, how can we have fallen? How can we have turned from the God who's so beautifully revealed in all things and for whom we burn with longing? Where does evil come from?

Makrina: [*Closing her eyes momentarily, breathing in deeply, and then composing herself with a wan smile*] Yes, it's a great mystery, I admit—and a monstrous one.

Perhaps it's because all creatures come from nothingness. Perhaps, until they're perfected and made steadfast in the good, they're of a changing and inconstant nature and so must gradually grow into their true selves.

Still, evil itself is incomprehensible. It doesn't come from God. God is Light... the one in whom there is no darkness (1 Jn 1:5). And, since all that exists comes from God, this would seem to mean that evil doesn't have any existence of its own. This isn't to say it's not real, mind you, but only that it's not a thing in itself. It's more like a shadow or an absence; it's a distortion or corruption of something real, something essentially good. It's not part of the life that God gives. Somehow it has arisen in rational natures. Somehow we've willed our separation from the God in whom alone we have our true rest, our only true home. All this we know. And yet evil itself, not being anything in itself, eludes both our understanding and our control.

Kallista: How, though, can we know this to be the nature of evil? I understand that all comes from God and that God is all goodness and all light.... I know it. And yet, when I see the sufferings of the world—of children especially—and see the depths of the evil of which human beings are capable... [*She pauses, casting her eyes upward and then lowering them to her hands in her lap.*] It's rather difficult to believe that evil is essentially... nothing.

Makrina: Not nothing, so much as nothingness. As I say, evil is quite real. So is disease, so is darkness. But evil is not a real existing thing alongside goodness. Darkness exists only as the absence of light. And we know this to be the nature of evil chiefly by contrast to the good that we've been shown. Only when we see the origin and end of all things unfolded before us in Christ and see that the nature of God is boundless love do we recognize the insubstantiality of evil.

Whatever the case, though, and however evil arose in the hearts of creatures, our faith teaches us to believe that the story we tell of all things has also been interrupted by a tragic discord between us and God, one that has diverted the whole created order from the end to which it's called.

This, too, is an event that can't be situated in time; it is the reality of fallen time and fallen nature as we know them, both of which seem like the only reality there is but which, are, in fact, only shadows.

The true nature of creation in its original innocence can't be remembered or found or seen directly. Even so, we know for ourselves that the truth of creation exceeds what we can see.

Kallista: [*Quietly*] How?

Makrina: By recognizing the love of God in Christ, but also by truly knowing ourselves. If we pause and meditate upon the deepest motives of our wills, our deepest longings, we must sooner or later realize that a natural longing for God always drives us on. It is a drive we can ignore but can't extinguish in ourselves. True, we're not always conscious of it, especially when we surrender to wrath, ambition, or hatred, but if we look for it within, we find it there always abiding—a deeper longing than words can properly express.

We see how natural it is to live in harmony with God and others. Despite this, we're divided in ourselves, yearning for the fulfillment of our natures in the love of God and yet unwilling to submit to that love. The reality of losing our original innocence is a truth we experience every day in our hearts. We are aware of the vast difference between the divine eternity that our deepest nature restlessly desires and the reality of the life we live here, in slavery to ignorance, suffering, and death.

Kallista: But then evil simply remains a mystery in itself?

Makrina: We might think in terms of shadow. We know a shadow's shape only by virtue of knowing what it's a shadow of—and, even then, we can't take hold of the shadow, but only of the thing whose shape it faintly mimics or deeply distorts.

Even while having no substance in itself, a shadow still has the power to obscure other things.

In terms of our own experience of existence before the mystery of God, we enter into the story belatedly; we can't simply remember either the reality of God in eternity or the reality of creation in its original goodness, or remember how it should have been before our loss of true communion with God, with other persons, and with the rest of creation.

Kallista: As I hear your words, I am remembering all the times I felt restless and felt that things weren't as they ought to be.

Makrina: Yes, it's beyond our powers of understanding because we're already estranged from our true nature, and are in need of return and restoration, true communion and peace.

We find ourselves in a reality marked by the first sin (Wis 2:23–24; Rom 5:12) because of which all have sinned and fallen short of the glory of God (Rom 3:23)

And we lack the resources to restore unaided what has been lost. Certainly, as far as our predicament in this world is concerned, the flesh is of no avail (Jn 6:63); indeed, flesh and spirit are at odds with one another (Gal 5:17), differing in their aims just as life and death differ from one another (Gal 6:8). Sin dwells within us. We wish to do what's right but aren't able. Prisoners to the law of sin, we often can't do even the good we really want to do, but instead we do the very thing we hate (Rom 7:14–8:14). We're lost and scattered (Ez 34:16; Is 49:21), wandering from sea to sea (Am 8:12); and we can't deliver ourselves from this body of death (Rom 7:24). Can we?

Kallista: I can't. And the others I've seen can't either... [*Again she pauses, then raises her eyes to Makrina once more.*]

PART NINE
The Fall

Makrina: Oh, dear one, that's not all we know.

Kallista: I know the goodness of God in my heart.

Makrina [*Nodding*] Yes . . . or else we wouldn't be able to feel how far removed we are from it. We see the consequences of our fall from communion with God in all the tragic divisions that disrupt our lives—divisions between persons and peoples, between the sexes, between classes, between humanity and the rest of nature—and of course between creatures and God.

Scripture too, again and again recounts those divisions and discords: of Adam from Eve (Gen 3:14–19), of Cain from Abel (Gen 4:1–16), of Isaac from Ishmael (Gen 21:8–20), of Jacob from Esau (Gen 25:9–23), of Joseph from his brothers (Gen 37:12–36), of Israel from the Nations (Dt 7:1–4), and on and on—ultimately the division of all of humanity from God (Rom 5:12–21).

Nature, society, and even personal consciousness exist in a state of constant disintegration. Violence triumphs over peace, fear over love, ignorance over wisdom, and death over life. Desire, when it has conceived, gives birth to sin; and sin, when it is full-grown, brings forth death (Jas 1:15) as its just wages (Rom 6:23).

So, then, the existence we know now is one enslaved to death, tending in every moment toward personal isolation and spiritual dissolution. Sin crouches at our doors, eager to control us (Gen 4:7). All are under its power (Rom 3:9–10), and everyone is its slave (Jn 8:34; Acts 8:23). Our minds are no longer filled with the memory of God, much less with our desire for him, but are instead confused by conflicting passions, selfish egotism, fear of our neighbors.

And this is a lethal condition. The mind set on the flesh is hostile to God; it doesn't submit to God's law, and indeed can't submit, and can't please God (Rom 8:7–8). Out of our hearts come evil thoughts, harlotry, theft, murder, adultery, covetousness, wickedness, deceit, licentiousness, envy, slander, pride, foolishness—evil things that arise from within us, defile us (Mk 7:21–23), and make us unable to enter the Kingdom of God (Gal 5:19–20; Rom 9:12; Col 3:6). And this isn't only a human tragedy; it's a tragedy for the whole of creation as well.

Kallista: Yes. But why does our fall affect all of creation, Mother? This I truly don't understand. Why is it that, as the Apostle says, our sin subjected all creation to decay (Rom 8:20)? How could we have such power over God's good creation?

Makrina: On account of that priestly role I spoke of earlier... the vocation that belongs to humanity within the Temple of creation. All creation is spiritually united. All of it lives by the one Spirit of God. God acts through that community of being, so all are responsible for all and all have their roles to play. And our role in the created order was one of particular responsibility.

Remember that human nature is—as it so pleases my brother to say—like a mirror, one that takes on any appearance and bears the impression of any form. In its most proper nature, the human mind is a glass in which the divine beauty is reflected and mediated to the entirety of creation; and creation is itself a kind of mirror of the mirror. And so, when human nature turned toward sin and abandoned the divine image it bore in itself, creation too was subjected to the deformity that humanity had conceived within itself.

Whereas, according to our true nature, we should each be to the other a reflection of the divine beauty, the reality of our fallen condition is one in which hatred, greed, envy, aggression, and every other disfiguring passion of the soul renders that beauty invisible in its every dimension: sacred, cosmic, social, personal. And we've passed this corruption onto the whole community of creatures.

Kallista: Well, once again... [*Kallista holds the cup to Makrina's lips. Then, when the latter has drunk from it, she resumes.*] ... the same question seems to arise, Mother. How can we know this to be the truth when that fallenness is all we've ever experienced?

Makrina: Well, once again, by contrast with what we've been shown. By contrast to the next moment in our story.

Kallista: Which is . . . ?

PART TEN

Salvation in Christ

Makrina: The moment of redemption, of course; the restoration of our nature and of all of creation. The moment of our rescue from sin and death. True, had God abandoned us to our fate, we might have never fully known how far we've fallen from our true estate. But God didn't—wouldn't—abandon creation to this estrangement from all it is created to be. And this part of our story may be the most difficult to capture and narrate in only one way.

Kallista: Why is that?

Makrina: Because there seem to be so many different ways in which one must describe it to make sense of it. Really, there are countless tellings of the tale—though it's one and the same tale in all its tellings. I mean to say, one can always recite the great epic of our Lord's heroic campaign of rescue: the liberation of captives (Lk 4:18; 2 Tim 2:26), the overthrow of evil's reign (Lk 1:51–52; Acts 26:18), the conquest of the unjust rule of malign and vindictive powers (Gal 4:3; I Cor 15:24; Col 2:15–20; Rev 12:10), the plundering of death's household (Rom 6:9; 1 Cor 15:26–28, 54–55; 2 Tim 1:10; Heb 2:14; 2 Pet 2:19; Rev 1:18, 20:13–14), and the restoration of a ruined earth (Rom 8:21–22; Rev 21:1–5).

Again and again, scripture speaks of the incarnate Logos as one who comes "from above" (Jn 8:23) or "from Heaven" (Jn 3:13; Jn 6:38; 1 Cor 15:47) into the darkness of a fallen order (Jn 1:5; Col 1:13) in order to penetrate into the depths of fallen creation's enmity to God (2 Cor 4:6; Col 1:21–22) and to overthrow the reign of death, spiritual and physical, in all things; and to "take captivity captive" (Eph 4:8) and set free the slaves (Gal 5:1); and to subdue the Powers and Principalities (Eph 3:10, 6:12); and to conquer the "Ruler of this world" (Jn 12:31, 14:30, 16:11; Eph 2:2). Our savior came to proclaim glad tidings to the poor and the oppressed (Mt 11:5; Lk 7:22; 2 Cor 9:9), to save and redeem from bondage (Lk 1:68; Rom 3:24; Gal 3:13, 4:5, Eph 1:7; Col 1:14; 1 Tim 1:15; Tit 2:14; Heb 9:15, 10:1–10; 1 Jn 3:4–6); to set all things under the just governance of the God who is above all (Rom 4:9–25; 1 Cor 15:24–28; Eph 4:6; Heb 2:5–8, 10:13). This is one of the chief ways of telling the story.

Kallista: This I know very well. Our God conquers not by violence, but by ceaseless compassion.

Makrina: It's a rescue of an extraordinary kind, isn't it? The story of Christ's victory over sin and death is also the greatest love story.

Sacred love is a self-abandoning love. It is the one true narrative of the "lamb slain before the foundation of the world" (Rev 13:8); and of the self-emptying of the eternal Son (Phil 2:7–8) out of compassion for God's wounded and dying creatures (Jn 3:16); and of a supreme act of divine humility in which the Logos willingly divests himself of his divine glory, assumes the state of a slave (Mt 20:28; Mk 10:35), goes about among his fellow human beings (Lev 26:12; Jn 1:11; 1 Jn 2:6) with no place to lay his head (Mt 8:20); and submits at the last to torture and death in pursuit of the lost (Mt 15:24, 18:11; Lk 19:10; Gal 2:20; Phil 2:7-8).

So we tell the tale of conquest, but tell it as it's never been told before.

Kallista: Christ our God does not conquer with the blood of his enemies, but with his own blood; he conquers by redeeming his enemies with that blood—offering himself as atonement on their behalf.

Makrina: And this is true not only of the divine Son. Neither does the Father delight in any kind of violence. Christ, our Passover, is sacrificed

(1 Cor 5:7), not as some sort of innocent victim slaughtered to appease the wrath of an offended God, but only as a price paid to buy us out of slavery to death. He takes upon himself the consequences of creation's separation from God, that is, in order to overcome that separation by his invincible love (Eph 5:2).

By his offering and sacrifice, Christ has sanctified us, and even perfected those who are sanctified for all time (Heb 10:12–14).

Kallista: This too, I must confess, often confuses me, Mother. If the Father doesn't desire the suffering and death of his Son, and if the violence of that sacrifice is contrary to his nature, how does the sacrifice of the cross reconcile us to the Father?

Makrina: The offering Christ makes on our behalf is simply the offering of perfect devotion to the Father, perfect love, and a willingness to endure whatever evil a fallen order visits upon that love, to the very end. That is the offering made by the Son. The cross isn't violence on the part of the Father, but rather the violence of this fallen world, the work of the Powers and of the darkness of this age, which the divine Son suffers in our stead. It's the place where God has taken up our burden of perfect devotion for us (Mt 11:28); and by taking up the human story for us, by suffering the wrath of the law in our place and yet overcoming it, he's left that wrath no place to come to rest.

Kallista: I have to admit, this aspect of the story shakes me to my core. The cross is the supreme symbol of the final defeat of all hope, but becomes instead God's supreme victory over evil and darkness.

Makrina: Even there, where the darkness of this world displayed itself in its fullest false majesty and might—its power to kill, as we saw with Pilate—the darkness still didn't overcome the light of that love (Jn 1:5).

The cross wasn't a defeat followed by a belated rescue in the form of an empty tomb; it was already the eternal victory of love (Jn 12:31–33, 16:33), confirmed and made triumphant in the raising of the Son in the power of the Spirit. This, too, is one of the necessary ways of telling the tale.

Kallista: Yes. Jesus is the one human being who lives out to the very end a life of perfect devotion to our heavenly Father, the pioneer and perfecter of our faith (Heb 12:2). Our Lord is the truest expression of humanity in its original goodness.

Makrina: And in this way, he begins anew the one universal story—the shared story that was lost in that ancient, unremembered catastrophe that separated creation from its God. He even tells the tale of our death for us so that we might die with him, triumph over death in him, and thereafter live for him.

Kallista: He died on behalf of all, and so in him all have already died; he has been raised on their behalf as well; and hence each person is in Christ a new creation, for the old things have passed away (2 Cor 5:14–17).

Makrina: Well said, Daughter—we've all been made new again (2 Cor 5:17; Rev 21:5). And even now he continues to draw all creatures into that restoration and will continue to do so until that story reaches its consummation in a fully restored creation, wholly united to the God who is all in all (1 Cor 15:27–28; Eph 1:22, 4:6; Col 3:11).

Kallista: The sacrifice of the cross isn't pleasing to the Father?

Makrina: Yes and no. The perfect love and devotion of the Son is pleasing to the Father. The return of all of humanity in the person of Christ is pleasing to the Father. The healing of our nature through its union with the divine nature in the incarnate Son is pleasing to the Father.

But the violence and cruelty of a world that crucifies and murders is, in itself, an abomination to him.

Remember, this entire story of salvation is also the tale of the restoration of the divine image within us.

Ultimately, that community of all people—that community of love—will come again to mirror the splendor of the Logos, as God intends it should from eternity.

Kallista: If all of this has already been accomplished, though, why has the Kingdom not arrived in its final fullness?

Makrina: Dear Sister, the divine beauty and grace that will radiate throughout all the members of the body, causing everyone to rejoice in his or her neighbor, is precisely the grace that animates the gifts of your service to other people, including this dying woman.

What's been accomplished in Christ must yet be worked out in each of us who are joined to him. The restoration of the whole created order will come to pass only insofar as each human will have been purified and made bright. All souls will shine together as one. We are saved, but we must still become, each one of us, what all of us have been made in Christ, just as you yourself are doing as you daily work to perfect your loving in God's Grace.

And then, too, there's that aspect of the story that encompasses not only us.

Kallista: How so, mother? Did the Lord become human not only for the sake of humankind?

Makrina: The entirety of the cosmos exists on account of the abundant love of God, and all of it is intended for glorification in him. The repair of our wounded nature in Christ is also the redemption of the whole of creation, in and through the glorification of the children of God (Jn 1:12; Rom 8:12–30; Eph 5:1; Phil 2:15; 1 Jn 3:1).

In Christ all the fullness of God was pleased to dwell, precisely so that, through Christ, all things might be reconciled to God, whether on earth or in heaven, that peace having been made by the blood of the cross (Col 1:19–20). In exalting Christ into the heavenly places, far above all Rule and Authority and Power and Dominion, and above every name that's named, not only in this age but also in that which is to come, God puts all things under Christ's feet, makes him head over all things, and unites all things in him, whether in heaven or on earth (Eph 1:9–10, 17–22). Becoming all in all (Col 3:11), Christ makes all things new (Rev 21:5).

Kallista: So the restoration of creation is something that occurs through us? I mean, if our fall was the fall of all things, then is our restoration also bound up with the restoration of all?

Makrina: Insofar as the restoration of all things in Christ is also our restoration as the priesthood of creation, yes, one must say just this. Surely, our salvation isn't only a divine gift, but also the renewal of our divine vocation—the renewal of the place of our human efforts in achieving the ends for which all things were made. In Christ, all paths are made straight, every obstacle is removed, and the rough ways are made smooth (Is 40:3–5; Lk 3:3-6).

The Way isn't easy, true. We must love our enemies and pray for our persecutors (Mt 5:43). The Christian is to be quick to hear, slow to speak, slow to anger (Jas 1:19). When reviled, he or she is to bless; when persecuted, to endure; when slandered, to seek reconciliation (1 Cor 4:12–13).

The Christian is to bear all things, believe all things, hope all things, endure all things (1 Cor 13:1–6). The Christian life is shaped by the love of God, love of creation, love of all others, and even love of ourselves in Christ. We're not merely spectators in the story we've been telling; we participate in its unfolding.

And when we find our place within the greater story, and come to see the world as God's freely given gift, we find that through our labors of love in the Spirit we enjoy genuine communion with God and with one another. This you know.

Kallista: Yes, Mother. I know the Way can be hard, but your presence makes it easier for me.

Makrina: Courage, Daughter. . . . And there is yet another way of telling the tale, then. At the last, it's the story of the final realization of God's eternal act of creation.

God becomes human in Christ in order that in him all persons might become "sons of the Most High" (Ps 82:6; Jn 10:33–36).

And this isn't merely a personal destiny (Jn 17:24; 2 Cor 3:17–18), but a cosmic one as well, the glorification of all things in God (Acts 3:21; Rom 8:29; Eph 1:3–4, 9–10; Col 1:19–20).

PART ELEVEN
The Last Things

Kallista: Oh, Mother, you make me burn with hope. [*Makrina coughs.*] At the same time, I can see how tired you are, and I worry that speaking is depleting you.

[*Makrina closes her eyes; Kallista waits and starts to retreat when Makrina opens her eyes again and manages a weak smile.*]

Makrina: I wish to continue. Do stay. I know you so well. . . we're on the precipice of something deeply important. Let's continue.

Kallista: [*Gently touches Makrina's shoulder.*] I'll gladly stay. But I barely know how to shape the next question.

Makrina: Just try.

Kallista: Mother, we are wading deeper into a mystery that I feel, but my imagination can't yet hold. Your loving kindness gives me the strength to try.

How is this end to be realized? I still don't entirely grasp what difference it makes for us now, in this world, to say that the judgment on evil has already occurred but is also yet to occur—or to say that we've already been raised with Christ into the heavenly places, but that Christ is yet to come again.

I don't doubt the truth of those claims. I believe all you tell me, and my heart knows they are true. Still, I'm not able to imagine the consummation of all things.

Makrina: No one can.

Kallista: Yes, but I don't just mean that I can't imagine what the Kingdom will be like. I don't just mean that it's too glorious to conceive. We all grant that. I mean, I don't even understand what faith says about what kind of event we're talking about.

Is the Kingdom something that will come in history, or is it beyond time altogether? [*Kallista falters and places her hand on Makrina's.*]

Makrina: What is it, Daughter?

Kallista: [*After a pause*] We're attended here by death, aren't we? [*She silently wipes her eyes.*] I'm wondering, does the answer come to each of us ... at death? Or to all of us at some single moment in the future, or both?

[*She pauses again, and Makrina reaches out to her, placing her frail hand on the younger woman's. Kallista falls silent before continuing.*]

Will it truly occur upon the earth or only there above, in the heavens? Again, is our normal understanding of the final judgment also like the story of Eden, a tale about something other than what just a literal understanding might be able to convey... something that we can't picture directly at all?

Mother, all these questions swirl around in my mind.

Makrina: [*Studying Kallista's face*] Don't be afraid. There is no fear in faith. You raise good questions but credit me with more wisdom than I possess. We're talking about realities that surpass the powers of our imagination.

Let's recall that all the promises of scripture come to us written in the language of symbols and must be read as spiritual truths that can be expressed to us in this world in no other way. We can experience what these symbols point to but only incompletely. What I think can be said with confidence is that, just as our story has two beginnings, it also has two endings—or perhaps, I should say, two horizons—one of which is in time and one of which is in eternity.

Let's wade into these waters together. In one sense, the story concerns the end of history. This part of our story is told in the imagery of judgment, the great tribunal of God's justice (Mt 3:11–12, 5:21–22, 25:31; Jn 3:19; Rom 2:3; 2 Tim 1:18; 1 Jn 4:17). Whatever the reality toward which those images point might be, it tells of the end of all the enterprises and intrigues of our fallen nature, and of the summing up within the bounds of time of all the violence and falsehood of history (Jn 9:39, 12:31; Rom 2:5; 2 Pet 2:4; Rev 17:1), and of a final reckoning for all of us with who and what we truly are (Mt 12:33–36; Jn 5:19–29; Heb 9:27; Jude 1:6), and of a divine discrimination between the real goodness of creation and the illusory power of evil that has long enslaved it (1 Jn 4:17).

The words of the Apostle tell of a making manifest and a "trial by fire" of all the works of humankind, revealing which deeds merit God's reward and which must instead be destroyed so that those who have done them might be saved "as by fire" (1 Cor 13–15).

It's the story of the present age passing away and yielding to the Age to Come (1 Cor 7:31; 1 Jn 2:8). This, at least, is the way the tale ends within the horizon of time.

Kallista: I can follow you. And the eternal ending?

Makrina: [*With great tenderness*] This ending is the ending of all sorrow. The eternal ending goes beyond our experience of time, and concerns the Kingdom of God "beyond all ages" (1 Tim 1:17; Rev 22:5) in which judgment is overcome by mercy (Tob 3:2; Rom 9:15, 11:31–32; Jas 2:13), where there is neither any sorrow nor any mourning, and where every tear has been wiped from every eye, because the former state of things—the rule of enmity and hate, separation and cruelty, ignorance and fear, suffering and death—has passed away (Is 25:8; Rev 21:4).

In the twinkling of an eye, the mortal puts on the immortal, the perishable puts on the imperishable, death is swallowed up in victory (1 Cor 15:51–55).

God truly becomes all in all (1 Cor 15:27–28; Eph 1:22, 4:5; Col 3:11).

Kallista: All those promises, though, are like words in a dream. When I'm hearing them, I feel I know what I'm hearing. But then, their meanings seem to slip away from me . . . and I feel as if I've lost something I had almost caught hold of. . . .

Makrina: [*Quietly and smiling*] Oh, I know about that. I know exactly what you mean, little sister. But one day, we'll all awaken into that reality and find that this life is the dream.

The final state of all things in God can't be imagined or captured in ordinary language. Our faith insists only that it will be a life of love—a shared reality, a communal and mutual indwelling of creation and God "so that God may be all in all" (1 Cor 15:28).

Scripture symbolizes that mystery as a heavenly feast (Is 25:6–7, 40:5; Lk 13:29), a celebration of the nuptial unity of God and his restored creation (Rev 21:1–2), the establishment of a Kingdom of Peace (Is 11:1–9, 65:25, 66:22).

Scripture also tells us that it's a reality in which all things created are called to share—all spirits and souls, the beasts of land, sea, and air, even the vegetation—all of it raising up a joyous hymnody to the creator and redeemer of all (Is 55:12; Ps 19:1–4; Rev 5:13).

To be joined to God, our story tells us, will be nothing less than a direct vision of the ultimate reality of all things in God, not as in a darkened mirror, but face to face, and we'll become co-heirs of the Kingdom (Rom 8:17; Gal 3:29; Eph 3:6; Tit 3:7; Jas 2:5). We shall, in sum, be like him, for we shall see him as he is (1 Jn 3:2;

Rev 22:4).

Neither death, nor life, nor angels, nor principalities, nor things present, nor things to come, nor powers, nor height, nor depth, nor anything else in all creation, will be able to separate us from the love of God in Christ Jesus our Lord (Rom 8:38–39).

—Which brings me back to my brother's sermon on slavery and slaveholding.

Kallista: Excuse me, dear Mother?

PART TWELVE

Living as Heirs to the Kingdom

Makrina: Yes? Have I lost you?

Kallista: [*With a slight laugh*] Well, the transition was rather abrupt, yes.

Makrina: But you're with me, yes? I long for us to keep going, as much is being offered to us right now. Let's continue as we can.

Kallista: [*Gratefully*] I understand well enough that we should live in the present as though the Kingdom were already dawning among us. I feel it dawning now in our time together.

Makrina: [*Gently touching Kallista's wrist again*] Oh Daughter, can you say why, then? Can you say it your way?

Kallista: Say it my way? [*Again, with a quiet laugh*] I'll try, mother. Our faith tells us that all things at the last will be restored to their original goodness and joined to God.

But it also tells us that this story is one in which we participate now, in the moment, in our lives with one another. It's not just a future we await, but also a reality we already dwell within.

We're to live both in time and eternity—in the body of death and already in Christ's risen body (Col 3:1).

Makrina: [*Quietly, but with surprising vigor*] Just so.

Kallista: Mother, there is more. . . . I've been turning your brother's words in my heart as we talk. I've been thinking about my having been a slave. May I share this in my own words?

Makrina: [*Especially alert, despite her weakness*] Daughter, I have been waiting for this. Please share any way you wish.

Kallista: Mother, I was born a slave, as you know. Slavery seemed normal to me. I knew that there were slaves in every prosperous household. Even though I had heard terrible stories about slaves being treated badly, I was not. I did what I was told and was given what I needed. I felt a part of the household, even if it was a restricted part.

In his Lenten sermon, your brother stated that not even God has the power to enslave human beings. When you asked me for his argument, I reported that he said divine gifts cannot be taken back. He went on to say that God's greatest gift to us is our restored liberty.

Makrina: [*With her eyes peacefully shut*] Yes, Daughter. Continue.

Kallista: Your brother was saying that freeing our freedom from slavery to sin is God's greatest gift to us. And what is that freedom? It's the freedom to love in union with Christ in God's own Spirit. It's the freedom to break out of all that would hold our freedom prisoner to anything less than the Kingdom of God's Love. I can see that now, and I can see that that insight is the key to understanding all the different ways the word "slave" is used in our sacred texts.

These different ways of using the word "slave" dance across the worldly and eternal tellings of our Christian story. In the earthly telling,

Christ freely becomes a slave subject to the powers of darkness, but neither torture nor death could deter his free consent to the Father's will to save us by healing and setting our freedom free. But, as our talking has made clear, God has no afterthoughts. So, in eternity God willed to create us free even though we were unable to handle it. We fell. We sold ourselves into bondage. But from before the beginning of time, God's love for us included his rescue of our freedom.

I realized your brother was speaking to me just as much as he was speaking to anyone else. Honestly, Sister, it frightened me when your mother freed me. Despite our household jubilation, I felt confused, even numb. I knew that I didn't know what being free meant. I couldn't read. I couldn't even dream of having my own opinions or sharing them in my own words. All I had ever focused on was doing what I was told and feeling grateful for any hints of approval I might receive.

Mother, my freedom had to be unfolded and tutored. It needed to be supported, engaged, and affirmed. I needed a model of healed freedom to learn to embrace my own. I can see that Christ is that model. I can see that healing our freedom in Christ is the meaning of our life in the monastery. And you, dear Mother, in your love for me in Christ, midwife my rebirth in freedom.

Makrina: [*After an extended pause, then speaking very softly*] Oh Daughter, details vary, but this is what it means to abide in the Body of Christ, to follow the Way.

Kallista: Yes, I can see that more clearly now. Being in the Body of Christ also includes our being together right now.

Makrina: Yes, right here, right now. . . . But also far beyond our convent. People everywhere are given the manifestation of the Spirit for the common good: wisdom, faith, healing, miracles, prophecy, discernment. All these are infused in us by one and the same Spirit, who apportions to each one of us individually as God wills (1 Cor 12:4–11).

Also, the search for wisdom and understanding—the search for the truth that sets us free—is a way of communion with God. And it's good to seek God's light wherever it's to be found, both in revelation and in all that is true and good in the religion and moral wisdom of humankind. We are called to water those seeds of goodness, which includes attending to the mysterious outpouring of God's graces outside the visible bounds of the church.

As your own life shows, our sharing in the story is perfected in works of love. The Son of man came not to be served, but to serve (Mt 20:28). The teaching and ministry of Jesus were devoted to service of God by way of service to strangers, orphans, and widows (Lev 19:9–10; Dt 24:17–27; Jas 1:27), to the poor, the ill, the imprisoned, the rejected, and the despairing (Lk 14:13; cf. Heb 13:3).

Christ explicitly told all who would follow him that their actions toward the destitute, the displaced, the infirm, and all who endure affliction are also actions directed toward him, and that he reveals himself to us in the faces of those who are in need, and in the presence of all those whom God sets before us on the way (Mt 25:31–46).

Christ's absolute concern for the poor and oppressed isn't merely an ethical practice for forming the characters of his followers, as you know; it's the concrete expression of what God's love is.

All are called to imitate Christ (1 Cor 11:1; Eph 5:1–2), to have the same mind and the same love as Christ himself (Phil 2:1–5), to present their bodies as living sacrifices (Rom 12:1; Phil 4:18), even to lay down their lives for their brothers and sisters (Jn 15:13).

All are commanded to be doers of the word, not hearers only (Mt 7:24–27; Jas 1:22–23).

And we are given this power to become coworkers with God by the gracious outpouring of God's own Spirit in us, and by way of those gifts that only the Spirit can impart.

Kallista: I worry you'll think me a stubborn fool if I ask this.

Makrina: I assure you I won't, Daughter.

Kallista: I still wonder, then, though I understand what you say about slavery and the justice of emancipation: Still, if I may, wouldn't it have been enough for your brother to tell his congregation to live in fraternal love with their slaves? To erase the boundaries between slave and free within their households, to live together—free and bound—as one family, knowing that in Christ these distinctions are as nothing and that in the Age to Come they'll be no more?

As long as charity governs our houses, what need is there to speak as if the bondsman must be set free as well? In every family, there are those who command and those who are commanded; but so long as all is done in love, and all both serve and are served, according to how God has apportioned them a place in the body of Christ, and according to their diversity of gifts, what need was there to speak so sternly about the normal institutions of our... our civic life?

Makrina: [*After a moment's thought*] I don't know if any answer I give can quite satisfy you, Daughter, since you're so stubbornly practical. And I know my brother's words are often much stronger than those that others use. I know, too, that the world he'd like to see come into being under the shelter of the church isn't one that human beings are very willing to make.

The gospel isn't easy. Or convenient, which you know all too well.

Yet, a good many Christians don't yet wish really to obey the gospel. They'd rather hear it spoken of in the basilica, and nod approvingly at what they hear, but then live lives according to the wisdom of the very Powers that Christ overthrew. And one of the ways of living with one foot in the world of the Powers and one foot in the church is to tell ourselves that we can continue on with the practices that make this a fallen world so long as, privately, we conduct ourselves charitably.

I don't know how to convince baptized persons truly to live as if they've died and been raised in Christ already.

All I can say is that, if they have been raised in Christ, they have to live as if this is so even when it is painfully inconvenient.

Kallista: Yes, Mother, I was being stubborn. You mean, I think, that works of love can't be limited just to individual encounters or to domestic harmony and equity. The peace of God's Kingdom is a concrete state of peace and love among persons, and the virtues it demands of us take the form of a true passion for justice, a willingness to denounce the accidental forms of injustice that a fallen world creates and then treats as necessary—like the power of Pilate to crucify.

Makrina: [*Very quietly, but firmly*] Yes, dear. That's it. It means loving resistance to those who rob the poor and the helpless, a protest against the abuse of God's children and creation. As new creations in Christ, all are given a ministry of reconciliation of all things (2 Cor 5:17–19), the things in heaven and the things on earth.

Above all, our highest calling is to love the Lord our God with all our heart, mind, and strength, and to love our neighbors as ourselves. All depends on this (Dt 6:5; Mt 22:37–40).

The life of those who are being conformed to God in Christ is a life shaped by the Spirit of God, who would have us all be truly one.

Works of love performed by those who have been reconciled to God are nothing less than the means by which human beings become "fellow workers" with God in the Spirit (1 Cor 3:9; Phil 4:3; Col 4:11; Philem 1:24; 3 Jn 1:8) and thus "work out their own salvation in fear and trembling" (Phil 2:12).

So it seems clear—at least, to my brother and me, as also it seemed clear to our dear departed mother—that this story we've been telling issues a call to all persons, within and beyond the visible bounds of Christ's body in the present, to a community of love that manifests the love that will, in the end, unite all creatures in the single body of the divine Son.

Kallista: Mother, this sounds very much like the foundation of our daily life here together, within these walls . . . and, of course, beyond them. The Body of Christ is devoted to the sacred dignity of each person made in God's image, no less than to the common good, right?

Makrina: Indeed. All are called, from the east and the west, from the north and the south (Lk 13:29). In the Kingdom, as can't be said too often, there's neither Jew nor Greek, neither slave nor free, nor is there male and female; all are one in Christ (Gal 3:27–28; 5:6). Love binds everything together into a single body, in perfect harmony—indeed, into a body prepared before the foundation of the world (Col 3:14–15; Heb 10:5).

You are knitting your brow again, Sister.

Kallista: I'm thinking beyond the human family of all creatures, of land and sea; the Garden, as it were. Are we not stewards of these also?

Makrina [*Smiling*] Yes. The same call that binds us all together in the totality of humankind, conceived in God's eternity before ever the world was made, is a call also to a renewal of that original stewardship that was humankind's unique privilege and duty in the beginning.

If this world is properly the Temple of the divine presence (1 Cor 3:16, 6:19; 2 Cor 6:16; Wis 9:8), and destined for glorification in the God who is all in all (1 Cor 15:27–28; Eph 1:22, 4:6; Col 3:11), then it's also a field of ceaseless moral action (Mt 26:41; 1 Cor 13:8; Eph 1:6; Col 1:9; 1 Th 5:16–19).

Kallista: We're called to be God's gardeners.

Makrina: Creation is forever crying out in torment at our abuse and neglect of the power we wield over it. As told within time's horizon, the story of this world begins in a garden paradise (Gen 2:8–9) and ends in a paradisal city at whose heart lies a garden where the very leaves of the trees are intended for the healing of all peoples (Rev 22:2).

It was in a garden that Christ offered himself up with perfect love to the will of the Father on behalf of all (Jn 19:11), and it was in the guise of a gardener that the risen Christ first appeared to Mary (Jn 20:15).

We're here to tend God's garden. To forget this dimension of our spiritual calling in the world is to forget the first story that Christianity tells about us and about creation.

[*Makrina falls silent. Kallista holds one of Makrina's hands and listens to her labored breathing.*]

PART THIRTEEN
The Church

Makrina: [*Smiling weakly*] We are approaching the end of the story. [*Kallista falls quiet.*]

Makrina: If there are questions remaining in your heart, this might be the chance to pose them.

Kallista: [*Earnestly*] How can we know, in this fallen world, that we are faithful gardeners and heirs of the Kingdom? All you've said helps me. I believe the Kingdom will come, yes, and I believe the Kingdom has already come among us and within us.

[*Even more earnestly*] Mother, I pray that God will also help my unbelief. I believe, but sometimes I can't feel my belief.

Makrina: One of our best assurances of all these things, in the end, is the church (Mt 16:18). The Kingdom hasn't fully arrived in time, and yet it's already present in the corporate life, the sacraments, and the liturgy of the community of Christ's assembly (1 Cor 10:16)—the body that's the source of unity (Rom 12:5), the pillar and ground of truth (1 Tim 3:15). The incarnate Logos isn't now present in the flesh, and yet is present in his mystical body (1 Cor 12:12; Eph 4:10), here and now.

In this life, the church issues a call to all peoples and persons to praise God (Heb 2:12), to turn again in sacrificial love toward God and neighbor (Col 1:24), to be joined to both in the love of God's Spirit (Rev 22:17). Yet also, in the life of the church, we enjoy a foretaste of that perfect community of love and knowledge that belongs to the Age to Come (Eph 2:7). The church is the pledge of a restored creation and the new reality of the Kingdom of God (2 Pet 3:13; Rev 21:1–2). The church, too, exists both in time and in eternity. It's at once creaturely and divine, at once a people redeemed by Christ (Col 1:18–20) and also the body of Christ (1 Cor 12:27).

In this age, it's in pilgrimage toward the Kingdom (Heb 11:13; 1 Pet 2:11); in the Age to Come, it's revealed as the fullness of the Kingdom in its universal embrace of all creation (Eph 1:22–23), the Temple of the divine presence and divine glory (1 Cor 6:19–20), the dwelling of all creatures in the God who calls them to himself out of nothingness (Jn 15:8), and the dwelling of God in his creatures as the One who is all in all (1 Cor 15:28).

Daughter, is there one more question you wish to ask? [*Laughing softly*] Could it have something to do with your love of practicalities?

Kallista: [*Smiling*] You know me so well. Thank you, one more?

Makrina: Certainly, Daughter.

Kallista: What does that all look like? In this life, I mean. I mean to say, yes, the glory of all things in the eternal body of Christ—the fullness of the communion of the saved—all that I believe.

But if, as you say, our perfection in Christ (Jn 17:19, Rom 6:23) begins in this life, in the body of the church, how does it reveal itself in us as individuals in this world? I know there are great and saintly persons, and signs and wonders attend them, and glory at times emanates from their faces, and...

Makrina: This question pleases me very much. Do you know what the greatest signs and wonders are, my daughter? Those that repeat the pattern of the everlasting Son of God among us. Yes, miracles and special graces have their place in moments of extraordinary revelation, but one sees the life of God in those who are becoming like God chiefly in their humility, their charity, and their love (Phil 2:1–18). This is the persistent revelation of the Holy Spirit working in us.

Kallista: Is the form of the slave assumed by the Son in this world a veiling of his nature, a masquerade?

Makrina: It was rather a revelation of that nature as boundless love. What was more miraculous than the God of all things bending down to wash the feet of his disciples?

What was more miraculous than the pure and immaculate God reaching out to lay his hands upon lepers, and breaking bread with the poor, and proclaiming liberation to those in bondage, and forgiving those who wronged him?

What was more miraculous than his humility before his accusers and persecutors and praying for those who crucified him? Yes, those who, by the Spirit, "participate in the divine nature" (2 Pet 1:4) are revealed at times by wonders and signs and works of power; but recall, even the devils can work wonders.

The truest signs of life in Christ (1 Cor 4:17) are humility, charity, caring for the poor, giving freely to those in need, caring for the weak, speaking for the oppressed (Mt 25:34–40; 1 Jn 3:16–18; Jas 1:27). . . . Love, my child, is the surest sign that one is being conformed to the form of God by him who did not disdain to wear the form of a slave. Love reveals God in us.

[*Lost in pondering, Kallista rises suddenly to her feet, pressing her hands to her heart.*]

Kallista: Oh, I've stayed much longer than I realized. I'll be late for evening prayers if I stay any longer.

PART FOURTEEN
A Final Blessing

Makrina: [*Tenderly*] Go then, Daughter. And thank you for staying with me. Your company is precious to me.

Kallista: Being with you is my joy. [*Starting to turn to go but then pausing, turning back, and whispering*] Your blessing, Mother.

Makrina: Yes, . . . and my love. [*Raising her hand in benediction*] Bless you—in the name of the Father, Son, and Holy Spirit. [*Lowering her hand with obvious weariness*] Remember me in your prayers.

Kallista: I shall, mother. I always do.

[*Refilling the cup beside the pallet, Kallista quietly departs. In only a very little time, Makrina has begun to sleep.*]

When the Fire Came

A RETELLING OF THE CONFUCIAN SACRED STORY

When the Fire Came

PART ONE
The Fire

The girl stood at the end of the driveway, looking across the wooded valley toward the part of the sky that appeared to be burning. As the day had drawn on, the red of the wildfire had spread across the horizon, consuming the forest of old-growth cedars, hemlocks, and pines, and pushing a wind carrying flecks of ash, some of which lay on the ground before her like small black moths. She nudged one with her foot, wondering what to do, where her mother was, before being mesmerized again by the horizon.

In the days prior to the fire, the valley and hillsides had baked dry in the late July sun and a tautness had permeated the village. It seemed people waited helplessly, the girl felt, for an errant spark from a car, a discarded cigarette, for the sun to set alight a dry blade of grass. At the grocery store, she heard an old man say that it only took an ember to burn down a house. Her mother had rolled her eyes and pulled her daughter toward their truck for the drive home.

Yet, the following day it had happened, the fire beginning with a nameless spark in a tindery patch of brown scrubland, then growing and sprawling until it was an enlivened mass as tall as local houses, and taller. The flames climbed cedars, licked up at the sky and huffed out smoke so that midday seemed like midnight. The distant townspeople felt their throats tighten and their eyes sting, but they were told the fire was heading away from them. Their forest of cedars had been a presence for hundreds of years, perhaps a thousand, creating a semblance of stability and security. Now, everything seemed out of balance, tossed into chaos and uncertainty. The girl was worried for the trees, though her mother was not in the mood to hear it.

"I won't be long," her mother had said this morning before getting in the truck. The fire had been doing unpredictable things, veering one way before twisting in another, exactly in the direction of her elderly parents across the valley. She left in a whirl of dust, her hand out the truck's window in what she had hoped was a casual wave. *I won't be long.* The girl was well aware, however, that four hours had passed, during which time it was not only the fire that had begun to do strange things, but her cell phone, also, which no longer worked, and the house, which was in danger, dark and hot inside.

The wind roared in the girl's ears as she turned back toward the house, which struck her as vulnerable and smaller than usual. It was a shingled cottage, which every few years her mother painted white and which had been chosen for its relative isolation. The closest house, stately and grey, was a quarter mile down the dusty track, beyond a stand of trees. The people who lived in it, a middle-aged couple who were professors at the university, were not only tutors for the girl, but a persistent interruption to her mother's attempts at seclusion. Mr. and Mrs. Z. were the source of summer vegetables—ripe tomatoes and zucchinis, bright peas and cabbages—left on the front porch and the neatly piled stack of neatly chopped wood that would suddenly appear in the firewood shack in autumn, and the repairers of winter water leaks that needed to be remedied. Often the girl or her mother would open the door to find that Mrs. Z. had left books she thought they might like. Once the girl found her mother holding a bundle of sunflowers from the Z's garden, glumly murmuring something the girl could not hear.

Now she stood in the little foyer of the cottage, trying to quell the panic that was brewing in her stomach. She longed for her mother and at the same time felt furious at having been left behind. The house underscored the absence not only of her mother, but her father, too, who had died when she was only four. Her mother sometimes reminded her that she was no longer small, though she felt miniscule against the scope of a burning forest. She imagined the sky over the next few hours darkening, and reddening, like blood spreading on a cloth. *You're fourteen!* her mother would sometimes say, which was another way of saying, *Why didn't you take out the garbage as requested*, but also, *You know what to do*. At school the girl had skipped ahead two grades as the teachers struggled to keep her occupied. Her peers, by and large, did not enjoy studying the way she did, but were learning to drive and preparing for college, things she felt unprepared to even contemplate.

All she could think of to do in this moment was to leave the house. After going outside and carefully shutting the door behind her, she began to walk toward the house of Mr. and Mrs. Z., who, she felt, would know what to do. Mrs. Z., a Confucian scholar, often seemed especially wise and was a comforting presence. The girl was immediately engulfed by the wind again; it was stronger and hotter than any she had previously experienced, stealing her breath as she walked. She began to jog a little, her sandals hitting the dirt road, then to run, then faster still, as if the flames themselves were right behind her.

THE SOUND OF THE WIND prevented Mr. Z. from hearing her frantic footfalls or her gasping for air, but he glanced up from where he stood by one of the gardens, dousing it with a hose. "Are you all right?" he asked, as she stopped beside him and drew in breath. She nodded, holding up her hand. "I don't know where Mom is. She—"

"Yes, she's getting your grandparents. She called us before she left." He studied the girl's face, stopping himself from saying that he had expected her mother to have returned by now. "The traffic must be stopped. I'm sure she's on her way back. . . ." He held the hose out to her, expecting her to take it, though she simply stared at him.

"It's not as useless as it seems," he said, continuing to extend the hose. Over the years, the girl had witnessed Mr. and Mrs. Z. tend the gardens as they worked methodically side by side, in all seasons. She had helped them uncover young trees crushed under the weight of snow in winter, and once helped Mr. Z. shovel the roof of their small barn, much to her mother's and Mrs. Z.'s consternation. Her hands hung limply at her sides, however, as if she didn't have the strength to take the hose.

"I'm scared," was all she could say, her words nearly masked by the wind.

"That's why I want you to take the hose."

He retrieved another one from a few feet away, and they both began to drench the shrubs lining the edges of the forest. She went between watching the water arc from the hose, unable to wrest herself from a sense of its futility—how this water was a laughable trickle compared to what was needed, that helicopters would have to drop water and retardant if they weren't doing so already—and watching Mr. Z.'s resolute face, how steady he was. She was just about to ask him how he could be so calm, when they both felt a change in the wind, the shift of it turning. There was a pause, a sudden strange lull of silence enveloping everything, even stopping the birds from flitting about. Mr. Z. stood very still, every part of him alert, as if waiting.

A RUSH OF HOT WIND barreled toward them, and the girl felt the power of it against her back. She looked in every direction but all she could see was the forest, the house, the sky with its roiling clouds in shades of orange and amber. The fire, she felt, was gaining strength as it ate its way forward, even if she couldn't see it. Mr. Z., however, simply continued to water. Water, Wood, Fire, Earth, Metal. And again: Water, Wood, Fire…

IN THE DISTANCE, she heard the sirens from the town below, signaling an evacuation that must be far too late for anyone to heed; it was, she thought, too late to run. Yet coming toward her was Mrs. Z, hurrying across the lawn. She was a small woman, with a delicate face and graying hair, and surprisingly fast.

"Come with me, dear!" she called, and suddenly the girl was being whisked toward the house. Mrs. Z., though extremely kind, had never once before called her dear.

"What about Mr. Z.?" she said, but Mr. Z. was continuing to water. He waved at her, as if it were a normal summer afternoon, and his wave not unlike the one her mother had given her.

"I want you to come in the house with me—" Mrs. Z. said as she hustled her over the dry grass, explaining how the basement would be cooler, how the air would be better there, how good it would be to get out of the wind.

And just like that the girl found herself in the Z.s' house, following instructions to gather blankets from the living room and bottles of water from the kitchen. Mrs. Z. filled a bag with things to eat and handed the girl a large flashlight; she herself carried a battery-powered camping lantern. She corralled their large golden housecat, who, sensing danger, was crouching down at her heels. "Follow me!"

The three descended into the basement along darkened stairs, and the basement itself was darker still. They could hear a sustained note, like the sound of a distant but oncoming train. Mrs. Z. walked to the far side and the girl followed, casting her flashlight beam tentatively around her. There were small windows up toward the ceiling that let in some light, but otherwise the basement was full of shadows, the dark forms of stacked boxes, some unused chairs and camping equipment. The cat hurried across the space and curled up in the shadows.

Mrs. Z.'s lantern was now sitting on a wooden desk and illuminating a tidy and charming area with a bookshelf, an office chair, and a small rug. On the wall there was even a painting. She would have been the first to note that the basement's environment might not be to everyone's preference, but she appreciated its burrow-like qualities, the earthiness of it. It grounded her and helped her think.

PART TWO

Learning about the Way

To learn the Way and from time to time renew your studies,
doesn't that bring great pleasure?"
—Confucius's *Analects*, Chapter 1, Verse 1

"You've not been down here, have you? I work here sometimes," she was saying, as the girl trailed her flashlight beam along a painted concrete wall and ceiling beams, cables and dusty cobwebs, and the large silver ductwork for the home's furnace, which was silent in the corner. Mrs. Z. was mentioning a lecture she was preparing for a summer seminar, *Confucian Virtue and Ethics*. "Soon enough you might be in one of my classes, and we'll compare Confucius to Aristotle and Kant..." Her face brightened but the girl could not see it. "When I'm at home, I work better down here, especially when it's hot. No one bothers me—no husband, no students!" She turned and smiled at the girl, but her smile faded.

"My dear, don't be afraid." She moved toward the girl and took her hand. Their faces appeared distorted in the contrasts of light and dark. She took the flashlight from the girl and set it on a box. The wind's growl reverberated around the house, a rumbling of thunder without end. The girl felt the resonance in every one of her bones, her body vibrating as though she were a gong being struck.

"It's an impressive wind!" said Mrs. Z. "Making a lot of bluster, just to scare us. The fire is farther away than you think. Maybe you didn't know this, but a rainstorm is coming by tonight." The girl watched her doubtfully. "I'm more worried about trees coming down in the wind, but we'll be fine here. The air is better, don't you think?" She turned to the desk and stacked some papers, then peered at her bookshelf in the light of her lantern. "Not something I'd usually say about the basement..."

The girl looked about her again. The sounds in the house above them sounded like furniture being moved, yet Mrs. Z. seemed unconcerned as she removed a book and opened it.

"It won't hold," the girl blurted out.

Mrs. Z. closed the book. "It's more helpful, perhaps, to believe that we will be okay."

"How will we be okay?" The girl's eyes filled with tears. "If this is global warming, there will be this fire and then another. And each one we'll have to survive."

"Yes, just that," said Mrs. Z. "We will survive. This fire and the next one and the one after that."

The girl continued to weep, afraid for herself, and for her mother and for her grandparents across the valley. She tried to picture what they were doing, where they were, but it only made her tears come faster.

Mrs. Z. put her arm around the girl for a moment; then moved a chair from the shadows, covered the seat with a blanket and nudged the girl onto it. She pulled her wheeled office chair away from the desk, sat down in front of the girl and watched her silently before saying, "You have to keep faith in what it is to be human."

The girl admired Mrs. Z. deeply—she had long been fascinated by the professor's demeanor, her books, her mysterious meditation practice, and that, beyond facts, she seemed to know things other people did not—but she had had quite enough. "Human? What does that even mean? Mrs. Z.! Humans are ridiculous. Selfish and cruel. We're not rising up when we should be—"

Mrs. Z. began to laugh quietly, surprising the girl, who felt her hands being enveloped by Mrs. Z's, which were strong and warm.

The older woman closed her eyes. It pained her deeply to see the girl's hopelessness, and she, too, was deeply worried about the girl's mother—and, truth be told, her husband also, who she hoped would join them shortly. "I'm sorry to hear that." She looked about her, as if the answer, what she might say to comfort the girl, lay in her papers on the desk or one of the boxes nearby. Where to begin? This morning she had risen at 5 a.m. in order to meditate in spite of the fire, though it had begun in earnest the day before. She had been determined to be undistracted from her daily practice. As she had sat on her cushion, she watched the lit candle before her, feeling that the single flame had accrued a larger, more dangerous meaning; after a few moments, however, she had grown newly curious about its movements, its lively energy; the same vibrancy filled everything around her. She considered the question: *What is the fire trying to say?*

She again picked up the book she had taken from the shelf. "Would you humor me if I read you something? We can pick up where we left off last week. We were talking about . . ."

The girl watched her. "Learning, actually. And you told me that I'm taking my studies too seriously and need to play more..."

"Did I? Well, that is true, but this is a different occasion." She closed her eyes. "There is a passage from Confucius that you might like":

> Is the virtue of humaneness distant? I yearn for it, and there it is right before me. (*Analects* 7.30)

The girl listened intently. Mrs. Z. often spoke of reality as what lay before them, if they looked with clarity. Mrs. Z. opened her eyes and began to read from the book:

> The Path is clear: Draw wisdom from history and the experiences of others; nurture our moral compass through education, introspection, and rituals; expand our circle of love and care from those closest to us to every being and the natural world; and recognize the sacred and moral tapestry that binds the universe, urging us towards righteousness. We should never forget that our past illuminates our present, while the fate of our future lies firmly in our grasp today through our commitment to care for one another and to serve the transcendent mandate of Heaven.

Mrs. Z. could see that the girl was pondering the words. She had shown a keen interest in history, had borrowed many of the biographies and works of philosophy from the upstairs library, and had an interest as well in environmental activism at her school. They had only just recently begun to speak about Confucius (or, Master Kong), however; the girl had announced two weeks ago that she wanted to study him to prepare for a fall class. Mrs. Z. was delighted, as Confucius was not only her main field of expertise, but also the source of her beliefs. The Sage had been born in 551 BCE in the small state of Lu in what today is northeastern China, during a time of great violence and tumult that heralded the Warring States period. Yet, he met the tensions around him with a response that she felt might seem mundane, certainly less spectacular, to some people: concern for morality, virtue, rituals, love of family, benevolence. She often remarked to her students that compassion and love were not the languages spoken during Confucius's time, and yet he was proficient in them. Because of this he had been a beloved teacher with numerous devoted students, certainly seventy, and as many as three thousand. Ten of these were close disciples, and his dialogues with them formed the foundation for the *Analects*, deemed a sacred text of Confucianism. Sometimes when she was embroiled in her news feed or concern for the natural world, she wondered how he had managed, in the tumult of his own period, to cultivate so thoroughly the promise of such outwardly quiet, yet defiant, ideas.

She slowly turned the page. "Here we are in this dark basement, wind howling—clearly dire straits..." She paused for effect, and the girl watched her warily, though the rise and fall of her chest was less dramatic. Last week they had been discussing some of the Chinese dynasties, in particular the end of the Song Dynasty; this era was long after Confucius's time but heralded the birth of one of his greatest followers.

Since the girl said nothing, the older woman continued, "Spin the globe within your mind so that you land in Southern China. Go back in time one thousand years. Let me paint a picture for you. I want you to imagine that you are witnessing parts of a famous debate between two Confucian scholars of the time and listening to their decorous exchange. At the same time, I invite you to join me, here in our basement, to enjoy some tea and together with me explore and reflect upon some of what they said."

Another roar of wind passed overhead, but the girl closed her eyes.

"This is a beautiful summer evening in the province of Jiangxi. The sun is still up."

There are distant mountain peaks covered in forests, and smaller hillsides blooming with wildflowers. The River Yunan winds its way, reflecting the foliage along its sides so that it's the color of green jade. On the east side of the river, across expanses of long grasses, there is another body of water: Goose Lake, which is still and reflective, a deep sapphire. This lake is unusual because at the water's edge there is a painted pavilion, and the pavilion belongs to the Goose Lake Monastery.

"What is the sky doing?" asked the girl, still with her eyes closed and longing to expel the image in her mind of the sky outside the house.

"Oh, the sky is marvelous, with a wide-open view of blue and only the odd cloud drifting through. The sun is sinking lower, but it's still above those distant peaks." She paused here, so they could both enjoy this image. "This pavilion opens on all sides to the view of the lake and valley. Inside it there is a long wooden table set with teacups and dinner plates in glazed celadon—"

She stopped and looked around, and the girl opened her eyes. "They're around here somewhere," Mrs. Z. murmured, standing up. "Hold on a moment!"

She took her lantern over to a stack of boxes under the staircase and rummaged until she found them. "Ah! These will do nicely!" She then arranged a box between their chairs and set two glazed celadon tea cups on the box with a flourish and laughed at herself. "I'm not done!"

Next she pulled a thermos from her bag. "It doesn't matter how hot it is, you know I always have to have tea..." She laughed softly. "This one is green and jasmine. You'll be happy to know that it's iced, made just before our power went out."

The girl reluctantly smiled as she watched the professor pour the tea into the cups. "That's absurd," she said, but accepted the cup the way Mrs. Z. had taught her to do, using both hands. They bowed to each other, which was the girl's favorite part. She enjoyed the feeling of the glazed surface under her fingers.

PART THREE

A Banquet at Goose Lake

"All right. The pavilion and the table. This is a large table, topped with food and wine, and with chairs for a dozen or so guests. Two musicians sit in a corner, one tuning a flute, the other an *erhu*—which is a stringed instrument akin to a lute. The sun sinks lower and eventually hides behind the mountains. However, the moon is full as it rises"—here, she picked up the flashlight and moved its round beam up the dark wall close to them—"and illuminates everything as the guests begin to arrive. They've come from different directions, as the invitations for this dinner party were sent to the far corners of China."

In the dim light, Mrs. Z. could see that the girl's expression had changed a little, perhaps becoming less fearful and more intrigued. A bead of sweat on her forehead glinted as she sipped her tea. Mrs. Z. continued:

One of the most important guests is making his way along the path to the banquet: He is a great Confucian master of the twelfth century, and his name is Zhu Xi, or, respectfully, Master Zhu. He is a man in his prime, exuding quiet self-confidence, both physically and spiritually. He embodies the Confucian intellectual: he is respectful of everyone he encounters; he is accomplished as a calligrapher, historian, philosopher, poet and statesman; yet he has humility, too.

Mrs. Z. had written extensively about Zhu Xi because of her interest in Confucian thought as it developed through the centuries. By the time of Zhu Xi's birth, Confucianism had long been the central religious, intellectual, and social institution in Chinese society, yet he transformed it for the next millennium. During Zhu Xi's era, Confucianism encountered new challenges from the growing influence of Buddhism and Daoism. Buddhism entered China in the second century CE, flourished during the Sui and Tang dynasties, and eventually became a mainstream religious force. The formalization of Daoist religion, beginning in the late Han dynasty, also became more prominent. Zhu Xi's significant achievement was his ability to synthesize these external influences and diverse interpretations of ancient Confucian texts. He developed a systematic Confucian philosophy that encompassed spiritual practice, metaphysics, ethics, and politics. One of Zhu Xi's notable contributions was compiling and annotating four major works from ancient Confucian classics into the "Collected Commentary on the Four Books." This work became a standard textbook for the civil service examination system in China, Korea, and Vietnam until these regions underwent modernization.

In particular, Mrs. Z. was drawn to Zhu Xi's thinking on *Qi*, or the vital life force. She devoted time daily to cultivating the quality of her own *Qi*, and understood the fire and winds to be aspects of the same energy.

"The last time we saw each other," said Mrs. Z., "you asked me about *Qi* (氣)."

The girl nodded and sat straighter. She had been intrigued by the mystery of this idea, which Mrs. Z. had told her was an all-pervasive cosmic energy. "You told me to think of it as the force that keeps everything going in the universe, including us."

"Good. You can imagine *Qi* as the force that keeps us alive and in fact is life. This is very much a sacred energy. Mencius, an earlier Confucian admired by Zhu Xi, who will also join this banquet later, teaches that we can harness and cultivate this cosmic *Qi* within our bodies. For instance, deep slumber or a certain kind of breathing practice can help us restore and replenish *Qi*. He felt that this is helpful not only in furthering our physical well-being, but also in making it easier to be a virtuous person, such as being kind and empathetic toward other people as well as animals.

"There is a seamless organic union between *Qi* and moral action, which I know you're interested in through your work at school. It is easier, isn't it, to know what to do when we are balanced and clear-thinking. *Qi* is part of everything, connects everything.

"But we were talking about the entrance of Zhu Xi to the banquet, and he is important with regard to *Qi*. He envisions the world as composed of both *Qi* and something called *Li*. *Qi* gives concrete form to everything in the world. It can be clear or cloudy. *Li* is the pattern underlying everything, and is pure and clear. For Zhu Xi, humans possess relatively clear *Qi*, and because of this, much of our principle or pattern, *Li*, shines through, like a pearl at the bottom of clear, unmuddied waters. Animals and physical objects have *Qi* too, but theirs tends to be cloudy and opaque, preventing the pure principle from shining through. So, according to Zhu Xi, the task of each individual is to clarify their *Qi*. Then the morally pure principles can shine through in the way one lives. He points to sacred texts and rituals as our guides in doing this."

Mrs. Z. had told the girl previously that the sages from thousands and thousands of years ago, such as the ancient Yao and Shun, or the Duke of Zhou, or Confucius or Mencius, possessed the most powerful and clearest *Qi*, so the bright patterns of their actions and thoughts were clearly visible. "Here is the really fascinating part: books have *Qi* too, and sacred texts such as the Four Books possess the strongest and clearest *Qi*.

"The idea of 'virtue politics,' though, starts with Confucius." Last week, they had discussed how Confucius had served for a time as a political advisor to several rulers of small city-state kingdoms in his region. "Virtue politics" meant governing through virtue and ritual propriety, which, in Zhu Xi's view, would be a particular kind of *Qi* that energizes the ethical nature of the world. According to Confucius's teaching, people with power, such as rulers, must follow the "Mandate of Heaven," or the "*Dao* of Heaven," *Ming*, which is to serve the people and to maintain the moral order of the world. "But, you know," said Mrs. Z., "he was largely unsuccessful, in spite of his steadfast perseverance. The rulers for the most part didn't take his advice."

"That must have been extremely disappointing," said the girl. She thought of how she and some of the other students at school had formed a group to share their concerns about the environment. Not many of the adults seemed especially willing to hear their voices.

"Indeed. But that didn't prevent Confucius from eventually wielding extraordinary influence. He came to be beloved by many. After he died, his home in the village of Qufu became a temple, so people could venerate his spirit." Mrs. Z. had visited the temple on numerous occasions. Over the past two millennia, it had been greatly expanded, with many buildings added by emperors from different imperial dynasties. By the end of the imperial era in 1911, the temple had become the second-largest classical architectural complex in China, just after the Forbidden City in the capital of Beijing. "It is known as the most sacred place in the Confucian tradition."

They could hear the sound of the wind rushing through the garden and the woods, and battering the sides of the house. The girl tried to ignore it, to stay with her train of thought. "There must be sacred places all around this area, but the fire could still burn its way through them all."

"Ignoring for a moment your assertion that all is lost..." Mrs. Z. smiled slightly. "When we talk about places being sacred we are talking about things that give life ultimate meaning and power. There is meaning in the fire, too." Mrs. Z. saw a flicker of anger in the girl's expression.

The girl raised the cup to her lips but didn't drink. Quietly, she said, "What is sacred then? And what is meaning?"

Mrs. Z. nodded and sighed. "Sometimes when you're despondent, you seem older than you are. Even you and I, here in this cellar, having this discussion, we are giving meaning to it." The question from her morning's meditation, *What is the fire trying to say?* arose again in her mind. She did not view the fire as something merely to fear, though she did fear it; she was also impressed by its energy, its expressiveness as it coursed over the landscape. Even as it was destructive and singular, it was connected to everything. It was part of the language being uttered by the world around them. Fire was one of the Five Elements making up the cosmos and mirroring the cosmos, also within one's one body:

Water, Wood, Fire, Earth, Metal. When in balance, the world, or the body, was at peace and in harmony. When out of balance—too much Fire, not enough Water—there was danger.

"Confucians believe in sacred connections and presences in the universe. This could involve the recognition of heaven, earth, our human world, and even the gods and spirits that were worshiped in ancient rituals before Confucius's time and after. It's interesting, but Confucians don't like to discuss the supernatural too explicitly.

"The *Analects* say of Confucius: 'The Master did not discuss strange occurrences, magical feats of strength, mysterious rebellion, and the existence of gods.' Confucians see the entire universe as sacred. And, you know, the sacred is hard to grasp or even discuss, isn't it? They engage with this sacred universe in a way that may seem too soft to be so potent, but is perhaps the most powerful practice of all: becoming better human beings in their everyday lives. For instance, in the face of challenging conditions like wildfires, how humans respond to them can reflect the sacredness of such natural occurrences."

PART FOUR

The Goose Lake Debate with Master Zhu and Master Lu

Above the dark cellar the girl could hear the strange moaning of the world above, and what she believed was the palpable splintering of wood. She clasped the tea cup in her fingers, shut her eyes and sipped.

When she opened her eyes, she said, "My mother was trying to be a better person. By going to get her parents." She was surprised by her own words.

"Yes. She was. Your mother didn't intend to leave you alone. We can only speculate about the traffic in the valley. I imagine she is frantic that she can't reach you. But I think she knows that we're here to help you."

The girl nodded. Mrs. Z. continued, "She would be proud of you. Do you want to get back to the banquet story? It's going to be the scene of a debate, and the question might interest you. . . . It's a conundrum, and it relates to our discussion last week about the personal versus the larger world: Should we prioritize listening to our individual moral compass, or should we be guided by the vast ocean of objective knowledge and seek wisdom through learning—in other words, the bigger picture? This is a question that has been on the mind of many Confucians, or *Ru*, of Master Zhu's generation."

"*Ru* . . . ," said the girl. "You said that those are followers of Confucius. Where does that come from?"

Mrs. Z. thought for a moment. "It literally means 'scholars,' 'the classicists' or 'ritualists.' In Confucius's time, this term referred to the specific profession of people who possessed knowledge of ancient classics and were able to conduct ancient rituals." She reflected on how Confucius had transformed his disappointment in the aristocrats' unwillingness to follow the *Dao* of Heaven by placing his energy into teaching. And, admirably, he taught anyone, or admittedly, any man. He is known to have said he would teach anybody, not just nobility who brought him a piece of meat, really meaning anybody, or any man, at all who had a passionate desire to learn. Although those students had not necessarily been born into nobility, they became *junzi*, which originally referred to 'son of kings,' now meaning 'perfected persons' or 'exemplary persons,' due to their cultivation of virtues; they acted with true nobility, dedicating their lives to serving society and serving Heaven. Confucius was dedicated to transmitting ancient culture and values to his students through teaching the classics and rituals. It was after his death that his critics began referring to his followers as '*Ru*,' a designation that these followers also embraced. "Much as in our time, older values can seem old fashioned. But followers of Confucius reclaimed the name and transformed it. Over two thousand years of history, two main meanings emerged. First, being a *Ru* means one's behavior is 'softened' (柔) by the performance of rituals, and second, due to the non-violent nature of ritual performance, a *Ru* can 'moisten' or 'nourish' (濡) people's lives to create a thriving environment for all living beings. So, philosophically, *Ru* can also be broadly translated as a 'civilized' or 'cultivated' human being.

"The word 'Confucianism' was originally coined by Christian missionaries in the nineteenth century. This term suggests that a religious tradition must revolve around a single figure, similar to how monotheistic religions like Christianity focus on one central authority. Since 'Confucianism' has become a prevalent term, many people who follow the Confucian tradition in different countries—across East Asia, Southeast Asia, and beyond—have chosen to center their religious practices around Confucius as a central figure. One may use either 'Confucian' or '*Ru*' to refer to followers of this twenty-five-hundred-year-old tradition, which, like any group and especially one that has endured for thousands of years, is diverse and complex.

"So," Mrs. Z. continued, "the question at the heart of the debate is: How does one become civilized or cultivated? Does it emerge from looking within or from looking without?"

The girl spoke quietly, "There are so many things to learn in the world, other than just trusting yourself. For now, I would love to know how to stop the fires, and I hope someone can provide the knowledge."

"Yes. Stop the fires. Or, maybe rebalance the Five Elements and tame the Fires? And what about the ethical issues surrounding the fires? For instance, how do we help one another during such disasters? Is objective knowledge enough to aid others and to stop the fires?

"At the banquet, Master Zhu has a clear stance. He champions 'the investigation of things.' He contends that true cultivation emerges when one delves deeply into the classical Confucian scriptures, looking at the deeds of historic luminaries and observing the world. Through these actions, one can uncover the guiding principle (*li* 理) that underpins all existence. Aligning one's intentions and actions with these principles, according to him, paves the path to true cultivation. For Master Zhu, the journey of self-improvement commences from the outside in."

Master Zhu takes a seat at the round wooden table. He is the picture of serenity as he waits patiently for the others to arrive: his head is held high, yet his back is relaxed; his posture is perfectly still as the light breeze rustles the wide sleeves of his silk robe. And he doesn't have to wait long.

In walks Lu Xiangshan, or Master Lu, a tad younger and dressed in simple robes. He greets Master Zhu with a courteous bow and inquires after the well-being of the senior scholar's family before settling in the seat across from him. But beneath the elegant courtesies brews intellectual tension. Unlike Master Zhu, Master Lu cares primarily about inner cultivation. He firmly believes that every human being possesses an innate moral compass capable of guiding one through every one of life's twists and turns. According to Master Lu, to become a better person means starting from the inside and then allowing that to transform one's outward actions.

The girl asked, "Are there just the two guests?"

"There are more! Now, I have to tell you that this is an imaginary banquet. In reality both Master Zhu and Master Lu were at the dinner that came to be known as 'The Goose Lake Debate.' But in our story, all the great Confucians join the banquet, some coming from a much earlier time—fifteen hundred years before Master Zhu—and some as many as one thousand years after Master Zhu."

"A multiverse! I like this. A banquet with guests who lived across twenty-five hundred years. This would be like having Socrates and Martin Luther King at the same dinner—I wonder what they would say to each other?"

"Exactly! Socrates and Confucius were near-contemporaries—Confucius died in 479 BCE, and Socrates was born in 469 BCE."

"So, who are the other guests?"

PART FIVE
Confucius Arrives

To have friends come from afar, doesn't that bring great joy?
—*Analects* 1.1

"They are almost here!" said Mrs. Z. "I will introduce them to you one by one."

Master Zhu and Master Lu greet each another like old friends, entirely comfortable in each other's company, and are able to readily speak their minds. But first they must wait for the most honorable guest to arrive. They sip tea in silence, seemingly lost in their own thoughts except for their attention to the stone path that leads up to the plateau where they are sitting. Finally, they see someone approaching through the line of evergreen pines and spruces: a tall man is arriving.

He is a bearded man dressed in a simple flowy white robe, with his collars delicately embroidered in silver threads with motifs of clouds. His steps are firm yet light, his countenance calm and kindly. Walking behind him are his ten disciples. They follow in a single line, walking steadily to the rhythm of his steps. When they reach the table, they greet Master Zhu and Master Lu warmly.

This man is Confucius (also known as Master Kong), who has spent the day visiting the sights of the famed Luliang waterfalls nearby. After exchanging greetings, Master Kong starts telling a story in a strong and resonant voice:

> *I must describe for you my visit to the waterfalls today. As you know, the waterfalls tumble down a long way along rough rocks to the river below where the water swiftly races and boils along for twelve miles after that. I was standing by the river admiring it when suddenly I saw a man diving into these tumultuous waters. I was greatly alarmed. This man seemed to be drowning, his arms waving above the surface as his head was submerged. My disciples and I wondered if the poor man needed to be saved from the river.*
>
> *However, this man quickly swam to the riverbanks and pulled himself up. He seemed energized by the incident as he strode toward me. Puzzled, I asked him how he had survived such turbulent water. The man looked me in the eye with a joyful smile. "I have no idea," he replied. "I grew up with Nature, and I let things come to natural completion with fate (ming). I go under with the swirls and come out with the eddies, following the direction of the water wherever it goes. I do not think about myself. I give myself over to fate. That is how I can stay afloat.*

Confucius finishes his story and laughs, shaking his head. "He was clearly a follower of Laozi! Even though Laozi and I both talk about the Way, or Dao, we have such different understandings of it."

Just as others are about to respond, another guest arrives: Mencius, or Master Meng, also a central figure in the Confucian tradition. He is younger than Confucius, and his robe is more extravagant, made of luxurious crimson brocade with intricate embroidery.

Mencius greets Confucius with a deep bow: "My Teacher," he calls out. "I have been fortunate to have studied with your grandson, Master Zisi. But it is the greatest fortune for me to meet you in this ethereal place, overlooking the timeless mountains and rivers." All the others stand in reverent silence as they listen to this greeting, for they know they are observing something extraordinary: the meeting of the two great sages of their tradition, who represent the eternal values of everything they believe in.

The girl was becoming aware of the prominent standing of both men. "Are Confucius and Mencius considered gods?"

Mrs. Z. thought about this. "They are often treated as gods and venerated with incense and other offerings in temple settings. This is especially true of Confucius, whose house was turned into a temple after his death. The temple for Confucius in his birthplace Qufu is China's second largest classical architectural compound, after the Forbidden City. Today there are still more than two hundred Confucius temples in use in Asia, mostly in China, as well as in places such as South Korea and Indonesia. The scholarly tradition of Confucianism venerated Confucius and Mencius as sages who transmitted ancient wisdom and taught humans to connect with the Way of Heaven. Given Confucianism's pervasive influence in society, there is no shortage of spiritual tales about them. According to a book written in the seventeenth century, when Mencius's mother was about to give birth, she dreamed of a god greeting her from one of the Five Sacred Mountains in China, Tai Mountain, while treading clouds over mountain peaks. She looked at this vision for a long time, and suddenly one of the clouds descended toward her. At the same time, her neighbors saw clouds of five bright colors landing on the house of the Meng family, enveloping it with their splendor. This coincided with the birth of Mencius."

"How about Confucius?"

"There is a mythical creature..." She enjoyed this particular legend about his birth, though the story was not accepted as part of the canon. "This creature is called a Qilin, and was said to have appeared to the pregnant mother of Confucius the day before he was born. Qilin were often described as colorful, possessing a dragon or lion's head, with a single horn on the forehead, scales...and the body of a deer. Despite being able to blow fire, they were a symbol of benevolence and gentleness, and the appearance of a Qilin was thought to be fortunate." She loved especially that the creature's ferocious nature was dominated by its mild side.

The girl was silent for a moment. Then she said, "I wonder about the deer and other animals outside. They must be terrified."

Mrs. Z. acknowledged that they must indeed be. "There is another story about the birth of Confucius. His mother and father prayed to the god of Mount Ni for a son, and their prayers were answered. A temple was erected on Mount Ni and dedicated to the sage, whose birth was seen by many as a miraculous gift from Heaven. Mount Ni has been considered a sacred site for Confucians ever since.

"Now, back to the banquet.... When Mencius meets Confucius, their mutual respect is evident. They share a common background, and something you will relate to," said Mrs. Z. On a few occasions she and the girl had spoken about the girl's father. The girl watched her and raised her eyebrows with interest. "Both Confucius and Mencius lost their fathers at a young age, and they both were raised single-handedly by their mothers."

The girl was silent a moment. "Yes. I know what that's like."

Mrs. Z. nodded. "At this fundamental level, you are connected to them."

Although he lived a hundred years or so after Confucius, from 372 to 289 BCE, Mencius experienced the same turbulent era later known as the "Spring and Autumn" and "Warring States," which spanned more than half a millennium. It was marked by intense political turmoil and significant cultural growth, leading up to the establishment of the first Chinese imperial dynasty, the Qin, in 221 BCE. Mencius is often referred to as the Second Sage because he dedicated himself to spreading the teaching of Confucius—the First Sage—during this crisis-ridden time.

When Confucius speaks at the banquet, he is diplomatic and concise, preferring to teach through personal example rather than rigid rules. He is as attentive a listener as he is a powerful speaker. Mencius, on the other hand, takes his time in expressing his thoughts. His discussions are lengthy and persuasive, and his teachings in the book The Mencius *remain sacred and central to Confucians.*

"Now I have to tell you about the Mother of Mencius!" Mrs. Z. said. "Most of Confucius's and Mencius's ideas have roots in the teachings of ancient sages, but they have roots also in their upbringing. When Mencius was a child, his mother influenced him greatly by emphasizing the conditions under which one could live a Confucian life."

PART SIX

The Story of the Mother of Mencius

"Was the mother of Mencius a Confucian too?" The girl asked.

"She was a widow, and it was very important to her to give her son the necessary ethical education so that he would grow up to be a virtuous person. It can be said that she saw the most important role in her life as that of being a teacher in her family." Mrs. Z. paused. "I would certainly say that she was a Confucian.

"There is a famous story of Mother Meng moving their residence three times in order to find the right social environment for the moral education of her son. At first, Mother Meng and Mencius lived near a cemetery. A young boy at the time, Mencius would play with other boys among grave mounds, imitating funeral rites performed in the cemetery. The boys would even compete with each other to do so, without any proper respect for these rituals. After she saw this, Mother Meng said to herself: "This is not a place where I wish to live and raise my child." So she moved their home away from the cemetery.

"Now their new home was near a marketplace. Young Mencius started to play with other kids by imitating how merchants busily touted and sold their goods, with no interest in anything else. Seeing this, Mother Meng said to herself again: 'This is not a place where I wish to live and raise my child.'

"For the third time, she moved their home, this time to a place near a school. Once they moved, little Mencius started to imitate how students in the school greeted one another and yielded to one another in social interactions. He also started emulating various rituals, including ways of arranging ceremonial utensils. This is something Confucius had done too, playing with rituals and learning about them in an innocent yet important way. Gradually, Mencius's behaviors and manners became gentle and cultured, and he talked and moved with clear intentions and reverence. This made Mother Meng very happy. Finally, she said to herself: 'This is really a place where my child can live.'"

"My mother did something similar for me," the girl said. "We moved here when I was a baby because my mother wanted us to be in a more natural place. So she persuaded my father to move here."

"I think your mother has a lot in common with Mencius's mother. They both care about giving their child an upbringing that will help that child become a good person. Or in Confucian terms, a virtuous person."

The girl seemed dubious. "What does that mean, exactly? I know what virtue is, and we have discussed Confucius's political ambition to urge rulers to be virtuous, but what is it really?"

"Being virtuous, according to Confucius, is like being the 'North Star standing in its place, with all the other stars paying court to it.' A person with virtue possesses moral power, and she has a gravitational pull over the world by the sheer example of her virtuous conduct. The greater one's virtue, the stronger one's moral charisma.

"Virtue (德), pronounced *de* in the Confucian tradition, means all the stable and desirable character traits—humaneness, righteousness, loyalty, filial piety, respect for ritual propriety, to name a few—that make a person kind and exemplary in conduct."

"How do you become virtuous then?"

"Confucians believe that you can cultivate virtue in many ways. You can rely on your natural, moral instincts and strengthen them through thoughtful reflection in everyday life. Or you can study the teachings of virtuous people and try to apply them to your own life. You can also choose to put yourself in a virtuous community and learn from those around you. Confucians believe that influencing someone through interpersonal relationships in person is much more significant than instructing with words."

"Mencius's mother probably used all these methods," the girl said, thinking about her own mother.

"There are countless temptations in everyday life, and it requires immense dedication to nurture learning and the pursuit of virtue. It couldn't have been easy for a mother on her own to do this for her child. You are so lucky to have such a good mother," said Mrs. Z.

The girl began to consider all the challenges her mother must have faced while raising her alone, after her father's death, and how they both had to overcome so many difficulties, sometimes alone, sometimes together. They didn't always succeed, but she knew how hard her mother tried. Her eyes began to fill with tears, out of compassion, gratitude, and love.

PART SEVEN

Meditating on Qi and Ritual under Fire

After a time, they heard a rapping at one of the basement windows and both looked toward the sound. Mrs. Z. stood up first and went to stand at the window, and the girl quickly followed. A shadow filled one side of the glass before they saw Mr. Z.'s face as he leaned down. He smiled at them. The window wasn't the kind that opened, so he shouted to them, though he was hard to hear.

Mrs. Z. smiled and said loudly, "We're holding up too."

"Good!" Then a string of half-muffled words, but they understood that he had gone to the girl's house and left a note on the cottage door.

"Oh, well done!" Mrs. Z. shouted. The girl thanked him, feeling another rush of relief pass through her.

Mr. Z. gave a thumbs-up and then turned to walk back across the yard. The girl could not help but smile. When she returned to the chair where she had been sitting, however, a despondency settled in again; the dark with its pools of light seemed desolate, the heat overbearing. Glimpsing Mr. Z. in the yard made her want to run out there and help him; or run down the road, yelling for her mother. She even wondered about her father, where he was in all this, if he could see her.

"Well," said Mrs. Z., looking at the girl. "I can see that you are upset. I've asked a lot of you. This situation is asking a lot of you."

She took the girl's sweaty hands into her own cool and steady palms, and had an idea. They had practiced meditation together before, though the circumstances had been wholly different, and unfettered by worry: a sunny Sunday afternoon in the Z.s' living room, a breeze coming through the windows and the old cat snoring loudly, making the girl laugh; another time, to celebrate the Lunar New Year; and once on a cool spring evening as Mr. Z. filled the stone firepit with hickory and apple wood and set it alight while they sat nearby on their cushions and breathed together.

The fire then had had a different character, with a sense of containment, or balance; the night sounds had been textured with the comforting snap of trapped steam bursting from the wood. The girl had opened her eyes to see Mr. Z. prod the logs and create a wave of sparks. Her heart had filled to see this, and she understood what Mrs. Z. had meant about the potent energy that was everywhere around her, enlivening each moment.

That particular moment, however, was far from them now. "Do you feel like we could do a breathing meditation together?" asked Mrs. Z. "It might be helpful."

The girl half-smiled, gesturing toward the cat who was curled beneath a chair. "Maybe he'll even start snoring."

"Would you like to guide us to start?" asked Mrs. Z.

The girl appeared hesitant; she closed her eyes and focused on her breath. "You always start by telling me to settle into my body. To sit with my back straight but relaxed, so that my shoulders can soften. And you say if I'm sitting on a chair to plant my feet firmly on the ground."

Mrs. Z. said, "Exactly right. We can pay attention to our breathing, and note that it has three parts: the inhale, the exhale, and a brief pause between the two. After we finish each breathing cycle, we'll continue to the next." The girl nodded in understanding, but her face was still tense.

Mrs. Z. continued: "Our breath is the most essential thing we have, but it is ungraspable. What happens if we try to hold on to it?"

"We can't. We would eventually have to let it go and breath in again or suffocate," said the girl.

"Yes, our breath has to come in and flow out, over and over. It does this whether or not we pay attention to it. But when we become conscious of this movement, something happens. Do you notice that it is difficult to focus on the breath and have a thought at the same time? If you place your attention on your breathing, your mind has a chance to quiet down, even briefly. If your mind is quiet for just one second, it is one second of freedom. When we pay attention to our breathing, this is one way of accessing or enhancing *Qi*, connecting us to the cosmic energy."

The girl nodded. They both sat breathing as the wind rushed outside. "Can we do the counting meditation?"

"Of course. Counting has a certain magic, doesn't it? Let's count each part of the breath to the number nine…

One: Inhale slowly, deeply.

Two: Exhale, letting air out of your lungs and relax into the breathing.

Three: Take a small pause, embracing the calm.

Four: Inhale again, filling your lungs with air, which is nourishing every cell in your body.

Five: Exhale, expelling the air that is not needed in your body.

Six: Take a pause, feeling the connection between you and everything around you.

Seven: Inhale, letting your body further relax and energize.
Eight: Exhale, releasing all tension.
And nine: Take a pause before the next breath, then take it and continue to focus on the air flowing in and out."

As they counted, the girl's breathing gradually slowed, becoming deeper and more controlled.

"How do you feel?" Mrs. Z. inquired after a few minutes.

"Much calmer. I can feel the connection between my body and the air. It's peaceful. I can feel it in my heart," the girl said. "Is this like yoga?"

"Yes, it is like our yoga, our prayer," answered Mrs. Z. "Different religions often have different forms of meditation. This is from our Confucian ritual tradition."

"Why is it called a ritual?"

"There is a passage in the *Analects* where Confucius asks people to 'enable yourself to return to rituals,' which he sees as the backbone of everyday life. We have three types of rituals: individual spiritual ones, interpersonal social ones, and official religious ones. Individual spiritual rituals are the daily practices through which we recenter ourselves, like engaging in the breathing meditation. Social rituals are all about showing respect to people, such as being polite to our elders or showing appreciation to our teachers. Religious rituals include 'three sacrificial rituals': the ceremonies honoring the spirit of Confucius; rituals of reverence to Heaven; and ancestral rituals that engage with the spirits of deceased family members. These rituals are like the glue that holds Confucian ethics and values together in our everyday lives."

The girl remembered something Mrs. Z. had said previously. "What about the rituals for family members who have died?" she asked quietly.

Mrs. Z. got up from her chair and retrieved a small box from the bookshelf. "Let me show you something." She removed some photographs from the box and handed one of them to the girl. The photo showed a large marble gravestone on a grassy slope, with inscriptions in Classical Chinese and offerings in front of the grave: fresh flowers, lighted candles, burning incense, dishes of fresh fruit and pastries, also plates of cooked fish and vegetables, as well as two cups of tea and two glasses of wine.

"My sister and I made these offerings to our deceased parents the last time I visited China," she said. "We brought all the food, drinks, flowers, incense, and candles to the grave, as a way to convey our love and care for them in the Underworld. We said prayers to them, and for them, sending loving thoughts and seeking blessings for the future of the family. No one fully understands what the Underworld is, but it doesn't prevent us from practicing these ancient rituals for deceased family members and the generations that went before them. In this way we can express our values and ethics; we find a connection between the present and the past, and also the present and the future."

"My memories of my father are mostly just fragments," the girl said, "but I do have one clear memory of him, in our garden. He was showing me the width of a cedar tree trunk and we both put our arms around the base of the tree until our hands met. I remember this. I can almost feel his hands. We don't talk about him very much at home. On the day of his death every year we just walk around the house, not knowing what to say or do."

The wind howled. She was suddenly aware of the basement elements again, the strangeness of the darkened corners and forms that she couldn't make out, but it no longer seemed so unfamiliar; the space seemed to breathe with her. "Maybe I'll tell Mom about the rituals you do. I think it would help us to do something like that. I might feel closer to him."

Mrs. Z. poured more tea in their cups. "I think that you might be right."

PART EIGHT

Moments of Awakening

"Our next guest is about to make an entrance," said Mrs. Z.

A diminutive man appears at the pavilion on the mountaintop, the esteemed Confucian Xunzi who lived between 310 and 220 BCE, about sixty years after Mencius. He settles in a chair beside Mencius and the two men nod to each other like old but somewhat distant friends. Xunzi speaks little and seems quite contemplative. Eventually Mencius and Xunzi get into a rather heated discussion about human nature.

If Mencius's worldview were to be contained in a phrase, said Mrs. A., it would be—using his own words—"human nature is good." Mencius believed that as newborns, people already have the seeds of goodness. They are like tiny sprouts of plants. With daily attention to innate goodness, these tender sprouts can grow into towering trees and forests of virtue.

For Mencius, the metaphor of agriculture was central. The "Four Sprouts" or four beginnings of virtue—(1) Benevolence or Love, (2) Righteousness, (3) Ritual Propriety, and (4) Wisdom—must be nurtured carefully in order to grow, for they can be easily stunted or even destroyed without daily care.

The most famous story in *The Mencius* concerns a child and a well, and it is about the innate goodness of human nature:

> The reason why I say that all humans have hearts that are not unfeeling toward others is this. Suppose someone suddenly saw a child about to fall into a well: anyone in such a situation would have a feeling of alarm and commiseration—not because one sought to impress the child's parents, not because one wanted fame among one's neighbors and friends, and not because one would dislike the sound of the child's cries.

"Hm. I'm not sure I think that human nature is inherently good," said the girl. "Present company excepted." She laughed.

"Thank you for that. Well, you'll be happy to know you're actually in good company, because Xunzi agrees with you."

Unlike Mencius, Xunzi believed that human beings have innate tendencies that, in their chaotic and disorganized forms, as a whole do not help us lead a good life. As a result, he believed that ethical norms were invented to help us trim, lengthen, reshape, organize, and prioritize our natural inclinations, which are neither inherently good nor bad.

In his view, cultivation of the self can come only through education and ritual practice. In his writings, Xunzi often employed the images of a carpenter or an artisan who works with materials from nature, such as wood, jade, or stone. The reshaping of raw materials through the tools of ritual and learning is Xunzi's metaphor for self-cultivation.

Mencius now begins to tell the guests a story about an ox. The others sit listening in silence, enraptured by his words. Mencius once advised a monarch, King Xuan of the state of Qi, on how to become a good ruler.

> *The king asked: "How do you unite the warring nations using virtue?" Mencius responded: "If you have loving care for your subjects, no one can stop you from conquering the world." The king said: "How do you know that I am capable of such loving care?"*
>
> *Mencius replied: "I was told that, once, in your palace, you saw an ox being taken to a sacrificial ritual. You said: 'Please release the ox, because it is trembling with fear. I cannot bear to see its suffering.' Is this a true story, my Lord?"*
>
> *The king acknowledged that it was, and Mencius said: "You have a heart that is unable to bear the suffering of an animal. And this is where the power of virtue resides. You will be able to govern with virtue, for your emotion of empathy is the root of your moral strength."*

The girl sat up and, her voice filled with emotion, said: "If anyone saw what happened to our valley now during the wildfire, do you think they would care at all? With humans and animals dying? Do you think they would feel empathy? People today seem pretty selfish, and so isolated in their own little worlds that no one really cares about the suffering of others."

Mrs. Z. thought for a moment. "I know what you mean. There is a Confucian concept called 'anthropocosmism,' which means that, although we think that humans are at the center of the world, we are always in deep relation with all of the cosmos, from animals to rivers and mountains. Confucians care deeply about rectifying our mistakes, such as the global warming created by human societies. Rectification is an important and freeing idea. Confucius once said, that "an exemplary human making a mistake is like an eclipse of the sun or the moon: when it takes place, everyone notices it, but when it is rectified, everyone thinks even more highly of them' (*Analects* 19.21). Let us hope that we take the rectification of our errors as a society very seriously."

WHILE THEY HAD BEEN TALKING, the wind had diminished. Then it surged again in a new wave of roaring before growing quiet again, which made the girl curious. She got up and walked to one of the windows. Mrs. Z. told her to use the nearby stepladder if she wanted to see better, so the girl climbed up on it.

From that height she could see across the yard to the gardens and woods on the far side. The world seemed the same as usual, even in these extraordinary circumstances: the grass was golden and dry, and the forest, even though it contained within it the ferocity of a wildfire, looked closed and dark. The only evidence of the wind that she could see from this vantage point was in the garden, where many of the tall flowers had collapsed onto others. And there was a dark orange glow to the sky, as if from a sunset that was too close for comfort.

She was captivated by the solemnity of the forest, however, by how the areas between the trunks appeared like darkening caves and the nearest branches of the firs were deep green compared to the yellowing of the lawn. There were shrubs and impressive blue grasses along the edge of the woods and these rippled in the wind; in one place, there was more rustling and the movement drew her eye. Part of the foliage seemed to swell and a large animal emerged from its center.

The red deer took a few steps onto the grass and stopped. The girl stood absolutely still as she watched. The deer had nearly grown antlers, and as he walked across the grass the girl noted that he did not run with panic, but strode slowly and steadily for a number of yards as if carefully balancing his rack. He stopped and held his head still, appearing to listen. The girl admired his reddish coat and the swatch of white under his chin and down his neck, which gleamed. The sculptural form of the deer was highlighted against the dark woods and the dusky sky. The silhouette was breathtaking.

"Mrs. Z.," she said.

"Yes?"

"A Qilin!" She half-whispered it. She said a little more loudly, "It's a Qilin . . . A fortunate sighting."

"A what?"

The girl turned from her perch and smiled. Mrs. Z. came to the window and the girl stepped from the ladder so the woman could look out. Mrs. Z. had been smiling with curiosity, but the girl saw her smile fade. "What is it?" she asked.

"It's just . . . beautiful isn't adequate. It is more than beautiful." Mrs. Z. continued to look out the window, entranced.

Suddenly there was the sound of the door at the top of the stairs opening and Mr. Z. came down the steps. "Hello, hello," he was saying. "How are you two doing?"

Mrs. Z. laughed and got down from the ladder. "We were looking at a mythical creature, actually." She couldn't help but clasp his arms. "How are things going out there? Can you see any of the fire?"

He shrugged. He was sweating and filthy from dark smoke, but when he smiled his teeth glowed in the dim light. "A few trees fell on the east side. I'm going to go down the road to see how those folks are doing. You're definitely in the right place. The air is abysmal."

He rummaged through the metal shelving along one wall for a box of masks and found them. "You might need these, too. Hopefully not." He kissed his wife and headed back up the stairs. "When this is over we're going to celebrate. . . . I don't know how yet, but it's going to be good." Then just like that he was gone again, and the dark reassembled itself.

Mrs. Z. remained at the bottom of the stairs for a moment, looking up, and the girl felt a wave of guilt as she realized that her tutor and friend was trapped in the basement because of wanting to protect her.

Suddenly Mrs. Z. turned, breaking the spell, and clapping her hands together said, "Our task is learning. Even here. Even now. Yes?"

The girl was growing tired, but at the same time she was having moments of real enjoyment. If her friends were to know how she spent her time during the fire, they would possibly laugh. Just as her energy was about to be depleted, she said, "I remember you read a quote to me about learning and something about how ice is made of water but is colder than water ever is. I liked that. It's very strange. And it's so hot down here."

Mrs. Z. laughed as she walked back to their chairs. "Oh, yes. It's from the Confucian Xunzi.

> A virtuous person (*junzi*) says: Learning should never cease. Blue comes from the indigo plant but is bluer than the plant itself. Ice is made of water but is colder than water ever is. A piece of wood as straight as a plumb line may be bent into a circle as true as any drawn with a compass and, even after the wood has dried, it will not straighten out again. The bending process has made it that way. Thus, if wood is pressed against a straightening board, it can be made straight again; if metal is put to the grindstone, it can be sharpened; and if the virtuous person studies widely and each day examines himself, his wisdom will be clear and his conduct will be without fault.

"Speaking of learning, I learned something from *you*," she continued, as the girl sat down again and picked up her teacup. Mrs. Z. brought out the boxes of cookies and a container of grapes and strawberries from her bag, arranging the snacks between them; she poured more tea, as the girl thanked her and delightedly began to eat.

"So, yes, I learned something from you, which is the joy of seeing the extraordinary and beautiful in a common animal. You called the deer a Qilin and something awoke in me."

The girl took great pleasure in this. "That's funny, because this is the best strawberry I've ever eaten."

Mrs. Z. laughed. "You have the knack, then, for appreciation; don't lose that." She thought suddenly of Wang Yangming, the most important thinker in the School of Heart-Mind, who, after terrible hardship and betrayal, had an experience of extraordinary awakening; Wang's conclusion was that this sort of awakening is not based on the accumulation of knowledge of external principles. Instead, he believed that in unusual moments of life, such as during deep meditation or in moments of distress, one can be suddenly awakened to one's original human nature, which he called "conscientious knowing.'"

"The lowest point of Wang's life was also spiritually the most enlightening for him, and he was convinced of the innately good disposition of human nature. This enriched Lu Xiangshan's thought and was certainly in contrast to Zhu Xi's notion of awakening, gradual step-by-step learning that involves understanding the interconnected principles of the world. It is also rooted in Mencius's belief in the innate goodness of human nature.

"Mencius had a method called 'cultivating the unperturbed heart-mind (*budongxin*).' He believed that if one practices meditation and is morally upright, one can live without fear and anxiety even in the most stressful situations. The word 'heart-mind' is the translation of the Chinese term *xin* (心), which refers to the core of human consciousness. Because the Confucian tradition doesn't advocate a sharp division between intelligence and emotion, the term heart-mind refers to both of them: our heart of emotions and feelings, and our mind of rationality and intelligence.

"Since our heart-mind can be motivated by varying intentions, in order to rectify or cultivate it, our intentions have to be authentic. 'Authenticity' doesn't mean just that we sincerely desire something. It means we need to line up our desire with the authentic values of things in the world. For instance, if we genuinely feel that reading sacred texts and classical books of learning can bring more joy than watching a television show, then we are valuing the prior activity more. As a consequence, if we intend to regularly practice such actions as a habit, our intention of doing so will be authentic. This then influences how intense and all-encompassing our feeling of joy will be.

"Moments of awakening (*jue*), large or small," said Mrs. Z., "are crucial to self-cultivation."

The girl nibbled some grapes; her mother had told her a story about when she and her father, newly graduated from college, had traveled to Asia to learn from various spiritual teachers about the idea of transcendence. "This sounds mysterious."

The cat had woken from his nap and, interested in the little branch that had held the grapes, sat at her feet and looked up at her.

She rubbed his head. "You said that your cat was the most enlightened being you know."

"I did," Mrs. Z. laughed. "He is."

The girl became thoughtful. "But what happens to someone's life after their awakening?"

Mrs. Z. laughed again with delight. "That is a marvelous question!" She sipped her tea and thought for a moment. "To a certain extent, the effort after one's awakening is even more important, and the Confucian tradition calls this effort 'cultivation' (修 *xiu*). For Zhu Xi, one needs to apply the general knowledge of the world obtained in the moment of one's awakening to the practical aspects of everyday life. This requires a continual process of inquiry and self-cultivation. For Wang Yangming, after being awakened to the true ethical standard of human behavior, one must continually rectify and improve things in the world according to that standard. After all, practice must be in constant unison with knowledge. In general, we can say that in the Neo-Confucian tradition, the effort put in *before* awakening leads to the moment of awakening, whereas the effort applied *after* awakening reinforces and renews the awakening."

PART NINE

Following the Way of Heaven

"What about praying?" the girl suddenly asked.

"Yes, we do pray," said Mrs. Z. "Let me introduce you to a very important concept called *Tian* (天), which can be translated as Heaven, or the Sky Above. It's essential to understand this deeply religious concept. Heaven, or *Tian*, is often seen as the source and enforcer of moral values, urging us all to act morally. What's important to understand is that this moral concept also carries a religious dimension. It's not an abstract idea but a divine force that drives human morality. However, it is worth noting that there is no single, agreed-upon definition of *Tian* within Confucianism.

"One day not too long ago, your mother and I were having tea together, and she asked me about suffering. . ."

The girl was not entirely surprised. "My mother isn't sure she believes in God. She said, 'If God is just, why is there so much injustice?'"

"In religious studies, the conundrum of God and justice is called 'theodicy.' Before Confucius's time, *Tian* was worshiped as a personal deity who dispenses divine retribution. For example, rulers in the early Zhou dynasty believed that if they were virtuous, *Tian* would reward them and legitimize their rulership. However, the tumultuous social changes around Confucius's time led people to increasingly ask: Why do good people suffer?

"Two trends of thought contributed to Confucian thinkers' responses to this question. Some argued that *Tian*, as a supreme deity, is too distant from human society to concern itself with our well-being. They believed that building a good and just human society should rely solely on human actions and virtues. According to them, if humans do not help themselves, *Tian* will not intervene; if humans do not reward goodness and punish evil, *Tian* will not get involved. Others acknowledged Tian's supreme power to cause natural phenomena like lightning and earthquakes, which evoke deep human feelings of awe and sublimity. *Tian* provides essential natural resources such as sunshine, water, and soil for the flourishing of human life. Proper utilization of these resources requires human effort. It is unfortunate that today humans, instead of preserving these precious resources, are destroying them through ignorance, greed, and carelessness. Nevertheless, even with these perspectives of humanization and naturalization, Confucian scholars have continued to recognize the supreme and transcendental status of *Tian* over humans.

"For Confucius and Mencius, I would say that *Tian* still maintains its original religious connotation of being the foundation of human morality and civilization, but they have shared some elements of the humanistic and naturalistic ideologies as well."

"It's interesting how meanings change over time," the girl said. At school last year, I was in a linguistics club. Now I wish I could learn more classical Chinese! I can see how important it is to understand the original meanings of words."

"I think you're understanding these ideas through translation well! It's worth remembering that scholarly interpretations represent just one facet of the broader tradition. Confucianism has shaped the lives of people in China and many others in Asia for over two millennia, and actual ritual practices have often been as important as theological and philosophical ideas."

"What kinds of ritual practices are you talking about?"

Mrs. Z. thought of her best friend and smiled. "I have a Confucian friend who believes in divine retribution. She believes good deeds are eventually rewarded, and wrongdoing is exposed. She sees this as the work of the watchful Heaven above. She identifies as non-religious, though, but she takes ancestral rites seriously—and she gets this from her mother. So, for instance, rather than buying ready-made paper money for offerings, her mother painstakingly handcrafts it, dedicating days to preparing offerings for spirits of family members who have died. Many Chinese people observe important ritual dates on the Confucian calendar, such as Qingming Festival, a sacred day for ancestral rituals, and the Lunar New Year's Eve, known as the Chinese Spring Festival. In addition to ancestral rites, my friend and her mother occasionally make offerings in Buddhist and Daoist temples, even though they don't consider themselves Buddhists or Daoists. This is common practice among Confucians in China: while they may not have a specific religious identity, they hold Confucian ethical teachings and rituals in high regard."

"So we can mix traditions if we want to? We don't have to pick one or the other?" the girl asked.

"The truth is that you don't have to choose. In China, for more than two thousand years, all the way to the beginning of the twentieth century, when the two millennia of imperial China ended (211 BCE–1911 CE), most people lived their lives as Confucians in their ethical outlooks and ritual life, while many also participated in Daoist and Buddhist practices. There has been a co-existence of different religious traditions. I'm not saying there is no tension between them, but the predominant mode of being religious in Chinese society is one of religious tolerance and pluralistic beliefs. Many of the guests at our literary dinner party would be at home in Confucian as well as Daoist and Buddhist traditions. There is an old saying that captures this well: "One lives as a Confucian when one is successful in social and civic life, and one lives as a Daoist when one retires from society."

She smiled to herself. For the famous Daoist philosopher, Zhuangzi, the *Dao*—or the path to life—meant wild, overgrown, and abundant Nature. "Confucius's *Dao,* or the Way," she said, "is the path that emphasizes thoughtful and meaningful actions of people, especially in moral and ritual matters, rather than merely following established patterns of nature. This is the reason why Confucius was determined to focus on learning when he was just a year older than you. The classics and the teachings of the sages—as well as ritual practices—were central to his fulfillment of *Dao*. According to Zhuangzi, the *Dao* is best found through embracing the wild nature that surrounds us. In contrast, Confucius believed that people have to prioritize thoughtful and meaningful actions and to exercise their own agency in decision-making. The Confucian *Dao*, therefore, can be seen as a uniquely humane approach that expands upon the natural *Dao* by incorporating humanistic values."

UP ABOVE THEY AGAIN HEARD the sounds of the wind and were knocked back into the world that was raging around them outside.

"I wish it would stop," the girl sighed, and the fear was back in her eyes again.

Mrs. Z. took hold of her hand. "Shall we continue our banquet story?"

The last guest to arrive, when the banquet is nearly over, is a serious-looking man with a mustache. He is dressed in the long black coat of a gentleman in the style of nineteenth-century China. He is Kang Youwei (1858–1927), who received a traditional Confucian education and became a high-ranking official. He was one of the first Confucian elites to blend Confucian ideas with Western ones, and he became a prominent political reformer. He wrote a letter to the emperor in 1895 to propose various reforms to modernize China, but his efforts failed. As a result, Kang had to go into exile for fifteen years, living in various countries including Canada, Sweden, and Mexico before returning to China.

In 1911, the republican revolution transformed China into a modern republic, abolishing the monarchy. Kang Youwei returned from exile and proposed new ideas for the nation, including making Confucianism a national religion. He believed it was vital for a stable Chinese state, but this proposal wasn't successful. However, he left a significant legacy, especially in promoting "The Association of the Confucian Religion," a group of grassroots organizations that spread Confucianism in everyday life. These organizations had a lasting impact not only in China but also in the Chinese diaspora in places like Indonesia and Singapore.

"Confucianism remains alive and evolving today, despite challenges in the twentieth century," said Mrs. Z. "Some intellectuals in the 1920s blamed Confucianism for China's slow modernization. During the Cultural Revolution in the 1960s and 1970s, Confucianism was seen as counter-revolutionary and detrimental to progress. It wasn't until the 1990s, with China's market opening, that Confucianism and its rituals returned.

"Confucian ideas also played a role in the development of Japanese capitalism in the nineteenth and twentieth centuries. The "Four Asian Tigers"—South Korea, Taiwan, Singapore, and Hong Kong—benefited from their diverse Confucian traditions during their economic success from the 1960s to the 1990s.

"Many in China see Confucianism as a vital spiritual resource for the modern world. Contemporary New Confucianism has produced three generations of thinkers, primarily in Hong Kong and Taiwan, during the second half of the twentieth century, with later influence extending to the United States and other parts of the world.

"There's even a school in America called 'Boston Confucianism,'" The older woman added. "This school was created by distinguished scholars in Boston, including both Confucian thinkers and Christian theologians and philosophers. These American scholars believe that Confucianism can be transplanted from its original Chinese cultural soil to the West, and the dialogue between Christianity and Confucianism, especially in terms of ritual life and ethics, could be beneficial to all.

"So," the girl asked, China is not the only country where Confucianism is important?"

"No, far from it! Korean Confucianism has a long and rich history, and today it remains one of the key religious, philosophical, social, and cultural legacies for people in South Korea. There is a long history of Confucianism in Japan as well. Confucianism is also very much present in other parts of Asia, especially Vietnam, Indonesia, and Singapore. The various forms all have great differences as well as great affinities. We should speak of 'Confucianisms' as a plural term, and I really like it.

"Let's move to the conclusion of the dinner party. Confucius was astounded by the global evolution of Confucianism. Yet, anticipating the myriad challenges humanity must confront to improve society, he brings the gathering to a close with his profound vision of an ideal society called 'Great Harmony.'"

When the Great Way was practiced, the world was shared by all alike. The worthy and the able were promoted to office and men practiced good faith and lived in affection. Therefore they did not regard as parents only their own parents, or as sons only their own sons. The aged found a fitting close to their lives, the robust their proper employment; the young were provided with an upbringing, and the widow and widower, the orphaned and the sick, with proper care. Men had their tasks and women their hearths. They hated to see goods lying about in waste, yet they did not hoard them for themselves; they disliked the thought that their energies were not fully used, yet they used them not for private ends. Therefore all evil plotting was prevented and thieves and rebels did not arise, so that people could leave their outer gates unbolted. This was the age of Grand Commonalty.

"Do you think we will ever get there, given how many conflicts, wars, and atrocities are being committed every day?" the girl asked. "Given that we can't even look after our own planet?"

"I think that all of the Confucians that we've met at this dinner party, from Confucius, Mencius, Zhu Xi, all the way to Kang Youwei, are hopeful, and believe that the Way of Heaven will prevail, no matter how long it might take or how difficult the process might be. The Way of Heaven is the way of interconnection and co-humanity. What we call "*Ren*" (仁) or benevolence is Love. Love is boundless in the Confucian tradition."

The girl brightened. "This seems like *agape* in Christianity or loving-compassion in Buddhism."

Mrs. Z. laughed. "That's exactly right! Very good. The term *ai* in contemporary Chinese is well translated as "love," although the equivalent term in classical Chinese, as well as in the Confucian tradition, is *ren*, variously translated as "benevolence," "love," or "co-humanity." One first feels co-humanity with those close at hand, such as one's parents, then it extends out to family members and beyond. The famous Confucian work *The Great Learning* states that one grows and strengthens one's sense of benevolence outward from oneself to one's family, to an ever-widening circle with the aim of becoming a cultivated individual, or even a sage, who is one with all under Heaven." Mrs. Z. smiled at the girl. "So that is love."

The girl smiled. "I think to end a story on Love is never a bad thing."

PART TEN
After the Fire

> Is the virtue of humaneness distant? I yearn for it, and there it is right before me.
>
> —*Analects* 7.30

The batteries in the flashlight were beginning to fade, but they both suddenly noticed that the world above them had been strangely silent and still for a while.

Then Mr. Z. appeared at the top of the stairs again, saying that he had a cell signal. Mrs. Z. and the girl jumped up as he came down the stairs. The phone glowed as he showed them the screen. "There are voicemails and texts from your mother." The girl held the phone and began to weep with relief, as Mr. Z. continued, "They're okay. Cell service is overwhelmed and texts are taking so long to get through. But I was able to let her know that you're here with us."

"Thank you." She couldn't find any other words. "Thank you." She held the phone to her heart before returning it to him, and felt Mrs. Z.'s arm around her shoulder.

Mr. Z. told them that the wind had passed and the rains were about to start; the fire was mostly out and the rain would do much of the rest. The elements were falling back in balance, the world was finding its way back to harmony, or as one of the Four Books canonical to Confucianism puts it, a middle way (中庸). He and Mrs. Z. gathered the food, the cups, and the lantern, and the girl cradled the cat in her arms as they walked up the stairs. She turned to look again at the basement, which seemed even dimmer now, though she had a different view of it than when she had entered it; she could see why Mrs. Z. considered it earthy and comforting.

The main floor of the house was notably smokey in comparison to the cellar, and the girl felt more scratchiness in her throat. She placed the cat on the floor and regarded the living room, the bookshelves, the large windows showing an unchanging view. She stepped outside onto the front porch. Apart from the downed trees and flecks of ash, the scene beyond the house was remarkably the same as ever, revealing little of the calamity that had been playing out around it.

Mr. and Mrs. Z. walked about the yard, checking on what had come down, but mostly marveling at what had stayed up. Enormous, promising rain clouds filled the sky around the dissipating plumes from the fire, and the girl couldn't help but think of the clouds that had heralded the birth of Mencius. She watched as Mr. Z. put his arms around his wife, how he pulled her to himself, one hand on her head, the other on her back, as if to bring her as close as he possibly could. She felt an ache of happiness, and of grief. She locked her arms around herself and, feeling longing and desperation to see the person who had been her bedrock, prayed for her mother to come home.

They were all about to return inside when a rumbling along the gravel could be heard. The dust-covered truck had barely come to a stop when the door opened and the girl's mother burst out and ran to her daughter. The girl found herself being rocked in her mother's fierce embrace, hearing the words, "I'm sorry, I'm so, so sorry," over and over in her ear. Behind them, the girl's grandparents were being helped out of the truck by Mr. and Mrs. Z., and soon the girl was enveloped by them also, as she wept with gratitude.

AS THE ENSUING DAYS UNFOLDED, the girl found there was a spirit of selflessness between the people of the marooned town. The fire had created its own weather and pattern of destruction, which came to a definitive end only with the advent of the rain. As people traded stories of the fire, there were accounts of motors melting, causing metal to trickle into street gutters; birds had dropped from the sky; gas tanks had exploded; people had died. The destruction had been capricious: where one apple tree in a garden survived, the one right next to it did not; where one house survived, another on the same street did not.

Yet despite the personal tragedies some of them had experienced, local workers and shop owners focused on the needs of others. The grocery store stayed open, running its generators, feeding the community, and restocking its shelves as soon as the immediate danger passed. The pizza shop and the coffee shop served their wares through the following day and night, stabilizing community morale as people fought the smaller fires that continued to break out here and there. The staff of the town's only hotel cooked meals for teams of firefighters, provided accommodations for many in need, and kept the bar open to help many settle their nerves. The girl, along with her mother, volunteered with a large group of people to help clean up the most damaged areas. It was community at its best, at its kindest.

The girl felt that this was what Mrs. Z. had been talking about: the practice of good works, of kindness, and of unity, respect, and, above all else, love for the people of their town and the natural world that surrounded it, no matter the religious or cultural differences among them. They had, each in their own way, borne witness to and survived the trauma and power of nature at its most destructive.

Through the pain of their own grief, their small community found a strength and drive in those who decided to stay; they would slowly, one small ritual action at a time, in community with others, day by day paying attention and nurturing the good in their community—all, come to think of it, Confucian ideals—rebuild the life they loved, despite the subsequent nervous summers during which they would have to be alert for wisps of smoke on the surrounding hills. They had received another message from the universe in the language of the environment, and their survival and prosperity would depend on learning to speak this language fluently.

A WEEK AFTER THE FIRE, and after the rains had come and gone, the girl noticed that a patch of dahlias and coneflowers close to the cottage was blooming. On a cooler morning, she and her mother picked an armload and carried them to the widest cedar in their yard, one that grew close to the house. In honor of the girl's father, they laid the flowers around the base of the cedar, carefully and methodically, one by one; then, putting their arms around the trunk, they found each others' hands. Standing linked in this way, with their cheeks against the cedar's bark, they listened to the sounds of the forest around them and the silence in between the sounds.

The girl eventually returned to the flower patch and selected enough blooms for a large bouquet, which she tied with a ribbon. She carried the flowers as she walked along the road to the house of Mr. and Mrs. Z., aware of how the gravel felt under her sandals and how she did not have to run but could take her time. Her heart was full as she recalled the day of the fire and the care that she had received. Tucked inside the bouquet was a small card where she had placed the words of Confucius, the ones spoken by Mrs. Z. on that extraordinary day; the words had traveled through time and reached her when she had needed them most.

Maitreyi's Quest

A RETELLING OF THE HINDU SACRED STORY

Maitreyi's Quest

At one in the morning, the New Delhi train station bustled with people. A cacophony of sound and pungent smells filled the station—people talking, yelling, laughing, children crying, and the ringing and pinging of phones. The acrid smell of diesel mixed with the distinctive spicy aroma of street food. Yet, all sounds were silenced by the intermittent train horns that wailed in the night like the goddess Kali, whose gaping mouth drowned all sound as she devoured hundreds of demons who threatened the world in the well-known story, the *Devi Mahatmya*.

Maitreyi thought of the *Devi Mahatmya* and its divine heroines, Durga and Kali, as she watched a train pull up to the station—its grand doors opening as throngs of passengers entered, as if into the mouth of the Goddess. The *Devi Mahatmya* was one of her favorite Hindu stories. She was partial to the dark goddess, Kali, because she reminded Maitreyi of the light that endures even in the darkest of times. Waiting for her train to arrive, Maitreyi felt as if she, too, was entering the Goddess, seeking illumination and purification during a time when the unknown cloaked her like the cold autumn mist of the New Delhi atmosphere.

Shivering, Maitreyi pulled her white sari tightly around her sloped shoulders and adjusted her woolen shawl over her graying hair. Her fingers gently clutched the silver locket around her neck, which held a picture of her beloved husband, Prem, with whom she had planned this pilgrimage (*yatra*) to sacred sites in India.

Maitreyi and Prem had lived and worked for more than thirty years as professors at a renowned university in California until his sudden death six months earlier. They had planned this pilgrimage as a journey to find a deeper meaning in life that had so far eluded them, despite professional and personal material success. They wanted to enter together the stage of Hindu life when, after fulfilling family obligations, one committed to spiritual study, reflection, and practice.

In her grief, Maitreyi wondered if she would be strong enough to make their pilgrimage alone. It had been decades since they migrated from India, and much had changed. The questions, however, about life's meaning that she and Prem often discussed had become even more urgent since his death. She saw the pilgrimage as a commitment to herself and Prem to pursue answers to these questions.

Her son Krishna—or "Kris," as he liked to be called—and her daughter Asha had flown with her to New Delhi from Los Angeles earlier that week. They had joined Maitreyi in a sacred ceremony on the bank of the Yamuna River to immerse Prem's ashes. Much to the chagrin of Kris and Asha, Maitreyi was determined to embark alone on the rest of her journey.

An air horn wailed in the distance. Maitreyi's train to Rishikesh approached.

"Mom, are you sure you should do this yourself?" Kris again asked as he pulled his mother's suitcase toward the train's platform. "I have another week of vacation time, and it just doesn't seem right for you to go without me." He zipped his iPhone and wallet into the inner pocket of his blue REI jacket.

Twenty-one and outspoken, Asha, accepting her mother's determination, scowled at her brother and argued, "Let her do this on her own, Kris. This is what she and Dad had planned to do after retirement. We need to support Mom's decision." Asha softened her tone and whispered to Maitreyi, "Be careful Mama, and please keep in touch. I'll miss you."

Maitreyi saw the fear in her children's eyes—especially Kris's—as he hoisted her suitcase onto the train, where a porter disappeared with the bag into the first-class carriage. She placed her cool hands on her children's cheeks and said, "Please don't worry. I'll be fine. I must go now. Be well."

Maitreyi gingerly lifted her sari as she climbed the single step onto the train. The same porter who had taken her bag had returned, and he quickly led her to her cabin.

There would be no time for extended goodbyes. *Perhaps it is for the best,* thought Maitreyi, as the brown leather couch squeaked beneath her when she sat down. Maitreyi looked out the window at the concerned faces of her children. She knew that her decision was painful to them after the recent loss of their father.

Kris was in his late twenties with a young family, and Asha had just started her final year at college. As the train pulled away from the station, both of them, in their ever-increasing smallness, appeared to be young children. Maitreyi felt her throat tighten and her eyes sting as she watched her family disappear into the distance. Never before had she felt so alone. She took hold of Prem's locket once again and swallowed her loneliness, contemplating the six-hour journey ahead to Rishikesh.

Maitreyi's thoughts returned to earlier that morning when, with Kris and Asha, she had gone to Yamuna Ghat. It was cool and misty, and they were surprised by the sight of so many seagulls flying near the surface of the water to feed. As the birds dipped in and out of the water, the golden rays of the rising sun shimmered off their feathers.

The priest, awaiting their arrival, signaled them to draw closer. Holding the small clay pot wrapped in red cloth containing Prem's ashes in her hands, Maitreyi led her children down the steps to the water's edge. The priest placed a handful of marigold flowers into the hands of Asha and Kris while chanting an ancient mantra in honor of God as Shiva.

> "We worship the omniscient Shiva, fragrant and nourishing, who liberates us from death like a ripe fruit separating from its vine. *Aum* peace, peace, peace."

As she remembered this, Maitreyi relived the heart-wrenching moment when, with trembling hands, she tipped the clay pot, and Prem's ashes gently fell and joined the flowing water of the Yamuna. Asha and Kris offered flowers to the Yamuna as the sacred river carried their father's ashes to the ocean.

Maitreyi silently prayed that, as raindrops from the sky reach the sea, Prem's soul would also find its way to unity with the divine. She held her children closely as they stood on the river steps watching the flowers disappear around a bend in the river.

FIRST *TIRTHA*: RISHIKESH

The Advaita Vedanta Tradition

Maitreyi and Prem had decided to start their spiritual journey at Rishikesh. They knew that Rishikesh has been a vital center of religious study and teaching since ancient times. Many of Hinduism's most renowned teachers lived here as disciples seeking the solitude and beauty of the Himalayan mountains and the sacred Ganges River. Prem had met Swami Anantananda several years earlier, when Swamiji had visited his university. He was attracted to Swamiji's eloquence and his style of teaching as he explained the tradition of Advaita Vedanta (non-dualism).

It was early morning when Maitreyi's train pulled slowly into Rishikesh. In the distance, she saw, for the first time, the Himalayan ranges and caught glimpses of the rapidly flowing Ganges. The trees in the forests along the way were green, lush, and vibrant, unlike the struggling, smog-covered ones in Delhi. Maitreyi opened her cabin window and felt the cool crispness of the morning air on her face.

The screeching of the train jolted her as it came to an abrupt stop at the train station. When she stood up, she glimpsed a reflection of herself in the window. It was strange to recognize herself dressed in the white garb of a Hindu widow. So much had changed in a short time for her. Lifting her well-worn bag, Maitreyi stepped down onto the narrow platform. The entrance to the train station was crowded with cycles and auto rickshaws. She made eye contact with an elderly Sikh rickshaw driver standing quietly to the side. "Can you take me to Swami Anantananda's ashram?" Maitreyi asked.

"Please come; I know the way," said the driver softly.

Maitreyi heard the sounds of temple bells and sacred morning chants as she made her way to the ashram. The road was narrow and crowded with pilgrims walking to temples. The driver skillfully maneuvered his vehicle to avoid hitting the cows leisurely strolling through the lanes. He slowed and turned left into a much narrower and winding road that led directly to the ochre-colored buildings on the bank of the Ganges itself. Maitreyi was warmly welcomed by an elderly monk (*sannyasin*) who served as the ashram administrator. He led her to her room, which was sparsely furnished with a small bed, a wooden table, and a chair. After a simple meal eaten while sitting on the ashram's dining room floor, Maitreyi walked along the shore of the Ganges. Here the river was young, and it roared as it flowed energetically toward the plains. She stooped near its edge, cupped her hands, and sprinkled a few drops of water on her head. In this way, she fulfilled the hope of every Hindu to see the Ganges and to receive her blessings. A sense of peace permeated her body and mind.

It was almost midday, and her first meeting with Swamiji was imminent. She walked to the small hut where Swamiji stayed whenever he visited his ashram in Rishikesh. There were sitting mats outside for visitors, and the young attendant, dressed in white, gestured to her to have a seat. Shortly afterward, the door opened, and Swamiji, wearing the ochre-colored robes of a Hindu renunciant, emerged from the hut. His robe covered his head, and his elegant beard was gray. His eyes twinkled as he smiled and welcomed her. "Maitreyi, I am very happy that you are here. I remember Prem well," said Swamiji. Maitreyi prostrated as Swamiji took his seat on a nearby armchair.

"Thank you, Swamiji, for the gift of your time to meet with me," said Maitreyi.

"My ashram is your home, Maitreyi. Let us know of your needs." Swamiji spoke lovingly. "What brings you to Rishikesh?"

"Swamiji, Prem and I always wanted to return to India after retirement to seek answers to a longing we both felt for a deeper purpose and meaning to our lives. Prem's unexpected death caused me unimaginable grief, but it also reminded me of life's uncertainty. It is difficult without Prem, Swamiji, but I had to make this journey." Maitreyi looked into Swamiji's eye as she spoke and saw deep understanding.

Stages of Life

"You made the right decision, Maitreyi," Swamiji assured her. "Our tradition understands life as progressing through several stages with different priorities in each stage. In the first or student stage (*brahmacharya*), we focus on gaining the knowledge and skills for a livelihood. During the second or householder stage (*grihastha*) we enter into marriage, raise our families, serve our communities and elders, and gather the resources we will need in retirement. The third or forest-dweller stage (*vanaprastha*) follows retirement and is meant for devoting more time to religious study and practice. A few people go on to a fourth stage (*sannyasa*) and become monastics, but for most, life progresses in three stages. You are in this third stage, Maitreyi, and your pilgrimage is appropriate."

Maitreyi felt affirmed by Swamiji's explanation that she was following an ancient tradition.

"Swamiji, Prem and I built a good life together in the United States. We both worked as professors with freedom in our classrooms and respect in our community. The births of Krishna and Asha brought us joy. We delighted in every phase of their growth. Our life was good, and Prem and I were grateful for the many blessings we enjoyed."

As Maitreyi spoke, Swamiji stroked his beard and occasionally nodded in approval.

"Prem and I supported causes about which we were passionate. We advocated for the homeless and volunteered in soup kitchens. We marched with neighbors and friends against police brutality. But something was missing, Swamiji. Prem told me that he identified with Narada in the *Chandogya Upanishad*, who confessed to his teacher that he experienced a sorrow he could not move past. I often thought of my namesake in the *Brhadaranyaka Upanishad*, who was offered ample wealth by her husband but who knew that wealth would not answer her deepest questions about life and death. What do we lack, Swamiji?" asked Maitreyi, furrowing her brow.

Maitreyi's question was interrupted by the loud sound of a bell coming from the low tent-like building near Swamiji's hut. He smiled and said, "It is our call to lunch." "I will join you there in a few minutes. Let us meet each morning after breakfast and evenings before dinner to continue our discussion."

Maitreyi walked across the pebbled courtyard to the food hall. She followed an elderly female monk, took an aluminum plate and cup from a table, and sat cross-legged on a jute mat on the floor. Soon after, Swamiji entered and sat at the end of the hall. His plate and cup had already been laid out by his attendant. Swamiji's entrance was the signal to begin chanting the fifteenth chapter of the Bhagavadgita, a custom before each meal at the ashram. The beautiful and metrical chanting moved and soothed Maitreyi:

> That brilliance that resides in the sun, which illumines the
> entire world, that which is in the moon, and in the fire,
> know that brilliance to be Mine.
> Permeating the soil, I support all beings with energy, and
> having become the watery moon, I cause all plants to
> thrive.
> Having become the digestive fire of all beings, I abide in all
> bodies and, united with the life breaths, I digest foods of
> all kinds.

As the chanting continued, cooks served a simple meal of rice, lentils, and vegetables. When the meal ended, Maitreyi followed others to the large sink, where they washed their utensils before returning them to the table. It had been a long day, and Maitreyi retired to her room for an afternoon rest.

That evening, as Maitreyi walked over to Swamiji's hut, the Ganges River and the mountains rising from its bank were suffused with the soft, cool light of the setting sun. Swamiji was already in his armchair, sipping a cup of tea and enjoying the serene beauty of the Rishikesh evening. The only sound came from the vigorous roar of the river as it made its way to the plains. Swamiji appeared to be in deep thought. "The Ganges," he said, as Maitreyi bowed and sat down at his feet, "is the flow of spiritual wisdom, adapting to diverse circumstances and challenges and always giving of itself to seekers. As teachers, we try to emulate the river by never turning away a sincere seeker who comes to drink from the fountain of knowledge. This is an obligation that we joyfully accept. Maitreyi, I recognize you to be such a seeker."

She was thankful for Swamiji's words, since she was not sure how he had received the personal predicament that she had described this morning.

The Goals of Life

"The dilemma experienced by you and Prem," continued Swamiji, "is a universal human one recognized in the Upanishads. The Hindu tradition is not otherworldly or life-denying. It is appropriate that both of you pursued wealth (*artha*). We acknowledge the need of every human being for access to those necessities that ensure dignified living. We affirm pleasure (*kama*) and love to celebrate life through music, dance, good food, and play. I was very pleased, Maitreyi, when you told me of the many ways in which you and Prem served your communities. This is the commitment to *dharma*, expanding our concerns beyond personal wealth and pleasure to include the good of others and the natural world.

Swamiji continued, "*Dharma* affirms the interrelatedness of life and the mutual obligations that follow. You shared a life with Prem that was rich in wealth, pleasure, and virtue."

"I am thankful, Swamiji, for the countless joys that Prem and I shared. I do not want to give the impression that I am disappointed with life." Maitreyi said. "With his passing, I am more aware of life's brevity and uncertainty. My predicament is a sense of lack and dissatisfaction in the midst of plenty. I know that my acceptance of Prem's death, whenever it comes, will not fill this lack."

The Limits of the Finite

"You state the fundamental problem well, Maitreyi," said Swamiji. "The goals of wealth, pleasure, and commitment to the common good are commendable but still finite. A life circumscribed by these ends will still leave us wanting. The gains of wealth and pleasure are transient. A great insight of our tradition is that human beings will not be satisfied with wealth and sense pleasure alone. You have discovered on your own what our scriptures teach: the finite will never fully satisfy us. You asked me this morning what you are missing. Let me tell you a story from my Advaita tradition." Maitreyi was surprised that Swamiji remembered the exact words of her question, and she sensed his love for story-telling.

The Story of the Missing Tenth Person

"This story, Maitreyi, was told by Shankara himself, the great teacher of Advaita. It is about ten religious students who were on a pilgrimage and came to a flooded river. They looked for a boatman, but not finding one, they went ahead and entered the raging waters. After being separated in the river while struggling to get across it, they reached the opposite bank. The students decided to take a count to confirm that everyone was safe. Each one counted and they concluded that they had lost a colleague—the tenth person. They immediately fell into deep sorrow. A woodcutter, returning home from a long day's work, saw the disconsolate students and inquired about their problem. After listening patiently, he asked the leader to repeat his count. When he stopped at nine, the stranger smiled and asked, "Did you count yourself? You are the tenth person!" The students immediately understood. The tenth person had been found!" The dinner bell sounded just as Swamiji finished his story. "Think about this story, Maitreyi; we will continue in the morning."

It was only the first day of her meeting with Swamiji, and Maitreyi felt she had learned much and had much to reflect upon. She decided that she would start early each morning with a visit to the ashram temple (*mandir*) for the morning worship. Then she would sit quietly on the bank of the Ganges, reflecting on the previous day's discussions with Swamiji. Her afternoons would be spent writing in her journal and resting.

Day Two in Rishikesh

The following morning it was still dark when Maitreyi walked the short distance to the temple from her room. The temple faced the Ganges and was dedicated to the divine in the form of Shiva as Gangadhareshvara (the one from whom the Ganges flows). The priest, who was already there, invited Maitreyi to join the few who were sitting in the front facing the icon (*murti*). He began the morning's sacred bath ritual (*puja abhishekam*) by pouring milk, honey, ghee, yogurt, and water over the *murti*. The *murti* is regarded as a living embodiment of divinity, and the priest would perform this obligatory ritual even if no one attended. The ritual ended with the priest gracefully waving a multi-flame lamp clockwise before the *murti*. Then he brought the flame to each person present. Maitreyi reverentially lifted her hands to feel its warmth and passed her hands over her head. The priest also offered each attendee a drop of Ganges water used in the ritual to bathe the *murti*. It had been a long time since Maitreyi had had such an intimate experience of worship in a Hindu temple. It awoke in her a deep sense of closeness to the sacred presence in the *murti*. That feeling stayed with Maitreyi as she walked down the steps to the river and sat in silent reflection.

Swamiji was already outside when Maitreyi arrived for her morning session with him. She bowed and took her seat on the mat next to his armchair. "Maitreyi, let us recite the prayer that teachers and students in the Upanishads say before studying together." Swamiji beautifully intoned the ancient Sanskrit prayer in his rich baritone voice and had Maitreyi repeat after him:

> May God nourish and protect us
> May we study together with great energy
> May our discussion be luminous
> May we not misunderstand each other

"Did you give any thought to the story of the tenth person, Maitreyi?" Swamiji asked.

She answered, "I thought a lot about it when I was sitting this morning near the Ganges."

"What did it communicate to you?"

"It is a beautiful story, Swamiji. They were searching for a tenth person who was never, in reality, lost. The tenth person was always there, but each one, in ignorance, forgot to count himself. In actual fact, they were searching for themselves, since each was the tenth person. Your story reminded me of the many mornings when Prem would come to me anxiously looking for his glasses. On each occasion, I would laugh and point out to him that he was wearing his glasses!"

That Thou Art: The Fullness of Self

"Indeed, Maitreyi," said Swamiji with a smile. "The predicament of the tenth person is a universal human one. Advaita, which is grounded in the Upanishads, teaches that the fullness that we seek, and that cannot be attained through finite gain, is, in fact, already attained. Fullness is the true nature of every being. The Upanishads speak of it as *ananda* (joy). This is what you are missing and searching for, Maitreyi; your own true self (*atman*). At the heart of this tradition is the teaching that the self is identical in all beings and one with the infinite *brahman*. You may remember hearing the famous sentence from the *Chandogya Upanishad*, "That thou art (*tat tvam asi*). 'That' refers to *brahman*, and 'thou' to the individual self (*atman*). The sentence acknowledges their oneness."

Maitreyi warmed to the teaching that she was the fullness that she sought. She remembered Prem speaking of "That thou art" as one of the great sentences of the Upanishads, but Swamiji's explanation also puzzled her. "If I am the full being, the joy that I am seeking, why is this hidden from me? Why do I not know who I am?" She looked directly at Swamiji with a perplexed expression.

"Good question, Maitreyi. This is where our story of the tenth person is also helpful. That person was never lost; he was always and immediately available. Yet there was a problem of ignorance (*avidya*) that had to be overcome and that was corrected by the woodcutter. In a similar way, we live under a condition of ignorance that causes us to misunderstand who we are. A teacher and teaching are necessary to free us from ignorance."

The Problem of Ignorance (*Avidya*)

"Swamiji, is ignorance then our fundamental problem?" asked Maitreyi. "Could you explain a little more about how it affects us?"

"Describing the basic problem as ignorance does not minimize its consequences," he said. "The Upanishads speak of the threefold knots of the heart, ignorance-greed-action, to explain the connection between ignorance, greed, and greed-motivated actions. Ignorance of the fullness of being we share with everyone expresses itself in alienation, ego-centeredness, possessiveness, and violence. It generates greed in a futile effort to achieve self-value. It manifests in social structures of injustice, inequality, disregard for the common good and our collective flourishing."

Maitreyi, listening to Swamiji, thought back to her and Prem's early years in southern California and their observations while driving through Los Angeles. Luxury stores proliferated on one street, while homeless people begged for food and money on the next. Swamiji was not pontificating. He was speaking of the world as it is.

"Maitreyi," Swamiji continued, bringing her out of her reverie, "the consequences of ignorance are evident also in socially constructed hierarchies of various kinds (race, caste, gender) that put human beings into categories of greater and lesser worth. We need to address the problem of ignorance both in our own hearts and in the world outside."

Maitreyi realized that, as social activists, she and Prem had focused exclusively on changing the world. They had not given any thought to the important connection between their inward spiritual transformation and their work in the world. The sound of the lunch bell brought the morning session to a close. She bowed and slowly made her way to the dining hall.

After lunch, Maitreyi found it difficult to fall asleep. She was enthralled by the Advaita teaching that she was the full being that she wanted to become, the idea that her understanding was clouded by ignorance, like the sun on a cloudy day. She was not separated by time or space from the joy that she sought. She needed only to know herself to understand more deeply her true nature. Still, many questions raced through her mind. Swamiji spoke of the self as one with the limitless *brahman*. What is *brahman*? What about the world in which we live? What is its source? Where did it come from?

She decided she would walk along the bank of the Ganges before her evening session with Swamiji when she would raise these questions. Huge boulders covered the bank, but the sand was soft and white, and she could tread between the rocks. Across the river, she saw roofs of temples and ashrams. On her side of the river there were also many ashrams, and she noticed monks sitting under the trees, absorbed in conversation and reading. Maitreyi found a comfortable rock to sit on and absorb the beauty of the setting.

Nature of Brahman

When she arrived at Swamiji's hut that evening, he was not yet outside, but his attendant was ready with his tea. It was not long before he came out and took his seat. His attendant gently poured him a cup of tea and added warm milk and sugar.

"Swamiji, I have a lot of questions to ask. I am sorry if I am asking too many questions," said Maitreyi.

Swamiji laughed. "No, Maitreyi, asking questions is encouraged in our tradition. Our sacred texts are structured as dialogues between teachers and students."

Maitreyi was encouraged. "You spoke this morning of *brahman* and the identity between the self (*atman*) and *brahman*. What is *brahman*? What is the origin of the world?"

"Your questions are all important, Maitreyi. They are the very ones discussed in the Upanishads. Many of the Upanishads begin with the existence of *brahman*, the limitless and timeless one, existing before anything else. *Brahman* is described as being-consciousness-infinite. *Brahman* is described as 'being' because it is not *a being*, distinct and separate from other beings, like an object existing alongside other objects. It is the truth and essential nature of everything that exists; everything receives its being from *brahman*. *Brahman's* nature as consciousness points to the fact that it is not inert; it shines in all beings as the self-revealing light of consciousness that enables all experiences. It is the light of all lights. *Brahman* is free from limits of any kind. It is the fullness, the unending joy that we all seek."

"Is it appropriate, Swamiji, to think of *brahman* as the creator of the universe?" asked Maitreyi.

"Yes, it is. The *Taittiriya Upanishad* describes *brahman* as 'That from which all beings originate, by which they are sustained, and to which they return.' We should understand, Maitreyi, that *brahman* does not create out of some other material but brings forth everything out of itself. The Upanishads speak of the universe as *brahman's* self-multiplication. Everyone and everything exists in *brahman,* and *brahman* is present in everyone and everything. In *brahman,* we are one with each other and the natural world."

Maitreyi was grateful for Swamiji's words. She remembered the many times she and Prem had stood with Indigenous communities protesting against the destruction of sacred sites to build roads and lay down oil lines and had lobbied the state government for legislation to control emissions. She understood better how creation is sacred because of *brahman*'s presence in the water, trees, mountains, and animals. She turned to look at the Ganges and the Himalayas behind her and felt a new harmony with them.

"Swamiji, in our family, we worshiped the divine in personal forms, such as Krishna and Rama. We observed their birth anniversaries and participated in festivals celebrating various events in their lives. Our relationship was a personal one. This morning, you spoke to me about *brahman* as being-consciousness-infinite. Should I understand *brahman* to be an impersonal reality?"

"Excellent question again, Maitreyi. Advaita emphasizes the unity of *brahman.* We may speak *of brahman* as love if we understand that love is not a quality of *brahman* but its very nature. We can surely describe *brahman* as personal as long as we do not imply divisions in *brahman.* We must always, however, be cautious with anthropocentric language and admit the limits of all descriptions of *brahman*, who transcends words and symbols. Our words, at best, are only pointers to the nature of the infinite."

The Meaning of *Advaita* (*Not-Two*)

"Is this why your tradition is called *Advaita*, Swamiji?"

"Yes, Maitreyi, it is indeed. The word *Advaita* literally means 'not-two,' and it is Advaita's way of characterizing the relationship between the infinite *brahman*, the world, and living beings. Describing *brahman* and the world as 'one' or 'two' is inappropriate. They are not 'one' because the relationship between *brahman* as cause and the world as effect is asymmetrical. The world, as an effect, originates from *brahman* and is dependent upon *brahman* for its existence. The relationship between *brahman* and the world is not 'two' since the world does not exist separately from *brahman*, and *brahman* is the being and truth of everything. The language of 'not-two' describes this unique relationship."

Swamiji had responded to all of Maitreyi's questions. She saw the tiredness in his eyes. In addition to meeting with her, he taught two classes daily on the Upanishads and met with visitors. The dinner bell sounded, and the session was at an end.

Day Three in Rishikesh

Maitreyi was up early the next morning. This was her last day at the ashram, and she made her way to the riverbank to contemplate the previous day's discussion. They had covered many topics, but Swamiji had not yet used the word *moksha* (freedom), which she knew to be the fourth and highest goal of human life. She thought she would use her final session with him to learn about the meaning of *moksha*.

It was a beautiful and serene morning. The mountain peaks reflected the soft light of the morning sun, the trees seemed greener than usual, and the river flowed in song. It filled her heart with joy to think that everything was enfolded in the one *brahman*. Maitreyi went earlier than usual to Swamiji's hut. She wanted to sit in silent gratitude before he came out.

The Meaning of *Moksha*

"What shall we talk about this morning?" asked Swamiji as he took his seat.

Maitreyi replied, "I know that *moksha* is the highest goal of human life. You have not yet used the word in our discussions."

"It is true, Maitreyi. I have not used the word, but I have been speaking of it. *Moksha* is overcoming our ignorance about ourselves and discovering our unity with *brahman*. It is a goal to be accomplished here and now in this life. It is more accurate to say that *moksha* is already accomplished, since the self is always one with *brahman* and the problem is ignorance. Clouds may prevent us from seeing the sun in the sky, but the sun is always there. Since *brahman* is identical in all beings, liberation is the discovery of our shared identity with all."

"Is *moksha* a private turning away from active engagement in the world?" she asked.

"Liberation, Maitreyi, frees us to embrace everyone in love. Ignorance is associated with hate and exclusion; liberation with love and embracing. Ignorance is a fragmented way of seeing the world; liberation sees the underlying unity of all in the infinite *brahman*. This unity and loving identity are inclusive and not circumscribed by religion, shared culture, ethnicity, nationality, or species. It is identification with *all* beings. To identify with others implies loving and valuing them as we love and value ourselves."

Maitreyi had never heard *moksha* described in this way. Swamiji's words went deep into her heart, but she still wondered if he was thinking only about suffering in a spiritual sense. Not for the first time, Swamiji continued as if anticipating her concern. "Love and commitment to the flourishing of others need not be limited to the *spiritual* well-being of others. We must not ignore the suffering of others when they lack the necessities for a decent living and when suffering is inflicted through oppression and injustice based on gender, birth, or race. Working to overcome suffering requires identifying the structures that impede human flourishing."

Maitreyi thought of the social justice work she and Prem had done and their motivation for it. They had never grounded their activism in

Hindu teachings. She now realized that there were teachings that would provide a deep justification for human equality, dignity, and ecological sustainability.

Swamiji fell silent, deep in thought. It was not a silence that Maitreyi wished to interrupt. She lowered her head and waited for what he would say next. "These teachings, Maitreyi, provide a strong foundation for transforming our world. Yet we often fail to bridge the wide gap between teaching and its practice. Even the best among us may fail to be agents of change."

Maitreyi was deeply moved by Swamiji's humility and confession.

Shankara and the Untouchable

"Let me tell you a story about Shankara, whom we revere as the greatest among teachers. One day, after bathing in the Ganges, he was walking toward the temple of Shiva when he saw an untouchable man standing in the narrow lane ahead of him. Fearing pollution from contact with the untouchable, Shankara shouted for him to move out of his way. To Shankara's surprise, the untouchable held his ground and asked him. 'O great one among the brahmins, what is it that you want to move away by saying, 'Go, Go'? Do you want the body made up of the five elements to move away from another body made up of the same elements? Or do you want the divine, dwelling equally in all, to move away from the divine?' The untouchable's astute questions, targeting the contradiction between caste practices and the teachings of Advaita about the oneness of humanity, were eye-openers for Shankara. He had failed to live out the social meaning of the tradition he taught."

Swamiji again fell silent. "It is a powerful story, Swamiji," said Maitreyi. "Religious teachings mean little if we are not transformed within and in our way of being in the world. I am grateful, beyond all words, for how much I have received from you."

Knowing it was her final day with him, Maitreyi had brought him a plate of fruits and a garland. She placed the fruit at his feet and took from the plate a small earthen lamp which she waved in front of him as an act of honoring him. Finally, she placed the garland around his neck and bowed. Swamiji whispered the sacred word "*Aum*" and touched her gently on her head.

"Where do you go from here?" he asked.

"Swamiji, Krishna has a special place in my heart. I have always longed to visit Vrindaban, the place of his birth and activities."

"You have my blessings, Maitreyi," said Swamiji. "You are always welcome to return to my ashram. Please remember what it means to understand our oneness with *brahman,* who exists in all and in whom all exist. You are never separate from Prem; he lives in you, and you in him. That oneness also means that Prem, like each one of us, is immortal. Death is not the end of our existence."

Maitreyi was not expecting these words of blessing from Swamiji. Her eyes filled with tears. In her rational mind, she understood through this insight that she was still connected to Prem. In her heart, however, she still longed for his physical presence.

She quickly joined residents for the midday meal and returned to her room to collect her bag and call Kris. She had not spoken to her children since leaving them at the train station in Delhi. "Mom," exclaimed Kris, "we have been waiting for your call. Asha is here with me on speakerphone. Are you still in Rishikesh?"

Maitreyi was delighted to hear that Asha was with Kris, but she was also aware of the anxiety in his voice. She reassured them that she was well and spoke of her appreciation for the beauty and serenity of Rishikesh. "I have much to share with both of you about my conversations with Swamiji. I am leaving this afternoon for Vrindaban. Asha beta (affectionate term for "child"), I know you are taking your MCAT exam soon. Please eat well and get enough rest. Mother Saraswati's (Goddess of Knowledge) blessings are with you. Kris, give my love to Emily and my little ones." Maitreyi's words did not surprise Asha or Kris. Despite being so far away, they felt the embrace of her love. "I will call again in a few days."

"Be safe, Mom. We miss you."

Second *Tirtha*: Vrindaban

The Vaishnava Tradition

Maitreyi made her way by rickshaw to the train station for her six-hour journey to Vrindaban. On the dashboard of the rickshaw was a small statue of Krishna with a weather-worn drawing of one of the saints of Vrindaban, Jiva Goswami. She smiled, thinking this must be an auspicious sign—she was on the right path. Yet, the rickshaw ride was bumpy and made her stomach churn. She gripped the handles of the rickshaw tightly and held her breath. Destitute children ran up and begged for money. *It's a Tuesday. Why aren't these children in school?* Maitreyi wondered as she pressed rupees into their soiled, out-stretched hands. Her natural inclination toward matters of social justice caused a painful knot in her heart for the plight of these children. Arriving at the train station, she walked into her first-class cabin, viscerally aware of her privilege.

She had reserved a window seat because she loved to see the villages and the landscape along the way. Her thoughts drifted to her childhood, to growing up in a small village outside Mirzapur in Uttar Pradesh. She had lived with her parents in her paternal grandparents' home. The household was a large and happy one with uncles, aunts, and several cousins. The village farms she saw as she looked out the window reminded her of days spent playing in the fields while her grandfather and uncles tended the land. The grazing cows in the fields she was looking at now took her back to the joy she experienced wherever she accompanied her mother to milk the cows. Before milking, her mother would tenderly call the cows each by name, stroke them gently, thank them for the gift of milk, and offer them freshly cut grass. She remembered the festival days when the cows were bathed, garlanded, and honored for their special role in the family.

She recalled the dusk ritual performed each day, with her grandmother lighting a lamp at the small shrine in the family home. It was from her grandmother that she had learned her first prayer, the one that she taught to Kris and Asha:

You are my mother and father,
Friend and relative,
Knowledge and wealth.
You are my all; my Supreme God.

Her grandmother would hold Maitreyi's tiny hands in her own as she waved the oil flame in clockwise motions before the icon of Krishna.

It was already dusk when Maitreyi arrived in Vrindaban. The only mode of transport to her guest house in the old part of the city was a horse-drawn carriage (*tonga*). "Radhe Radhe," said the driver, invoking the name of Krishna's beloved devotee as he took her bag and helped her up to a seat. The road was narrow and full of bicycles, scooters, and pedestrians. Stray dogs sat on the sidewalks near food stalls for scraps. She noticed many shops displaying icons of Krishna and Radha in various sizes and poses, along with colorful garlands, incense sticks, and other devotional items. The lilting sounds of sacred music emanated from several shops all along the way.

When she arrived at the guest house, the night watchman opened the iron gate, greeted Maitreyi, and gestured to the door. The guest house was small and simply furnished. "Radhe Radhe," the elderly receptionist greeted her. Maitreyi immediately noticed that she was of similar age and dressed in a white sari like her. Another widow. She smiled and approached the desk.

"Welcome to Bhakti Sadan (House of Love), the receptionist said. You must be exhausted after your long journey. I am Lalita. Please have a seat while I complete your paperwork." Lalita carefully recorded, by hand, the details of Maitreyi's passport in a huge, worn notebook. She walked her to her room on the ground floor, handed her a large key affixed to a piece of wood, and said, "Ramu (the guest house caretaker) will bring you a pot of chai and some biscuits. You must be hungry."

After thanking Lalita, Maitreyi walked into her room. There was a single bed resting on wooden slats, a small vanity, and an armchair. Hanging above the bed was a familiar painting, Krishna's ecstatic dance with the cowherd girls (*gopis*) of Vrindaban. A small adjoining bathroom had a bucket and bowl for baths and an Indian-style squatting toilet. She had not used one since childhood and wondered how she would now manage using it with her arthritic knees. Maitreyi had chosen to live simply on this pilgrimage, forsaking the luxuries that she could have afforded. She felt that simplicity was much more in accord with her spiritual journey and united her with others on a similar path. Her journey was both search and practice.

Day One in Vrindaban

The next morning, her younger cousin, Govinda, came to visit her. She had not seen him since her teenage years, but they had occasionally exchanged letters. "Radhe, Radhe, Didi (elder sister), welcome to Vrindaban, land of Krishna." Govinda chose to address her, not by her first name, but respectfully, as an older sister, since she was ten years his senior.

Govinda's head was shaved except for a small tuft of hair. On his forehead, he wore the *urdhva pundra*, the traditional marking of a Vaishnava (a devotee of God as Vishnu) consisting of two vertical lines of sandal paste with a red dot in the middle. He wore a yellow dhoti (a long robe tied at the waist) and shawl. Strung on his shoulder was a cotton bag, and wrapped around his right wrist was an ochre-colored rosary *(mala)* bag. Maitreyi had not previously known that Govinda had become a novice monk in the Vaishnava tradition. His boyish smile, however, reminded her of the playful, mischievous young cousin she had known.

Memories and images of celebrating Holi, the colorful festival to welcome spring, flitted through her mind. It was her favorite festival. The band of cousins equipped with water guns filled with colored liquids and powder marched through the village to douse their victims. There were no barriers between boys and girls, men and women, the young and the old. The spirit of play ruled. Maitreyi would wear one of her oldest salwar-kameez since she knew that she would be completely drenched in rainbow colors by the end of the night. Villagers offered *thandai*, a cool refreshing drink made of milk, almond, saffron, and rose water, as well as tasty snacks. Govinda, dressed as Krishna, took particular delight in smearing her face with colored powder. It was always a riotous and joyful festival celebrating the divine play of Krishna with Radha and the cowherd girls.

"Didi, it is a special joy for me to show you Vrindaban, where Krishna, the lord of my heart, lived and played, but I do not want you to be disappointed."

"What do you mean, Govinda?" Maitreyi asked, looking puzzled.

"Didi, as you may know, the *Bhagavata Purana,* the preeminent scripture for devotees of Krishna, describes Vrindavan as a village of cowherds amidst forests abounding with sweet fruit, clear rivers, and natural beauty. Writings going back centuries describe Vrindavan as a pilgrimage town replete with temples surrounded by the forested plains of the Yamuna River. For devotees, Vrindavan is a *dhama,* the Lord's home on earth that provides us an opportunity to be with him, in this life and in eternity."

Tears welled in Govinda's eyes as he continued in sadness. "Today, the forests are mostly gone, and the Yamuna's waters are among the most polluted in the world. Some pilgrims resign themselves to this as a sign of our decadent iron age (Kali Yuga). Others organize campaigns to save Vrindavan as an act of service (*seva*) to Krishna's sacred land."

"What I want you to know, Didi," continued Govinda with fervor in his eyes and a smile lighting up his face, "is that Vrindaban is a special space saturated with love. One needs eyes anointed with love to see Krishna's play. Here, the supreme Deity, Krishna, plays as a small child, setting aside his awesome power in favor of the intimacy and vulnerability of love."

"Every pilgrim," he added, "attempts to gather what is at the heart of Vrindavan, namely, *rasa*—transformed relationships of love between humans and God and between one human being and another. This is the Vrindaban that is ever available, and I hope you will discover it." As Govinda poured his heart out to her, Maitreyi started to understand what had attracted him to Krishna.

Visit to the Krishna-Balarama Mandir

"Let us walk together, Didi, and allow me to show you some special places." Maitreyi and Govinda stepped out of the guest house into the street, which was bustling with activity. It was mid-morning, and Maitreyi felt the heat of the brilliant sun.

"Govinda, I see people from different parts of the world dressed in *dhotis* and colorful saris."

He nodded and said, "We are just outside the famous Krishna-Balarama Mandir, a temple of the International Society for Krishna Consciousness (ISKCON) and my spiritual home. Let's go inside."

"The temple is already full, even at this time of the day," exclaimed Maitreyi with surprise.

"Yes, people are here to see the *murtis*, the sacred icons of Krishna and his brother, Balarama. Seeing them is called *darshan*. It's the most important reason people are here."

"Living in the United States, it was always difficult for Prem and me to explain the meaning of *darshan* and our temple practices to our Christian friends. Many equated our *murtis* with idol worship." Maitreyi remembered with sadness how she and Prem made their devotional lives more private over the years, afraid of what their American friends would think. Here, in Vrindaban, she felt pangs of remorse—how could anyone be ashamed of loving God?

"I understand," continued Govinda. "Our devotees are not worshiping anything in place of God, nor are they worshiping stone or metal. They are worshiping God, who is merciful enough to descend into a physical form that we can see, worship, and love."

They slowly made their way to the central shrine where the icon of Krishna was installed. "Didi, this form of Krishna is described in great detail in the *Bhagavata Purana*. As you see, He stands in a graceful dancing posture, with a flute to his lips and a peacock feather on his head. His complexion is black, and his brilliant yellow clothes look like lightning in the night sky. Indeed, the very word 'Krishna' means 'all-attractive.'"

Govinda and Maitreyi brought their palms together and bowed their heads in worshipful silence. As Maitreyi opened her eyes and looked into the luminous black eyes of Krishna, she felt that she was indeed in God's loving sight. She remembered a similar feeling in Rishikesh when she gazed silently at the Himalayan mountains and the flowing Ganges and thought of *brahman* pervading everything.

The sounds of singing and clapping brought her back from deep absorption in *darshan,* and she smelled the heady fragrance of red roses and white jasmine flowers. "Isn't this *kirtan* singing, Govinda?" she asked, noticing several devotees dancing in ecstasy as they sang the names of Krishna. She remembered listening to *kirtan* cassettes during her pregnancies with Kris and Asha. The music had calmed her, and she had felt that the sacred sounds were spiritual nourishment for her unborn children.

"Yes, Didi, the music is *kirtan,* the devotional singing of God's holy names. To sing Krishna's name is to be in his presence, for there is no difference between Krishna and his name. We believe that calling on his name cleanses the heart of negative qualities, relieves us of suffering, and gives us happiness."

"Let us go to a quieter part of the Mandir. There is someone I want you to meet. This is a *murti* of my spiritual teacher, Swami Prabhupada. He is our beloved guru who shows us the way to God, so we give him a seat of honor in the temple. He lived as a monk in Vrindavan for many years and then, at the request of *his* guru, he traveled to America to teach Krishna's message to the world."

"Govinda, wasn't this in the 1960s? I remember my parents reading the news and talking about the crowds joining in his singing."

"Yes, Didi, many people took notice of him when George Harrison, one of the Beatles, popularized *kirtan.* 'Hare Krishna' became a household word."

"Ah!" Maitreyi said emphatically, "I remember hearing the Hare Krishna mantra in George's hit single, *My Sweet Lord.* Now I know where he learned it!"

Govinda continued, "When Swami Prabhupada returned to Vrindavan with his American disciples, the people here found it a sight to behold. Not everyone in this traditional village looked kindly on the idea that anyone—white, black, or brown, man or woman—could worship in the temple and teach from the scriptures. But Prabhupada insisted that Krishna did not care about a person's caste, nationality, or other divisions created by human beings, for these labels do not apply to the *atman,* the eternal self. Krishna is interested in the quality of our hearts."

"It is wonderful, Govinda, that Vrindaban is a global pilgrimage center and that so many are attracted to the divine as Krishna."

"Let us go outside, Didi. It is a tradition here to circumambulate the temple, and we can do that while continuing our conversation." Maitreyi and Govinda joined a line of worshipers walking slowly around the temple in a clockwise direction. Some repeated Krishna's names as they walked, while others were engrossed in quiet conversations.

"A question, Govinda," said Maitreyi. "Why does God take birth on earth?"

"Excellent question, Didi," said Govinda. "For us, God descends to earth—he becomes an avatar—for our benefit. We learn from the Bhagavadgita that whenever there is a decline in righteousness, God manifests among us to re-establish righteousness and to protect the virtuous. Krishna is known as Dina Bandhu, the friend of the weak, the downtrodden, and the poor. He shields those who have no shelter."

Radha and Krishna

"Is the relationship between Radha and Krishna an example of the love about which you speak?" asked Maitreyi.

"Yes," explained Govinda. "Her love for Krishna is unmatched in intensity and purity, as is Krishna's love for her. They are the original, divine couple. For a Vaishnava, there is no higher destination than to serve Radha and Krishna. In truth, there is no difference between them—in the Bhagavadgita, Krishna says that he is the father and mother of creation. As the supreme mother, Radha is especially dear to devotees. She embodies divine grace."

"I understand now," Maitreyi said, while nodding in agreement, "why everywhere we go in Vrindavan, people greet each other by calling out 'Radhe! (O Radha!).' She is in every temple, with Krishna right beside her. The divine feminine is central to so many Hindu traditions."

"Yes, Didi," Govinda said, happy that she understood the significance of the relationship between Radha and Krishna. "My prayer, in all humility, is to become a servant of the servant of Sri Radha. To be a devotee of Krishna and Radha is to serve all, and especially those who are poor and marginalized." By this time, they had completed their third circumambulation. Now they paused at the temple entrance for a last look at the *murti* and to receive *prasadam* (food blessed during worship) before leaving.

Maitreyi cupped her hands and received the sweetened wheat flour on a square of white paper. She reverently touched it to her forehead, recognizing it as a gift from Krishna. She took a small morsel as she and Govinda left the temple to return to the guest house. She had barely walked a few steps before she felt a thump on her shoulder, and, in the twinkling of an eye, the *prasadam* was snatched from her hand by a small brown monkey who scampered away to the neighboring rooftop.

"Did you see that?" she exclaimed. Govinda burst out laughing.

"Sorry, Didi, I forgot to warn you about our mischievous monkeys who are always on the lookout for *prasadam*. As you know, it is our custom to share *prasadam*, and today you shared yours with a little monkey."

Maitreyi joined him in laughter. "My little granddaughters would have enjoyed this sight."

"Didi, are you comfortable finding your way back to the guest house? I will return in the morning."

Maitreyi nodded, knowing that Govinda had generously spent most of his day with her and had evening responsibilities at the temple.

As Maitreyi made her way back to the guest house, she was struck by the number of women, young and old, wearing the white color of mourning, walking purposefully in small groups. This unsettled her, since it reminded her of her own widowhood. She resolved to ask Lalita at the guest house why there were so many widows in Vrindaban.

By the time she got to the guest house it was the dinner hour. Lalita invited Maitreyi to join her, since she was the only guest in residence. Maitreyi was famished and had not eaten since breakfast. After a quick wash, she took her seat with Lalita at one of the small dining tables. Ramu brought two plates with steaming rice, dal, potato curry, and rotis. The simple meal was delicious, and she enjoyed every morsel.

"Lalitaji," said Maitreyi, "I noticed groups of widows walking on the streets of Vrindaban. I have never seen so many widows in one place. Is there some reason for this?"

Lalita nodded as a sadness shadowed her face. She took her time before replying in a quiet voice. "Bahanji (sister), the reasons are painful. Most of these women came from poor families who could not support them after their husbands' deaths. Here in Vrindaban, there are several government and privately run shelters where they are given accommodation and meals. Some younger widows are able to find employment in the city, while the elderly ones live out their days in ashrams in prayer and religious practice. I was married at fifteen and lost my husband when I was forty. We had no children and had been living with his parents and brothers. After his death, I was asked to leave and made my way to Vrindaban. I was fortunate to find work at this guest house ten years ago. It is a lonely life, Bahanji, since we widows are also regarded as inauspicious and not allowed to participate in festive occasions. I have resigned myself to my fate."

Lalita fell silent, and Maitreyi was not sure what to say. Maitreyi was a widow but knew she would never have to deal with rejection and social stigmatization. She thought it was an injustice that widows were treated so poorly in a tradition that honored the divine as feminine. She recognized it as an expression of a patriarchal culture that was contradictory to religious teachings. Her thoughts returned to Swami Anantananda speaking to her of ignorance and its manifestations in social inequality. Maitreyi reached out and clutched Lalita's hand. "I am sorry, Bahanji, that you have to experience so much suffering. Let us be friends; I will not forget you." Silent tears streamed down Lalita's cheeks. It had been a long time since someone had noticed her and spoken to her with such empathy. Maitreyi retired to bed with sadness but also with gratitude for her children, her family, and her friends who would continue to be sources of comfort and support for her.

Day Two in Vrindavan

Maitreyi woke very early the next morning with the edges of a vivid dream lingering in her mind. She had been dreaming of Prem sitting in his favorite armchair in their home, sipping coffee and reading the *Los Angeles Times*. The rays of the morning sun streamed through the large bay window. It had been his morning habit to read the news and discuss items of interest with her while she was busy in the kitchen. The warm feelings that the dream evoked were replaced by an intense wave of loneliness when she awoke to the fact that it had been only a dream. When Ramu brought her morning chai, she took it downstairs and sat with Lalita, two widows sharing their loneliness.

Govinda soon came and greeted them both. He was ebullient, warm, and smiling. "Today, Didi, I want to take you to one of Krishna's favorite places on the Yamuna River." They walked together through narrow winding lanes and alleyways, passing many small and ancient temples, before arriving at the river's western bank. These temples were very different from the modern ISKCON one that she had visited the previous day. Govinda led her to a majestic tree overlooking the river.

"This *kadam* tree, Didi, is one of Krishna's favorite haunts. He loved climbing its branches, delighting in nature and playing with his friends on the riverbank. By his example, he calls us to revere, reciprocate, and enter into a personal relationship with the natural world. We should care for the earth in gratitude for all she gives us."

Maitreyi sat in quiet reflection, absorbing what it means to sit where the divine Krishna sat and look at the river where he played. She understood more clearly that the personalization of the earth is an important pathway to sustainability, whereas the objectification of the earth is a sure pathway to its destruction.

"Govinda, I can feel the spirituality of this sacred place, and I want to learn more about your own experiences with the Vaishnava tradition."

"Didi, as you may know, Krishna was my *ishtadeva* (favorite form of God) growing up, and I wanted to understand better what it meant to be His devotee. I came to Vrindaban, studied with several Vaishnava teachers, and have been living the life of a novice monk. Each day I continue to learn more about what it means to be His devotee."

"Could you share with me some of what you have learned?" she asked softly.

"I am happy to do so, Didi. Sharing spiritual wisdom is one of the ways in which we serve God. Our tradition has long understood that if we want to know God, we must begin by knowing ourselves. Once we know ourselves, we can know others, since we are all interconnected, and we can know our relationship with the divine. Hindus agree that we are the *atman,* the spiritual self that is eternal, conscious, and blissful. Yet, this eternal, blissful *atman* finds itself in a temporary and often miserable world. That is the paradox, Didi, the struggle of the human condition. That is the angst that drives our quest for something better."

The Cycles of Birth, Death, and Rebirth

"Do we have just one life to fulfill our quest for something better?" Maitreyi asked, thinking of Prem and recollecting the blessing of the priest who, at their marriage ceremony, had wished them seven lifetimes of happiness together. Her heart longed for reunion with Prem in a future birth.

"No, Didi," Govinda answered. "Each of us has been through many lives, many births, and many deaths. For us, the opposite of life is not death but rebirth. In each life we experience the fruits of choices made in previous lives and create the conditions for our future lives. This is our teaching on *karma*, emphasizing our human responsibility and the necessity for thoughtfulness about our choices."

As Govinda spoke, Maitreyi recalled the famous verse from the Bhagavadgita recited by the priest before Prem's cremation.

> As a person changing used clothing enters another that is new,
> so the dweller in the body leaves a used body and enters into
> others that are new.

Seva (Service) and Happiness

"I thought, Didi," continued Govinda, "that I could be happy by gaining the things of this world: a new house, a new toy, a better position, more respect, more power. But alas, when I found something good, it slipped through my fingers like sand. At other times it did not turn out to be as satisfying as I thought it would be, and death snatched away those I loved. Experiencing all this, I decided to seek a remedy. I learned a fundamental truth in Vrindaban: the soul can be satisfied not by the pursuit of more material goods or power but through service (*seva*). The innermost nature of every living being is to serve God and each other. When we are situated in service, we are happy. This is the paradox of our journey: if we want to be happy, we must stop trying to make ourselves happy and instead *work for the happiness of others.*"

"*Seva* is a beautiful teaching, Govinda. Prem and I had hoped to do more of this after retirement." Maitreyi could see how much Govinda loved to share his devotional life and the depth of his faith. She asked him to explain further the uniqueness of *bhakti* (love of God) as a way of loving and serving.

Govinda smiled, his voice increasing in intensity as he described the meaning of *bhakti*. "The *Bhagavata Purana* defines *bhakti* as selfless, constant love. When love has these two qualities—selflessness and continuity—it completely nourishes and satisfies the soul. *Bhakti* is a radical departure from self-interested relationships based on a desire for profit, position, and personal pleasure."

"I have seen and learned so much from you," Maitreyi said. "I am grateful for the person that you have become."

Govinda accompanied her to the guest house, and she thanked him profusely for his *seva* to her. She invited him to visit her in Los Angeles.

"If Krishna permits, I will surely come," he smiled. "Where do you plan to go next?"

"I will be traveling to Ganeshpuri in Maharashtra to learn about the divine as Shiva and the Shaiva tradition," said Maitreyi.

The following morning after an early breakfast Maitreyi sought out Lalita to say goodbye. Lalita accompanied her to the gate for her taxi to the airport. Her flight to Mumbai took two hours, after which she boarded a bus for the four-hour journey to Ganeshpuri.

Third *Tirtha*: Ganeshpuri

The Shaiva Tradition

As Maitreyi settled into her seat, she once again thought about the reverence for nature central to the Hindu tradition. She reflected on the iconography of Shiva residing in the Himalayas amidst lush and verdant vegetation. She pictured Nandi, the bull, sitting happily next to him, the snakes playfully adorning his neck and the moon shining as a jewel on his head. The Ganges River flows peacefully through Shiva's luxuriant hair, suggesting the necessity of maintaining our forests in order to prevent destructive flooding. If only, Maitreyi thought, we human beings could express this kind of sacred reverence for nature by becoming better custodians of our natural resources.

The window of her bus was open, and the gentle wind lulled a weary Maitreyi into a deep sleep.

> Prem walked to the bank of the Ganges hand in hand with Maitreyi to watch the sunset. "I'm so glad we decided to do this together," he said. "Being here fills me with a sense of self and reminds me of who we are."
>
> Maitreyi looked off into the distance and saw a small boat appear through the thick Varanasi air. A boatman waved at her as the boat approached. "Prem," she said, "Let's take a boat ride and watch the sunset together. It's the perfect way to end our pilgrimage." Prem nodded and smiled.
>
> The boat pulled up to the dock and the boatman said, "There is room for only one person, Madame; I am sorry."
>
> "Oh, that's okay, then, we'll just wait for the next..." But before she could complete her sentence, Prem got into the boat and it started pulling away without her. Prem began to disappear into the mist.

"Prem! Prem!" She cried. "Don't leave me! Prem!" Maitreyi stood alone on the dock, staring into the misty twilight.

"Prem . . . Prem . . ." Maitreyi mumbled as she felt someone shaking her shoulder. She awoke with a start to see a young woman sitting beside her and staring at her with concern. "Madame! Madame, are you alright? I think you are dreaming."

Maitreyi felt slightly disoriented and embarrassed as she positioned herself upright on her seat and secured her loose hair back into a bun at the nape of her neck. "Oh dear, yes, I am alright."

When she got into the Ganeshpuri bus early that morning, she felt reconnected to God, but now her grief and longing for her husband only grew stronger. Her calls with her children and grandchildren did not fill the void that Prem had left when he died. How she longed to hold his hand, to hear his voice.

The bus ride to Ganeshpuri was difficult, because several of the roads were unpaved. The bus jostled back and forth, and her stomach began to jostle along with it. She was also weary from travel and missed the comforts of home. The bus suddenly came to a screeching halt. Maitreyi looked at the young woman who had woken her earlier and asked, "What is going on? Why have we stopped?" She was anxious to arrive at her guest house, where she could nap and have a proper meal.

The woman stood up, took hold of the sash of her bright pink sari, and walked to the front of the bus to talk to the bus driver. When she returned she said, "Madame, there is a roadblock, and we must detour. It will be about another hour before we reach Ganeshpuri."

"Oh no!" exclaimed Maitreyi. She was tired and carsick and felt she could not bear being on the bus for much longer.

"Please, Madame, don't worry. Who are you meeting in Ganeshpuri? My name is Maya. I live in Ganeshpuri and can help you." Maya seemed genuinely concerned, and Maitreyi was touched by her generosity.

Shiva and Shakti: The Transcendent and Immanent

Maya reached across Maitreyi to open the window and said, "Did you know that Ganeshpuri is the home and resting place of the saint, Bhagavan Nityananda, affectionately known as 'Bade Baba,' or 'Big Father'?"

"No, I didn't," said Maitreyi, "I have heard of him, but Bhagavan Nityananda's history is mostly unknown to me. My husband and I had heard of the hot springs and the many Shaiva temples in the area, which is why we wanted to come." Sweat dripped down her forehead as the bus traversed the hot, rocky terrain.

Maya said, "My family is Adivasi—India's tribal people—and we Adivasi came to know of his holiness and healing power during the years when he wandered by foot from south India up to Ganeshpuri, where he was drawn to the hot springs." Maitreyi was stunned for a moment. Rarely in her academic life had she had occasion to speak with an Adivasi. They were India's "first" Indigenous people, otherwise known as "scheduled tribes," who were often discriminated against for being illiterate and destitute. Maya, however, was articulate. She continued, "Bade Baba taught most through his actions that evoked the Shaiva belief that the divine can be found in both transcendence and immanence. The divine is beyond our intellectual understanding, yet it can always be experienced as ever-present in the world."

"Ah, yes," said Maitreyi. "I have read about how Shaiva notions of the divine are expressed in the natural world and the human body as Shakti (divine female power), who travels within the subtle body, mind, and emotions to reunite with her beloved Shiva (transcendent consciousness). Their union is a metaphor for the union between the transcendent and the immanent, between God and the embodied self." Maya nodded her head, looking somewhat bemused at Maitreyi's academic response.

Their bus rumbled toward the foothills of Fire Mountain. The landscape changed from temple shops, farmland, and huts to a dense, humid jungle. Fire Mountain is a dormant volcano. It generates geothermal heat that bubbles up across the landscape as hot springs, rich with minerals, creating fertile countryside. There is a wildlife sanctuary where leopards, tigers, and deer roam freely. Banana plants, teak, *kadamba*, and coconut trees still grow there but must compete with bush burning, chopping down teak trees for fuel and trade, and longer, hotter summers. The fragile biodiversity of Ganeshpuri impacts the tribal villagers who depend on rice paddy cultivation. Industrialization, climate change, and social inequity have impoverished them. Maitreyi looked up at the landscape and reflected on humanity's common condition: ignorance of our interconnectedness, which threatens the survival of the world.

Encountering a Siddha

The bus rolled to a stop at the base of the mountain near a small food stand to make a long pit stop for lunch. Maya asked Maitreyi, "Do you mind walking over to say hello to my *guruji* (beloved teacher)? He is a Siddha—a perfected being—who lives and carries out his spiritual practices here. From the village you can sometimes see his fire burning at night as it illuminates the night sky."

After getting off the bus, Maitreyi and Maya meandered through a roughly worn path to a temple on the side of which was a small hut. Maya signaled Maitreyi to enter as she pulled aside a curtain across the door. Inside was an older man with a shock of white hair and a kind expression on his face. Maya said to him, "*Namaste*, Guruji. I have brought a friend to meet you." His smile lit up the room as he greeted them.

"*Namaste*! Welcome! Come inside!" He waved them into the hut toward a small shrine with a picture of Nityananda and a Shivalingam, an obelisk form of Lord Shiva that has its origins in the rich, long history of Shiva's divinity in India.

Maya whispered, "Many years ago, when Guruji was just a boy, Nityananda instructed him to practice yogic austerities. Guruji followed Nityananda's instructions his whole life, took vows of celibacy and poverty, and moved to Fire Mountain. Since then he has lived like a yogin (a practitioner of yoga)—mostly outside the hut during all seasons, engaged in ascetic practices such as soaking in the stream in the cold months and living off one spoon of soaked legumes per day for forty years!"

Such a life would be unbearable for many, but Guruji seemed full of joy and gratitude. Maitreyi and Maya bowed to Guruji and Nityananda, and Guruji led them outside to a stream behind the hut, where they were to bathe before approaching the shrine.

After returning to the hut, Maitreyi observed Guruji moving around quickly, sweeping, making tea, and preparing the shrine. Maitreyi was inspired by Guruji's energy and devotion to service and thought that his solitary life in the mountains threw into relief her own attachments. She watched how his actions seemed to help preserve the essence of the divine in its most natural element. Maya said, "Guruji's days are filled with meditation and keeping the stream clean for bathing—he even feeds the cats and deer. He does this for Shiva, who is both creator and creation, immanent and transcendent."

After washing up, they settled on mats in front of the shrine. Guruji approached both of them, chanting in a low voice, "*Om Namah Shivaya*," before leading them in a simple mantra that they were to chant inwardly. He explained, "When you meditate on God, say to yourself, *so'ham, hamsa,* or 'I am that,' with every breath. If you chant this regularly while rooted in your breath and focused on God, over time, you will remember that you are never separate from the divine. You will remember that the divine lives in you and *as* you. Even if you forget this mantra, it does not change the fact that you are eternally one with God."

Maitreyi's mind, as it was wont to do during meditation, drifted to Prem. Guruji's words penetrated her grief, because ever since Prem's passing she had often felt separated from God. Eventually, she allowed the repetition of the mantra to envelop her thoughts, and she fell into a rhythmic, effortless awareness of her breath and mind as they synchronized.

Guruji rang a bell, bringing Maitreyi back into an awareness of her surroundings. Time seemed to fall away, and her car sickness and fatigue vanished. She opened her eyes. A silence filled the hut and her mind.

Guruji noticed Maitreyi's white sari and gazed at her in wordless acknowledgment of her husband's death. She did not need to ask him her questions. Guruji seemed to know what her questions were before she did. He sat, pensively stroking his prayer beads, and said:

> "At the dawning of time, Brahma, the creator, could not create humans who would live symbiotically with the earth and each other. He called upon Shiva to help him with this task. Shiva encompasses all diversity and is both Great God and Great Goddess. For creation to unfold, Shiva separated into two entities—male and female (Shakti). The separation of Shiva's unified self into two beings brought about the cycle of creation. The Great Goddess, who was in substance and identity the same as Shiva, became known as Sati, 'The Real.' Once Shakti was incarnated in human form as Sati, she was subject to the same limitation as Shiva. Sati was willful and had a mind of her own. Furthermore, she was unable to remember her own divinity and indivisibility with her beloved, Shiva. From this point on, 'difference' was born in the world. The sense of individuality, difference, and separation from God are the three impurities of consciousness, which each person must transcend to attain freedom." Since we are all children of Shiva and Shakti (Sati), we have inherited this divine capacity to see and know the divine absolute that resides within all of us. However, as we transmigrate from life to life, we are subject to long bouts of self-forgetfulness, just like our divine mother and father."

Maitreyi asked, "Guruji, how can the divine become forgetful? It seems as if the divine should be all-knowing and never forget who they are."

Guruji replied, nodding, "When Shiva decided to divide himself, he purposely concealed his divinity and limited his omniscient power. Just as in the Vedas when the cosmic person, Purusha, sacrificed his own body for the birth of the world, so does Shiva sacrifice his own totality so that we may know and experience absolute freedom."

Maitreyi contemplated where she had experienced such self-limitation for the sake of others. She thought of her and Prem's decision to settle down and embrace their life as householders for the sake of their family. While she was pregnant with Kris, Prem was given the opportunity to work as an independent scholar and author, which would have brought him great inner joy and satisfaction. Instead, he opted to take a tenure track position at UCLA for the sake of their growing family. That decision had a profound impact on their lives. With much hard work and sacrifice, they both earned a good living, but Prem became prone to bouts of insomnia due to stress, and he could never fully immerse himself in his own research and writing. His plan was to put aside his own creative and intellectual work until he retired. Maitreyi shut her eyes, feeling the sting of regret and guilt.

Guruji's gaze fell on Maitreyi as he continued. He added, "Despite many incarnations of forgetfulness and separation, Sati and Shiva have never really been apart. They are always united. The whole drama of life, death, and rebirth is a part of Shiva's divine play. Like Sati, our own liberation entails remembering that we can never be separated from the source of our fullness and bliss, which is God."

Shiva and the Marginalized

"Guruji," Maya interjected, gazing down at her bare feet, "I sometimes identify with Shiva as the Dark Lord who is a bit of an outcast. I sometimes feel like that—like I'm not 'good' or 'pure' enough to engage in yoga practices or like I don't fit in at the temple. How can Shiva seem so subversive yet divine at the same time?"

Maya was alluding to the long-standing convention that those of low-caste and Adivasis are barred from entering certain temples because of their perceived "impurity." Maitreyi felt a great deal of compassion for Maya. The heartfelt question she had asked reflected how certain doctrines could be interpreted in ways that disenfranchised people.

"Shiva is all-powerful and exists beyond human binaries!" Guruji emphatically explained, "Yet, knowing of humanity's tendency toward delusion and bias, Shiva often tested people. He would frequently appear in human form as a destitute, wandering mendicant with matted hair, naked and covered in ash. Shiva was also known to hang out with a rough crowd—ghouls, social miscreants, and the seemingly 'impure.' He knew that all beings were reflections of the absolute. Through contemplation, the yogi is granted divine sight that pierces through appearances. It is to these yogis Shiva reveals his inner, resplendent nature.

"Because of Shiva's association with ghouls and social miscreants, Sati's father Daksha did not invite Shiva to his ritual ceremony to the divine. Who could imagine not inviting God to his own ceremony? But Daksha, deluded by his ego, was too concerned with outward appearances and was blind even to Shiva's brilliance.

"Yet despite Daksha's rejection and discrimination, Shiva and Sati were resolute in their union. The desire between Shiva and Sati represents the wish to grow and realize the true Self, who is forever united with the divine. However, like Daksha, people are prone to forget their own divine nature and act out of this limitation. Shiva, who is pure consciousness, exists everywhere in all people, and exclusion of anyone from the worship of the divine is caused by the same ignorance that led Daksha to exclude Sati and Shiva from his ceremony."

Guruji then anointed Maitreyi and Maya with turmeric and gave them flowers and fresh baby coconuts as *prasadam*. Maitreyi looked for a long time at the photograph of Bhagavan Nityananda, who appeared to gaze back at her. She was no longer concerned about the delay in her plans and thought this adventure might be part of God's divine play. She pressed her palms together and gave obeisance to Guruji, knowing that she would likely never see him again.

"Maitreyi," Maya asked as they returned to the bus, "you are traveling alone from the United States?"

"Yes, I am. I was supposed to come with my husband, Prem. But as you can see, he is no longer with us."

"I see that, Madame, and I am hopeful that I will be like you one day—brave and capable of doing things independently with or without a husband. Because of Bade Baba and the schools started in his name, all the village women and children in Ganeshpuri are educated. I hope to attend college someday and maybe see more of the world. You inspire me."

Guruji's lessons about the transcendence and immanence of the divine were brought to life as Maitreyi looked at the tall young woman walking ever so slightly ahead of her. Maya exuded such strength and hope despite the limitations that had been placed upon her since her birth.

While not everything Guruji said made sense to her, Maitreyi understood enough to know that to find God, she needed to cultivate her ability to see God in everything and everyone around her—especially within herself.

Maitreyi's long and arduous pilgrimage through India continued, but she felt rejuvenated after a few days in the quiet hamlet town of Ganeshpuri. Maya took Maitreyi to several Shiva temples, and Maitreyi continued to do the internal recitation of the mantra known as *japa* that Guruji had taught her, which gave her a sense of safety and inner peace. She did it for much of the seven-hour plane ride from Pune to Pondicherry, where she planned to attend the Durga Puja festival in Auroville.

Fourth *Tirtha*: Aurobindo Ashram, Auroville

The Shakta Tradition

Auroville was a *tirtha* of Maitreyi's choosing, since she had felt called to celebrate Durga, the Great Goddess, ever since she was young. Durga, as a preeminent manifestation of *shakti*, inspired and uplifted women around the world. Her followers speak of themselves as *shaktas*, worshippers of the divine as *shakti*. In the *Devi Mahatmya*, Durga did what no other god could—she saved the world from demonic destruction, wielding the power of eight gods. The story identifies the Great Goddess with ultimate reality, pure consciousness, and the infinite ground of being. Durga Puja is a celebration and a reminder that light always prevails over darkness.

Maitreyi also admired the Auroville ashram's founder, Sri Aurobindo. Aurobindo was an early twentieth-century philosopher saint involved in the anti-colonial movement in India. Like her, he had been educated outside of India. He studied at King's College, Cambridge University, UK. Upon returning to India, he became deeply conflicted about British colonization and the desecration of its four-thousand-year-old spiritual heritage. He became a freedom fighter for India's independence. While in custody for his anti-colonial activities, he had an epiphany. He left liberation politics for a contemplative life dedicated to understanding the human predicament and the nature of the unfolding cosmos. He was joined in this work by Mirra Alfassa (1878–1973), who became his early disciple and collaborator and was known as the "Mother of Pondicherry." Together they created this ashram for his disciples.

Maitreyi exited the plane in Pondicherry to a warm, balmy sea breeze. She took a deep breath and filled her lungs with the ocean air. A car was waiting for her outside the airport. "Hello, Maitreyi?" said the woman from the driver's seat.

"Yes, that's me," replied Maitreyi.

"I'm Nandita! It's so nice to finally meet you!" She stepped out of the car and embraced Maitreyi. Nandita was a guest services administrator at Auroville, and the two had been emailing for months. Nandita knew of Prem's recent passing and had been a source of unexpected support. Nandita gently but firmly gripped Maitreyi's hands and said, "I'm so happy you are here to experience Durga Puja with us. It is truly a wonderful time to celebrate Shakti."

Maitreyi looked around with wonder at Auroville as they drove into the ashram. It was getting dark, and the central temple, the Matri Mandir, was illuminated with colored lights. Crowds of people surrounded the mandir anticipating the final day of what is known as Dusshera, ten days dedicated to ten different forms of the Great Goddess. Durga Puja occurred on the tenth day and drew many people from around the community.

Maitreyi saw many pilgrims sitting in silence around the shrine. Exquisite red, pink, and yellow floral decorations adorned the raised white marble area that marked the memorial. One woman had used some of the vivid floral offerings to create an intricate mandala and intersecting geometric forms. Nandita explained, "These designs, or *yantras,* represent visual frequencies of the powers of the divine feminine."

The air was filled with the aroma of sweet rice, pineapple, and ghee—*prasadam* for Durga Puja. Maitreyi became acutely aware of her hunger as her stomach growled.

After Maitreyi dropped her bag off in her room, Nandita said, "You must be ravenous. Let's get you something to eat before visiting the contemplative heart of the ashram."

Inner Awakening and Social Responsibility

As they walked through the grounds of Auroville, Nandita said, "Sri Aurobindo saw this place as the fulfillment of the Earth-embracing, life-affirming, justice-rooted theology of Shakti. He described the Divine Mother as the 'Conscious Force that dominates all existence, one and yet so many-sided that to follow her movement is impossible.' Shakti creates and exists within and as all beings."

Maitreyi thought about Maya, the Adivasi woman she had befriended in Ganeshpuri, and asked, "How much can a theology of Shakti influence the disadvantaged? While I find spiritual richness in the idea that Shakti is the divine power that pervades all things, I sometimes feel such ideas have little practical impact on the environment and those most in need, especially marginalized women. I also see the degradation of the environment, which, like women, suffers despite the rich spiritual traditions of the world that venerate woman as earth and as mother."

Nandita nodded and said, "Shakti teachings emphasize a reverential attitude toward nature. In practice, however, the sacredness of nature has not translated into good environmental practices. Our rivers are polluted, and deforestation is growing. To honor Shakti is to practice active compassion and to care for those in need. Sri Aurobindo emphasized that our journey is to see the divine not only in oneself but in all. He taught that we must seek not just our own liberation but the liberation of all. If there were only more people like you, perhaps the world would be different."

Nandita and Maitreyi walked and continued their conversation. Nandita said, "This ashram has nurtured generations of contemplatives and a global community dedicated to inner awakening. Aurobindo's Integral Yoga posits that our path to realization is fulfilled when spiritual knowledge returns us to awareness of the divine in embodiment. It is fulfilled in responsible relationship to each other and the world. The idea that the divine is deeply immanent—organically, radically present—is foundational to Shakta theology. This is one reason why we celebrate Durga Puja."

Maitreyi, however, had seen so much social inequity. Her years as an activist had made her somewhat cynical. It was a trait that Prem frequently warned her about. She recalled a heated discussion with him many years ago when she had had a crisis of faith and refused to go to Durga Puja at their neighborhood temple:

> "Mai (mother)," as he used to call her, "Why don't you want to go to the temple with me and the children?"
>
> Maitreyi had been spending weekends volunteering at a women's shelter and was troubled after having seen so many women and children struggling to survive. "I don't know," she replied. "It all seems so detached from reality. While we wear our new clothes and fill our bellies with *prasadam*, people are going hungry. Where is their liberation in all of this?"
>
> Prem's voice grew grave. "You are quite correct about the disparity between our life and the lives of many others. Yet these festivals remind us of the nature of the divine—wise, beneficent, and ultimately compassionate. They also serve to remind us of the importance of being in joyful interrelationship with the divine. A life of service is honorable, but we must serve with joy and gratitude for all that we have been given.
>
> Perhaps by attending *puja*, more people will be inspired to exhibit these same divine qualities, just as you do already."
>
> Maitreyi agreed to attend Durga Puja that year and every year afterward.

Nandita looked at Maitreyi thoughtfully and said, "It's late and you must be tired. Tomorrow morning is the immersion of Durga's icon into the ocean in Pondicherry. Would you like to go and celebrate Durga Puja with the Shakta community?"

"Yes, I'd like that very much," said Maitreyi.

"Wonderful," said Nandita. "I'll see you in the morning."

Day Two in Auroville: The Immersion of Durga's Murti

The next morning, they boarded the bus to Pondicherry, eager to watch Durga's immersion. Maitreyi saw women gathering and fashioning flowers into mystical designs, and women performing the sacred Dhunuchi fire dance. The aroma of incense filled the air and made Maitreyi a little lightheaded, as did the sounds of rhythmic drums and music emerging from the many shrines lining the streets.

They exited the bus and approached an intricate, larger-than-life icon of Durga in a large temporary shrine. Durga stood, resplendent, bejeweled, and richly decorated with flowers. The sight transported Maitreyi into a transcendent sense of time and sacred space. The sound of the music, the scents and sights brought her into communion with the Divine Mother. Though Maitreyi was not one for crowds, she felt surprisingly at home in the center of such activity.

The icon depicted the scene in the *Devi Mahatmya* in which the goddess destroys injustice, cruelty, and negative passions. The eight-armed goddess towered above Maitreyi, with each of her hands wielding a weapon that was a gift from the gods, including a sword symbolizing sharp intellect, a discus symbolizing the world, a conch shell symbolizing the sound of the universe (OM), and a trident, symbolizing the three qualities of the world—purity, action, and inertia. She rode a large lion, at whose feet lay a demon personifying evil aspects of the human psyche. These include greed, jealousy, violence, and other human traits that cause destruction and damage to the fabric of the living world.

A group of men gathered around the base of Durga's icon and lifted it onto a large platform behind a truck. "Ah!" said Nandita, "We are about to experience *visarjana*. Durga's icon will be returned to the sacred waters of the ocean, from whose clay it was lovingly crafted."

The two women followed the procession to the beach. Maitreyi listened to the liturgy for *visarjana,* which states that the Mother of the Universe is pervasive in Her creation and not limited to any "form." Maitreyi watched the same icon of Durga that had been adorned with flowers the previous night hoisted from the truck bed onto the shoulders of several strong men. Her sari and her hair danced in the breeze as she was carried toward the ocean. A deep longing and sadness overwhelmed Maitreyi as she experienced a profound, sweet communion with the goddess descending into the water—returning to her own primordial essence.

Over a loudspeaker, a woman began chanting verses from the *Devi Mahatmya*. Maitreyi knew it well and was able to recite the chant from memory.

> To that Goddess who abides in all beings as peace:
> Salutations to Thee
> To that Goddess who abides in all beings as compassion:
> Salutations to Thee
> To that Goddess who abides in all beings as strength:
> Salutations to Thee
> To that Goddess who abides in all beings as Mother:
> Salutations to Thee

Maitreyi felt infused with the energy of the Divine Mother. She felt the cells of her body renewed as the Mother's presence manifested in her.

While they were sitting on the bus waiting to head back to the ashram, Maitreyi noticed a woman much like Maya tending to a roadside shrine in front of a tree. She watched as the woman carefully picked up garbage around the base of the tree trunk and tenderly adorned with flowers the shrine before which she knelt and bowed. Maitreyi thought again of her disagreement with Prem that one morning before Durga Puja. She recalled his words as she observed the woman honoring spirit and matter in her worship. The hymns sung during Durga Puja replayed in Maitreyi's mind as she recalled the many Durga Pujas she and Prem had attended and helped organize: "Mother, I bow to Thee again and again, destroyer of worldly sufferings, embodiment of bliss, dispenser of wisdom and devotion." She closed her eyes and saw Prem dressed in his best clothes and making offerings to Durga with Kris and Asha when they were only children. He beamed. Maitreyi savored her memories, filled with joy.

Fifth *Tirtha*: Belur Math, Kolkata

Sri Ramakrishna and Swami Vivekananda

Early the next morning, Maitreyi settled into her window seat for the two-hour IndiGo airline flight from Chennai to Kolkata.

She was looking forward to meeting Sumit again. Sumit was one of Prem's closest friends. They had known each other from their undergraduate days at Kolkata University, where they had both studied philosophy. Sumit had visited them a few times in Los Angeles and guest-lectured in some of Prem's classes. He had special expertise in the life and thought of Sri Ramakrishna and Swami Vivekananda.

Sumit was waiting for her outside the domestic terminal. He scanned the passengers as they exited and was quite shaken to see Maitreyi in her white sari. She had visibly aged and was gaunt in appearance. She looked so different from the Maitreyi he had known in Los Angeles. As he approached her, his eyes filled with tears, and he held out his arms. "Bhabi (sister-in-law), I am so sorry." They hugged in silence. Maitreyi also started crying. She had barely cried since losing Prem. She wanted to be strong for Kris and Asha. Here, in the presence of Prem's dear friend, the wall that had been holding back her tears of grief broke. Sumit led her to a nearby bench where they sat down. Several minutes passed with neither of them speaking.

He was the first to break the silence. "Bhabi, I am happy that you made this journey, as difficult as it is. I know Prem wanted to show you the city of his birth, especially the places associated with Sri Ramakrishna and Swami Vivekananda. When you called to tell me of Prem's passing, I never thought you would still want to visit."

Maitreyi said, "Prem always spoke very fondly of his college days here and shared so many of his memories with me. With a gentle smile, she added, "Being here brings me closer to him." Sumit took note of her smile. He recognized her desire to re-visit tender memories of Prem.

"Bhabi, I remember so fondly the first time Prem spoke to me about you. He said that he had met you outside the American Embassy in New Delhi. Both of you were in line to apply for student visas to the United States. He told me that he had met the girl of his dreams and would marry her. I was astonished, since Prem had never been interested in dating or marrying."

Maitreyi broke into startled laughter. "I had not heard that before. I remember our conversation that day. Prem seemed very interested in my desire to study literature at UCLA. To my surprise, his parents, soon after, contacted my family about marriage and came with Prem to visit. We met several times over the next few weeks, and I realized that I also wanted Prem to be my life partner."

"I still remember your grand wedding ceremony, Bhabi," Sumit reminisced. "I recall the colorful tents across the street and the throngs of guests. It seemed as if your entire village was in attendance. I joined Prem's *baraat* (wedding procession), with musicians and drummers as we all danced around Prem seated on his white horse. I can still see him struggling to keep his balance, since he had never ridden a horse before. The drummers came too close and the horse was startled. I had to move quickly to help the handler steady the horse. Prem, who was dancing on his saddle, then gripped the reins firmly for the rest of the procession."

Maitreyi smiled, remembering the joining of their garments as they walked around the sacred fire seven times making their vows.

Let us take the first step to become each other's nourishment
Let us take the second step to become each other's strength
Let us take the third step to become each other's wealth
Let us take the fourth step to become each other's joy
Let us take the fifth step to become each other's family
Let us take the sixth step to become each other's delight in
    every season
Let us take the seventh step to become each other's lifelong
    friend

Prem then applied a touch of vermillion on the part of her hair, signifying her new status as his wife.

"Sumit *bhai* (brother)," Maitreyi said," Prem and I honored the vows of our married life and grew deeper in love. I am so grateful that we shared those years together."

They slowly made their way to the parking lot and to Sumit's car. "Bhabi, I know you had an early start this morning. I will take you to the Belur Math Guest House so that you can get settled and have some breakfast and rest." Although the distance was only five miles, it took Sumit close to ninety minutes because of heavy and chaotic traffic. Horns blared as cars moved without signals from left to right, seeking to advance. Maitreyi held onto the seat firmly as Sumit repeatedly braked to avoid cars cutting in front of him. Strangely, no one gestured in anger or shouted at another driver. It was quite different from road rage in Los Angeles.

Belur Math was an oasis of green and calmness after the noise and congestion of city traffic. It was spread out on over forty acres of land on the west bank of the Hooghly River, a tributary of the Ganges herself. The guest house was nestled amid tall, gently swaying coconut palms and shorter banana trees with their broad green leaves. Colorful parrots flew from branch to branch squawking loudly.

"Bhabi," said Sumit, "I have a class to teach, but I will be back later this afternoon to show you around. I would like you to meet my guru, Swami Tapasyananda."

The reception area of the guest house was adorned with large, garlanded photographs of Sri Ramakrishna, Sri Sarada Devi, and Swami Vivekananda. After a light breakfast, Maitreyi retired to her room to rest. There were several colorful booklets on the small table outlining the history of Belur Math, the headquarters of the Ramakrishna Order of monks. She took several booklets to read in her room.

The Ramakrishna Order and Mission

In the booklet, Maitreyi learned that this new order of Hindu monks and nuns is based on the teachings of the sage, Sri Ramakrishna (1836–1886). It was established by his renowned disciple, Swami

Vivekananda (1863–1902). Swamiji, as devotees call him, was one of the first Hindu teachers to travel to America. He spoke at the World Parliament of Religions in Chicago in 1893. For some time after that he remained in America and, in 1894, he established the first Vedanta Society in New York. Swami Vivekananda's pioneering interreligious stance and expansive erudition led to his leaving a strong imprint on American religious history. In 1897, he returned to India, where he founded two monasteries—Belur Math in West Bengal and Mayavati in the foothills of the Himalayas—as well as the Ramakrishna Mission. Today, the Mission is the largest relief organization in India, with its headquarters at Belur Math. The Mission runs schools, orphanages, and hospitals throughout India.

According to Swamiji, selfless service to God, who exists in all beings, is a path to liberation. God is worshiped as Daridra Narayan: God in the form of the poor.

Maitreyi was especially happy to learn of the work of the Mission in education, health, and childcare. The booklet slipped from her hand as she fell into a deep sleep. She was awakened by a loud knocking on her door. It was the guesthouse doorman informing her that someone was waiting for her downstairs.

"Bhabi, I hope I did not disturb your rest," Sumit said apologetically.

"No, Sumit bhai, I had a good sleep."

"Prem and I often came for walks around Belur Math," Sumit said. "We enjoyed its peaceful atmosphere, and we would sit and have long discussions about philosophy while looking at the river and the boats sailing by. Let me show you around." Images of a youthful Prem flashed through Maitreyi's mind and she was momentarily distracted.

"Yes, yes, of course," she replied. It was a beautiful afternoon. The sunlight was soft, and the buildings were surrounded by trees, green lawns, and blooming flowers. It was easy to see why Prem would be attracted to such a place.

Exploring Belur Math

Sumit first took her to visit the room where Swami Vivekananda lived and attained *mahasamadhi* (union with God) on July 4, 1902. The room was simple and furnished with the few items used by Swamiji. It looked out on the Ganges. Maitreyi saw his clothing, footwear, and cane; she noticed his large photograph on his bed. It was a powerful experience to be so close to the living space of this towering spiritual teacher. Then she and Sumit walked over to the Swami Vivekananda Temple at the river's edge, constructed on the spot chosen by Swamiji for the cremation of his body. They stood in silence before his large marble *murti*.

Sumit took her next to the temple of Ma Sarada Devi (spouse of Sri Ramakrishna), also facing the Ganges. It was built on the spot where she was cremated in 1920. Sarada Devi guided and served the disciples of Sri Ramakrishna for twenty-four years after his passing. Devotees regard this spot as an abode of feminine divine energy.

The spiritual atmosphere of Belur Math moved Maitreyi deeply and filled her with gratitude for lives devoted to spiritual seeking and service. She could connect with the disciples of Sri Ramakrishna who had come to him looking for deeper meaning, as she was doing on this journey. Visiting the various temples constructed on cremation spots made more vivid for her the inevitability of death. Death, she understood with greater clarity, is a natural and inevitable part of life and not an aberration. Maitreyi recalled that even the *murti*s of the divine worshiped during festivals like the Durga Puja are eventually immersed in water like the ashes of our loved ones.

"Let us now walk over to the Sri Ramakrishna Temple, where we will meet my guru, Swami Tapasyananda, and attend the evening *arati* (waving of lights) ceremony," Sumit said.

Approaching the temple, Maitreyi was struck by its appearance. It almost resembled a European cathedral, but instead of steeples, it had the distinctive domes seen in many Hindu temples. Sumit explained that the temple deliberately combined the architectural styles of many different religions (Hindu, Buddhist, Christian, and Islamic).

As they entered the main hall of the temple, they heard the voices of the singing monks, some dressed in ochre and others in white robes. Instead of the traditional sounds of the harmonium to accompany the devotional singing, Maitreyi was surprised to hear the deep and rich music of the organ. The chanting was slow, meditative, and melodious. A white marble *murti* of Sri Ramakrishna, seated in *samadhi*, or absorption in God, was at the far end of the hall and the focus of the evening worship. Behind the monks, rows and rows of devotees sat. Maitreyi sat on the cool marble floor near one of the side doors. For many of these devotees, Sri Ramakrishna was not only an enlightened sage but an *avatar* (divine incarnation). The visible intensity of their devotion as they sang with the monks reminded Maitreyi of the devotees of Krishna at Vrindavan.

After the *arati*, Sumit and Maitreyi made their way to the shrine to meet Swami Tapasyananda. Sumit bowed and touched his guru's feet in reverence. He introduced Maitreyi to him as his dear friend's wife who had come on pilgrimage.

Swami Tapasyananda greeted her by saying, "Maitreyi, I welcome you to Belur Math in the names of Sri Ramakrishna and Sri Sarada Devi. May they bless your pilgrimage. Let us go over to the guesthouse for *satsangh* (spiritual conversation), where I take questions from our visitors who want to know more about this tradition."

On arriving at the guesthouse, Maitreyi and Sumit found several visitors and, together with them, sat in a semicircle at the feet of Swamiji.

Religious Pluralism and the Ramakrishna Mission

"Swamiji," asked Maitreyi. "I saw that the Sri Ramakrishna Temple uniquely incorporates the symbols of many religions. I have not seen this elsewhere. Could you explain why this is so?"

"Our pluralism," explained Swamiji, "does not stop with Hindu traditions. Sri Ramakrishna drew also from Islam and Christianity. He believed, as a direct result of his own experience, that these were all different paths to the same Reality. Hindus have revered the leaders and saints of other traditions as important spiritual figures. There is no limit to where truth can be found or how it can be realized, because ultimate reality is infinite."

"Swami Vivekananda," explained Swamiji, "was the first Hindu teacher to the Western world. When he spoke there, he cited sacred texts from both the Shaiva and the Vaishnava traditions. He quoted from the *Shiva Mahimna Stotra*":

> As the different streams having their sources in different
> places all mingle their water in the sea, so, O Lord,
> the different paths that people take through different
> tendencies, various though they appear, crooked or straight,
> all lead to Thee.

Social Service and the Ramakrishna Mission

Maitreyi, who had been listening intently, asked, "Swamiji, I have read that the Ramakrishna Mission runs schools, orphanages, and hospitals all over India. This work has truly impressed me. How does it fit into your worldview?"

"Very good question," replied Swamiji. "The motto of the Ramakrishna Mission, as authored by Swami Vivekananda, answers your question. These words are *atmano mokshartham jagat hitaya cha* (for one's own liberation and for the welfare of the world). The first two words, 'for one's own liberation,' emphasize the necessity for our individual spiritual growth. The next words, 'for the welfare of the world,' express his passionate call for us to see the religious life as finding its true expression in a life of service. The balance that Swami Vivekananda envisioned sprang from his core conviction that God exists equally in all beings. One will not find God by turning away from one's neighbors who are in need and by deafness to their cries for help."

These words resonated deeply with Maitreyi and reinforced her desire to find ways of continuing to serve others after her pilgrimage.

Swamiji closed *satsangh* and said, "If you all would like to join me tomorrow, after morning *arati*, we can cross the river to Dakshineshwar, where Sri Ramakrishna practiced *sadhanas* (spiritual disciplines). Let us conclude *satsangh* together with prayer." Swamiji then led the group in the beautiful prayer from the *Brihadaranyaka Upanishad*:

> Lead us from untruth to truth
> Lead us from darkness to light
> Lead us from death to immortality
> *Aum* Peace Peace Peace

Day Two in Kolkata: Visit to Dakshineshwar

At daybreak, with the sun just shimmering over the tranquil waters of the Ganges, Maitreyi joined the devotees who had hired a boat to go upriver to Dakshineshwar, the temple where Sri Ramakrishna served as a priest of the Goddess Kali. The boat trip itself was a serene and sacred experience. A mist rose from the river, and the only sound was the "chug, chug" of the boat's small engine. The devotees fell into a meditative silence.

After disembarking from their boat, the pilgrims first visited one of the shrines to Lord Shiva. With the help of the priest, they offered milk, which they poured over the Shivalinga. As they turned, they saw a ginger-colored cat enter into the temple, clearly drawn to the milk.

Swami Tapasyananda, who had accompanied them, proceeded to tell them a story. "You know, after Sri Ramakrishna had his first vision of the Divine Mother, he saw Her presence everywhere. While he was performing the daily *puja* at the main shrine, he took some of the food offered by the devotees and fed it to a cat, seeing the Divine Mother's presence in the cat. The devotees were offended and complained to the temple establishment. But Sri Ramakrishna said, 'I see Her in all beings. What else can I do?'"

Swami Tapasyananda then exclaimed, "Maybe this cat is a descendant of the one that Sri Ramakrishna fed!" The group laughed but then lapsed into silence, realizing that this small living being, this hungry cat, could be a living link to Sri Ramakrishna himself. Maitreyi smiled as she recalled the incident with the small monkey in Vrindaban.

Kali as Divine Mother

The group then gathered at the central temple for *darshan* of the Divine Mother in the form of Kali. This was the very same *murti* before which Sri Ramakrishna did his daily worship and poured out his heart in song. This is where he experienced Her living presence and where many of his famous dialogues with his disciples occurred.

Maitreyi gazed at the *murti* of Kali—dark skin, open mouth with white teeth and red tongue, three piercing eyes, multiple arms, her neck encircled with a garland of skulls, standing on the chest of the supine Shiva.

"Swamiji," she asked, " from childhood I have been familiar with the *murti* of Mother Kali. Her appearance is quite fierce. Yet, I have read that Sri Ramakrishna revered her as the gentle and loving Divine Mother. I would love to get your thoughts on this paradox."

Swami Tapasyananda nodded in acknowledgment of Maitreyi's comment and said, "The Divine Mother is beyond all form and all ability of the finite mind to comprehend. She appears fierce in this image because she is protecting us from our negative tendencies. Kali is a purifier, taking all impurity upon herself. When Sri Ramakrishna had his experience of Kali, he saw her as a limitless, infinite, effulgent Ocean of Consciousness. He experienced her as a universal mother of infinite and tender love."

"Did Sri Ramakrishna remain a devotee of Kali throughout his life?" Maitreyi asked.

"Yes," said Swamiji. "He practiced many spiritual disciplines but saw the forms he experienced as forms of the Divine Mother. He taught that the eternal *brahman* is the same as the Divine Mother. Kali and *brahman*, for Ramakrishna, are one."

With these words, Swamiji gestured toward the adjacent small room, which had been used by Sri Ramakrishna, and invited the group to enter and sit in silence for a few minutes.

The Four Yogas

Later that evening, after supper, the devotees reassembled for another *satsangh* with Swamiji. Maitreyi felt revitalized and wanted to learn more. She asked the first question. "Swamiji, I have been learning on my pilgrimage of the many paths to liberation taught in the Hindu traditions. I learned about the paths of wisdom, loving devotion, and meditation. What is the path recommended by Sri Ramakrishna and Swami Vivekananda?"

Swami Tapasyananda replied, "Perhaps Sri Ramakrishna's most famous Bengali saying is *yato mat tato path*. 'Each religion is a path to the same goal.' We believe this is his most important message to the world: that there is no point in fighting about religion. Religions should coexist peacefully. We should all learn from one another how to know God better in many ways and forms. As the *Rig Veda* says: 'Reality is one; the wise speak of it in many ways.'"

"Can you elaborate further on the different paths, Swamiji?" asked Maitreyi eagerly. Swamiji said, "Among the major paths, or yogas, are *jnana yoga*, or knowledge of *brahman*, and *bhakti yoga*, or loving devotion to God. There is also the royal path or *raja yoga*, which consists of meditation, or *dhyana*, the process of calming the waves of the mind to know one's true Self." He continued, "Then there is the path of selfless service, or *seva*, known as *karma yoga*, in which we live a life dedicated to the well-being of all. We worship God by serving all living beings. None of these paths, in practice, is mutually exclusive. They all interpenetrate and flow through one another."

"We are many human beings," Swamiji concluded, "practicing many traditions and holding many worldviews. But we are also one family. The *Maha Upanishad* teaches us that *vasudhaiva kutumbakam*—the world is one family. We must learn to appreciate the truth and the value of the diverse views and ways of life of others."

Swamiji clasped his hands together prayerfully and inclined his head forward, signaling that the *satsangh* was over. He quietly left the guest house. Maitreyi and the other devotees sat for a while in contemplative silence before returning to their rooms.

Maitreyi's Realization

Maitreyi stepped out into the jasmine-perfumed night air for a walk along the Ganges. It was a starry night with a full moon, and the river flowed silently. A cacophony of crickets was the only sound. She experienced a deep inward stillness and oneness with the world. She was overcome with emotion as tears streamed down her cheeks. She saw herself and all things clothed in divinity. God was present everywhere, and creation rested in God. All of nature was suffused with a divine love that tenderly embraced her. She felt her own heart expanding in an all-encompassing love. Gratitude coursed through her with the realization that she had found what she had been seeking through this pilgrimage—a transformed way of seeing that brought new purpose and joy to her life. As she closed her eyes and breathed deeply, Prem's radiantly smiling face appeared in her mind. It was as if he had also participated in her realization of this world as pervaded by the divine. Her pilgrimage had blessed him too and was transforming her grief into loving gratitude.

Maitreyi's journey had come to an end. The challenges of travel, change of place, and diet had taken their toll on her body. At the same time, she was deeply fulfilled; she had completed her pilgrimage. She was grateful for the love so generously expressed by her teachers, friends, and guides. It was a love given unreservedly, a wisdom shared without expectations. She would continue to reflect on what she had learned, grateful for the spiritual transformation that was now under way.

Kindred Spirits

A RETELLING OF INDIGENOUS SACRED STORIES

Kindred Spirits

INTRODUCTION

There are more than five hundred and seventy Indigenous nations recognized in the United States today. Yet even with this large number of tribes and our different traditions and sacred histories, we continue to share deep spiritual roots. All our early ancestors imparted a respect and deep reverence for this earth and for all beings. Over our many millennia on this land—even in the face of adversity and injustice—we have continued our care for the natural world and continue to look for ways of maintaining and ensuring a healthy and sustainable earth for future generations. We seek to continue a healthy and ongoing creation.

We are created of the elements of our cosmos, earth, and waters. We share this with the rest of humankind and with non-human lives. The first lessons passed on by the Elders has to do with living together in peace and as caretakers of everything in this world that has life, from beneath the earth to the world above. This is what it means to live as part of the sacred and compassionate mystery of creation. It is a guiding principle that comes to us from our ancestors and is what unites us with all other Indigenous cultures here on our continent and with Indigenous peoples throughout the world. This understanding remains universal to all traditional Indigenous peoples and is how we ground ourselves as individuals and in community with our nations. It is more important in our fragmented and dangerous time than it has ever been before.

Our own spiritual traditions and sacred stories, as well as the journals of the early European invaders, comment in detail on the profound beauty and richness of our forests and fields, our abundance of food crops, our earthen structures that date back thousands of years, and our care for one another, the land, and even the newcomers.

As with all people, we have our origin stories, starting with the creation of the cosmos and then of everything in it. The stories reveal the sacred law and ethos that have been an integral part of the natural world from the beginning. For Indigenous peoples, human beings are humble lives in the immense web of creation.

Our purpose here is not to document our ceremonial traditions or describe our medicine people's healing arts, but rather to recount some of the key stories of our collective ancestors and so tell of how we hold this planet and every living thing on it as a sacred being in itself.

In many origin stories, human beings are the last to be created. We have survived with the help of animals and plants, which we see as being like ourselves, as intelligent persons. Knowing our place in creation, we embrace all other forms of life—and even what may be considered inanimate—with respect and reverence.

OLD GRANDMOTHER

Many years ago when I was still a boy, I would go down to the small cabin in the bottoms where the woman we all called Old Grandmother lived. On days when she felt like talking she would plant a red pole in the rich earth near her garden. The pole stood straight and tall, ringed by grasses and colorful wildflowers. At the top of the pole there was a flag with beads, ribbons, and horsehair that rippled in the valley breeze. Eager to hear her words, we would be on the lookout for the flag. When we saw it, we would rush through our chores in order to run down the hill and leap over the creek to get to her cabin, while older folks would slowly walk the red dusty road to her porch where she often sat and watched the world around her. In my memory, the grasses remain green—even under the snow, because Seeing Glass Creek ran past her place year-round on its way to Bear River.

Most days a great tortoise would make a path through the grasses, moving them aside as it slowly went forward. Sometimes an older tortoise would also appear. Soft mosses like the ones on the shady side of the creek grew on its back. I always greeted the two tortoises when I arrived. Old Grandmother watched me from her sagging porch, approving of my greetings to her friends.

She sat on the willow chair my Papa had made for her. Her legs were skinny as a cricket's, and she kept her skirt smoothed across her bony knees. Although her kind face revealed early years of hard times, her bright eyes held a radiant smile. All of us—young and old—were eager to hear what she might say.

She spoke about other Native people she had met in her life and the many stories they had told her during her years of traveling the country by wagon and train. Some of her journeys took place during the Great Depression, a time of a devastating drought in the Great Plains caused by the destruction of trees and natural grasses. She traveled during "the times when mothers cried," as we called the boarding school days, and cared for the many children on trains bound for schools far from home. Most could not speak with one another, because they had different languages, but in their hearts they were all badly hurting. Many were still too young to be without the milk of their mothers. Some, seeing a woman who looked like they did, would hold her tight and close as if she were a relative. "We **are** all relatives," *she told us. Their sorrow was her sorrow.*

Grandmother had had the same experience, but at the time none of us knew this. Sometime later, my father told me that that when she was a young child she had been taken to boarding school but she later returned to the Carlisle School as a teacher. As a teacher she had students write about the forbidden: their lives before all the stories other teachers tried to erase. She wanted the students to preserve their heritage, their identity, their stories, their people. She wanted to give them back their cultural traditions. Like their languages, all these things were too important to lose.

Later in her life she wrote books about Indian lives. For a long time she was a reporter.

Sitting by the curious tortoise near her porch, I took in all she said to us. Her words and the visions they created in my heart and my mind informed my own life journey of learning, listening to others, and looking for works and people who might help unbury our histories.

BEGINNINGS

Every day is a god, each day is a god
and holiness holds forth in time.
—*Annie Dillarld,* Holy the Firm

Down in the small cabin where our town Grandmother lived and worked, she had a wealth of knowledge and happiness dwelling within her. She lived in her words and actions. They defined her. Of course I was young when I first saw the red pole and went to listen to her, but even then I saw her inner self as she spoke of our Indigenous ways of life and their connection to the spiritual world. She never called it "religion"; the term she used was "spiritual." She lived in her songs as she gardened, and she was the Elder who greeted each morning with prayers, with tobacco or a meal offered to the four directions, and speaking with our words I almost understood. One day she spoke to all of us about the creation of our worlds—not only ours or the people we come from, but those of many nations:

I have been thinking of how to talk about this sacred world. There are so many of us Native peoples, each with our own stories and traditions. Each tribe has its versions of the creation. A people's understanding of their beginning derives from something that has been told and trusted, as with the biblical versions. It also comes from the land on which a people live. Tribal peoples come all over the world, from snow-covered mountains or from deserts blooming after spring rain. Many dwell in the far north, stepping carefully across the ice floes. Others live in rain forests nourished by clouds and the drops of water dripping leaf to leaf and eventually creating flowing waters. Others live on ocean islands to which they sailed from other lands, and still others in lake country or on the edges of the largest river in this part of our continent.

I've heard many origin stories. In all of them, even the Christian beginnings, all was at first darkness, all emptiness. One or more mysterious creators used words, songs, or thoughts to bring light to the darkness, to settle the empty universe with wondrous shining stars and with planets. The sun and moon were set in place, and there was a soft rattling sound as of seeds shaken inside a gourd. That was the first heartbeat of life. In these and many other ways, the earth, its waters, and all life forms were created in the Time Before Time and, even now, these all remain a mystery.

On this particular day, Old Grandmother she said that only one book of the Mayans wasn't burned by the Spanish invaders. That book still exists. It is known as the Popul Vuh, *which means, "The Book of the People."*

Their written words tell us that the Mayan people existed as a community, and to this day, they understand themselves not as only single individuals but as a part of the whole, as "We."

For ancient Mayans, there were two creator spirits, The Maker and The Feathered Serpent. Putting their minds together and thinking hard, these two spirits imagined everything into being. They created the sun, the moon, and the stars. Together they thought up the earth, our mother, her many waters of life, and the growing plants. Just think what fun it must have been to imagine the animal people. Try imagining something like a giraffe! Even the insects, the reptiles, and the great flying birds that took to the air all came from the spirits' imagination.

The last creation of all was those of us who walk the earth on two legs. The others who were already here took pity on us. We needed them in order to survive. They nurtured and cared for us and taught us everything we know. They offered themselves as food. They loved and cared for us—and what strange beings we must have seemed to them.

She laughed as she said this, and her laughter was like the sunlight, sparkling as the beads she wore. I realized that her inner radiance and joy came from her fulfilling life. I was grateful to hear the stories of creation because we'd just been taught in school that there was one way—only one, and no more.

Old Grandmother wanted us to remember the Feathered Serpent because, as I later learned, it is a constellation most Indigenous people across the world recognize. It not only lives in the night sky but it also inhabits sacred places on land.

According to the Popul Vuh, the Mayans were much like our people, water travelers who lived near one another. It is thought that, after being attacked by Spaniards, several Mayans settled in Florida and shared their knowledge with us. Archeological evidence found there points clearly to Mayan influence. Northern peoples also created animal-shaped earth mounds. Their influence may have been how we knew to create an immense city with a pyramid larger than any in the Americas.

Old Grandmother shifted in her chair remembering something, then began speaking:

The oldest of our kin in Australia also have many tribes. They too acknowledge the world around them as alive, but their first world was dry and flat, with no mountains, no water, not a single tree. One day the earth moved. Then it moved even more. Soon the Rainbow Serpent pushed herself up from under the dry ground. She was a large, beautiful creature, a shining rainbow. As she moved, she formed gorges in the land. Feeling lonely for her own kind, she went searching. Soon the gorges she left behind became filled with water that streamed from one gorge to another. Ridges and mountains came into being as she journeyed. Trees, brush, and ancient grasses began to grow, their roots soaking up the sacred waters flowing where she had passed. In her loneliness she called out for others like herself. Instead, different animals appeared, some with fins to swim through the coursing waters, other with wings that took them to the sky. Four-legged creatures appeared, grazing on the lush grasses. She made rules that her sacred creations were to obey. Those who obeyed became humans. Others became the strong red mountains, the land, and many amazing caves that people later used for art and stories.

After a time, the exhausted Rainbow Serpent curled into a spiral under a large body of water and went back to sleep. She has lived there and will continue stay there until it is time to rise again. She is called the God of Water, but many believe she created all things in the universe. She gave to every life and all the features of earth their own songs. Theirs is a world of songs, and these songs have become a map of their continent.

Even here, in our own lands, each place has a song or a story. This is one reason why the land is our teacher. We learn from observing and listening to each part of the land around us. It has always been our guide.

What Old Grandmother said was true and worth contemplating. To observe and know the land around us is the first step toward a true understanding of it. It was the beginning of an intelligent science that came from observation. By studying the behavior of plants and animals that helped us, we have learned that each one has a spirit, its own knowledge, and the ability to communicate. These spirits speak with one another and would also speak with us if only we could listen and speak with them. Many accounts tell of such communication, even with stones.

I had been taught in school that our continent was formed as a result of geologic plate movements that caused great shifts, with water trading places with the land. Enormous turtles swam through inland oceans, and birds resembled flying reptiles filled the skies.

Old Grandmother then spoke to us of our ancestors.

The oldest people I know are still too young to understand all that our earliest ancestors originally said or passed down. Our songs are older than our singers. Still, we know them. When settlers forced us to leave our homelands, much was forgotten in the chaos and onslaught of violence and numerous wars against us. We somehow survived the first times of "Indian-hating" during which Europeans fought even each other for our lands, which for us were spirit-inhabited, but for them were merely "property." They never seemed to have time for peace, and then even the peace we once had with each other no longer existed. We ourselves broke our original laws when we had to trade animal furs and skins for weapons in order to survive.

Many stories changed with this terrible loss, yet each song is still the living breath of its singer. It comes from the heart and is shared with reverence and love. Most of the ancient songs and prayers we still have are of this earth and its incredible brilliance. They are a reminder of our human place and our responsibility for creation. Even our personal songs are not for our being only, but are for every being as part our sacred journey to benefit all. We live now in a time when it is particularly important that we and all future generations continue to take care of The Great Holy.

Old Grandmother then went on to tell us of the Indigenous people of our own continent, tribes dwelling along different parts of the large arteries of water traveling down the continent.

There have been two principal origin stories telling of how humans arrived on the surface of the earth. For tribes living in the Northeastern regions of the continent, the Anishinaabe and Haudenosaunee, the first world consisted of a boundless sea of water alive with cloudlight by day and paths of light following the moon at night. From an opening in the clouds, a sky-dwelling woman came down to earth, falling through the air toward the water. She was saved by geese who caught her and carried her to a safe landing on the back of the Water Turtle called Earth and for us in Native America, Turtle Island.

Hearing this, Old Grandmother's tortoise came closer. I knew the tortoise had been listening to her words and understood her. It wasn't the first time this had happened. Once, as it was leaving through her gate, she warned the tortoise of the dogs. Immediately it stopped, turned around, and came back to the safety of her home.

Old Grandmother continued with her story about Sky Woman.

The Sky Woman carried seeds for planting a green, forested world. But there was a problem. On Turtle's back there was no earth. What was Sky Woman to do? The water animals held a conference. All of them wanted to help. After arguing over who was most fit, Beaver plunged into the depths but came back with no precious soil. Smooth-furred Fisher also had no success. Marten returned empty handed, saying that the water was too deep. Loon remained under water for a long time, then came up gasping for air; it had been too dark to see, he said. All the water animals had hoped to fill her need. Knowing the ways of water, none blamed the others. They all cared only about how they could help this mother of humans.

Finally, the modest Muskrat, so quiet and humble, said he would try. He dove in and brought up mud and earth. Soon the creation of the realm of plants was set into motion. With Sky Woman's dancing, the world on turtle's back began to grow green and forested. Nesting birds arrived, and deer approached to graze on the new grasses.

In the Haudenosaunee versions of this story, Sky Woman gives birth to twins. According to an Anishinaabe version, Sky Woman had a son, half man, half spirit, who was able to change into different beings. He and Wolf became traveling companions. Together they walked the earth, learning from plants and animals. The natural world became their teacher, imparting wisdom about harmony and balance.

Indigenous people in another part of the continent had a different origin story. Native tribes dwelling in the Southeast and Southwest lived in caves along the shores of marshland or the sacred waters of Blue Lake. Their origin story begins with human beings living underground in the dark, wet womb of earth. From darkness they could see the brilliant, hypnotic starlight of the night skies and the sunlit days above. Fascinated, they climbed toward the light. When they emerged and studied the surface world, they moved into caves and safe ledges above the Mississippi River, which they named Missa Sipokna, the Old Person.

Like the human beings in other Indigenous origin stories, they were aided by animals and even insects. The humble spider helped. When it grew cold and others tried to help, it was meek Grandmother Spider who succeeded. She walked across the surface of the water to an island where a lightning-struck tree was burning. Using her ability to weave, she made a basket so that she could carry a burning coal across the water. On her back she brought fire to the people who needed it for warmth and cooking. She is venerated still by many tribes for her abilities, even in the area of medicine. With her eight legs and the shining thread that comes from her body, she is a brilliant creator and teacher. Some nations call her the Creator Goddess, the woman who taught. It is often considered a blessing to have a house or kitchen spider. Out of respect, an earthen mound was created in her honor. It's an example of our ancient mound art.

Stories like these tell of how the Animal Persons care for us and how we care equally for them, the walkers and flyers in our lives. We have had agreements with them. We have had treaties with them. Traditionally minded Indigenous peoples continue to understand that intelligent lives around us are part of the same creation to which we belong. Through their actions they have taught us humility and love.

In my dreams I glimpsed ancestors from the early world in tall skin boots that protected them from thorns and thistles in the thick forests. I dreamed of our time in the Black Prairie, the place where light comes not just from the sky but also from the ground where glow-worms answer the stars. When we lived there, we made friends with the Grandmother animals to keep them from walking across us. I saw night-shining mushrooms and flowers and dreamed of making canoes by carving and burning them into shape, and I also saw the flatboats that carried our breed of horses. I dreamed one night of beautiful music that had never before been heard on earth. These dreams came from the old ones.

From the various origin stories Grandmother told I learned about the beginning of the universe and human existence. These stories came alive in my sleep, but I remember them in my blood and marrow. I know them in my heart.

From earliest times, as Old Grandmother said, people from other backgrounds have joined us on our good red road to protect the lands and the living creations upon them. Over time we have all learned the same lessons: We are part of creation. We are this earth.

> *We forget and we consider ourselves superior, but we are after all a mere part of the Creation. And we must continue to understand where we are.*

We stand between the mountain and the ant, somewhere and only there, as part of the Creation.

—*Oren Lyons (Onondaga),*
United Nations Human Rights Commission

The mountains,
I become part of it.
The herbs, the fir tree,
I become part of it
The morning mists, the clouds, the gathering waters,
I become part of it.
The wilderness, the dew drops, the pollen,
I become part of it.

—*Navajo Chant*

THE LIVING SKY

Every day was as a beginning of some new thing
and every evening ended
with the glow of the next day's dawn.

—*Inuit (Arctic) Poem*

One day when I saw the flag flying on the red pole I ran down the hill to Old Grandmother's. I arrived after the two land turtles had begun to walk away.

I had thought often about Old Grandmother and her words. What she told us conveyed the important qualities of humility and the mysteries of creation, but also, I felt the greatness of the immense and breathing universe.

Our earth is only a small planet in the tail of the Milky Way. It is easy to forget how small we are. Old Grandmother had mentioned our being enchanted by the sky world when we lived inside the dark earth.

On this day, Old Grandmother spoke about sky beings. She wore her silver braids wrapped around her head in the way of our Elders, and she'd wrapped herself in a soft white shawl to warm her arms as a cool breeze began to rise.

Having told us stories about the universe and its creation, she turned now to how, from ancient times, Indigenous traditions have understood the sky and the stars.

We have always been practical and intelligent. Some believe we first arrived on this continent thousands of years ago by crossing the Bering Strait on a land mass called the Bering Land Bridge. Evidence indicates that there were many migrations. With our canoes and sky knowledge, we could easily have come by sea. Today, in the far North, Alaskan Natives continue to have reunions with their Siberian relatives, sharing words and dances.

The First People learned about the sky long ago and used this knowledge to travel oceans and riverways. The constellations allowed Polynesians to find this continent half a century before Europeans arrived. Vikings had already left instruments behind that told of their early presence here. Chinese cartographers made a perfect map of our continent even before that time. All these things happened before Europeans arrived. People of our Southeastern nations traveled across the Gulf along with the Mayans.

While we were using the sky to navigate, Europeans still had to find their way back to land by following caged birds they would release. Lost on their long journey, when they reached our continent, they believed it was India.

In the many millennia of our existence we accumulated knowledge not only about the sky we could see but also about the cosmos and about the earth, and we passed that knowledge on to our young. We were always concerned with sustaining a healthy environment for future generations. We fostered equality and friendly trade between nations.

In contrast, Europeans were creating new forms of warfare and powerful weapons to conquer other lands, take resources from newly found continents, and enslave the people they found living there. I understood from history books I read that this was true, that they had no history of peaceful times.

I lay back, listening to Old Grandmother and looking up at the late afternoon sky. It was clear enough to view the first star of evening. I wondered if I could ever learn astronomy and how it was that we traveled in those times.

We live in between sky and earth. The sky tells us much about earth because in every culture there is a relationship between the two. In Indigenous cultures, stars and planets are named after the lives around our Indigenous lands or in our stories. We honor the stars as living beings. After all, we are made of star dust, so we offer the moving night sky our gratitude.

One simple connection that is easily seen is the way the moon governs the waters of oceans and even our own inner waters. Tides move with the cycles of moon, but in the seventeenth century even Galileo was still claiming that the moon had nothing to do with the tides.

If you learn the constellations you will never be lost. They are our map for traveling, planting, and social events. And the North Star is our constant.

For the Northeastern people, the Anishinaabe and Haudenosaunee, the sky reflects the earth. Grandfather (Chomis) Chief Dominique Rankin, Hereditary Chief from the Algonquin First Nation tells of how they see the sky in ways useful to inner human growth. The heartfelt connection between sky and people is expressed in these words:

> The stars are our ancestors. We look at the beauty of night sky and see our connection with them. Grandmother Moon is there with the Wolf who carries the feelings in our hearts up the mountain to sing away our painful emotions.
>
> The Sky also tells us the weather by the height of clouds or a halo around the moon. In early fall, summer weather

> often returns briefly for a time. Some call it "Indian Summer." We are a nomadic people, and this weather tells us it is time to begin our journey home to prepare for winter.
>
> Grandfather Sun helps; if he is hidden by mist or fog, we prepare for strong winds and stay away from lakes or rivers.
>
> Before spring, the snow begins to melt and newborn beavers tell us the sweet season is coming. As the snow melts, the land again turns green, and when the sky clears, it is time for us to celebrate. We have a large spring feast to thank Mother Earth and the Sun's light for their gifts to us. This feast reminds us to have gratitude for nature's gifts and to care for the environment.
>
> Stars are reference points in life. We wish to become more conscious of them. Each day, the stars help us in our human journey.

As he said, the cosmos offers help for our human becoming.

Over many centuries Indigenous sky watchers studied the universe. The Navajo knew that when one of the constellations, The Feather, touched the horizon, creatures would come out of hibernation. The stink bug came first, then the four-legged animals. With the First Thunders, there is a celebration.

The Skidi Pawnee were once considered to be the most intelligent astronomers. They learned from the stars how to structure daily life. Their plan for the Council of Chiefs was inspired by the ring of stars now called The Pleiades.

The people who plant see the Pleiades as seeds whose appearance is a reminder that it is time to plant or harvest. They are also a marker in social life as the time for traditional dances such as The Green Corn Ceremony. For those in Pueblo villages, the Pleiades are a time for starting the all-season Corn Dances that take place throughout the entire growing season. There is a logical reason why the Pleiades are called Planter. The Pueblo dancers are barefoot as they spin and leap in dry heat to offer their human energy to the corn and other plants. For this work, this offering, healthy plants feed the people in abundance as a returned gift.

The Skidi Pawnee regarded the North Star as a planet whose role was to oversee the relationship between humans and animals. Animals would relay to the North Star God, Tirawahat, anything humans did that needed to be revealed and changed. Tirawahat was also the name for a great bison. Its black fur was the dark night sky that revealed stars and constellations like flakes of snow against its hide. It was part of the Mystery of Creation for the Buffalo People, Native Americans who relied on buffalo for sustenance and survived because of them. Some Plains nations saw all the constellations together as one buffalo, with each cluster of stars being a different body part. The bison was their God, deeply sacred for those called "People of the Buffalo."

Most Pawnee households kept sacred star bundles to remind them of the meanings of night sky. Their villages and homes, like ours, were laid out by the patterns in the sky. This helped people stay in balance with the rest of creation, a desired state of being.

The lives of the people in these communities changed when they were forced to give up their lands to settlers. Like others, they disappeared into Oklahoma, then called "Indian Territory." They suffered the loss not only of their traditional surroundings, the intimate ecology, but also of their children, who were captured and sent to boarding schools to become assimilated and Americanized. Most were young and forgot their language and the knowledge embedded in it. After life in the schools, they were no longer their own people. Few returned home.

The Milky Way lies stretched out on its back,
making a humming sound.

From the door of my house I recognize in the distance
Nahut, the stick used to beat Coyote, and Kashlapish,
the ringing stones. I look up.
Look: Antares is rising.
Altair is rising. The Milky Way,
Venus is rising.

—*A Pawnee Song*

The Southeastern people were known as expert astronomers. Over thousands of years, they traveled waters and inland rivers guided by the sky. Most importantly, their sky knowledge added scientific and mathematical data to the measurements of the constellations as well as to the architectural designs used for building earth structures and mounds that remained undamaged for centuries. These were constructed between 1 CE and 400 CE, long before warring invaders arrived, and before we were people of two minds, one Indigenous and one of Western ways.

I sat straight up, shaken by this information. To this day I think of the moving, breathing sky and hear Old Grandmother's voice speaking about our people. I never doubted that the sky was the pulse of life and part of the creation. I understood the pain of stolen children unable to go home to the people they came from, but I listened to her words with fascination as she spoke of the built creations I'd actually seen with my own eyes. As she spoke, I saw how our constellations reflected what lived with us. The clusters of stars, even the earth works, all named for our world: alligator, cougar, spider, the plants, two entire worlds joined with our own. One above. One below. And we humans in between.

We watched the movements of shining bodies of planets, cycles of the moon and the Milky Way. From ancestral times we celebrated the equinox, solstice, and constellations. Indigenous people studied sky beings that traveled from horizon to horizon.

The Great Serpent is far more important than I indicated when I was speaking about the creation of the universe. It is a large constellation known across the entire world, the most obvious curve of stars stretching across darkness, a holy being in almost all Indigenous lives. Its shining red eye is sometimes called Antares. But as a serpent it has horns like an elk, a curved body, and a coiled tail. Its form is depicted in ancient rock paintings and on walls in Chaco Canyon. Its likeness is carved into the ancient trees of California, and even now the Pueblo dancers in New Mexico wear the image of the Serpent on their regalia and clothing. We all recognize this constellation because in our eyes it is the most obvious.

For Mayans it may be the Feathered Serpent Creator God I mentioned in talking about origin stories, and it is similar to the Rainbow Serpent of Australia. On that continent its image is painted on cave walls.

Whether they see snakes as objects of reverence or fear, all Indigenous peoples consider them important. The Hopi still have snake dances, which are now closed to all outsiders, as is the case with certain ceremonial practices of other nations.

With their shining scales, snakes are the beautiful guardians of waters. They are often found near the stones and grasses by watering holes. In early Europe they were associated with healers and healing, as evidenced by use of the caduceus, the image of a staff with two snakes on insignia symbolizing medicine. Moses in the Bible also turned an ordinary walking stick into a snake that healed those who looked at it.

Because they shed their skin, growing and renewing themselves each lunar—sometimes solar—year, snakes emerge fresh and shining, leaving behind perfect skin and even perfect eyes.

In the deserts of the far South and Southwest the sidewinder, a type of rattlesnake, is seen by Native Americans as symbolizing agility, resilience, and the ability to survive in harsh conditions—like the Indigenous people themselves. The thirteen-hundred-foot-long Serpent Mound in Ohio built by them more than two thousand years ago is recognized as the largest serpent effigy in the world.

All people recognize the Milky Way, that glowing spiral in the darkness of night. People of the Desani Nation in Central America view the entire sky as a single image. For them it is the image of a brain. The star-filled sky is considered a rational mind, a thinking brain. The line of light that is the Milky Way separates the two hemispheres.

For most other Indigenous peoples it is the path on which spirits journey after death to the next world. For the Anishinaabe and Southeastern nations, the spiral galaxy leads us to the village where souls live. For our Chickasaw people another constellation—The Great Hand—is also viewed as important in the time of passing from life to what is next. This constellation is not hard to see. The wrist is what Europeans call Orion's Belt. As the hand moves west it meets our human souls at the horizon and lifts them gently up to the spiral pathway. This care and gentleness at the end of life is a tender indicator of our people's depth of feeling for those who are gone.

Old Grandmother still had much to say, and it was growing dark. I wanted to stay and watch the sky change as I listened. I could see the hand. It was easy to see. Then I glanced across from where I was sitting and saw my father, who had arrived to walk me home in the dark, but I noticed that he was also listening. We both stayed. Later that night we went out together to look at the sky.

On one occasion, Old Grandmother related the story of Fisher's mission in the sky as told by the Anishinaabe peoples of the Great Lakes.

One spring no birds appeared. A competition was held to determine who among the animals would investigate their disappearance through a hole in the sky. Bear wanted to climb a tall cedar but was too big. Porcupine was too timid. Then Fisher volunteered. He was able to climb to the top of a tree where spindly limbs allowed him to leap into the cloud world. There he found an angry cloud spirit holding the birds captive. Fisher began to spin his tail. This broke up the clouds. Soon the opening allowed the birds to return to earth. This made the cloud spirit angry and it shot an arrow at Fisher. Fisher was releasing more birds while trying to evade the arrows. Unfortunately, he was hit, and he fell to his death. The other animals and birds gathered around his body to honor him. Great Spirit, watching from above, reached down to earth and picked up nine stones to throw into the sky. For his bravery and courage, the Fisher constellation was created. It is now called the Big Dipper.

The amazing effigy mounds created by Indigenous people seem to be a written language used by humans to speak to the universe.

Poverty Point in Louisiana is the oldest known mound creation. Constructed before 1600 BCE, the mound was first uncovered in the nineteenth century, but it was not until a hundred years later that its amazing shape—that of an Eagle—was noticed when a small plane flew over the site. The design can be seen only from the sky, and the mystery of its creation rivals that of the Nazca lines in Peru.

Earthworks connect sky and land, but the Great Serpent Mound, which was mentioned earlier, directly connects to the constellation with curves that relate to set points of the moon. The head of the serpent aligns with the sunset at the summer solstice, and the tail points to winter. In this way it has cosmological connections.

The sacred architecture of most earthworks is based on alignments of the constellations. Monks Mound, a pyramid in Illinois constructed by Native Americans known as the Mississippians, is the largest earthwork in America. The mound was part of a then thriving city, Cahokia. The top of the pyramid was for astronomer priests and not for kings, as Europeans coming from feudal cultures believed. Although the city was built on a floodplain where several rivers meet, it withstood major flooding as well as the Great New Madrid earthquake of 1064 and many violent storms.

Built by ancestors of the Southeastern nations, Cahokia at its peak in the twelfth century CE had a population larger than that of Paris or London. Travelers were guided there by markings on trees, paths, and stone walls along rivers. Nations from the entire continent gathered in Cahokia for ceremonies, drama, dance, copper work classes, art, and trade, but most importantly for the exchange of knowledge.

Cities and villages were created in relation to the shape of the measured cosmos. But for me, what was most important was that the people were egalitarian; all were equal.

As for us who dwell between earth and sky, we feel the power of both worlds. We express that energy and beauty in our work. We may do it through art, poetry, prayer, or singing. We call this part of the good red road, the path of life. Along this road, we have learned the sacred realms our ancestors passed down that show us how sky and earth dance together, closely joined, and we humble people are invited to join and to dance for our own and future generations, for the future of our planet among the rest of the living universe.

We sing with our light
We are the birds of fire...
Among us are three hunters
Who chase a bear
There never was a time
When they were not hunting
We look down on the mountain
This is the song of the stars.
—Algonquin Poem

THE ROOTED EARTH

The British saw the Big Dipper as The Plow. We saw it as canoes with singing, happy people journeying in it.
—L. Hogan

Old Grandmother was thoughtful and seemed preoccupied with her own feelings about the past, but I knew she'd been hard at work that day and wondered if typing and yard work hurt her bent fingers. Even if that were so, she remained busy outside. I'd glimpsed her earlier working at her table. Still she had time for us. Being tired must have helped her speak from the heart.

This is what some in the Northwestern nations said:

> We do not like to harm the trees. Whenever we can, we always make an offering of tobacco to the trees before we cut

> them down. We never waste the wood, but use all that we cut. If we did not consider their feelings and did not offer them tobacco before cutting them down, all the other trees in the forest would weep, and that would make our hearts sad, too.

A few years ago, I worked with young people. They planted a medicine garden on dry land not far from here. It was beautiful to see them work, devoted as they were to their circle of plants. They used pails to carry water from town to the garden, and they covered it with straw to retain moisture.

On a certain day one of our Elders came to visit. She opened her medicine bundle and took out corn kernels that were at least two hundred years old. These she gave as a gift to the young people so they could plant the old corn for the future. Her care for the future touched and moved us all. The young attentively nurtured the plants. They planted squash and beans around the corn. Nearby were herbs and other plants that quickly sprouted and grew.

When the ancient corn rose toward the sky, it was as if we too had emerged from our roots in ancient times when we had followed shining stars from our dark earth origins. We gathered in a circle around the garden and took part in a prayer ceremony led by the Elder. Seeing all the green life, some wept for the beauty of it and the realization that the corn had survived more than two hundred very hard years of our history and trauma.

As the prayer continued, I looked down at the earth. A trap door spider had woven its door with different colored straw in a perfect design. The entire morning became one of awe in the presence of plant holiness, spider intelligence, and the growth and survival of the ancient corn which for so long has been an important staple for our people.

Old Grandmother told us there were thousands of kinds of corn. Corn flourished across the continent from the far South to the North. Each region developed a type of corn for its location. Pueblo nations in the hot dry Southwest learned to preserve moisture for their corn by using special practices for drought conditions, including terracing and planting on hills that easily absorbed rainfall. Earthen walls were made with depressions for holding morning moisture. Seeds were planted deeper so they could benefit from the winter snow that would seep down. Without certain bees or insects, the people had to go from plant to plant to pollinate them, and so, even today, a few very old planting locations still have some vestigial corn plants emerging. Corn, so many varieties in a plant that cares for us, also supports and shades its relatives, the beans and squash planted with it.

As corn in the drought country of the Southwest, so too was wild rice in the Northern areas for the People of the Waters. There they have grain that grows on water. The lakes are filled with rice and fish that have sustained people for millennia.

Old Grandmother told us an Anishinaabe story about the half man, half spirit, Nanaboozhoo.

One evening, Nanaboozhoo came home empty-handed from hunting. He warmed up his kettle of water and, by chance, he noticed that a duck was sitting on its rim. The thought of duck soup entered his mind, but, to his disappointment, the duck flew away. When he looked inside the kettle, he saw grains of rice floating in the water. And when he boiled the soup and ate it, he found that it was the best soup he'd ever eaten. The duck had left behind wild rice. Later Nanaboozhoo, went out and, following the direction the duck had taken, he came to a lake filled with wild rice. After that, he always knew where to find food for the others.

Old Grandmother was quiet for a time after telling us this. I was always happy for the silences. They spoke, too, and we were a culture of listeners. We could hear through the silences. A breeze blew against her skirt, and it seemed like she listened to inner voices before she looked at us and told us the stories of what we called the old days of our tribal lives.

My heart yearns to tell you today about our old forests. We carefully nurtured and loved the ancient forests. The trees and the earth returned that love by giving us many foods: chestnuts and hickory from the taller trees, and black walnuts. These we traded with other nations, especially chestnuts and hickory. The hickory was sweet as a milk and in demand. It was the most desired trade item. We flattened it, rolled it tight, and waterproofed it inside thin hide for the trade journeys.

In the forest we created areas of light so that other plants could grow. In the first area of sunlight grew medicinal plants and berries. At the edges were sweet grasses to attract the wildlife, deer, elk and other animals.

Plants, like all other earth beings, speak. They are living spirits that respond to one another and to human beings. They remember if someone harms them, and if someone helps. They attract birds and smaller bees. Our forests once were filled with birdsong. I long to be one with those old growth forests, where I could see the incredible beauty of the red light of dawn on their enormous trunks, and at sunset the golden light on their leaves. They had such dignity and brilliant majesty. Our Elders knew the sounds of the trees, and just by the sound of a breeze or a wind passing through them, our Elders could identify them.

The hearts of our ancestors fell to the ground when they saw the forests cut down by newcomers to our world. The trees were suddenly gone. On the entire continent, nothing like forest clearing had ever taken place before. This is how much we differed from those who had left their own continent. Our forests became nothing more than timber in Nashville, a place of sawmills as far as the eye could see. Trees—what we call sacred and from the earth—were taken there. Taken. Stolen. The new people didn't see the real wealth this world offered. They believed in another kind of wealth. It breaks my heart.

Farther south, Germans who were hired to cut down our cypress swamps wept at destroying such beauty. The swamps were silent except for the glide of birds on water, the languages of animals and winged lives there. The workers didn't want to do that work, but they had to earn wages. It's the dilemma of American ways, so unlike our own ways that sustained us for so many thousands of years. The hired men cried at having to kill these unique trees, the likes of which they'd never seen before. They knew what would happen. The animal life hidden within the thick, dense world where our Holy Cypress grew would disappear. This was the beginning. There would be no more ivory-billed woodpeckers dwelling in those regions. Extinct—a word we'd never before heard. Those birds meant so much to our people. From earliest times, our artwork contained images of them carved on shell and etched into ceramics. We worshiped that large bird.

My heart and my mind linger on what is rarely seen today. I smell the roots and the soil, even the trees, like the thick circle of black walnut trees that surrounded Monks Mound. In the leaves and branches lived heath hens, ivory billed woodpeckers, and passenger pigeons. These kept the trees and the whole region free from insects and night-time predators, encircling the area with protection. The trees are now only stumps, and the birds have vanished—all disappeared into history.

The Onondaga Faithkeeper and philosopher Oren Lyons once said, "What your people call natural resources, our people call relatives." Consider this: even the word "resource" implies that the source will be available in the future, that it is inexhaustible. It is a word that often lies.

I have lived long enough to know many intelligent people, and I have learned from them. My old friend Dennis Martinez coined the term "kincentric" to denote the reciprocal relationships between the many lives of our world.

He also told me of at least one Rainforest nation that remembers the sounds of birds that are no longer there. The Native people continue to sing the songs to keep open a space for when the birds return.

Outside Old Grandmother's cabin her garden was a mixed one, containing both vegetables and flowers. She pointed out a tall plant with velvet-soft leaves close to the ground and a tall candle of seeds growing from its center toward the sky. After slowly rising from her chair and going down the stairs to the mallow plant she said:

"This one is a healing plant. It is one to remember. Its leaves placed on wounded skin are, like honey, an antibiotic. The plant has healed many a cut arm or leg. Some pull it up as a weed. They do not even offer an apology."

She was careful with the plant. I was happy to see her walk, still so graceful, so lovely to me, this grandmother of our town, her heart filled with care for us all and what we would learn and what we would become.

Old Grandmother looked out over the hills, lost in memory that day. I too regarded the wide view, imagining what was present to her but unseen by me. Still gazing out, she said to me:

A Shoshone grandmother once told a visiting student, "When you look out at these fields, you see nothing but weeds. But I see at least seventeen medicines." She picked one she thought would be useful to someone. She had no meal or tobacco to give the plant, but she took a quarter out of her pocket and left it there in in thanks. I would remember this in the future, to always leave a gift, even if it was not a traditional one.

I remember hearing about the Plains and grasslands rich with plenty. These provided for the people's survival, until the plow with oxen was brought to that land. It was a time of shock and dismay for people who had already seen so much destruction. The grasses alone called forth the deer, the buffalo, and other important sources of protein. Digging up the earth devastated everything in and beneath the soil, all of which was essential. This is the reason for droughts, the reason European and other countries have failed to feed their people. It is the reason why at one time Chinese men were kidnapped and compelled to go to islands where birds lived in large numbers. The men were sent there with shovels to collect and send back to China large shiploads of bird guano, a fertilizer. No one had previously paid attention to their own soil or thought of it as the primal source of all life.

Every time she spoke, I learned from Old Grandmother about the ways we are we all part of the same single planet, relatives of the plants as well as other life forms.

People failed to remember that the planet does not exist only for human beings but for all the forms about us. Our ancestors knew how to show gratitude. They sang when they planted. They thought of seeds as sacred, and they responded from their hearts. Many of our young forgot this when they were sent to boarding schools and taught other ways. The result was a ghost world in that time and after it. Yet the trees remembered. Like the land, they know our stories. And out of our own necessity we too are learning again the ways of our old ones.

It seemed to me that we evolved together and that the damaged relationships are being mended. We again sing to the seeds as we plant, imagining their future. We sing and pray as we gather in the harvest. Even non-Indigenous nations and peoples have joined in the effort of learning the intelligence of the planet. All are working for survival, coming together on the red road and moving forward to care for it all. For us, our cultural and spiritual survival depend on this collective work.

> *The whole of nature touches and intertwines in one great embrace. The wind that brushes against my skin, the sun that kisses my face, the air that I breathe, the fish swimming in the water, the far-off star, and the gaze in which I hold it are all in contact.*
>
> —*Ernesto Cardenal,* Abide in Love

THE FOUR-LEGGED

We went to Geneva, The Six Nations (Haudenosaunee) and the great Lakota Nations, as representatives of the Indigenous People of the Western Hemisphere.
There is a hue and a cry for human rights, they said, for all people.
And the Indigenous People said, What are the rights of the natural world?
Where is the seat for the Buffalo or the Eagle?
Who is representing them here in this forum?
Who is speaking for the waters of the Earth?
Who is speaking for the trees and the forests?
Who is speaking for the Fish and the Whales, for the Beaver, for our Children?

—Oren Lyons, Onondaga Faithkeeper, 1990

It was a warm day in late fall. I was working at Old Grandmother's. She was standing outside the fence feeding an autumn apple to her horse and brushing the mare's long mane and tail. I asked if she needed help. I'd seen how hard she worked for the horse, but they were companions. They understood one another in ways I hadn't yet learned. I worried about the day she might lose her sister mustang.

It had been a long time since I'd seen the pole with its ribboned flag waving in the breeze outside her cabin, but it was the busy season. It was autumn. Her garden was drying and only small red tomatoes remained. The leaves of the trees were scarlet and gold. Even the road was red. But I knew she'd been busily working in the cabin, typing on the old typewriter with her strong fingers.

Today she had let her hair fall in a long, thick braid. She'd been too busy to pin it up. Before anyone else arrived, we greeted one another. I sat and spoke with the turtles. Old Grandmother had turned her face up toward the sun and was basking in the light. Suddenly she spotted a hawk high up in the sky, and then another. She was so happy. I thought of the story in which the sun is a woman. In the nations that worshiped it as a fiery female planet, she would easily have fit, her face and yellow dress reflecting light. But sometimes I thought she could fit at any time or in any place.

Soon the others arrived, some walking through the drying grasses and the younger ones running along the old rust-colored road ahead of their families, all looking forward to hearing what she would say.

As the seasons were changing, the animals came by all our places more often. Now the sound of the walking and visiting people sent them out of hiding and away from Old Grandmother's place to get away from other people. I heard the deer, then saw them pass by. A fox came in from the prairie region, stopped to look at us, then quickly moved on. Of course, the tortoise was there. It was, as always, attached to Old Grandmother.

When she began to speak it was again about those she had known or heard in her life, which my father once said had been full of much loss. She was the last of her family. But, he said, she had had a wonderful, exciting life.

She spoke first of a man she had known, Joseph Old Coyote. She smiled at us, only slightly, a little tired. I was growing older now, and I had begun to notice a hint of autumn sadness that came to many elders at this time of year. I wondered if she, too, felt it, but I always saw the happiness of her spirit.

Sometimes I think of the many stories I have heard. My heart and mind stayed with the Northern Cheyenne man who told me about the turbulent times they faced when they were being driven out of their homelands and forced to relocate to Oklahoma Indian Territory. They had escaped the army, the settlers, and the Indian-haters many times. A clan mother and chief went to the wolves and requested their help, asking that they remember and safeguard the songs that belonged to the people in case they didn't survive. Years later, the two of them returned and the wolves sang the songs that belonged to the people. The kinship formed between the two different types of beings was still alive. The relationships existing between humans and plants exists, and an even stronger one exists between humans and animals. This kindred care is what connects us, and it needs to be respected and cherished.

I think of the people I have met along my life's road. Anyone who heard Mohawk Elder Jake Swamp's Thanksgiving Address sending greetings and thanks to the natural world could never forget it. The beautiful words of that address are still spoken at all our gatherings to remind people of what we are grateful for. Re-mind is the right word. By hearing the words, feeling them, making them our own and sharing them with one another we pass on the gift of the ancient soul for all tomorrows.

She was quiet again for a moment. I was always glad for the silence. I wanted to take in this deep meaning and absorb it.

We express gratitude for all that exists in our environment, for the earth and all grasses and rooted lives, the winged insects and the many-colored birds. Then we turn our minds to the air we breathe, to those with four legs, and we thank all the rest that dwell among us. This is the time we think not only of today but the times of tomorrow.

In the Thanksgiving Address swimming lives are mentioned, and this reminds me of a dear Canadian friend, and Algonquin chief, speaking of the Walleye. These are his own words:

> The animals never go backwards. They teach us always to walk and look forward. We don't forget the spirits living in water, in lakes and rivers. Fish is pure food because the fish live in water. It is the purest food, and it can also be medicinal or restorative. For instance, the Walleye has delicate white flesh that provides nourishment for us, but that is not all. In the past, our ancestors didn't have eyeglasses. When they reached old age and their eyesight was no longer good there was no science to help them, and they had to find their own remedy. So, they turned to the Walleye with its strong eyes,

and it helped them to see. The Elders told me about this, and they taught me how to remove the lens of this fish eye so it becomes like a magnifier.

In our culture, everything we do is related to spirituality. Everything we experience in the forest is spiritual. We respect all the animals. I think of what we give to animals and what they give us in return. Last night, the rain was falling on the roof of my cabin. It was like Mother Earth was taking me into her arms. So my spirit is completely open to speak to you about our beliefs and our way of living.

As Anokiwini, my mother and father taught me always to begin with gratitude, to give thanks. The word "Anokiwini" means many things, not just the one who hunts or traps for his family and others, but the one who helps Mother Earth when she suffers. This word is deeply related to love of Mother Earth and other spirits.

As for hunting, before we go to hunt we must have a dream. We don't choose the animal we are to hunt. We don't run after it. It must come to us in the dream.

I don't like using the word "animal." In my language we call them spirits. Preparing to go trapping, I begin with a vision in the morning. I give thanks in advance for the food this spirit is going to give, and for the medicine it may provide.

Here, we mainly trap Amik, which is Beaver. I sit a long time before and after setting the trap. At sunset I return home in peace, knowing that this spirit will offer its life for us. I say, "Thank you, *migwech*," to my ancestors for teaching me this. and to Amik.

The next morning, when I open the trap and lift out lift the beaver, circles of water move outward as it moves from the beginning of life into the universe. I ask The Mother to bless the spirit of this beaver. I stroke him like a child and offer prayers, telling the animal spirit that I will reverently care for its body.

After the prayers, I make certain the body is healthy. I check the liver. If it is not well, I must cremate the animal, but if all is fine, I respect the commitment I made to him. Every

> part of the body is sacred, and we use it all. Some parts are not our food but a medicine, much like penicillin.
>
> On a psychological level, Amik teaches us about balance, because it is a spirit who lives half his life on earth, half in water. Beavers are very spiritual, intelligent beings. They teach us perseverance and creativity. If a careless person destroys their dam, the Amik goes back to work re-creating his home. Like us, he is a forest person who knows how to cut trees not for only himself but also for his children. The Amik loves to eat the top leaves of the tree, those at the ends of the branches. We are grateful for the rest of that tree because we use it for making snowshoes and sleds, or for building. I am especially grateful for the medicines provided by this Amik.
>
> As for me, I have two cultures within myself. The culture of the First Nations and the culture of the white people. It's very rich. When we are sad, it's because we're not connected with the earth, the forest, and the animals.
>
> —Chomis (Grandfather)
>
> ″

I am happy he calls animals "spirits" because it is what they are.

In our Chickasaw language, the animals are called "Nan Okcha." It means "All Alive." Those two words are significant. My heart remembers them daily as I see the spirits around the cabin early in the mornings.

As always, Old Grandmother had much to say about our love for the All Alive. It was one thing she made sure we would learn. I liked to sit in the front and close to her, but looking up I could see where we lived, and I would think about how we carry all this within us. As I grew older, her words became even more important to me, and I struggled to keep them inside myself all the time. At this particular moment, though, my heart felt love for every spirit living here, those in the nest of the tree, the old tortoise, the flying insects.

Old Grandmother reached back to move her hair and made herself more comfortable.

Not many years ago, a Lakota man named Alex worked for Native Fish and Wildlife. He was one of the first who worked hard for the return of the bison to Native land where the Lakota lived. Returning them was no small work. I visited and went to watch. I thought I'd write about it. When the bison were released from the large cattle trucks, they just stood like great spirits come from another world. They were giants, like mammoths on the dry, tired lands. After they were restored to the large amount of land that had always been theirs, they remembered how to live. The Elders who watched said that it wasn't long before the weight of their hooves brought streams and creeks of water shining up to the surface. The Elders had not seen water on that land since their childhood. Soon insects and birds returned to the new marshlands. Wild foods and flowers began to thrive again, and tall, green grasses covered the earth. Deer and elk arrived for the grasses.

It is important for us to know that waters inside earth can return to the surface. We have seen that, with the return of Native lives, regeneration takes place on earth that has been devastated, usually by cattle, and no longer has streams, springs, and creeks; they can be found only in the old stories. When we remember older ways, we find possibilities for our future. We are reminded that we live in a world still connected to the web of life, a world just waiting for us to bring it back into a whole.

Old Grandmother told us of how Charles Eastman, a Native American who had been born on a Dakota reservation wrote about the Great Mystery.

He simply called the creation "The Grandfather." Eastman spoke and wrote of the lives he knew as a boy when the buffalo and other large animals still roamed earth. He attended Boston University from which he earned a degree in medicine in 1890. As the only doctor at the Pine Ridge Reservation during the massacre at Wounded Knee, he took care of the few bleeding survivors, his own people. It hadn't even been a situation where tribal people started any trouble. This slaughter took place because a new young Indian Agent feared the religious Ghost Dancers and ordered U.S. Army troops to shoot. They murdered almost three hundred persons, old people, women, and children.

After the massacre, Eastman helped in the search for survivors who might have been covered with night snow while trying to escape the gunshots. They searched long distances for bodies, looking for bloody trails.

Much later, he became a public speaker, then a writer. Dr. Eastman wrote that animals are regarded as part of the Great Mystery. They were killed only to provide food. He studied and learned the manner and ways of living of the animals and with them. For his people it was sacrilege to know the secrets of animals and use that knowledge against them, so most Elders and others who knew the animal people stopped hunting. These are sacred actions for conscious human beings.

Dr. Eastman, through his words and work as a writer, not only relayed important information but also kept a tradition alive. His words alone could be considered ceremony. He authored many books. Even in the books some consider as having been written for young people, he laid out the original ethics for the treatment of all lives. In Red Hunters and the Animal People, he reveals what we might call the ethic of our own deep lives. In one place he wrote of speaking with a man who had many eagle feathers. He said, "You must have killed many eagles to have so many feathers." The response of the man with feathers was to say that he had killed none of them but had managed to capture many in his lifetime and keep only a few feathers from each.

Dr. Eastman knew much about death and about life. He knew about Americans and their capacity to harm the Indigenous, but he tried to live his daily life as ceremony, as a right way of living in the time after so many massacres that changed our histories and people across the continent.

He eventually moved back into the woods from which he had come. One day as he was writing, there was a knock on his door. When he opened it, he found large tortoise waiting to enter. It was as if all creation had come back to him, with another life to share with his.

THE WORDS, OUR WORLDS

We are still trying to heal ourselves from the long-enduring epidemic of being colonized. Some few of us are academicians and some have forgotten to speak for those from which they come.

—John Mohawk

Indigeneity assumes a spiritual interconnectedness between all creations, their right to exist and the value of their contributions to the larger whole. At the core of Indigenous thinking is that coexistence relies on the ability of all peoples' and living things' voices be heard and heard equally.

—LaDonna Harris, Founder and President
of Americans for Indian Opportunity

Magic Words, Songs

In the very earliest time,
when both people and animals lived on earth,
a person could become an animal if he wanted to
and an animal could become a human being.
Sometimes they were people
and sometimes animals
and there was no difference.
All spoke the same language.
That was the time when words were like magic.
The human mind had mysterious powers.
A word spoken by chance
might have strange consequences.
It would suddenly come alive
and what people wanted to happen could happen—
all you had to do was say it.
Nobody could explain this:
That's the way it was.
—Nalungiaq, Inuit woman interviewed by
ethnologist Knud Rasmussen in the early twentieth century

On this day, Old Grandmother was holding a handful of reeds and grasses. She began talking to us about baskets. Long blades and stems of grass lay across the stones beside her. Her old hands began weaving as she spoke:

When a basket is put together it becomes a living thing. It doesn't dry up and crack apart as the materials do if left uncared for on the ground.

This is the way of our stories and our traditions. When we pass on our words, our knowledge of the sacred remains alive. Our traditions are a gift of love, so we have to take care to keep them. They are the spirit of the people and food for our own growth.

She seemed older to me this day. I thought about how losing her would be a great loss—not only for me, but for all who had come into contact with her soul and the words that came from it, those who had read or heard her words, knew of her life and the way her heart connected with those of others. I was concerned, but she continued. She was still herself.

As in the creation, we each began in darkness, in the natal waters of our birth mothers. Water will always be part of our existence and our stories. Then we move into the element of air. The breath of the maker whirls us into existence and our lifetime of growth, learning our land, our waters, and our people's ways. Many centuries travel within each of us. We carry our peoples' history within us. It is our bone and blood. The ones before us passed on their words to tell us of the beautifully woven world around us, the world web that shines through each story, song, and prayer. Words. Through them we often remember ourselves as dwellers in ancient forests or on desert dunes. Our Elders teach us, but so does our own observation. Each element, each place, each movement around us is part of our human journey. We learn songs, like those the Northwest people sing for the salmon who swim up stone embankments to go back to the source where they were birthed and to bring forth young.

The star world and the currents of wind tell us of the coming weather. As planters we learn what soils support our foods. Our bodies hold the magnificent world of water that fell tenderly from rainclouds. When we learn to listen and to watch, that single act of attention opens within us a spirit of awe, which is so important on our path along the good red road we call right living.

When I speak of right living, it has to do with our spirituality and religions that were forbidden by American law until 1978 when the Religious Freedom Act was finally passed. Before then our rituals, dances, and practices were illegal in this country. Even so, we held our ceremonies on dark nights in hidden places. Stories help us to keep our sacred and traditional ways. Stories from centuries past also tell us how to create a sustainable future. It is remembered from centuries past.

Our planet needs human tending and care. This is especially true now, in this time of environmental breakdown. Still, we struggle with oil pipelines on our own sovereign lands, with miners who are sometimes our own people, with loggers, even with other governments. Working to care for our habitat has become a full-time endeavor for many people. But the earth is changing and such work is essential. Climate change has uprooted the Caribou People of interior Alaska and others, forcing them to move their homes and villages. It has turned sand into plastic beads that no life can inhabit. If each person tackled only one part of the harm being done, it would make a huge difference.

At a hundred years of age, my friend Meridel le Sueur said, "We must re-member the dismembered." She meant that we must put back together that which was taken apart. This includes the land and all that is woven together with it, like a basket capable of holding inside it our way of singing the earth and not of signing it away.

Old Grandmother looked at the clouds moving across the sky above us while she searched for the right words. Then she returned her attention to us. All the while her hands were weaving, as if demonstrating what she was saying.

I prayed to the ancestors, asking how I could speak to you about what we have learned from the stories and how we grow from words. Stories are not always told in words. The botanist William Bartram, who wrote several centuries ago, told of an experience he had while staying in a Chickasaw village where he was studying plants. A group of people had gathered one night. They sat in a circle, the fire lighting their faces. Each person shared something with the others. One sang. Another told a story. Each sharing was a gift offered to those gathered. All spoke in words until one woman stood and danced her story. With graceful motions she danced how her husband had been killed as she watched, and then with her movements related the sufferings of her own life as she was taken into slavery. She had a fluid grace and such deep emotion that everyone wept in grief at her body's story—a narrative of her history, with her sorrow so powerfully expressed that it became theirs.

The dancer told her story wordlessly. Knowing the power of body language is why we dance to the heartbeat of the drum or the rattle like the one that long ago marked the first moment of the creation of our universe by The Maker.

I remember Old Grandmother's words when I think of the new science that says memory exists in our blood, genes, and cell structure. According to John Trudell, a Dakota poet and activist for Native American rights, "All human beings are descendants of tribal people who were spiritually alive, intimately in love with the natural world, children of Mother Earth. When we were tribal people, we knew who we were, and we knew our purpose. This sacred perception of reality remains alive and well in our genetic memory. We carry it inside of us, usually in a dusty box in the mind's attic, but it is accessible."

Our bodies are containers of memory, but words are what we use to follow back to how our ancestors existed and endured. Perhaps this why so many of us have returned to the early bountiful circle of life, learning again our original ways and restoring what was untended for too long. Some have gone to work helping medicine plants or animals, birds, and other species to survive. We need to learn again to care for the waters and the soil. We also need to care for our own inner lives, which have been injured. Like the salmon, we are coming home.

Old Grandmother then spoke of reverence.

The most meaningful and important teaching is told in the reverent language of prayer and ceremony. Indigenous people throughout the world have preserved ceremonies and rituals that keep us in balance with the earth and with other spirit beings. One example is the many long songs of traditional Navajo Chantways. These ceremonies include chants, prayer, and action expressing the desire to create harmony and balance as part of healing. A singer may know only one song, one ceremony that sometimes lasts for many days and nights. Often herbs, water, and traditional medicines are used. The outcome is to create balance between an individual and the rest of creation. It begins small, but like a stone dropped into water, the ceremony expands to the plants, the insect visitors, the animals that pass by. It continues outward to the sky and the universe, placing the person inside the wide cosmos. When we feel ourselves in that place, we are in balance; a healing has occurred and we stand in the circle of life.

Songs and prayers live at the border between the holy and the human. The connection between the two gives us the strength needed for our journey from birth to our last breath.

Much is offered from our ancestral past and is meant to be carried forward. For some this includes such religious rituals as the Sun Dance, the Thirst Dance in Canada, the Native American Church, and Southeastern Stomp Dances. Sweat lodges are now found across the continent, although some are led by people who are not properly trained and authorized. Many of our ceremonies incorporate elements of Christianity. Some Indigenous people combine Catholicism with the traditional rituals, like the Yaqui Easter ceremonies.

I now turn to a consideration of our religions and my own sense of the world, the enchantment of the deep forest with its smell of sweet daily rains. Each place, each spirit has a story, something silently known that perhaps needs to be spoken. The word is powerful.

Maybe our ancestors had an inner map they followed to live more solidly, more widely with the earth and the human self. I sift through all the stories I've been told by Elders. Observation of the environment (now called ecology) played a key role in our early science. We came to understand the now almost unfathomable kinship that exists between life forms. But without the stories, what could I have learned?

As for what Old Grandmother told us, some may have called it myth, but it is a language of the deepest parts of our inner world, and it is also a way of contemplating the sacred mystery. As in ceremonies, it is meaning that makes us whole. Myth leads us to find balance with everything else. We grow more insightful, more capable of understanding deeper meanings as we travel along the path of our human journey. Story or just simple speaking of words may lay out for us teachings like the Haudenosaunee Great Law of Peace, instructions for living that are so important that the American people based their Constitution, in part, on the same manner of ethical living.

We also share with one another our human spirit, our lives, our actions. For the moment I think not only of the many new writers and writings, but also of the old ways we used to keep our ways of knowing. For instance, one of the Acoma Pueblo writers, Simon Ortiz, once said, "It's a way of decolonizing ourselves." We are in the difficult process of decolonizing ourselves by using words, but then our peoples always had writing, whether in letters like the Mi'maq who used pine needles to punch words into birch bark long ago, or using older methods, like tying knots in strings. Even older are the images carved in wood or painted on stone. And, as Old Grandmother said, the animal earth effigies and the great mounds are another form of writing. They are an expressions of love to the universe.

We have infinite ways of speaking. Times and events, even prophecies, have to be recalled.

Wampum belts remain one of the most significant types of writing. These beaded works record treaties and events, tell stories, and are even used for correspondence. All the writing is done with woven beads made from the shells of water animals. Many of these belts—

too many—are still in museums and not with their people. Yet many of the people have kept them.

Chomis, from the Canadian North, speaks of wampum belts they were given:

> We are protecting four very ancient wampum belts. There's one I would like to talk about specifically. It's called the Wampum Belt of the Seven Fires, and it encodes prophecies that have been handed on for hundreds of years. These prophecies are predictions of the future, with each prophecy referring to a time period—an epoch—called a fire because it involves radical change. The prophecies contain crucial teachings that must be received by human beings so that they may make right choices.
>
> Traditional leaders believe that we are now in the period of the Seventh Fire. This is a critical time that involves not just Indigenous people but all of humanity.
>
> Technology and globalization have led not to greater unity but instead to disunion, disharmony, discord, even violence. The natural world is radically out of balance. We see the effects of this everywhere: extreme weather events resulting in droughts, flooding, wildfires, loss of species, hunger, displacement of people, expanding diseases.
>
> We are at a crossroad, and the future of all of us depends on the choices we make. Those choices will lead either to further destruction or to a new vision that will bring about healing and peace.
>
> These teachings are part of our education. They help us and our relations know where we are among seven sacred fires. The wampum belts that we protect were created about seven hundred years ago by people who had a vision of the future. This prophecy is important as it allows us to search for a new vision today.
>
> The last fire speaks of a promise of a new era with light and harmony on the land. The Seventh Fire asks us, are we the people who will light up the Eighth Fire? The fire of peace and unity? This is the reason why it's important for me to

deliver the message of this prophecy to everybody in the world. Because all the peoples in the world are included in this prophecy. It says that something beautiful is coming. . . . Let's be ready.

At the end of his words, Old Grandmother simply said, like trees we remember the old growth we came from.

Her basket was finished.

Stories are strong with life energy. That energy is felt from both above and below. The stories nourish us, holding our connection with all that surrounds and enriches us. Once again, the earth and sky are our teachers and we remember. This is the way we flourish.

—*Linda Hogan*

CIRCLING BACK

In our Anishinaabe language, we call the lake *zaaga'igan*. When we say this word, we are in fact talking about love, because *zaaga'igan* comes from the word *zaagi'* which means love.

One day, a spirit we call Ma'iingan, the wolf, came to this lake. Contemplating this vast stretch of water, Ma'iingan decided to touch it with his paw. As he did that, he discovered it was creating circles on the lake. They became bigger and bigger.

Ma'iingan realized life was there. After that, there appeared another spirit, Mikinak, the turtle. I remember the Elders saying that when Ma'iingan arrived, all the other animals came too, because they wanted to see what would happen.

Mikinak's arrival was how all that is feminine arrived on the Earth.

Mikinak is very connected to water, as well as to the Earth. Her shell is like a mother's womb. She speaks to us of all that lives within us in the silence, in the invisible realm and in gestation. That is why she speaks to us about everything that is feminine.

As soon as *Mikinak* arrived, Mother Earth began to speak. That was when women started giving life. Human beings were created through a little drop of water. It was woman who received that little drop of water. That's why we say women are water carriers, because they give life through water, like Mother Earth.

Contemplating the way all beings were created, our people began to share the same vision. They began to be connected to all of nature: rivers, lakes, forests, mountains, and all the rest.

That is why I know where I come from. I know we cannot be disconnected from the Earth.

I thank the Elders who passed on the stories to me. Every morning, I thank the ancestors. It is something I never forget—to say thank you to each moment for all the gifts of Creation.

—Chomis

From any journey or experience,
we return carrying a bag
filled with nothing but the story.
—Linda Hogan

Season of Remembrance

A TELLING OF AN INTERSPIRITUAL SACRED STORY

Season of Remembrance

INTRODUCTION

> *All who seek to participate in Ultimate Reality are united in the same fundamental search. They relate to all of genuine value in every spiritual path. They resonate to human values wherever they can be found, whether in religions, science, art, friendship or service to others.... The most precious value that we have in common is the accumulated experience of the spiritual journey....As teachers of the various spiritual disciplines pool their common experiences, resources and insights, the benefit to contemporary seekers and to the world will be immense.*
>
> —Father Thomas Keating, *The Common Heart*[1]

Interspirituality, in this sense, has existed as long as humans have traveled under the stars and shared stories around a fire. Often, religions are thought of as separate and distinct entities; in truth, they have always been connected, evolving together through the centuries in a variety of ways. Today they are coming into closer and closer contact, spurred by technological innovations and changing cultural demographics. Thus, the world's great contemplative traditions have entered into an intimate dialogue with one another, sharing their deepest experiences of reality and giving birth to what has been called "interspirituality."

The word was first coined in 1999 by Brother Wayne Teasdale, a Roman Catholic monk and Christian *sannyasin* drawn to India and

1. Father Thomas Keating, in *The Common Heart: An Experience of Interreligious Dialogue*, ed. Netanel Miles-Yépez, (New York: Lantern Books, 2006), 125, 126.

dialogue with both Hindu and Tibetan Buddhist spirituality.[2] Teasdale used the word *"interspiritual"* to point to a more intimate engagement between traditions and practitioners of varying religious and spiritual traditions—an intimacy that happened primarily at the contemplative or experiential level. Interspirituality represented a sharing of our most profound experiences of reality, among both individuals and religious traditions. Where interreligious dialogue might ask, *"What do you believe?* interspiritual dialogue was more likely to ask, *"How do you encounter or experience awakening, or divine union, or simply the sacred?"* And its participants would often invite one another into those experiences.

The word "spiritual" speaks here to the totality of our human experience and possibility. "Being spiritual," Teasdale wrote, "is a personal commitment to a process of inner development that engages our totality."[3] *Inter*-spirituality then expresses the deep, interconnected roots of our individual spiritual journeys, as well as those of our religious traditions, on both physical and spiritual planes. Interspirituality, Teasdale wrote, "conveys a fundamental truth—the essential spiritual inter-dependence of religions. Spiritual inter-dependence among the religions exists because an essential inter-connectedness in being and reality exists."[4]

Interspirituality also names or, in its adjectival form, perhaps describes many of the complex experiences of our great cultural convergence. It covers and connects the inclusive values of those who are committed to one tradition but who honor all; and it also covers and connects "hyphenated" religious identities, like those of Christian priests who have become recognized Zen *roshi*s, or Jewish rabbis who have become Sufi *shaykh*s; it covers and connects the "threshold" experiences of people who walk liminal paths between complex religious and cultural identities, saying, "I am not *in* any tradition," or even *"between* traditions"—I am simply *interspiritual.*

---

2. Wayne Teasdale, *The Mystic Heart: Discovering a Universal Spirituality in the World's Religions* (Novato, CA: New World Library, 1999).

3. Teasdale, *The Mystic Heart*, 17.

4. Teasdale, *The Mystic Heart*, 27.

Thus, interspirituality names the complex spiritual relationships that exist among our diverse religious and contemplative traditions, as well as the complex religious and spiritual identities that many people hold today.

The Story of Interspirituality offered here[5] is a compilation of true stories, historical accounts, personal narratives, and myths from many different religious traditions and spiritual paths, placed in a fictional framework. It is not meant to be *the* story of interspirituality, but merely *a* story of interspirituality, one among many, with many more to come. The story does not try to explain interspirituality but rather to illustrate its inner meaning without diluting its complexity and diversity of meanings by unifying them in one synthetic story. It is a series of stories set within one overarching narrative that represents the dialogue between them and highlights the relevance of interspirituality to the spiritual journey more broadly.

All of the stories are ultimately stories of Love. They help us to understand our mutually entangled histories and interconnected roots and the community formed by them. They also affirm the diversity of our spiritual journeys—as well as the multifaceted religious, cultural, and ethnic identities that belong to them. Together these stories reveal a shared ground of love and spiritual actualization that has always existed among and between our religious traditions: a sacred ground that continues to percolate today.

---

5. A note from the authors: Ultimately, this work reflects the perspectives and concerns of our particular team of interspiritual authors, and may omit important perspectives and concerns that other colleagues might include. We also wish to acknowledge that our project as a whole has its origins in the United States, and thus a certain U.S.-centric (as well as a broadly North and South American) perspective. The setting for our narrative reflects this, being located in the United States, and representing its particular diversity as well as its local concerns.

Everything is an avenue leading to the experience of Ultimate Reality.
The divine communicates itself in all things.
There are infinite ways to encounter the source.
Ultimate Reality may be experienced in virtually anything.
There is no place, no activity that restricts the divine.
It is everywhere.

—Wayne Teasdale

PART ONE
The Fire

The Bearers of Remembrance

The first time I came to the Fire, I was not yet twenty-three, and not really sure I wanted to be there. I had come at the invitation of my grandmother, who had been the Fire-Keeper for many years. When I was a child, I saw her often, and we had a special relationship, the kind that bristled with a sense of magic. I felt as if there was a secret between us that no one else shared.

But when I was twelve, my parents moved us out of state and I saw her less and less. We visited occasionally, and she sometimes visited us; but by then I was a teenager beginning my own stumbling exploration of life and somehow forgetful of all the magic that had once existed between us.

So, by the time I came to visit her just after my college graduation, I was disturbed to find that our relationship now felt stilted and awkward. The special "secret" we had once shared now seemed like an empty box I had treasured and kept for years without knowing why. Had she always been this person, or was it me who had changed?

I stayed with her for a week, unsure of how to relate to this eccentric old woman who felt like a stranger. Whenever possible, I made excuses about work to be done for my classes and hid in my room talking to friends. But on the last night of my stay, on the Day of Remembrance, my grandmother insisted I come with her, saying that it was "time" I came "to the Fire."

Of course, I had heard about the Day of Remembrance my whole life—which is not to say that I knew what it was, exactly. It was just something that was mentioned often enough in my family to be familiar. What it was really about, or what was actually done on that day, I had no idea.

We drove an hour or so north from San Francisco into the high country along the coast, finally parking in the late afternoon near a collection of cars outside an old outpost. Together, we began to walk up an uneven dirt path to the escarpment overlooking the Gulf of Farallones.

The place of the Fire was less "ritually exalted" than I had imagined. It was an ordinary fire pit with a well-stacked pile of wood and kindling in it, the ground around it set with chairs.

The whole thing seemed a bit silly to me. I felt like the adult, my grandmother a child I had to indulge. I was surprised, however, to see people of all ages there. I had supposed it would be a gathering of my grandmother's friends, all of a similar age and in need of similar indulgence. But these people were different from what I had expected, and I found them interesting for reasons I could not quite express. The respect they showed my grandmother surprised me, and unexpectedly moved me, even as I struggled to understand all that I was seeing.

When the ceremony began, my grandmother motioned for me to take a seat where I could observe from outside the inner ring of chairs, as I was not a member of the Circle. I sat down on an old redwood stump, feeling it touch my sit-bones through my jeans. As the sky darkened, she was handed a special torch, and it was then that I saw my familiar grandmother transformed, assuming the face of a dignified elder rising to light the "Fire of Remembrance." I learned later that she was the eldest of the Circle, with the longest memory of past Fires.

The night was cold and growing darker now, and I welcomed the fire's warmth, a feeling that perhaps made me a little more vulnerable to its primal charms—its light dancing on my grandmother's lined face, transforming her into the priestess of an ancient rite, the "Fire-Keeper," ready to tell the story of the "Bearers of Remembrance."

"This is the Place of Remembrance," she said, pointing to the fire and drawing a circle around it with her finger, looking at all of the assembled.

"This land was once inhabited by peoples who called themselves *Me-Wuk*. Here they fished salmon, collected acorns, and hunted *'uwu:ya*. Here they gathered in small communities, performing rituals to restore balance to life, to the land and all its inhabitants—animals, plants, spirits, people. We acknowledge their sacrifice in maintaining the sacred balance of life here. We *remember* their gifts, and acknowledge their suffering and loss as a result of our ignorance and greed.

"Here, tonight, the past, present, and future are woven together, bringing meaning to our 'today' and our 'tomorrow.' Here, we remember *who we are,* and what we came to do. Here, in this very place, are told the stories of our ancestors, stories that may guide each of us on our walk through life.

"A hundred years ago, we came perilously close to destruction in our ignorance. In the years after, people began to gather in small Circles like this one at various sacred places around the planet. We come from all over, but many live in this area too. All the Circles are similar — made up of people who live near the place of their Fire, and others who are connected to that place and return to it from afar. Some come to speak at the Circle, others just to listen. It is the same all over the world.

"In the beginning, one of our elders remembered how the *gauchos* of Argentina used to gather in the highlands around a fire and share the stories, songs, and poetry of their people; and we decided to do the same. Thus, year after year, we gather in a circle around a fire and bring stories—the stories of our ancestors, the stories of how we are all connected—and we remember what makes us one human family.

"We have been meeting for a century now. Our beginnings were small, but the Circles grew over time. On this night, we celebrate the ties that bind us, and revel in the firelight that dispels the dark illusions of estrangement and mistrust.

"We meet on this Day of Remembrance, light the Fire, and speak the Words.

"In order to 'remember,' our ancestors explored the history of their peoples, cultures, and traditions, as far back in time as they could reach. They impressed them on their memories and stitched them onto the 'fabric' of their existence. Then they did the same with the story of the planet and the story of the universe. They hid nothing from one another, and they did not attempt to distort the truth, no matter how complex or painful the story.

"When they knew their story and the paths they had walked, they realized that they had made great mistakes, and that some of those mistakes had almost led them to destroy themselves and the planet. So they wept for a long time and repented.

"After this period of contrition, our ancestors asked forgiveness, and they were forgiven, and forgave themselves. Forgiveness was found in the valuing of all their experiences, both positive and negative, as parts of a necessary learning process. They chose to unite all the knowledge they had acquired with what they called 'The Sacred Thread of Existence,' sewing together and arranging all the panels of 'fabric' they had once stitched with their stories.

"In time, our ancestors realized that they could combine the panels of their stories and memories in new ways, forming larger and larger pieces of the whole, until they seemed to form a great unity, until one could not really tell they had ever been separate. Thus, all the panels eventually connected, like panels in one great quilt—beautifully translucent, and comprised of all the colors of life, saturated by the shimmering flow of the Sacred Thread.

"This Quilt of Remembrance belongs to all of us, and all of us know that parts of our own stories exist within it. We know that our actions are written on it, so that we may remember our connection with everyone and everything and not forget to play the parts we have come to perform. Our ancestors discovered their connection with all of the beings of the Earth. They knew, as human beings, that they were the eyes and ears of the planet, the awakened consciousness of creation on Earth. Their mission was to love, to care for, and protect the world and its beings.

"The great Quilt of Remembrance was a clue, a secret our ancestors needed to uncover. Following this clue, they began to embrace the deepest experiences and testimonies of one another. They discovered beauty and harmony in the varied expressions of religious and spiritual life throughout the human family. Like the Quilt of Remembrance, they discovered that Love permeated all of their stories, and that radiant truths might be learned from one another. They understood that this was also true of the Earth and all of her myriad creatures: they, too, were living stories woven into the Quilt of Remembrance.

"Their discovery led them to uncover more and more mysteries, until they recognized their connection with the invisible universe, and indeed, with all universes. They realized that they themselves were an intersection between physical and celestial realms; and they knew themselves to be one with everyone and All Being.[6]

"Since then, we have come to care for the planet and all its beings, whom we consider sacred and perceive as Love manifesting in matter; but we also bear witness to the spirit of life in the universe, to its evolutionary creativity and many varying expressions.

"This is the reason why our ancestors, who join us on this consecrated evening, began to call themselves 'Bearers of Remembrance.' They had remembered who they were, where they came from, and that we are all one family. They recognized their interdependence, their shared belonging to the Earth, to one another, and to Love itself.

"Generation after generation, we relive this remembrance within our own hearts to reacquaint ourselves with this realization, so that for each one of us, the reality of our oneness with all being becomes a living experience. Life is a gift that gives us a unique opportunity to develop and share our lives and experience with one another.

"Today we bear witness to and affirm the presence of the sacred in the world; for it is ours to bring awareness into a living universe, to contemplate the sunrise for a sun that does not know it dawns, to admire the grandeur of the mountain for a mountain that does not know its majesty, to appreciate the fragrance of the flower for a flower that does not know its own perfume, to gratefully experience the Earth and all her creatures, to affirm one another in the depths of our being, and to drink deeply from the sacred wells of our shared experience. We do this by telling our stories, speaking and listening from that place of Love that binds us all.

"The stories are important; they are how we remember, and by remembering we survive."

Then the "Fire-Keeper," my grandmother transfigured, added with ceremony—"Come to the circle and remember."

---

6. The basic story of the "Bearers of Remembrance" is adapted from an account of a personal vision reported by Alejandra Warden in her book, *Remembrance: A Vision of the Sacred Feminine and the Renewal of the Earth* (Boulder, CO: Albion-Andalus Books, 2022), 25–29.

I don't know why exactly, but I trembled a little as she pronounced these final words. I cannot say I understood the entire metaphor of the "Bearers of Remembrance" then—the "Quilt" and the "Sacred Thread"—but something about the parable impacted me, something about the sacredness of life, the valuing of all our human experience, and learning from our collective mistakes.

She then turned away from the Fire and slowly took her seat.

PART TWO
The Circle

The Mother Who Loves All

As my grandmother sat down in front of me, a dignified woman of about fifty, with wavy black hair laced with silver threads and wearing a multicolored blanket, stood up slowly, carefully laid her blanket down on a rock, and lifted her hands toward the warmth of the fire in the crisp night air. Realizing that I was cold too, I zipped up my wind-breaker. It seemed that the storytellers were not constrained by any particular order, but instead rose and approached the fire according to their own inspiration.

"Today," she said in a clear voice, "I traveled the long road up from Los Angeles," pronouncing the city's name like a native Spanish speaker.

"As I was leaving home, I passed a building upon which a mural had been painted. It was Our Lady of Guadalupe. All over the world, people know her as the 'Mother Who Loves All' and revere her, no matter what religion they follow. But the old ones tell us of when and how she first appeared.

"It was just ten years after the bloody Spanish conquest of México. In that year—1531—an Aztec convert to Christianity, Juan Diego, was climbing a hill associated with the Aztec mother goddess,

Tonantzin. As he climbed, he heard someone call his name, and he looked up to see the most beautiful young woman he had ever seen hovering in the sky, a 'woman clothed with the sun' and standing on the moon. She was a woman of his people, brown and serious, and yet, *not of his people,* being also like the daughters of the newcomers.

"Suddenly, she spoke and told him that she was the 'Mother Who Loves All,' adding that 'All who sincerely ask my help in their work and in their sorrows will know my Mother's Heart.'

"She then sent him to tell the Spanish bishop about her appearance. The bishop, however, dismissed Juan Diego as an ignorant peasant.

"But the woman sent him back again. This time the bishop asked for some 'proof' of her having appeared. So she had Juan Diego collect all the wildflowers he could find on the hill and place them in his *tilma*—his cloak made of cactus fiber—and she arranged the flowers in the *tilma* and sent him to the bishop once again with this 'sign' of her appearance.

"When Juan Diego opened his cloak before the bishop, the wildflowers were all gone and Castilian roses from Spain fell to the floor. On the cloak itself was an image of the Mother of All, just as Juan Diego had seen her in the sky—just as she was in the mural I passed today. Then everyone believed him and a church honoring Our Lady of Guadalupe was built on the ruins of the Temple of Tonantzin, at the place of her appearance.[7]

"To the Spanish Catholics, she seemed to be an appearance of Mary, the Mother of God, in the form of the Black Madonna in the monastery of Guadalupe in Spain—a sign that the Madonna and her blessings had followed them across the ocean to this new land. To the Aztec people, however, she seemed a sign that Tonantzin, the mother goddess, was still with them, even if she now dressed in the strange new clothing of the Spanish.

"Because she appeared to Juan Diego as a *meztiza,* a 'mixed one,' being *morena*—dark haired, and having some of the coloring of the

---

7. Although the story of Our Lady of Guadalupe is well-known, this version draws upon Mirabai Starr's telling in *Our Lady of Guadalupe* (Boulder, CO: Sounds True, 2008), 3–8.

native people, but with European features—she became a symbol of a long process of healing for a land that had been bathed in the blood of conquest. She became the 'Matroness' of México, the mother of the *meztizos*, a symbol of a new people.

"But today, as I looked at her—painted as a mural on the side of a liquor store—and thinking of how the peoples of the planet have embraced her and seek her healing—Mary, Mother of God, and Tonantzin, goddess of Sun and Moon—it seemed to me that she had come not only to heal México, but to build a bridge between heaven and earth, to heal the great divide between the *conquistadores*—who sought the secrets of the heavens and desired to encircle the earth—and the *indígenas*—the people of the earth, who lived close to her breast and womb, preserving the mystery of life.

"I remember aloud the words that are recorded about her in the *Nican Mopohua* . . .

I am truly your
Compassionate Mother,
Yours, and of all people
United on this land,
And of all the different races of peoples—
All those who love me,
All those who cry out for me,
All those who seek me,
All those who trust me.
I will listen to their weeping and their woes,
Remedy and cure their misery,
Their troubles, and their suffering.[8]

"The story is important; 'The Mother Who Loves All' knows no boundaries in her love. She is simply 'Mother' . . . to all. On this Day of Remembrance, let us remember that we are *all* her children."

---

8. See Starr, *Our Lady of Guadalupe*, 65.

The Hall of Worship

I had of course seen the image of Guadalupe many times while growing up in California, but I had never really understood her significance. Now she took on a new meaning for me.

As someone who also had a complex racial and cultural identity, I recognized her "mestiza consciousness" in my own story. I wondered how my professors and fellow students studying systems of cultural oppression and colonialism would react to such a story. Not too kindly, I thought. From their perspective, it might all seem a little too easy, washing the blood of conquest away without a reckoning.

And yet, the story touched me in ways my academic studies had not; I remembered how often I was left feeling angry, cynical, isolated, and helpless as I learned about the past. But now, somewhere deep in my heart, I felt a resonance, as if hearing a truth long forgotten or remembered at the edge of a fleeting dream.

I was curious to see who would follow this dignified woman. It was a slender man in carefully ironed clothing, with delicate brown features and a refined manner. He rose from his seat hesitantly and stood thoughtfully in front of the fire before speaking.

"My name is Seyyid Barkat Ali, and I am professor at the university here. I am, I confess, a man of books, most at home among dusty tomes in the library—unused to campfires at night. But, in those books is also a kind of light and warmth, which I find congenial in the cold stacks of the university library. In them, I find the tracks of our evolution and the evidence of our humanity, sometimes preserved only in tiny print, in footnotes of which I am the keeper. I become a discoverer and preserver of treasures, treasures important to our past, important for an understanding of ourselves, and treasures that may yet give us hope for the future.

"Close to my heart are the remnants of a sliver of time, a brief open window in the complex and troubled history of my home country —Bharata—or India, as it is mostly called today.

"In 1575, the Indian Mughal emperor, Akbar the Great, erected a special building in his capital called the 'Ibadat Khana,' the 'hall of worship.'

"The emperor had a special admiration for the learning and discourse of scholars. He had a keen mind and an extraordinary memory, and he loved to dialogue with various scholars of religion and to hear them dialogue with one another.[9]

"It was for this purpose that he built the Ibadat Khana.

"Though he began his life as an orthodox Sunni Muslim, in time, the emperor came under the influence of more liberal Sufi scholars and practitioners, and he eventually conceived the idea of inviting Muslim leaders and scholars of various sects to dialogue and debate in the hall of worship.

"Perhaps not surprisingly, they often disagreed and argued, and sometimes fights broke out in the hall of worship.[10] But even as he witnessed this sad display, it occurred to the emperor that the reason the scholars fought was because they were so *close* in opinion that they felt compelled to distinguish themselves by 'splitting hairs' over things on which they basically agreed, all in order to be 'right.' [11] So he grew curious as to what would happen if he brought together people who were not so close in their beliefs, the leaders of all the known religions in India—Muslims, Hindus, Christians, Zoroastrians, Buddhists, and more.

"In a letter to King Philip II of Spain, the emperor Akbar wrote of how he often enjoyed the company of 'learned people of all religions,' profiting 'from their exquisite discourses and exalted aspirations,' adding that few people are willing to investigate the truth of re-

---

9. John F. Richards, *The Mughal Empire* (Cambridge, UK: Cambridge University Press, 1996), 35.

10. Saiyid Athar Abbas Rizvi, *A History of Sufism in India*, 2 vols. (New Delhi: Munshiram Manoharlal Publishers, 1983), 2:81.

11. Satish Chandra, *History of Medieval India* (New Delhi: Orient Longman, 2007), 253–54.

ligion, instead following 'the religion in which they were born and educated, thus excluding themselves from the possibility of ascertaining the truth, which is the noblest aim of the human intellect.'[12]

"Unfortunately, the emperor found that the 'learned men of all religions' also argued. Nevertheless, in their discourse, he discovered something unexpected: they had many practices and teachings in common.

"The discovery of these commonalities was so inspiring to him that he began to talk about the 'Tawhid-i-Ilahi,' the 'divine unity,' or what some later called the 'Din-i-Ilahi,' the 'divine religion.' By this was meant that, perhaps, there was in the religions of humanity a kind of core that was shared by all, and even a set of ethical teachings and practices upon which all might agree and practice together, even if they maintained their commitments to particular traditions and communities.

"It is a footnote in our history, I know, but one to remember, I think, on this Day of Remembrance. It is one thread of the story of how we began to come together."

He then added with awkward solemnity, "The story is important; it is how we remember."

The Hyphen

I was charmed by the gently refined scholar, erudite and yet clearly uncomfortable without the protection of his books! And his footnote, was amazing to me; I had no idea that so long ago others had had such insight into religions and had made such noble efforts to make peace between them.

I was beginning to understand somewhat better now the diversity of faces around the circle, and what connected them. They were people who recognized, spiritually, something that I had been struggling to articulate from a sociological standpoint—the profound implications of our human diversity and our complex

12. Greg Considine, "Finding Tolerance in Akbar, the Philosopher-King," *Huffington Post*, April 10, 2013.

identities, as well as our common aspirations for peace and happiness across cultures and religions.

As I was thinking about this, I looked up and saw that an elder, perhaps in his early eighties, was now being rolled up to the Fire in a wheelchair. I realized that this man had actually spoken to me before the ritual began, his eyes twinkling as he welcomed me to the Fire, and I had shivered with a strange feeling of déjà vu. Now, as I sat outside the Circle, taking it in like an anthropologist, I noted his well-trimmed white beard and traditional Ottoman vest worn over a nicely ironed white shirt. And I saw two silver pendants hanging from a single chain around his neck, each glinting with light from the Fire. With surprising strength, he began speaking and said:

"In the past, like others, I have shared stories about the lives of saints who have inspired me, or moments in history that have served as foundations for us and that give us hope. But tonight, seeing that this is likely my last Fire, I want to share my own story. Today, my story is perhaps less unusual than it once was, as I am one of those whose life has been called 'hyphenated,' itself being a meeting-point between two religions, a 'calling' that early on I did not understand.

"My mother was Turkish, raised in a devout Sunni Muslim family. When she met and fell in love with my father, a committed Roman Catholic Christian traveling in Turkey, it created quite a stir. Her parents were distraught and refused to support the marriage unless he converted to Islam. But my mother and father actually loved one another's devotional life, and did not want either to have to convert. So they eloped and moved to the United States, settling in North Carolina. In time, my grandparents 'came around'—especially after I was born—visiting from Istanbul every couple of years; and we went to see them, as well.

"Both my parents actively practiced their faith. My dad attended Mass weekly, and my mom found a small, progressive mosque where she attended Friday *jummah* prayers. Occasionally they even joined each other in worship. So I grew up with *two* traditions: I was baptized and received communion in the Church, and I also joined my mom in fasting for Ramadan when I was twelve. We celebrated both Eid al-

Fitr and Christmas. I prayed both the Fatihah and the *Pater Noster*. In fact, as a child, I thought that everyone's parents belonged to different religions!

"I was in truth both Christian *and* Muslim. I loved and participated in both traditions. My parents never made it an issue, and so I never thought twice about it . . . that is, until I started high school. As I got involved with student groups, my friends became aware of my dual 'affiliation,' and I was told that there was no such thing as a Christian-Muslim or a Muslim-Christian. It was as if *I* didn't exist. My identity, my experience, my *lived-reality* was a contradiction and somehow invalid.

"Sadly, as one is wont to do in those tender years, I listened too much to my friends. I also began to believe I could not be both. I started to feel as if I had to choose between them. In a rather simplistic manner, I reasoned—'Well, the Prophet Muhammad came *after* Jesus, so Islam is the more *up-to-date* revelation.' It superseded Christianity. *Decision made.* With a heavy heart, I stopped attending church and became a Muslim . . . *only* a Muslim.

"With the zeal of a newly minted convert, I tried to convert my poor dad. You have to understand for *my choice* to be 'right,' my dad's choice had to be 'wrong.'

"Thank God, he was patient with me, and even supportive as I refused to attend Christmas or Easter celebrations, which we had always celebrated together as a family. Secretly, I missed those liturgies—the smell of the incense, the music, the candles—but I was committed to being a 'real' Muslim now.

"Then one year, while home from college, I decided that I was confident enough in my Muslim-only identity to join my dad at church. I thought, 'We don't do much together these days, and it'll make him happy.' As we settled into our pew, the organ prelude began, and much to my consternation and surprise, I found myself fighting back tears. Looking around, I saw the community with whom I had grown up. . . . People who loved me, people I loved, people from whom I had intentionally cut myself off in order to keep my religion 'pure.'

"When the time came for everyone to walk forward to the communion rail, I found myself longing to join them. I could almost taste that wine from where I stood, remembering my First

Communion—which my good Muslim mother had assured me was okay, as it was *'sacramental wine,'* and only a sip. *'Intention is everything,'* she said. Yet I was a 'better' Muslim than she was now—a 'real' Muslim—and so I stayed put as my dad walked forward to take communion, alone.

"But something inside me started to crack and give way as I sat in that pew; a wall I had constructed in my heart was beginning to crumble. The truth was, my 'double-belonging' had never been wrong, never been a lie. It was as organic to me as my own body, soul, and spirit. It was a fundamental fact of my being and experience. Christianity and Islam, church and mosque, were different worlds, but I had grown up with 'dual-citizenship.' No one could take that away from me unless I let them. *Why had I let them?*

"It took a few weeks, but later, back at school, I found my way to the local Catholic church and slipped into a pew. I hadn't consciously planned to, but when the time came, I found myself stepping into the communion line. After receiving the bread and wine, I didn't bother fighting back the tears. A connection that had nourished me for years returned, and along with it, an exiled part of my heart.

"It felt wonderful... *and confusing.* Did I now have to give up Islam? I decided then and there that I wasn't going to even entertain the idea. I didn't know exactly how it all fit together, but I was ready to start claiming both halves of my soul. And so, come Friday, I was back in the lines of prayer at our Muslim Student Association *jummah;* and then on Sunday, back in the pews for Mass.

"Because I was still a student, I began to research the lives of others who had identified with more than one religion. I found the writings of Swami Abhishiktananda—Henri Le Saux—a French Benedictine priest who, a hundred years before me, had experienced a struggle similar to mine, bridging the Christian and Hindu traditions in himself. These words of his leapt off the page and poured themselves into my heart—I've kept them on a scrap of paper in my wallet all these years....

> It is precisely the fact of being a bridge that makes this uncomfortable situation worthwhile. The world, at every level, needs such bridges. The danger of this life as a 'bridge' is that we run

> the risk of not belonging to either side; whereas, however harrowing it may be, our duty is to belong wholly to both sides.[13]

"It was as if an invisible weight had been lifted from my shoulders. *I* was not a contradiction; *I* was a bridge! And it was okay. Indeed, it was good—*needed*—and I began to recognize it more and more as a 'calling,' a vocation.

"A bridge, of course, connects two places that might otherwise remain unconnected—and allows something to flow between them. I found that dialogue between contemplative traditions, with their emphasis on profound realms of lived experience, was far more fruitful for my own integration than dialogue at the level of theology. Working over the years with Sufi Muslims and Christian contemplatives, I saw how both tended to point beyond the words to direct experience, to a meeting-place in the *guha,* the 'cave of the heart,' as Swami Abhishiktananda often called it. More and more, I feel that is where my own path has led. Hence, my story had never been one of conversion, as I once thought, but rather one of *'convergence.'* We are—all of us—points of convergence.

"Today, I wear these two pendants over my heart—one, a cross, a symbol of my Christianity; the other, the *Bismillah,* 'In the Name of God, the Infinitely Compassionate, the Infinitely Merciful,' written in Arabic calligraphy—words that open each *surah* of the Qur'an, and ideally every conscious act of a Muslim. There, two traditions, with long histories of mistrust, hatred, and violence between them—embrace on the ground of a single heart."

The Face of God

I was moved by the fact that tonight might be this fascinating man's last Fire, and honored that I would be among those who would now remember his story. His emphasis on lived experience challenged much of what I had learned in my studies, but it struck me that perhaps this

---

13. James Stuart, *Swami Abhishiktananda: His Life Told through His Letters* (Delhi: ISPCK, 1989), 213.

was also part of the meaning of the parable of the Bearers of Remembrance. We are a living testament of all that connects us, and for all that has been before us; it is our remembrance that holds us together!

Before I could let this sink in, a woman of dignified bearing, dressed in an elegant gray pin-striped suit with a bright purple shirt —which seemed somewhat out of place in the rustic surroundings— stood and approached the Fire.

"I was brought up," she said, "in Memphis, Tennessee. Our neighborhood church was strong in those days, and my parents raised me to be a good Christian. And though I 'backslid' some in my late teens, the values with which I was raised stayed with me, and eventually brought me back to the church.

"In time, I went to school and obtained my bachelor's and master's degrees in the social sciences. I taught for a while in a community college before eventually deciding to enter the seminary. Being a part of the African Methodist Episcopal Church, I attended Turner Theological Seminary in Atlanta, which is now more than two hundred years old, and then took up a position as a pastor in Nashville. After a number of years, I was elected bishop of my district, and an opportunity arose for me to go with a group of my fellow bishops to South Africa.

"Of course I wanted to go. Long before, I had learned that some of my ancestors may have been Zulu from South Africa, and so I viewed the trip as a kind of 'homecoming' and reclamation of a lost inheritance.

"For me, the trip was everything I had imagined, and I began to open my mind to other ways of looking at the world.

"In Soweto, I heard about a Zulu healer who said that she had actually seen God, and had even made a picture of God shortly thereafter.

"Well, all my life I had heard the 'Word,' and I had taught that 'Word,' the love of Jesus Christ, our Lord and Savior; but, I tell you, the moment I heard about this woman who had seen God's 'face,' I simply had to know what it was she had seen . . . to know what she *understood* that perhaps I did not.

"So I hired a guide and a translator to take me to this healer. When we arrived in her village, she came out of her hut, and I must admit I was surprised that a woman who had seen God appeared so ordinary. She was about my height and lighter skinned than I, wearing cheap sandals, a simple pair of trousers, a blue jacket, and a faded yellow shirt. I don't know what I expected her to look like, but it was not this. The only thing special about her was a circlet of rolled brown fabric set atop her head and a large beaded necklace.

"But she smiled in a friendly way as we greeted one another. Then, the three of us—myself, the translator, and the healer—all sat down on stumps around the cold remains of an old fire. I asked my translator to tell the healer why we had come, and to ask to see the picture of God she had made . . . and, if she was willing, to tell us what had happened when she had seen God.

"As my translator made my request, the healer looked at me and smiled. She then went into her hut and came back after a moment with a child's lesson book. When she handed it to me, I felt nervous. What would her 'God' look like? I wondered.

"I opened the battered old lesson book and found that it was part journal and part sketchbook. I turned the pages carefully, on each page expecting to see something extraordinary. And finally, there it was...*and it was extraordinary.* Though perhaps 'bizarre' would be a more honest descriptor of my impression at the time. I had never seen anything like it.

"There, in colored pencil, was an odd arrangement of heavy black lines. A horizontal line at the top of the page with a large black V-shape below to form the 'face,' I suppose. Inside and near the top of the V shape were two large cartoonish eyes, and what looked like a dark mustache or huge whiskers fanning out from the face, almost like fly wings! The face also appeared to have a very long nose, like on a toy I had once seen. 'God' also had a red-colored pate, and maybe something like black insect legs at the bottom, or a neck with fancy necklaces on it!

"This is 'God'?" I thought.

"Through my translator, I asked the Zulu healer to tell me where she had seen this 'God.'

"The woman pointed to a nearby mountain. 'There,' she said, 'one could meet God; but that one should not go there 'unprotected.'

"'And is this really what God looks like?' I asked, trying not to sound incredulous.

"The healer laughed unexpectedly, as if this were a silly question. . . . 'No, sister!' she said seriously through my translator, 'You cannot see *God;* you can only see *God's image,* as it appears to the eyes! This is a drawing of God's image as it appeared to me on the mountain that day. Some people think that it is dangerous to see God, but it is not dangerous, because we are not seeing God, but God's image. God's image allows us to *be* with God; otherwise, we could not *be* with God, because God is everywhere and all things. The only danger is in how we approach God and how we deal with God's image. Looking at God is not dangerous; drawing God's face is not dangerous. But when the "artist" is gone, and all there is to look at is the drawing—with no artist to tell you *how* to look at it—that is when looking at God becomes *dangerous.*' [14]

"As the Zulu healer spoke these profound words, I was taken back to my theological studies, to words I had hardly understood at the time, from Nicholas of Cusa, the German Renaissance theologian, who said:

> 'Oh Lord, how marvelous is your face, which the young will see as young, the old as old, the face beyond all faces and all concepts which can be formed of a face. In all faces is seen the face of faces veiled in a riddle of our own making. How could it ever be unveiled except we enter into that secret and mystic silence, where there is no knowledge or concept of a face? In that cloud darkness, beyond all knowledge or concept, the darkness itself reveals your face beyond all veils.'[15]

"So it was that I learned something important about how I had viewed God up to that point, and how I had judged the 'faces' of God that others had 'drawn' through the centuries, with no artists left to explain them to me—until, that is, I met an artist of the Zulu, who

---

14. Adapted from an encounter with a South African healer in the documentary series by Ronald Eyre, *The Long Search*, British Broadcasting Network, 1978.

15. Adapted from a work by Nicholas of Cusa, *De Visione Dei*, trans. Emma Gurney Salter (New York: E. P. Dutton and Co. 1928), 25–27.

could tell me that we were sisters in the spirit, despite the differences that separated us. Without ceasing to be a Christian, I left the village that day believing that this Zulu healer had indeed seen God's *image,* and did not mistake it for God, as I and so many others had done through the long centuries of our separation.

"The story is important; it is how we remember, and by remembering we survive."

By Many Names

What the Zulu woman had said stretched my capacity to understand; but I knew that I had heard something important . . . something I had never considered in my somewhat judgmental critiques of religion. . . . God is not our idea of God, and maybe we have been confusing the two all along!

Now someone of medium height, soft brown facial features, intelligent eyes, and reddish hair, approached the Fire. They were wrapped in a cream colored shawl with a rust-colored stripe along the edge, and spoke as if surprised to find themselves speaking at this particular moment.

"I did not originally intend to participate this evening; but it seems to me that these encounters, as much as they might appear to be 'between religions,' are actually experiences that point to a transformative internal experience that heals a divide in our consciousness. This is so in the heart of Juan Diego, overcoming the divide between the Virgin of Guadalupe and Tonantzin; this is so in the heart of Emperor Akbar, who sees the possibility of the *Din-i Illahi;* this is so in the convergence of Christianity and Islam in the cave of a single human heart; and forgive my presumption, sister, but it also appears to be so in your meeting with the Zulu healer, too, discovering God beyond God's masks. And I think this is perhaps the most important aspect of these 'meetings.'

"In my own order, the Ramakrishna Order, we celebrate the examples of the great saint Ramakrishna Paramahamsa and his wife, Sarada Devi, the 'Holy Mother,' who lived long ago.

"Ramakrishna was born into a poor but pious Bengali family of Brahmin priests devoted to the god Rama. By the time he was six or seven, Ramakrishna was already having natural experiences of *samadhi,* or meditative absorption. One morning, while walking the narrow ridges of a rice paddy, eating rice from a small basket, he saw a flock of milky white cranes flying against the backdrop of heavily laden black clouds that covered the entire sky. He stared in wonder at the marvelously compelling sight and lost all consciousness, later waking amid spilled rice on the ground.[16]

"In his late teens, Ramakrishna went to Kolkata, where a wealthy low-caste woman named Rani Rasmani had built the now famous Dakshineswar Kali Temple, following a vision of the goddess Kali. The problem was that no Brahmin priests were willing to serve at a temple built by a low-caste woman—that is, except Ramakrishna and his brother.[17]

"Soon after, Ramakrishna's brother died, leaving him as the sole priest of the temple. After arriving in Dakshineswar, Ramakrishna became increasingly devoted to the goddess Kali. Daily he begged her to reveal herself to him in a vision, sitting before her image absorbed in her, singing devotional hymns to her with profound emotion and longing.[18]

"As his devotion and desire to see Kali increased, Ramakrishna spent more and more time in meditation, freeing himself from all attachments to worldly things for her sake. When the sun went down each evening, he would cry out in anguish, 'Mother, another day is gone and still I have not seen you!' . . . 'Are you true, Mother, or is it all a fabrication of my mind, mere poetry without reality? If you do exist, why can't I see you?'[19]

"Eventually, Ramakrishna's devotion increased until, desperate to see and know Kali directly, he cried out in agony, 'What is the use of

---

16. Swami Chetanandanda, *Ramakrishna As We Saw Him* (St. Louis: Longman's, Green and Co., 1990), 13.

17. Swami Saradananda, *Sri Ramakrishna*, The Great Master, trans. Swami Jagadananda (Sri Ramakrishna Math, 1978), 14, 114–20, 134.

18. Saradananda, *Sri Ramakrishna*, 135–39.

19. Chetanandanda, *Ramakrishna As We Saw Him*, 403.

this life?!' Suddenly his gaze fell on the sword that hangs in the temple. He decided to end his life with it, then and there. Like a madman, he ran to it and seized it. At that very moment, he had a marvelous vision of Mother Kali and fell down, seeing houses, doors, temple, and everything else around him vanishing into emptiness. Later, he said:

> What I saw was a boundless infinite conscious sea of light! However far and in whatever direction I looked, I found a continuous succession of effulgent waves coming forward, raging and storming from all sides with a great speed. Very soon they fell on me and made me sink to the unknown bottom. I panted, struggled, and fell unconscious. I did not know what happened then in the external world—how that day and the next slipped away. But, in my heart of hearts, there was flowing a current of intense bliss, never experienced before, and I had the immediate knowledge of the light that was Mother.

He was later found on the ground uttering the word, *Ma*—Mother—repeatedly.[20]

"Now maybe this is not the kind of intense 'spirituality' some people want today; but it should be remembered that it is these experiences of the great mystics, and especially the transformations that follow them, that cut and clear the broad Path that others can then follow. Whatever their desires or purposes, the destination of that Path is a unity where all desires and purposes come together. This is why we gather, and how our gathering connects to the great spiritual purpose that we all share!

"And this is what Ramakrishna Paramahamsa sought, too. After his great vision, he was captured by this unity, so that everyday experiences became profound realizations, transforming his awareness of the ordinary world. 'One day,' he said, 'it was suddenly clear to me that everything is Pure Spirit. The utensils of worship, the altar, the doorframe—all Pure Spirit. Human beings, animals, and other living beings

---

20. Chetanandanda, *Ramakrishna As We Saw Him*, 14, and Saradananda, *Sri Ramakrishna*, 140–41.

—all Pure Spirit. Then like a madman I began to shower flowers in all directions. Whatever I saw I worshiped!' On another occasion, he reported: 'I had been plucking flowers when it was revealed to me that each plant was a bouquet adorning the universal form of God. That was the end of my plucking flowers. I look on people in just the same way. When I see a person, I see that they are God, walking on earth!'[21]

The young monastic then stretched out a hand from under their shawl and pointed at us with their finger.

"You see, this Circle is not *'just a circle,'* any more than the practices of our traditions are just a 'means of relaxation' in a hectic world. The ritual and the practices are tools of transformation! They are the means of transforming our awareness, so that when we look at the world we see God, and when we look at each other we see God! And when we *really* see God in each other, then petty meanness and divisiveness has no place in our interactions. This is the realization of the unity at the heart of our diversity.

"For Ramakrishna, that realization did not end with flowers and people, but also extended into his relationship with other religions. For him, this was not an intellectual exercise; it was a part of his devotion. The goddess Kali, the Mother, was *shakti,* 'divine energy' taking diverse forms throughout the Cosmos—in flowers, people, religions. Thus, the individual paths that these religions represent became for him a means of knowing different aspects of the one Mother. He practiced diligently the spiritual paths of different religious traditions, and achieved through them his own unique realizations.

"Of course, he meant no disrespect in this. He did not mean to say that he represented those traditions; he only wanted to know more and more of God through them. No matter what their differences might be, for Ramakrishna they were all still expressions of the one Reality.[22]

"Ramakrishna's experience gives light to all of us as we pursue our paths; but perhaps because of its intensity, his wife's journey has

---

21. Adapted from *The Gospel of Sri Ramakrishna*, trans. Swami Nikhilananda (New York: Ramakrishna-Vivekananda Center, 1942), 396.

22. See Swami Atmarupananda in *The Common Heart: An Experience of Interreligious Dialogue*, ed. Netanel Miles-Yépez (New York: Lantern Books, 2006), 55–57.

often been a more accessible model for me to follow. Sarada Devi, or the 'Holy Mother' as we call her, was also born into a poor Bengali Brahmin family, and lived the simple life of an Indian village girl. But she was also fascinated by traditional Hindu folklore and stories and had a deep childhood devotion to the goddesses Kali and Lakshmi. It is said that she meditated even as a child and sometimes experienced visions too.[23]

"Worrying that Ramakrishna's spiritual life was becoming too intense, his mother and older brother proposed a match to the serious and kind young Sarada Devi, who they hoped would have a steadying effect on him, bringing him into the responsibilities of marriage.[24] So, when she was eighteen years old, Sarada Devi came to live with Ramakrishna at Dakshineswar. Being older than she was, he instructed her in meditation and explained aspects of the spiritual life to her.[25] To Ramakrishna, who was a *brahmachari*, or 'celibate' spiritual practitioner, she was the goddess herself, and he treated her as the Divine Mother, calling her always 'Sri Ma.'[26]

"In this spiritual marriage, Sarada Devi became a great practitioner, rising at 3:00 a.m. to make her ablutions in the river, and practicing *mantra-japa* and meditation until daybreak. Ramakrishna taught her the sacred mantras she used, and he instructed her in how to initiate and guide others in the spiritual life. Over time, a number of dedicated young students flocked to learn from Ramakrishna, and to them, Ramakrishna and Sarada Devi were father and mother.[27]

---

23. Swami Ghanananda and John Steward-Wallace, *Women Saints: East and West* (Hollywood: Vedanta Press, 1979), 95–98.

24. Carl T. Jackson, *Vedanta for the West* (Bloomington: University of Indiana Press, 1994), 18.

25. Gayatri Chakravorty Spivak, *Other Asias: Occasional Essays* (Malden, MA: Wiley-Blackwell, 2008) 207–8.

26. Romain Rolland, *The Life of Ramakrishna* (Hollywood: Vedanta Press, 1929), 59.

27. Ghanananda and Steward-Wallace, *Women Saints,* 102; Sharada Sugirtharajah, *Imaging Hinduism* (Oxfordshire: Routledge), 129; Swami Nikhilananda, *Gospel of the Holy Mother Sri Sarada Devi* (Chennai: Sri Ramakrishna Math, 1984), Introduction.

"After Ramakrishna's passing, Sarada Devi made a pilgrimage through northern India, accompanied by a party of Ramakrishna's disciples, both men and women. Later, at Vrindavan, associated with the god Krishna, Sarada Devi experienced an extraordinary meditative state and thereafter began to serve as *guru* to many disciples.[28] Shortly before her death, she said to her devotees, 'I tell you one thing—if you want peace of mind, do not find fault with others. Rather, see your own faults. Learn to make the whole world your own. No one is a stranger, my child: this whole world is your own!'[29]

"This was her last message, that there are no strangers in the world—no strangers in this Circle—because the world exists in our consciousness! All the petty differences we insist upon exist inside of us! Thus, it is with ourselves that we must make peace, and refuse to be divided outside.

"The story of the Path and the Goal is important; it is how we remember, and by remembering we survive."

Liminal Roots

As the monk of the Ramakrishna Order turned to sit, it occurred to me that I had never really considered why someone might undertake such intense practices; but here it was, in the experience of Ramakrishna and Sarada Devi. They wished to see God "walking on earth," to transform their awareness of seemingly ordinary things, seeing their special beauty and sacredness at all times—instead of living in ignorance of the hidden divinity, as we so often do. For the first time, I began to realize that there was a 'spiritual path' available to me, a path whose goal was a kind of maturation of consciousness, taking one beyond the things that divide into a sacred unity and love for all creation.

---

28. Ghanananda and Steward-Wallace, *Women Saints*, 107–8; Christopher Isherwood, *Ramakrishna and His Disciples* (New York: Simon and Schuster, 1964), 314.

29. Adapted from Ghanananda and Steward-Wallace, *Women Saints*, 115–16.

As I silently pondered my own "spiritual path"—or lack thereof—a thin Black woman with large owlish eyes approached the Fire. The movements of her hands from under her shawl were small and delicate as she rubbed them together for warmth. When she spoke, it was in a precise manner, intellectual, and deeply thoughtful.

"Tonight, I wish to share a remembrance of one of my own spiritual ancestors, the Reverend Dr. Howard Thurman, whose blessings and guidance are still sorely needed. Dr. Thurman is one of the greatest contemplatives our country has ever produced. His book, *Jesus and the Disinherited,* has been a treasured companion throughout my life, shedding light on and guiding me along the spiritual path from the unique perspective of oppressed peoples.[30] You see, Dr. Thurman's deeply transformative spirituality was never separate from his struggles for justice. Living as a Black man in the twentieth century, in a racially divided and oppressive society, he simply didn't have a choice to separate justice from his spirituality.

"If you've never heard of him, Dr. Thurman was a Black American mystic and a mentor to many in the American Civil Rights era, including the beloved Reverend Dr. Martin Luther King Jr. In fact, it is rumored that Dr. King carried a copy of *Jesus and the Disinherited* with him wherever he went. Thurman often said: 'Life holds a crown over my head that I'm always trying to grow tall enough to wear.'[31] This has been a comfort to me in hard times, and humbling in times of triumph.

"I like to tell people that he was a mystic from Daytona Beach in Florida! It reminds them that mystics are not from some faraway place, but right next door. Howard Thurman was born in 1899. His greatest influences in childhood were his grandmother, a former slave, and Nature Herself. His grandmother more or less raised him, and from her he learned a fierce dignity and sense of divine worth that would forever form the core of his mystical life. From Nature, he learned of a transcendent mystery, one he could feel in Her rhythms

30. Howard Thurman, *Jesus and the Disinherited* (New York: Abingdon-Cokesbury, 1949).

31. A saying of Howard Thurman repeated in many contexts.

and modes of life. The woods and the rivers befriended him, giving him a sense of belonging he failed to find elsewhere. One particular oak tree became 'a close friend,' and still stands to this day. The dark and quiet night became his secret refuge, and he would spend long hours listening to the sounds of the ocean tides. In them he discovered a 'sense of timelessness,' and experienced an existence that reached beyond 'the ebb and flow of circumstances.' Through this, he developed a fundamental rootedness in Life itself, in Nature.[32]

"It was to this rootedness, deep in the center of his own being, that he credited his ability to survive as a Black man in America. These experiences of the 'root of his being' allowed him to live

> beyond all the ravages inflicted upon it by the brutalities of the social order. To live under siege, with the equilibrium and tranquility of peace, to prevent the springs of my being from being polluted by the bitter fruit of the climate of violence, to hold and re-hold the moral initiative of my own action and to seek the experience of community, all this to whatever extent it has been possible to achieve it, is to walk through a door that no person can shut.'

"In 1936, Dr. Thurman traveled to India as part of the first African-American contingent to meet with Mahatma Gandhi. At the time, Thurman had already developed a distinctly African-American approach to pacifism and non-violent resistance. He and Gandhi had much to share. They spoke of the brutalities of oppression, the means of resistance, and the place of spiritual power—what Gandhi called *satyagraha,* 'truth' or 'soul force'—in bringing about change in the world.

"As their time together came to an end, Gandhi said to Thurman that it may be through Black Americans 'that the unadulterated message of non-violence will be delivered to the world.' Nearly twenty years later, the queer Black organizing genius Bayard Rustin recounted these words at the founding of the Southern Christian Lead-

32. Peter Eisenstadt, *Against the Hounds of Hell: A Life of Howard Thurman* (Charlottesville: University of Virginia Press, 2021), 23–46.

ership Conference in 1957—which went on to become the vehicle for Martin Luther King Jr.'s work.[33] You see, my friends, those liminal roots among our traditions have often grown especially strong amongst the oppressed.

"During his trip to India, Thurman also had a spiritual experience that guided him for the rest of his life—one that I find particularly pertinent for our ritual here tonight. While traveling over the Khyber Pass in the Hindu Kush mountains, in what are now the borderlands of Afghanistan and Pakistan, peering out into the endless depths of the inner Himalayas, he had a vision:

> All that we had seen and felt in India seemed to be brought miraculously into focus. We saw clearly what we must do somehow when we returned to America. We knew that we must test whether a religious fellowship could be developed in America that was capable of cutting across all racial barriers, with a carry-over into common life, a fellowship that would alter the behavior patterns of those involved. *It became imperative now to find out if experiences of spiritual unity among people could be more compelling than the experiences which divide them.*[34]

"This vision brought a powerful focus to Dr. Thurman's life: Could human beings overcome their differences through spiritual experience? Could the power dynamics of race, class, gender, religious difference, and more be transcended—and even healed—through a sharing of spiritual experience? Some years after returning from India, he went on to found one of the first interracial, interreligious churches in America—The Church for the Fellowship of All Peoples—not far from our Circle tonight in San Francisco, and later became dean of Marsh Chapel at Boston University, the first Black man to be so named at a major majority-white university.[35]

---

33. Eisenstadt, *Against the Hounds of Hell*, 7–8.

34. Howard Thurman, *Footprints of a Dream: The Story of the Church for the Fellowship of All Peoples* (New York: Harper and Brothers, 1959), 24, emphasis added.

35. Eisenstadt, *Against the Hounds of Hell*, 218–307.

"At the Church for the Fellowship of All Peoples, he was able to experiment. He tested the question: Are spiritual experiences of unity more important 'than all the concepts, prejudices, ideologies, fears that may divide' us? He learned that if you can multiply 'these experiences of unity' over extended periods of time—coming together regularly in sacred spaces, then 'you can undermine any barrier that separates one person from another,' just as we are doing tonight.[36]

"One of the commitments of the Church was a vow that has been a guiding light in my own life—'I desire to share in the spiritual growth and ethical awareness of men and women of varied national, cultural, racial, and creedal heritage united in a religious fellowship.'[37] There is a story from the Church that I always think of when I recount this vow. . . .

"Dr. Thurman tells of sitting with a young Japanese secretary in the office of the Church, as they listened together to radio reports on the day the U.S. dropped an atomic bomb on Hiroshima, Japan. The young lady had family in Hiroshima, and the two of them sat in silence, listening to the reports throughout the day, unable to speak. But something was being shared between them that ran deeper than words and bridged any distance between them. As he put it: 'We could establish no psychological distance between ourselves and the horror of the moment. The experience flowed together as a single moment in time. This was the Fellowship Church, not in action but in *being*.'[38]

"This was also what it meant to *'share in the spiritual growth'* of others in a diverse religious fellowship. It meant being present to one another in the most trying of times, and developing the inner resources

---

36. See Thurman, *Footprints of a Dream* for a detailed account of his work with the Church for the Fellowship of All Peoples.

37. Thurman, *Footprints of a Dream*, 158.

38. Howard Thurman, *With Head and Heart: The Autobiography of Howard Thurman* (Boston: Houghton Mifflin Harcourt, 1981), 162. To learn more about Howard Thurman, see the filmed "Conversations with Howard Thurman: Howard Thurman Talks with Landrum Bolling," made available by the Howard Thurman Educational Trust.

necessary to do so. We continue on in that spirit of sacred Fellowship here tonight, some of us the great-great-grandchildren of congregants in that very same church.

"The stories are important. They are how we remember our ancestors and bring forth their blessings. They are how we recognize one another and affirm one another in the 'roots of our being.' Each life is an embryo of unique gifts for the good of the world. And each life is entangled with our own, somewhere down in those shared, liminal roots. As Thurman's mentee Dr. King said: 'We are caught in an inescapable network of mutuality, tied in a single garment of destiny. Whatever affects one directly affects all indirectly.' And thus, 'injustice anywhere' will always be 'a threat to justice everywhere.'"[39]

The Pipe and the Prayer Book

The thin woman turned to take her seat again. While I wondered if Thurman's Japanese secretary had understood the significance of that moment in the same way,[40] I realized that I had never considered that there might be a deeper connection between spirituality and activism. For me, they were largely separate—a notion reinforced in the academy. Even when I learned about the Civil Rights Movement, and the involvement of Black churches throughout the American South, I had somehow thought of their involvement as "social," not spiritual. Why had I assumed that? Was it because I did not know a

---

39. Martin Luther King Jr., *A Testament of Hope: The Essential Writings and Speeches of Martin Luther King, Jr.*, ed. James M. Washington (New York: HarperCollins, 1990), 290.

40. Eisenstadt, *Against the Hounds of Hell*, 247: "In March 1945, answering an urgent need of Thurman's, the church hired Ayoka Murota, recently returned from the [Japanese-American detention] camps, as its first secretary. A few months later, Thurman was sitting in his office, holding her hand 'from 8:30 in the morning until 2:00 in the afternoon while the tidings of Hiroshima were coming across the air. Her aunts, her uncles, her nephews were all there. Now and then, the grip of my hand would tighten on hers, or the grip of her hand would tighten in mine. There were no words for words were raspy noises, unuttered in the discipline that would make manifest what was stirring in our hearts.'"

spirituality of depth or didn't have a contemplative life of my own? As I looked around the Circle, taking in its marvelous diversity, I had the sense of something missing in my life. For here were the very roots of the change I had so hoped to see in the world, not passionately proclaimed as I had so often done, but clearly embodied.

While I pondered this lacuna in my own life, a man wrapped in a colorful blanket rose from the shadows and approached the fire. He was an Indigenous man, and I instinctively called him "grandfather" in my head, though part of me wondered if I was stereotyping him. While his hair was jet black and youthful, tied at the back, his face was older, with the hollows and lines of long experience. He wore old-fashioned half-lens glasses like those I had seen in movies, and held a sacred pipe in the crook of one arm and what looked like a small black leather book with gold-edged pages in the other.

"In the memory of my people," he said slowly, "are many important stories, stories we must remember if we are to continue together. Among them is one we did not understand for many long years, and which we are still trying to understand, but that has nevertheless long since spread far and wide. Another is less well known, even among our elders, but is no less important, I think. Both concern our ancestor, whose people called him "Heháka Sápa,"—the Holy Man who, in the language of the Wasi'chus-who-changed-our-future, is called Black Elk.

"When Black Elk was nine years old, he took sick and lay in a fever for many days, during which he was visited by the Wakinyan, the Thunder Beings, who showed him a great vision. Years later, he told his vision to the medicine man, Black Road.[41] He told of how he had arrived at the highest mountain in the center of the world and made four increasingly difficult ascents that signaled the changing fortunes of his people and the breaking of their 'sacred hoop.' But there was hope, too; for he said:

---

41. John G. Neihardt, *Black Elk Speaks* (Lincoln: University of Nebraska Press, 2014), 13, 29, 100.

> I looked ahead and saw the mountains there with rocks and forests on them, and from the mountains flashed all colors upward to the heavens. Then I was standing on the highest mountain of them all, and round about beneath me was the whole hoop of the world. And while I stood there I saw more than I can tell and understood more than I saw; for I was seeing in a sacred manner the shapes of all things in the spirit, and the shape of all shapes as they must live together like one being. And I saw that the sacred hoop of my people was one of many hoops that made one circle, wide as daylight and as starlight, and in the center grew one mighty flowering tree to shelter all the children of one mother and one father. And I saw that it was holy.[42]

"All his days, Black Elk struggled to understand this vision and his people's place in it. He embraced all things that he believed might be in accord with his vision and which might restore the sacred hoop of his people and of all people. This was because he was a 'holy man.' And for this reason, he made peace with the ones who changed our future, and even embraced their cross. And yet, he did not abandon the ways of our people and kept the sacred pipe close to his heart, even as he prayed with his rosary.

"So it was, we are told by his granddaughter, that one day he was visited by his friend the priest in the springtime. The priest knocked at the door, and when he entered, he saw Black Elk preparing to smoke the *chanupa*, his sacred pipe. At once, the priest marched up to Black Elk, grabbed the pipe from his hands, and said, 'This is the work of the devil!' He then threw the *chanupa* out the open door and into the dirt!

"Black Elk did not say a word, but simply arose and took the prayer book from the priest's hand and threw it out the door into the dirt as well! For a long time, the two men just looked at each other. Then both walked outside. The priest picked up his prayer book and carefully brushed the dirt off it, and Black Elk lifted his *chanupa* from the ground and lovingly dusted it off. The two men looked at each other again until an expression of understanding passed between

42. Neihardt, *Black Elk Speaks*, 26.

them; then they smiled, shook hands, and entered the house together as friends.[43]

"Today, my friends, I bring a sacred pipe and a prayer book to the Fire as testimony to the truth of how things *are,* that both are now joined in the destiny of my people. It is important to respect the sacred gifts and ways of all. Though the road of their friendship has been hard, and there is much yet to learn, we must enter the house in peace, respecting the prayer book and the pipe in the same circle of life. Here in this Circle, we see what Heháka Sápa had hoped to witness all the days of his life, the sacred hoop of his people joined with the hoops of all peoples in peace.

"This story is important to my people; it is how we remember, and by remembering we survive."

Only Yesterday's Dream

I swallowed, unable to understand my own reactions to the story. My body was beginning to ache from the long sitting, too. I thought of the horror of the Christian boarding schools, and the near genocide of his people, and wondered how the pipe and the prayer book could possibly exist in peace. But maybe my understanding was not required. After all, it was not my story. I found myself looking at the elder who had returned to his seat, holding both the pipe and the prayer book in his hands, and I instinctively bowed my head.

After a moment, a young woman wearing a mustard-yellow shawl over black robes came forward with a determined step. She had an almost military crispness to her manner, but in the firelight, I could see that she had an intense and honest face, intelligent blue eyes,

---

43. Adapted from Hilda Neihardt and Lori Utecht, eds., *Black Elk Lives: Conversations with the Black Elk Family* (Lincoln: University of Nebraska Press, 2000), 137. And incident witnessed by Nicholas Black Elk's granddaughter, Esther. The priest was Father Placidus Sialm. Also discussed in Joe Jackson, *Black Elk: The Life of an American Visionary* (New York: Farrar, Straus and Giroux, 2016), 440.

and a mass of naturally wavy—almost crimped—blonde hair. She began somewhat formally. . . .

"This story, friends, happened more than two hundred years ago, not far from where we gather this evening.

"In May of 1923, a Zen master and a Sufi master met for the first time in San Francisco. The Zen master was Nyogen Senzaki, one of the principal students of Shaku Soyen, who had first visited the United States in 1893 for the World Parliament of Religions. Senzaki Roshi, a Japanese immigrant, lived an unassuming life in San Francisco, working quietly in hotels and other establishments, the guests having no idea that a Zen master and scholar of profound accomplishment was operating the elevator or clearing their tables!

"Of course, there were some who were aware of his accomplishments, and Senzaki Roshi—who was among the earliest Zen teachers in America—taught Zen to small groups of Americans in his 'Floating Zendo' located in cafes, libraries, and any other place that would accommodate them. He also often spent time in discussion with learned people in the great city.[44]

"Thus, he discovered that a great Sufi master was soon to be visiting San Francisco—Hazrat Inayat Khan—who was himself the first Sufi master to come to the West. Inayat Khan had arrived from India teaching a Sufism that was universal in orientation, being, as he said, a 'religion of the heart.'[45]

"Senzaki Roshi often used the library of one of Inayat Khan's students, Murshida Rabia Martin, who was herself the first American-born Sufi. Murshida Martin felt that Senzaki Roshi might be interested in meeting her own *murshid*, Inayat Khan, and thus invited Senzaki Roshi to meet Inayat Khan at her home.

---

44. Roko Sherry Chayat, ed., *Eloquent Silence: Nyogen Senzaki's Gateless Gate and Other Previously Unpublished Teachings and Letters* (Boston: Wisdom Publications, 2008), 5–8.

45. Netanel Miles-Yépez, *In the Teahouse of Experience: Nine Talks on the Path of Sufism* (Boulder: Albion-Andalus Books, 2021), 15–16.

"On his way to the appointment, Senzaki Roshi bumped into another acquaintance, Dr. Hayes, a psychologist.

"'Where are you going?' Dr. Hayes asked.

"'I am going to meet Inayat Khan,' he replied.

"'Oh, that Sufi teacher?'" said the doctor. 'I attended his lecture this morning at the Sufi Temple. It was such a tiresome ceremony—the lighting of candles, much bowing, and all that. The lecture bristled with too much about *God* and *Love*. There was nothing new in it, and I had to pay one dollar for admission. Still, I'll come along with you to meet him.'

"'If you do not feel like going,' Senzaki Roshi replied, 'you need not come with me; I am not asking you to do so.'

"'Well,' said Dr. Hayes, 'At least they won't charge anything for an interview. I'll go with you.'

"Thus it was that the two men went to the home of Murshida Martin.

"When they arrived, they were ushered into the meditation room. It was dimly lit by a lamp covered with a green silk cloth, while fragrant Persian incense filled the room.

"Murshida Martin then introduced Nyogen Senzaki Roshi to Hazrat Inayat Khan. After shaking hands in the American fashion, they all sat down at a square table, with Murshida Martin facing Dr. Hayes, and Inayat Khan facing Nyogen Senzaki.

"The psychologist, Dr. Hayes—taking a cigar out of his pocket—began talking to the Sufi master, asking how he liked America and its people, evidently unsure if he should light a cigar in a Sufi master's presence.

"Inayat Khan did not answer him, but smiled at Senzaki Roshi and asked him, 'Mr. Senzaki, will you tell me what the significance of Zen is?'

"Senzaki Roshi looked at him in silence for a while, and then smiled.

"Inayat Khan smiled back at him.

"The dialogue was over.

"The psychologist, not having understood what had just taken place, said, 'You see, Mr. Khan, Zen is Japan-ized from Sanskrit. Its original meaning is *Dhyana*, which means meditation, and…'

"At that point, Inayat Khan waved his right hand gracefully and stopped the psychologist's explanation.

"Murshida Martin then interposed, saying, 'I will get a book that describes Zen very well. It is an English translation from Japanese of *The Twelve Sects of Buddhism.* I will get it for you.'"

But, again, before she could rise from her seat, Inayat Khan waved his hand gracefully—this time his left hand, stopping the *murshida.*

"He then glanced at Senzaki Roshi, his eyes suddenly full of tears—not tears of the world—tears from the Great Ocean, calm and transparent.

"Senzaki Roshi then recited an old Zen poem:

No living soul comes near that water —
A vast sheet of water as blue as indigo.
The Abyss has a depth of ten-thousand feet.
When all is quiet and calm, at midnight,
Only the moonlight penetrates into the waves,
And reaches the bottom easily and freely.

"At the end of the poem, Senzaki Roshi said, 'Murshid, I see a Zen in you.'

"'Mr. Senzaki,' the Sufi master replied, 'I see a Sufism in you.'

"Both men smiled at one another.

"Murshida Martin interrupted again. 'Mr. Senzaki, you should practice your English; why don't you talk more about Zen?'

"At this comment, both the Zen master and the Sufi master laughed out loud.

"Murshida Martin and the psychologist joined in the laughter, too, but without knowing why.

"The happy interview was over. But the psychologist seemed to want to go on talking with the Sufi master, explaining as much as he asked, while Murshida Martin showed off her collection of books. So they remained there the whole evening, discussing a wide range of subjects.

"Senzaki Roshi noted that Inayat Khan used the Nyaya system of logic in making affirmations, and this made him feel very much at home with the Sufi, as Buddhists use the same system.

"Inayat Khan then told them of his ideal of Universal Fellowship, which he believed would be established in time, and which he also believed would transcend all national and ethnic boundaries, as well as harmonize all religions to the extent that they could work together in harmony for the uplifting of humanity, and for the advancement of the spiritual world.

"Inayat Khan—who was among the greatest Indian classical musicians of his day—also expressed the wish to attend a concert of Japanese classical music. Senzaki Roshi could not find any that were billed for that week, so he went to Madame Nakamura, who taught the *koto* in her home, and he asked her to invite Inayat Khan to hear her play.

"She consented gladly, and Senzaki Roshi proceeded to the Sufi Temple on Kearney Street to tell Inayat Khan about this arrangement. It was about two o'clock in the afternoon, and the Sufi master asked the Zen master to meditate with him in a secluded room where his pupils received personal guidance from him. They then sat down to meditate together; but before even one stick of incense was consumed, both entered *samadhi.* Thus, they were surprised when Murshida Martin suddenly called them, saying that it was already dark!

"The two masters looked at each other in surprise, but nodded a knowing assent. The incense was completely consumed, and had been out so long that no fragrance remained in the room. Both Sufism and Zen had become only yesterday's dream.

"Shortly thereafter, Inayat Khan visited Madame Nakamura's studio, accompanied by Senzaki Roshi. The simplicity of Inayat Khan's manners and conduct on the way impressed Senzaki Roshi. Wearing a Turkish hat and a long black mantle, and carrying a cane, the Sufi master rode the streetcars with a simple air of dignity and majesty.

"The concert at Madame Nakamura's was a great success. The first number on her program was *Chidori,* which she played on the *koto,* accompanied by another *koto* played by one of her pupils and a *shakuhachi* played by a Japanese youth.

"The Sufi master's attention to the music was keen, and he observed an almost breathless silence.

"When the performance was over, Inayat Khan praised Madame Nakamura warmly, saying that she was 'music itself, not only with her *koto,* but also in drinking tea or in walking around the room.' Madame Nakamura appreciated this comment, as the Sufi master was a poet and a musician who was not given to flattery.

"Inayat Khan then left the studio, saying that he would tell European musicians about the deep impressions this music had made on him.

"Having reached the street corner where they were to part ways, Senzaki Roshi turned to Inayat Khan and said, 'All sounds return to one, and where does that one go?'

"Inayat Khan stopped walking and offered his hand to Senzaki Roshi, saying, 'Goodnight, Mr. Senzaki.'

"They shook hands, eyes meeting with welling tears. 'Goodnight, Mr. Khan.'

"A moment later, they went their separate ways.[46]

"May we learn to recognize one another beyond words, and may depth commune with depth in the silence that speaks."

Life Revealed as Love

As the young woman in robes turned back to her seat, my head was still echoing with the question, "All sounds return to one, and where does that one go?" I wasn't sure I understood what it meant; but I loved the understanding between these two old masters of different cultures and traditions. I felt intuitively that wisdom was a well from which anyone could drink. But how does one find that well? And why do so few seek it? My own questions showed me that I was clearly far from the "silence that speaks" . . .

I thought this must now be the turn of the younger folks because a youthful-looking man came forward. He wore jeans with a nice sport coat, showing the designs of a t-shirt underneath. His manner was easy and relaxed. I thought he might be a young professor of physics or philosophy at my university. Stopping at the Fire, he took a

46. Adapted from Nyogen Senzaki's first-person account in his article "Sufism and Zen" found in the archives of the Sufi Ruhaniat International. A less complete version is found in *Eloquent Silence*, 242–43.

moment to look at everyone, a smile on his face, and then began in a tone more casual than the others. . . .

"I wasn't sure if I was going to speak tonight. The truth is, I don't like speaking about my personal experiences or talking at gatherings. But I find myself now moved—I guess you'd say—to share some of my own story tonight, or at least a few experiences that have been important to me and seem relevant now.

"When I was twelve or maybe thirteen, I heard a priest give a wonderful sermon about God being 'like a friend'—in fact, the 'best of friends.' 'When you have a best friend,' he said, 'there isn't even a need to speak to one another on some occasions. You can just hang out, relaxing in one another's presence.' Thinking about this later that night while lying in bed, I decided to try it. I remember asking God, a bit sheepishly, if it was okay to simply 'hang out,' with no words of prayer. I didn't want to be blasphemous—despite my often mischievous behavior—not this time, at least. But much to my surprise, I didn't feel any judgment or that I was doing anything wrong. I felt the opposite. I was *immediately* embraced by a loving, calming presence, which saturated the room. It was something I had never felt before. God really *was* my friend—and willing to hang out in my bedroom! After that, I often thought of God as my 'best friend,' someone I could hang out with without the need of either of us to speak; and we did hang out, sometimes for hours!

"Though I had never heard of a 'spiritual journey,' a transformative path was already beginning to unfold itself before me. But it wasn't until college, really, that I discovered what a spiritual journey meant . . . reading about people from all walks of life who described some kind of 'Path' leading to a transformed consciousness, much like what our friend said about Ramakrishna earlier. It made sense to me, seeing how all these people from differing epochs, cultures, ethnicities, races, and religions could describe something so eerily similar—that *something* along these lines *had* to be true. It's not that what they described was the *same;* nevertheless, their descriptions of spiritual transformation resonated through the most profound human differences. I became 'sold' on such a 'contemplative project.' It seemed to me the most consequential thing a person could do in this life, and the best way one could serve others and the wider world. So I devoted myself—body, mind, and soul—to a spiritual path.

"Years later, on a languid summer's evening—it sounds funny to say it . . . but I was observing the mosquitoes buzzing around me, when I suddenly found myself asking God sincerely, 'What possible use is there in a mosquito? . . . How many countless people have suffered and died because of them?' It was a funny question; but there was a seriousness in it for me.

"A few weeks later, I got my answer. I was meditating under a tree sometime after midnight, when a mosquito came buzzing around. I watched silently as it bounced among the hair follicles on my arm—frolicking, it seemed to me, biting and sucking my blood as if I wasn't there watching it the whole time. It seemed blissfully unaware of the consequences of its actions, caught up in its dangerous game of survival.

"For some reason, the whole situation suddenly struck me as a cosmic joke. *Silly mosquito!* I thought. *Innocent and daring, flying around and biting people!*

"In the middle of a laugh, a revelation suddenly descended on me. *This is how it is with all of us.* The vision was overwhelming. I saw that we are all wandering this Earth, mostly unaware of our actions, hurting one another—and at some profound level—*innocent.* We are like the mosquito, ignorant of the worlds in which we are living—frolicking about—heedless of the consequences of our actions . . . for each other, for the planet, and for the many dimensions of reality with which our own lives are profoundly entangled.

"Just then, another wave of revelation washed over me, and I saw that despite my ignorance, somehow, all that I had done in my life had arisen out of Love—for Love was all that existed.

"There was *nothing* other than this Love. Everything, at its core, was simply an outpouring of Love. There was nothing *doing* the outpouring; there was *only* the outpouring—a divine, dynamic *emptiness* at the center of everything—including 'me'! I was eternal, primordial, and death was but an ignorant dream. It was a mystery known only to experience, and yet was, in some profound sense, *always already known*. It wasn't even 'me' seeing it, but rather the dynamic emptiness blissfully and joyfully aware of itself—an emptiness of fullness out of which Life itself poured—and in its glory, Life itself was revealed as Love.

"I have meditated much on this and other experiences over the years, and wondered at times how to categorize them within our religious traditions. Are they Christian? Are they Buddhist? Are they Hindu? They are all and none of them. Perhaps they are simply potentials of human experience, possibilities of human consciousness. Later, I went on to have teachers from all of these traditions, as well as others, and found many descriptions in many traditions that resonate with my own experience of Life. Yet I never found myself within any one tradition exclusively. And my teachers—bless them in their wisdom—never asked whether I was 'Christian,' 'Hindu,' or 'Buddhist.'

"My experiences were my own, and what mattered to my teachers—and to me—was not who I was at a conventional level, but who I was in the depths of reality itself. It was my spiritual growth and maturity that was the point of our teacher-student relationships—not my religious identity. What was important was the realization of more love, more compassion, more wisdom, and more justice in the world. As a result, I now see myself and my path as 'interspiritual,' existing in the spaces among and between religious traditions, and in the liminality of our most basic human experience."

He was silent for a moment, and the fire's crackling filled the air.

"For me," he started again slowly, "the *interspiritual* is more an atmosphere than an identity, more ambience than label. It is found in the liminal spaces of diverse spiritual traditions existing in mutual harmony and intimacy. The *interspiritual* is the level at which we are all meeting right now."[47]

He then turned to sit down, reflective, his energy now quite different from when he had begun.

---

47. Adapted from the personal recollections of Charis Foundation for New Monasticism and Interspirituality co-founder and story co-author Dr. Rory McEntee.

The Peace and Dignity Journeys

There was a kind of incongruence between the man's casual demeanor and the stories he told that baffled me. Yet, as he sat down, I began to feel a stinging sense of longing. Though I could not remember having had any such experiences, there was a sense of familiarity about them—a nostalgia. Memories of childhood flitted through my mind, tinged with a similar awareness . . . but I could not quite retrieve them. Was this part of the "secret" I had shared with my grandmother so many years ago?

I was suddenly reminded of something my grandmother had said to me recently while talking about religion. I was arguing with her, and I don't think I was really paying attention to what she was saying. But now it seemed important: "A mystic is not a special type of person; every person is a special type of mystic."[48]

At this point, I was beginning to feel uncomfotable with my own level of involvement in this ritual. My hard edges were being worn away, and I wasn't sure I liked the process. Nevertheless, I found myself hungry for each new story.

In the middle of my confused longing, a man of about fifty, with grey-blue eyes and silver strands of hair highlighting his temples, came into the light of the Fire. He wore a black jacket and black shirt, over which hung a colorful Peruvian scarf. In his right hand, he held a long staff with shreds of cloth tied to it. He began speaking.

"In the time of my 'spirit-grandmother'" he said, "there was much talk of the prophecy of the Eagle and the Condor, and of the Peace and Dignity Journeys that were begun to fulfill that prophecy.

"At the time, my spirit-grandmother—she is not my *actual* grandmother, but that's what I call her because she comes and talks to me—

48. A statement quoted by Carmelite hermit Tessa Bielecki and attributed to Brother David Steindl-Rast.

was only just beginning to feel her vocation as a *curandera*, a traditional healer, and to come into relationship with her spirit guides.

"The prophecy of the Eagle and the Condor came from the Indigenous peoples of South America, though there were similar prophecies from native folks in other parts of the continent too.

"Prior to colonization, says the prophecy, we, the *indígenas* of the Americas, were taught to fly in balance as human beings. We were taught to cultivate both our 'Eagle' and our 'Condor Wings.' The Condor Wing is feminine, intuitive, connected to the Earth and to compassion. The Eagle Wing is masculine, connected to the intellect, and to doing things in the physical realm. Regardless of gender, all human beings need both wings—the wings above and below—to fly in balance in life. We were taught to cultivate both these wings in ourselves, and in our communities, so that we would not harm the planet.

"The prophecy of the Eagle and the Condor spoke of a five-hundred-year period of *imbalance* during which those who had destroyed their own 'Condor Wing' and their own medicine people would fly out of balance with just their 'Eagle Wing.' Without their Condor Wing, which had been destroyed or atrophied, they would take over the Earth and cause great harm because of their own imbalance. The 'medicines' of the Indigenous peoples would have to be hidden, because it would become dangerous to practice those things outwardly for many centuries.

"But the prophecy said a time would come after five hundred years when there would be an opportunity for humanity to come back into balance. At that time, the medicine that had been hidden could reemerge to help us restore the 'peace and dignity' of Indigenous peoples—and indeed, of all peoples. As our friend mentioned earlier, we are all part of one 'sacred hoop,' and all the colors of humanity have to come back into relationship with the medicine. This means rituals remembering our ancestors, remembering our ties with the land, and remembering the source of our sovereignty and of our true peace. That time was the time of my spirit-grandmother. It was a time when great shifts in cycles were occurring on the Mayan and Toltec calendars.

"In 1990, more than two hundred representatives of Indigenous peoples from North, Central, and South America gathered in Quito, Ecuador, and began to talk about their various prophecies of this time of shift, and about the urgency of the Indigenous peoples' need to come back into their 'peace and dignity.' The time had come to help people remember their essential unity once again, and to begin to shepherd a great transition for the human family.

In response, the Peace and Dignity Journeys were then initiated to reunite the Eagle and Condor Wings of our people, with individuals running in stages from Alaska on the 'Eagle Route,' and Argentina on the 'Condor Route' over a period of six or seven months until they finally met in Central America. Along the way, in each of the communities through which the runners passed, ceremonies were conducted and prayer staffs were collected representing prayers for those communities and all humanity. And so, by the time the runners reached Central America, they were carrying prayer staffs from Indigenous tribes all over the Americas, from north and south and from all across Abya Yala, 'Turtle Island.'

"The runners carried prayers for the healing of the planet, for the healing of Indigenous peoples, and for the healing of traditional ways, imploring us all to remember how to be in right relationship with the Earth and with each other. They reminded us of the importance of ceremony and lost medicine in helping to bring us together again and fly in balance. The Peace and Dignity Journeys were run every four years until healing and reunification were accomplished.

"My spirit-grandmother was also a runner in those journeys... *though a reluctant one at first.* An anthropologist by training, she was well aware of the cultural traditions of South America concerning our ancestors—but it was something else entirely when her own grandmother, who had died when she was young, began to speak to her in dreams and visions!

"One day, seemingly out of nowhere, she heard the voice of her grandmother saying, 'You must be part of the Peace and Dignity Journeys in 2012,' their twentieth anniversary. As a person of Indigenous heritage, she knew of the journeys, but now she was being asked by her dead grandmother 'to contact the organizer for Nicaragua,' the land of her own ancestors. She had not been to Nicaragua since she was a child, and now she was supposed to go because a voice was telling her to? It seemed a little crazy.

"Nevertheless, she thought—*Why not?* So she contacted the organizer as her grandmother had asked and said 'I know you don't know me, and as strange as it may sound, my ancestors—my grandmother, really—is telling me I have to help you.' To which the Nicaraguan organizer responded unexpectedly, 'Oh, I was praying at the fire recently, and my own grandmother told me that she was going to send someone to help me...I guess that's you! It seems that our grandmothers are talking and hatching plans together!'

"Despite feeling a bit uneasy, my spirit-grandmother went to Nicaragua to help in the organizing. Once there, she was approached by a young man who said, 'Today you have to run!' The young man came from an Indigenous tribe in Colombia, and he had been selected by the council to be the leader of the Condor Route.

"Well, my spirit-grandmother had not planned to run, and since she was not in particularly good health, running was not only unexpected but also seemed a little dangerous! Thus, she responded in a worried tone, 'No, I'm just here to help!'

"But the leader of the Condor Route said, 'The spirits are telling me that you have to run.' My spirit-grandmother was humbled by this, for to run is to carry prayers for the people. It is a great honor. Every foot that drums the Earth in the running sounds a prayer dedicated to peace, to dignity, to healing. So she decided to carry a staff for her people in Nicaragua that day.

"But the next day, the young leader of the Condor Route approached her again, saying, 'The spirits are telling me you have to run *again;* and you now have to carry the Condor Staff.'

"Well, this was an even greater responsibility, and my spirit-grandmother began to cry, saying, 'No, no! There are other people who have been running in South America, and they haven't yet had a chance to carry the Condor Staff!'

"The leader of the Condor Route responded, 'I don't decide who carries the Condor Staff; the *ancestors* do. I pray every morning, and the ancestors tell me who is supposed to run, and who is supposed to carry the Condor Staff. The person who carries the Condor Staff has to carry it with a loving heart for all of humanity. For whatever reason, maybe because your ancestors were from here, they want *you* to carry the Condor Staff. You will be okay; I will tell you what to do.'

"You see, carrying the staff in prayer cannot be done from a place of ego or pride or hatred for other peoples; it has to be done from a place of humility, of wanting the peace and dignity of all the original peoples, and of all humanity. The runner must remember that we are all one human family, and must desire to re-unite the Eagle and the Condor Wings of humanity to bring all humanity back into remembrance of their forgotten Condor Wing.

"Now, the previous day when my spirit-grandmother had run, the length of the run had been short and the terrain had been flat and easy; but this day, the run was longer and uphill. In addition to not being in the best of health, my spirit-grandmother had not trained to run as others had, and she was no athlete. So she struggled. Her knees were in pain and threatened to give out, and she felt the tears coming. She was afraid that she would fall and fail to carry the Condor Staff to the end of the journey, that she would fail in this great honor!

"At that very moment, her own grandmother and spirit guide showed up beside her and spoke again for the first time since she had sent her there: 'Thank you for coming when I asked you to come; thank you for being part of this ceremony and this prayer for humanity. Do not worry; you are not doing any of this alone. . . . I am going to help you up this hill!' *And the rest of the run was easy, for she felt like her grandmother was carrying her!*

"On that day my spirit-grandmother was initiated into a larger world of spirits and healing, magic and mystery, and she went on to become a *curandera* herself, performing many ceremonies for the healing of her ancestors and the planet. But it was this moment, carried by her grandmother's spirit, in ceremony with Indigenous peoples, on the land of her ancestors, that forever changed her life.[49]

The man fell silent for a moment. He then said in a gentle but strong voice, "May we all cultivate both our Eagle and our Condor Wings, and may we learn to fly in balance with one another."

When he said these final words, a shiver ran through me and the hair on my arms stood on end. I felt washed in that shiver by a

---

49. Adapted from the personal recollections of story co-author Brenda Salgado on The New Monastics podcast episode "Every Step a Prayer: Walking with All Our Relations with Brenda Salgado," October 2022.

knowledge that bypassed my intellect, and I knew that I had somehow lost touch with my own "Condor Wing" in the years since childhood. It was not my grandmother who had become childish and naïve, but the imbalance of flying with only my "Eagle Wing" that had caused me to judge her so, and to judge my childhood with her as such, emptying the "treasured box" of our relationship of its "secret"! I stood then and cried in silence from my place outside of the circle . . . because I truly was outside of this Circle.

PART THREE

The Future and Now

The Sacred Feminine

Something had now shifted, and I felt the ceremony begin to approach its completion.

There was a movement in front of me and I saw my grandmother beginning to rise. I leapt up and took hold of her arm. I felt the warmth and texture of her embroidered wool shawl. Out of a woven bag hanging from her shoulder she took a white envelope from which she extracted a handwritten letter. She asked me to take up a nearby lamp so that she might read the letter. The Circle seemed aware of a certain ritual significance in this moment.

"Every year," my grandmother said, "I look forward to this day. In the weeks preceding it, I am always filled with a feeling of 'coming home.' This hundred-year anniversary is especially significant for me, as my own grandmother was present at our first gathering and offered us the story of the Bearers of Remembrance there."

I was stunned. How could I not have known this?

"This year, I have brought something very special to me, a letter she wrote to me when I was still a child, not even able to read it. I would like to read it to you tonight.

> My dear Alba —
> I want to leave you with something you will not be able to appreciate until you are older. It is a part of my own story, one I believe will be of help to you one day.
>
> When I was thirty-seven years old, I had an experience that changed my life, and which set me on a profound journey. I had moved from Argentina to the United States with my husband and young children that year, and one night, I fell asleep while praying. That night I had a dream—actually, a vision—in which a woman with very fine, almost transparent features, visited me. Somehow, I knew that she was the embodiment of 'the sacred' and 'the feminine.' As I looked at her, I saw a golden substance pour from her hands, which formed a subtle mantle made up of all the colors of the rainbow. The substance was 'Love,' and the colors were the many forms that Love could take in life. The Mantle of Love then became a Golden Thread that ran up to the moon, and to each of the stars. Then I saw the ocean filled with life, and the Golden Thread diving into it and connecting each lifeform in the ocean.
>
> The Thread then emerged from the water and spread over the land, connecting and enlivening every plant, every tree, and everything it met. It created a brilliant web that became larger and larger, until it encompassed the sky and the waters and all the lands of the Earth. And then I saw a mother with a child in her womb, and the Golden Thread joined the heart of the mother to the heart of her child; and when the child was born, the thread became the milk that flowed from the mother's breast into the baby's mouth.
>
> This vision removed a veil that had obscured my understanding of myself as a woman, and the meaning of the word "feminine." The 'sacred feminine' I encountered was cosmic

in scale, and sacred in every way. I saw her as the incarnation of Love and Wisdom, and as the soul and body of existence. She was the universe—Earth, nature, women, men, and neither—and I felt a sense of belonging and inclusion that was intrinsic to her very being.

In time, I came to understand that the interconnectedness and interrelatedness of all things—the core-essence of the Feminine—had come to me in many ways already, and had been a driving force throughout my life, without my knowing it. She was present when, as a young adult, I felt drawn to go beyond the teachings of my Catholic school education by reading the sacred texts of all the world's religions, without losing my devotion to Jesus, or to his mother, Mary. She was present when I founded my first school and developed a world-focused curriculum, emphasizing ecology and education and peace—where the connections between animals, plants, humans, history, mathematics, science, and other subjects, became central to everything we did.

I have come to recognize the great role her wisdom has played in so many of the changes that have taken place in recent history, especially regarding women's rights and their role in society, and indeed, the rights and roles of all peoples who have been oppressed. I have seen how her energy of unity and interconnectedness is not in accord with the energies of oppression, how it continually seeks to redress these wrongs and to bring the body of the planet and its beings into a healthy awareness of one another. It is a gradual work and will take time.

In the years that followed that dream-vision, I dedicated myself to spiritual practice and eventually became a spiritual teacher. As I look back on those years and the message I shared with my students, I can see now the strong role the dream-vision played in the evolution of my teachings. Over the years this vision increasingly colored my teachings with the sacredness and beauty of nature, and the energy and wisdom of the Golden Thread of Love that weaves together the fabric of all existence.

When the sacred Feminine showed me her truth—that all is one and everything is interconnected and interrelated—each spiritual path became, for me, but another expression of this truth.

Now, I want you to understand, Alba! In saying this, I am not belittling or trying to erase anyone's tradition or path! I am only sharing my own experience with you, in the hope that it may be of some help to you on your own spiritual journey. This Feminine has manifested itself in many forms and is venerated in many traditions, as Mary the Mother of God, as Kali Ma, as Mother Earth herself.

With the experience of the Feminine, I began to see the diversity of spiritual paths as many threads of connection. I recognized even more profoundly that our interdependence is also an invitation—an invitation to share with one another the fruit of our own paths. Sharing our stories of spiritual experience and transformation forges a solidarity among our diverse religious traditions, enlivening our interconnectedness with Love.

The insight that I had always been, that *we* have always been, in some sense 'interspiritual' has given me, and all of us, permission to embrace all the various parts that make us whole.[50]

I pray that you will find your own path my *nieta*, and may the Sacred Feminine provide help and protection to you along the way.

With love, always,
Your *abuela*.

"The story is important; it is how we remember, and by remembering we survive."

---

50. Adapted from the personal recollections of story co-author Alejandra Warden.

The Conference of the Birds

As my grandmother folded the letter and carefully placed it back in its original envelope, I found myself quietly crying, both for what the letter had touched upon, and out of shame for how I had allowed my relationship with my grandmother to deteriorate, distancing me at the same time from this precious inheritance.

Gently, and without the slightest judgment, my grandmother removed my hand from her arm and gestured for me to return to my place just outside of the Circle. She was the Fire-Keeper and had a final duty to perform.

Just as she had told the first story, the honor of telling the final story—the story to bring all the stories together—fell to the Fire-Keeper. She lifted her arms ceremonially, allowing the long, dark fabric of her dress to drape from her outstretched arms. They looked like black wings in the firelight. Then she began to speak in a story-teller's tone . . .

"Once, in a far-off land, the birds in a certain tree began to whisper about a 'Great Bird'—one that flew with the utmost majesty and grace, with a wingspan that dwarfed all others—though only a few of the birds knew more than rumors. But the soft orange and white hoopoe, with her crown of ink-stained feathers, was well-traveled and wise, and it was thought that she might know of the Great Bird. Thus, it was decided to seek her out, and when she was found, they asked her about the Great Bird.

"The wise hoopoe did indeed know of the Great Bird, which she called the Simurgh. She shared with them all that she knew and told them many stories that only hoopoes tell of the Simurgh, though some of the stories were hard to understand. Her stories fascinated all the birds assembled, and yet somehow always left them wanting more. Indeed, the more they heard, the more dissatisfied they felt with the lives they were living. The Simurgh haunted their dreams, and whispered of a greater life beyond their own. Noticing this effect, the hoopoe now said, 'The Simurgh is indeed greater than all birds; but in truth, the Simurgh cannot be known or described in words, but only experienced.'

"'How then do we experience the Simurgh?' asked one curious bird.

"'Well,' said the wise hoopoe, 'first we must *seek* the Simurgh; indeed, we must all take the journey in search of the Simurgh together.'

"Then all the birds in the tree began to chirp and twitter excitedly, for they took the hoopoe at her word. Some were ebullient, for flying and sighting is what they do best! Some were nervous, fearing that the journey would be long and hard; thus, they fretted and made excuses to stay behind. Some even talked boastfully of how they could see the Simurgh without the journey! But the wise hoopoe, with patience and understanding, answered them all according to their need, until every one of them was inspired to seek the Simurgh together.

"'Lead us in search of the Simurgh,' they cried, 'we want to see the Great Bird!'

"'Well,' said the hoopoe, 'it may be a long journey, with many twists and turns; we must fly high and descend low into numerous valleys; and there will be much privation. But having been brought low, we will in time get high enough to see the Simurgh.'

"So the motley assortment of birds—nightingales, parrots, peacocks, ducks, partridges, homas, hawks, herons, owls, and finches—set off with the hoopoe in the lead. And as they flew, other birds joined them, until they were a vast throng of birds, a monstrous murmuration in the sky!

"But after some time the birds landed in exhaustion—complaining of the vast wastes and distances without water, of the tiring flight, of cold rough winds on high peaks, and of the heat of the sun—and they began to squabble among themselves.

"For these complaints and the petty squabbling the hoopoe admonished them—'Did I not tell you that the journey would be long and hard? And how will you find the Great Bird without leaving your comfortable perch and flying beyond Kaf's mountain peak? For though the Simurgh is always near to us, we live far from it! Come now! Let us fly beyond Kaf's mountain peak!'

"So the birds took courage again and flew off in search of the Great Bird, flying over forgotten regions and desert lands, through the Seven Valleys and beyond, until—flying high and beyond any mountain range they had ever known, they came to a vast yellow plain. Then, as the sun beamed down in the sky above them, one observant bird happened to look down and saw an extraordinary sight . . . *the form of an enormous bird gliding over the yellow plain, head and wings and tail all majestically outstretched—exalted, imposing, and dignified it flew!*

"'The Simurgh!' the bird cried out, and all the birds looked down, seeing the Simurgh for themselves. The site was breathtaking—an incomprehensible harmony of movement and grace. Its beauty left the flock spellbound, and only slowly did it dawn on them what they were seeing.

"'The Simurgh!?' they cried together

"Yes,' answered the wise hoopoe, as they watched the shadow of the vast host flying along the ground, '*we* are the Simurgh, the Great Bird, greater than all birds. What we have sought has always been among us—the one whose power to do good surpasses all individual powers, whose truth stands over all truths. Only when we learn to fly together are the Simurgh present and the balances restored. This is what we must all remember!' "[51]

As my grandmother said these final words, she lifted her arms high, looking directly at me, and I knew what she intended, just as I had always known her mind as a child. Pushing aside my own inhibitions, I stood up then and stepped into the Circle and embraced her. The secret between us was restored and as sacred as ever. Perhaps one day, I imagined, I might also become a Fire-Keeper.

The ritual of remembrance was now complete, and brought to a close with a final poem from Howard Thurman, "The Time of Recollection," recited from memory by the thin woman who had spoken earlier…

---

51. Adapted from the classic Sufi parable, best known from the Persian work Mantiq-ut-Tayr (Conference of the Birds) by Farid ad-Din Attar, itself based on an earlier work by Ahmad al-Ghazzali.

Again and again, it comes:
The Time of Recollection,
The Season of Remembrance.
Empty vessels of hope fill up again;
Forgotten treasures of dreams reclaim
their place;
Long-lost memories come trooping back to me.
This is my season of remembrance,
My time of recollection.

Into the challenge of my anguish
I throw the strength of all my hope;
I match the darts of my despair
with the treasures of my dreams;
Upon the current of my heart
I float the burdens of the years;
I challenge the mind of death
with my love of life.
Such to me is the Time of Recollection,
The Season of Remembrance.[52]

---

52. Anne Spencer Thurman, ed., *For the Inward Journey: The Writings of Howard Thurman* (Richmond, IN: Friends United Press, 1984), 257.

Surrendering to the Merciful Will of God

A RETELLING OF THE SACRED STORY OF ISLAM

Surrendering to the Merciful Will of God

Wedged into a window seat in an airplane somewhere over the Atlantic Ocean, Zahra curled her shoulders inward and crossed her arms over her chest. Trying to contain her roiling emotions, she studied the small screen above her dinner tray. It showed a map and, inching across it, a plane with its nose pointed toward Saudi Arabia.

The plane was speeding southeast at five hundred miles per hour. But she felt like she was hurtling backward in the dark, into a past life. She dabbed at the tears pooling in her kohl-lined eyes—she knew not what she was mourning, yet she felt flooded with grief. Hours earlier, she had stood on the curb at JFK International Airport in New York City with her suitcase and watched her husband Raheem get behind the wheel of the car and disappear into traffic without looking back.

Her gloom was familiar, and festering.

They'd barely spoken on the way to the airport; a stifling silence had filled the car. Stuck in traffic, he stared straight ahead, tapping the steering wheel impatiently. She stared out her window and thought of all the times she had suggested they go to marriage counseling. The more she asked, the more resolved his refusal became. She wondered now about this haze of tension that had settled over them—when exactly had it set in? All she knew was that she could no longer see him through the thick fog. She sensed herself, too, becoming blurry. And it wasn't just with him that she felt this way. It was with her daughter Maryam as well.

Because the thought of flying had always made her feel her mortality, the night before she left she'd invited Maryam, who studied political science at a nearby university, to come for dinner. *Inshallah* (God willing), she would return home safely, but one never knew. The Qur'an says, "No soul knows what it will earn tomorrow, and no soul knows in what land it will die: but God is omniscient, completely aware." With that in mind, she intended to leave her family with one last pleasant memory.

She'd made Maryam's favorite, *Yayla Corbasi*—Turkish yogurt soup. Maryam burst through the door, nearly half an hour late, apologizing as she sat down and putting her phone beside her where she could eye it as she ate. Had her parents seen the news? Another young Black man had been murdered by police, his last desperate moments captured in a cell phone video. Of course, Zahra had not seen it; she would never subject herself to such brutal footage. Maryam described it in vivid detail anyway.

Zahra was determined to not ruin another family gathering. A bitter taste still lingered from the last time this subject had arisen in conversation. Maryam had cursed the police, and Zahra had reminded her of the risks they took, the good work they did, and that most didn't engage in brutality. When her daughter insisted that all police officers were bad, Zahra had tried to explain that dehumanizing an entire group of people went against her religion.

This time she would not pull down her Qur'an from her bookshelf to read: "Believers, be upstanding for God as witnesses to justice; and do not let the hatred of some people hurt you so much that you are not fair. Be fair; that is kin to conscience. And be conscious of God, for God is aware of what you do."

"But Mom," Maryam had shot back, "it's hard to see religion as a force for good. We see Christians justifying slavery, or Muslims justifying terrorism, or Jews justifying occupied territories." That conversation had ended badly: her daughter storming out angry, her husband withdrawing into silence.

So this time, Zahra ate quietly as Raheem and Maryam talked politics, their voices steadily rising as they moved from police brutality to Black Lives Matter, from colonization to American foreign policy. By the time they had reached the subject of white supremacy, Zahra's bowl was empty. She quietly left the table, feeling ethereal as a ghost.

"Don't you find it disturbing," she said to Raheem later that night, "that she's so angry? And so rigid? And so dismissive of religion?"

He avoided her gaze. "She's young and idealistic," he said. "She cares about justice. Give her time."

Now, as the tiny plane icon on the screen crept closer to her native Turkey, vivid memories of her childhood in Istanbul resurfaced: the *adhan* (call to prayer) drifting in through open windows; the cat curled up and purring in her lap as she sat in the mosque listening to the Friday *khutbah* (sermon), the sound of her father's gentle voice reciting Qur'anic verses, their subtle rhyme and rhythm a lullaby to her young ears.

She recalled her last phone conversation with him. She'd asked how he was doing, and his predictable reply—*Alhamdulillah* (Praise be to God)—with its soothing sound, had calmed her, drawing her out of her self-absorption into gratitude. After a pause, that same gentle voice had delivered a blow to her heart.

"*Canim* (darling)," he said, "I'm not well. It's cancer."

Panic welled up in Zahra, and her mind began to race. She fired a staccato of questions at him: What kind? What stage? What doctors have you seen? What treatments are they proposing?

"*Babam* (father), you must come to the United States," she said. "We have two university hospitals nearby. World-class doctors. You need a second opinion."

He thanked her calmly. "*Canim*, that's not the trip I am planning," he said. "But I do need to see you. That's why I'm calling. I want to go on one last pilgrimage *inshallah.* Will you join me?"

"Of course, *Babam*," she'd said—the same way she responded to all her father's requests. He sounded delighted. He told her this sacred journey was his gift so they could both benefit from the blessings. After they ended the call, one question troubled Zahra: his response to cancer was to go on a pilgrimage to Mecca?

For each of their five daily prayers, Muslims around the world turn toward the Kaaba—their holiest mosque, visited by millions of pilgrims each year. Muslims are obligated to complete the *hajj* (major pilgrimage) once in their lifetime if they are able, and many also complete *umrah*, a voluntary minor pilgrimage that is shorter and less strenuous and can be done any time of the year, unlike the *hajj*, which can be performed only at a specific time of the year. But Zahra had a fear of pilgrimage crowds, and until that conversation with her father, she had never imagined going to Saudi Arabia.

And why, she wondered, had he chosen her as his travel companion, when he could have invited her half-brother Emir, who lived nearby in Istanbul? What did her stepmother think of this plan? She was the only mother Zahra had ever known; hers had died in childbirth. And though she loved her stepmother dearly, she had always felt like she stood on the periphery of her father's second family.

She wondered if her father would have the strength and the stamina to complete the pilgrimage, even though he deeply desired to do so. Over the phone he sounded determined. To allay her fears, her father added that he would reserve hotel rooms within a short walk of the Kaaba. But, she wondered, how would he handle the second part of the pilgrimage, when they would sleep in tents and spend an entire day under a blistering desert sun on Mount Arafat?

Later that evening, when she told Raheem about her father's cancer, his face softened with compassion, and light broke through the clouds between them. He opened his arms, and she leaned into his embrace. She pressed her cheek to his chest, her tears moistening his crisp white shirt. He, more than anyone, knew how much she adored her father and how hard it was for her to live so far away. Over the years her commitment to visiting him regularly never wavered—not even when she had to travel with young children, or their budget was too tight to allow for any other vacation.

When Zahra told him about the pilgrimage, his eyes widened in surprise. He also knew about her fear of crowds—and how alienated she sometimes felt around Muslims who practiced their faith differently. He recalled her frustration after her last visit to the local mosque; she'd been directed away from the main entrance and up a flight of stairs to the women's prayer space. On a short-circuit television, she'd watched the sermon being delivered below, straining to hear the words over the cries of babies as toddlers ran in circles around her. The arrangement didn't sit well with her; when she was growing up in Istanbul, men and women normally prayed in the same space, albeit separated. And, as her father had told her, during Prophet Muhammad's life, men and women were not segregated for prayer. "I'm not going back," she'd declared to Raheem that day. And she hadn't. She was content to pray at home. And she had already found spiritual community among a few close Christian and Jewish friends, whose prophets she also embraced, and whose beliefs she largely shared.

Now, still within her husband's embrace, she confessed to him that she'd agreed to join her father in Mecca as it would also give her time to persuade him to come to the United States for a second medical opinion and treatment. Raheem smiled knowingly. This sounded more like the Zahra he knew.

AT WORK THE NEXT DAY, Zahra requested time off, without mentioning the pilgrimage or Saudi Arabia. As the company's only Muslim employee, she already felt self-conscious about closing her office door to pray. Her boss, after having seen the Post-it note on her closed door ("Praying/Back in five minutes"), let slip that he had no idea she was "such a devout Muslim." He acted as if praying made her a zealot.

She shared her travel plans only with her Jewish friend and colleague. Hannah's face lit up when she heard about Zahra's upcoming pilgrimage—not only with excitement for Zahra but also because her news reminded Hannah of her own pilgrimage to Jerusalem; she would never forget pressing her folded prayers into a crack in the Western Wall. She sensed Zahra too would be deeply affected by her sacred journey. "Only God knows what gifts await you," she told Zahra, squeezing her hand. "I want to hear all about it when you get back."

To her boss, Zahra simply said she needed time off to visit her ailing father. Taking ten days off, her boss pointed out, would use all her vacation days for the year. Little did he know about the importance of this journey. And little did *she* know how much it would change her life.

By the time she booked her flight on a Saudi airline, she was relegated to a seat in the last row of the plane. When she boarded and found her seat, she was surprised to discover a generous open prayer space behind her. At least six seats likely had to be removed to make room for that carpeted area, which had a digital screen pointing to the Kaaba and curtains on either side for privacy. How extraordinary, she thought, that an airline would sacrifice profits for prayers.

Hours later, as sunlight streamed into the cabin and the flight attendants moved up and down the aisles serving coffee, the pilot announced that the plane was approaching the *miqat*, or boundary, before which pilgrims must enter into a ritual state of purity and set their intentions for pilgrimage. The man seated beside her awoke with a start, stood up to retrieve a bundle from the luggage bin overhead, and joined a growing line of men holding similar packages. One by one, the men slipped through the closed curtain into the prayer space behind her.

Zahra could hear the rustle of cloth, the murmured prayers, the sighs and creaks of bodies folding to the ground and rising up again. Each male pilgrim emerged with a white unstitched cloth wrapped around the lower half of his body and draped over his right shoulder, wearing sandals but no wrist watche or jewelry. With all signs of status, wealth, or lack thereof erased, the men looked surprisingly similar to one another. (Female pilgrims simply wore floor-length robes and headscarves, with only their faces and hands exposed.)

AT JEDDA AIRPORT, Zahra waited in the baggage claim area to meet her father, trying to tamp down her anxiety as she prepared herself to see the ravages of age and illness on his face. In her childhood, Kareem had been an imposing figure with a deep, sonorous voice and a booming laugh that shook his broad girth. She recalled how, as a little girl, she had clung to him in the crowded marketplace, gripping the fingers of his warm, heavy hand, half-running to keep up with his long strides.

It had been almost twenty years since she'd said goodbye to him in an airport like this one before catching her flight to the United States to attend university. That day she had no identity separate from her family and community: no ambition, no personal style, no desires apart from theirs. Her sudden loss of home and belonging had been shocking. To survive the separation, she had walled off part of herself, learned to be independent, and become engrossed in her studies.

She felt a hand land gently on her shoulder. Spinning around, she was stunned to see her father. He was so much slighter than she remembered—and somehow also brighter. His bare shoulder looked pale. His hand felt bony and light as a bird in hers as she raised it to her lips. The sandalwood prayer beads wrapped around his wrist rattled softly as they slid down his arm. She raised his hand to touch it to her forehead, discreetly wiping away tears. She had missed him terribly.

"*Canim*, I'm so glad you're here," he said, his hands reaching out to hold her face. "Let's take this journey to the House of God together. I trust it will bear many fruits, *inshallah*."

The touch of her father's gentle hands on her cheeks caused a breach in the dam inside her. Grief flooded in for lost time, along with gratitude for their reunion. As frail as he was, he insisted on pulling her suitcase behind him as they walked to their bus outside. Watching him weave through the crowd in the garments of a pilgrim, Zahra couldn't help but smile through her tears: he looked like Gandhi on a business trip.

THEIR BUS TO MECCA was crowded with pilgrims. Slipping into a seat beside her father, Zahra asked him about his cancer. Before he could answer, a passenger began to chant a prayer, and others immediately joined in. "Later, *Canim*," he whispered, resting his hand over hers. The pilgrims sang:

Here I am, O God, here I am!
Here I am, O You without any partners, here I am.
All praise, all blessings, all dominion are Yours,
Oh You without partners.

Her father mouthed the words softly along with the others—Nigerians, Jordanians, Americans, Malaysians, Pakistanis, and Chinese among them, all chanting in unison. They were men and women, young and old, rich and poor, and brown, black, and white. The bus carried a geographic and demographic microcosm of humanity. Zahra recalled a verse from the Qur'an: "O humankind, We created you from a male and a female, and We made you races and tribes for you to get to know each other. The most noble of you in the sight of God are those of you who are most conscientious."

She had always understood this verse to mean that tribal, religious, and cultural differences were opportunities for people to learn from each other, and that Muslims should vie only to excel in nobility and piety. More often than not throughout history, Muslims peacefully coexisted with other religious communities. Muslims honor all the known prophets—and the Qur'an specifies there were countless other, unknown prophets too, sent to all human communities. And Muslim scholars and sages always traveled to faraway lands to learn from great thinkers of other communities.

Now she considered how this verse applied to diversity *among* Muslims. If only we could value our differences more, she thought, and judge one another less. It moved her to look around the bus and see the diversity of faces singing in harmony, finding unity in their faith and in the oneness of God. Hearing all these disparate voices become one in worship, Zahra wondered if this was the beginning of what it meant to know one another: to discover the deep longing we share as part of our human nature, to not be so hypnotized by our superficial differences.

Her father was chanting beside her, his eyes closed. Zahra felt a tinge of embarrassment to realize she was the only one on the bus who didn't know this prayer by heart. Familiar refrains began to repeat in her mind: *I don't belong. I am not enough.* Then, looking around, she realized that if everyone else here belonged, she must as well.

Zahra closed her eyes, took a deep breath, and began to listen. Eventually her lips began to move, and the quiet trickle of her voice joined the mighty flow. Closing her eyes, she repeated the prayer again and again, her voice blending with those of all the others. Opening her eyes, she turned to the window and watched the parched brown desert pass by. *Here I am, O God*, she thought, with sudden wonder.

KAREEM HAD RESERVED ROOMS at a hotel just across the plaza from Masjid-al-Haram, also known as the Sacred Mosque, which contains the Kaaba. The hotel's revolving glass doors shut out the din of the crowded street. Pilgrims standing on the gleaming marble floor of the lobby were lined up to check in. Others sat on plush couches book-ended by striking flower arrangements. Above the registration desk, a large display screen broadcast a live webcam from the Kaaba. Zahra thought it odd that her frugal father had chosen such luxurious accommodations, but when they stepped into the elevator and he declared his intention to perform all his prayers at the Kaaba while in Mecca, it made sense. It wasn't the luxury that drew him; it was the proximity to what he valued most.

"Prophet Muhammad, peace be upon him, said one prayer at the Kaaba is worth a hundred thousand prayers elsewhere," he told her.

Zahra did the math in her head; by that accounting, he would rack up millions of extra acts of worship. How, she wondered, would that benefit such a kind and faithful man? Islam taught her that God was, above all, merciful. *In the name of God, the Compassionate, the Merciful,* the Qur'an begins, and Muslims also begin anything of significance by reciting the same phrase. The Arabic word for mercy (*rahma*) is derived from the root word *rhm*, which means "womb"; the closest thing on earth to God's mercy is a mother's love for her child. A God that merciful, Zahra believed, would never turn away from such a good soul.

Zahra felt exhausted from travel, but Kareem seemed energized. They agreed to rest in their rooms for an hour and meet back in the lobby so they could be at the Kaaba before Asr (afternoon prayer.) Alone in her room, she fell back onto her bed and stared at the ceiling. She briefly considered calling Raheem, then was relieved to realize he would already be asleep.

She felt she was traversing new terrain, uncharted yet filled with light. She had left behind all her comforts, her roles and routines, her sense of normalcy in the daily grind that was her life. She felt disoriented and raw. She also felt something deeply stirring—a heightened presence, a spark of wonder—that needed time to unfold, to grow, and to be grasped fully. The ground was shifting beneath her, and a yearning was arising within. She recalled a quote her Christian friend once shared from the *Confessions* of Saint Augustine: "Our hearts are restless till they find rest in Thee."

She rolled over, looked out her eighth-floor window, and watched construction workers on the roof of an unfinished building laboring under the open sky. An impulse to check her work email was immediately followed by anxiety: Had she overlooked something or forgotten a task before leaving? She resisted the impulse. The software company where she worked as a project manager had recently been acquired by another firm; the inevitable round of layoffs had followed; those who remained took on additional responsibilities. No matter how hard she worked, she could not dig herself out from beneath a deluge of email and other documents. She prepared reports nobody acknowledged reading, wasted too much time in meetings that tested her patience. She came home exhausted—yet unsure of what, if anything, she had accomplished. Her work seemed bereft of meaning. To make matters worse, she feared she might be laid off. And what then? How would she and Raheem pay their bills or save enough money to retire?

Back in Brooklyn, such worldly concerns consumed her. She found small pleasures in cooking and sharing a meal with Raheem, or watching a film with him, or going on a quiet evening stroll through their neighborhood. But mostly she felt untethered, adrift without an anchor as a storm gathered on the horizon.

Too restless to sleep, she got up, performed her lustrations, and selected a clean *abaya* (floor-length gown) from her suitcase. She wrapped her scarf neatly around her head and studied her face in the mirror. Growing up in Istanbul, she had always covered her head for prayers at home or when she went to the mosque. Now she felt that same heightened sense of devotion, the same elevated intention she had always associated with covering her head.

She waited for her father in the lobby. Kareem stepped out of the elevator, his cheeks flushed with excitement—more for Zahra than for himself. He couldn't wait for her to see the Kaaba for the first time.

"Think carefully about your prayer," he said, holding her gaze, just before they stepped out into the street. "I've heard that the first one you make after laying eyes on the Kaaba will be accepted."

Pilgrims buzzed around the entrance to the mosque like bees around a hive. Kareem reached for Zahra's hand.

"Follow me," he said. "Look down—don't look up until I tell you to."

Gripping his hand tightly, Zahra kept her eyes on the ground as they maneuvered through the crowd. When they passed beneath the threshold of the sacred mosque, the light changed and the crowd grew thicker. Any sense of personal space disappeared. The last time she'd been in such an overwhelming crowd was when she and Raheem had taken the train into Manhattan on New Year's Eve to watch the ball drop at Times Square. The flashing neon lights overhead, the drunken revelers, the relentless pop of fireworks: all that barely contained chaos had been too much for her.

Though much larger, this crowd moved calmly, and with a shared purpose. Each time she saw no room to take a step forward, someone yielded space. Finally, Kareem came to a stop and pulled her close beside him.

"Look up," he said, and she raised her face. There it was, straight ahead: a cube covered in black silk embroidered in silver and gold, a stunning square island in a swirling sea of pilgrims. As she took in the magnificence of the simple structure, tears welled up and trickled down her cheeks. It was as if her long journey had been a delirious dream, and her fever now broke. The significance of the moment washed over her.

She turned to her father, and his eyes were glassy too. How many times in her childhood had she aligned her prayer mat to face this precise place? How many times had she put her forehead to the floor, facing toward this symbol of the oneness of God?

The cubic shape of the Kaaba, which faces every direction, including above and below, is a metaphor for God's omnipresence. It is covered in black—the sum of all colors—just as God unites all diversity into singularity.

Given its prominence in her religious life, Zahra was heartened to see how majestic the Kaaba appeared beneath the open sky. All around it, high-rise buildings towered, and construction cranes hovered in the air. Just beyond the walls of the mosque, modernity continued its march of "progress"—but in this sacred space she entered another dimension, joining a slice of humanity in a timeless devotional choreography of praising the divine.

The last time she had felt this—Islam as an energetic reality that permeated her body and altered the air she breathed—she was listening to a thunderous recitation of *salawat* (blessings on the Prophet) at the breathtaking Blue Mosque in Istanbul during Ramadan. But things had changed dramatically in the United States since September 11, 2001. On the one hand, people became more curious about Islam; on the other, being Muslim became a liability. Zahra's intellect became her best defense. Endlessly explaining and defending her faith exhausted her. It also obscured the *felt* reality of Islam. Now, standing in front of the Kaaba, she experienced it again, with a joyous intensity: this melting of her separate self into a vast belonging, this surrender to the awesome mystery of God, this heart ablaze with love and longing.

On their short walk from the hotel, her mind had raced with all she would request in her first, potent prayer at the Kaaba: for her father to be healed; for intimacy, understanding, and healing in her marriage; for a more meaningful job; for her daughter's heart to soften. But these appeals vanished the moment she laid eyes on the Kaaba. The only prayer on her lips was this: *Forgive me.*

Zahra prayed for forgiveness because she had lost sight of the most important truth: that God is the only constant in this changing world, the unmoving center around which all of creation revolves.

She had drifted far away into worldly concerns and ignored the reality of God within and around her. According to Islam, there is no such thing as original sin—quite the opposite. Muslims believe in original goodness, the purity of the *fitra*, the innate nature of humans ("We have made man in the finest order," the Qur'an says), which recognizes the oneness of God. But human beings are forgetful creatures, prone to error, with a tiny black spot within the heart that can grow, with abuse and wrongs, until that spot completely covers the heart. Human heedlessness makes the heart vulnerable to temptation, which, with the ego, enables the devil, human desires, and the fleeting aspects of the world to lead people far astray.

And do not pray to any other deity besides God—there is no other god.
All things perish but the purpose of God,
to whom belongs the judgment and to whom you will be returned.

IN THIS WORLD OF TESTS AND TRIBULATIONS, it's only human to forget our true nature. Drowning in temptations and distractions, we forget God; people do it all the time. And in Islam, forgetting creates a precious opportunity. The moment we turn our attention from our own faults to God's greatness, and repent, we can receive God's forgiveness and mercy. "My Mercy extends to all things," God promises in the Qur'an. God loves to forgive—so much so that Prophet Muhammad, peace be upon him, reportedly said that if human beings did not sin and seek forgiveness, God would have swept us from existence and replaced us with creatures that did.

According to the Qur'an, when Adam and Eve disobeyed God by eating from the forbidden tree, God taught them about repentance, and forgiveness, and inspired them to say these words: *Our Lord, we have wronged our own selves. If You do not forgive us and have mercy on us, we will certainly be among the lost.*

The moment she uttered her first whispered prayer for forgiveness, Zahra felt the mercy of a benevolent God wash over her, prompting her second prayer: *Alhamdulillah* (Praise be to God).

Broadcast through the crackling speakers overhead, a man's plaintive voice rang out above the crowd, reciting the call to prayer. "*Allahu Akbar* (God is greater)," he began and repeated, his voice rising higher with each word, like the birds above, sailing aloft on gusts of wind. Countless times in her life Zahra had raised her hands to her ears at the start of her daily prayers and spoken those two words. Now their meaning hit her with full force. God was indeed greater than her troubled marriage, her stressful job, the horrible news headlines, or anything else she could imagine in all of God's creation.

Catching Zahra's eye, Kareem winked and smiled. They had made it in time for their first prayer at the Kaaba. As the crowd surged forward, Zahra was shuffled along into a prayer section where women were lining up in neat rows. She nodded politely to the woman beside her, trying to respect her personal space even as the crowd pressed in. But the woman tugged at Zahra's sleeve, drawing her closer until their shoulders touched. She noticed that Zahra had no prayer mat, so she turned hers sideways in front of them, creating just enough space for both their foreheads to rest on it in prostration.

As far as Zahra could see, rows of pilgrims began to pray in perfect choreography. When thousands of pilgrims dropped to the ground in prostration, the sound of their falling bodies cut through the air with an audible whoosh, as if they were one body, moved by divine will. For the rest of her life, she would recall and reflect on this spellbinding sight and sound.

Touching her forehead to her neighbor's mat, she breathed in lingering traces of the stranger's perfume. On either side, she heard the sound of lips moving as women silently recited their prayers. With her heart elevated above her head, she felt a heaviness roll off her shoulders and a heat radiate from her chest. "Oh, it is by remembrance of God that hearts are satisfied!" the Qur'an asserts. In prostration, Zahra felt the power of divine remembrance as it calmed her, and her heart came to rest.

Not every prayer had this effect. In recent weeks and months, Zahra had struggled to make her five daily prayers on time. The prayer times came during her commute, or staff meetings, or when she was hurrying to get dinner on the table, or after she'd already settled into bed with a book, exhausted. When she delayed a prayer, she felt guilty—and when she rushed one, she felt nothing at all.

Now she reminded herself of a Qur'anic verse stating that God is always aware of what is within a person: "We did indeed create man, and We know what his ego suggests; and We are closer to him than his jugular vein." Prayer was for her benefit—a way to liberate herself from all the distractions that made her forget the divine. Now, as those diversions and distractions left her during her first prayer at the Kaaba, she felt awash in gratitude. There was no need to ask herself why or to enumerate her blessings; this feeling did not reside in her mind. It poured from her heart into her limbs. It pooled in her eyes as tears. What sweet relief it was to give her worries to God and surrender to the mercy that had brought her here.

THE NEXT MORNING, after their dawn prayer, Zahra suggested to her father that they complete their first pilgrimage ritual: circling the Kaaba seven times, known as *tawaaf*. The previous evening she had studied that powerful current of humanity swirling around the Kaaba the way a sailor studies a stormy ocean, trying to determine if it was safe to set sail. There appeared to be an especially dangerous undertow around the corner with the Black Stone.

According to Islamic tradition, the Black Stone dates all the way back to Adam, the primordial man who was shown where the temple of God should be built. (It became black over time, as it took on the sins of those who kissed it and prayed for forgiveness from God.) Most pilgrims today who circle the Kaaba wave as they pass by, while some still touch or even kiss it.

To Zahra's relief, the sea of pilgrims was calmer in the blue-black light of dawn. She clutched Kareem's arm as they waded into the crowd and became part of the devotional wave. Seven times Zahra raised her hand to the Black Stone as she passed, feeling mystified each time she did. Her father did the same. He seemed bleary yet blissful.

After they completed their seven rounds, they walked back to their hotel in silence. Zahra felt melancholy and reflective. She'd been Muslim her entire life, yet in Mecca she felt keenly aware how much she still had to learn about Islam. A recurrent theme in the Qur'an is the paramount importance of lifelong learning. For as long as she could remember, her father had sought wisdom and understanding by studying Islam with learned scholars (*shaykhs*). He taught her by example that Islam ignites the intellect as powerfully as the heart.

Her love of learning had begun with her religion. By the time she was ten years old, she wanted to join her father when he attended evening lectures at the mosque, or when he hosted esteemed Islamic scholars for tea and wide-ranging conversations about family, society, philosophy, or politics. But Zahra was not invited. On those nights, she lay in bed craning to hear those convivial male voices. She crept into the hallway to spy on them—and discovered that her stepbrother, younger than she, was welcomed among them. Around that time, she redirected her intellectual energies to her studies, eventually becoming an engineer.

After breakfast, Zahra told her father she was headed to the open-air market around the corner from the hotel to find a prayer mat. She also wanted time to herself. She made her way slowly down the sidewalk, taking time to examine the offerings on display—prayer beads, robes, headscarves, incense—anything a pilgrim might desire.

As she admired a delicate strand of red prayer beads the color of fresh blood, Zahra thought about Ada, her stepmother—the only mother she'd ever known. Ada often told Zahra the story of meeting her father when he was a young widower with a baby girl. Ada joked that his proposal sounded more like a plea.

"If only I had a son," he had said to Ada. "I might be able to raise him. But what do I know about girls? This baby needs a mother."

To Ada it was a heartwarming story of how they had become family. But all Zahra heard was her father's preference for a son. A few years later, when her stepbrother was born, her father got what he wanted. Looking back, Zahra could see how long and hard she had tried to prove her worth to him.

When she came to the end of a row of shops, Zahra found stacks of folded prayer mats in different colors and textures. As she ran her fingers over one covered with intricately embroidered flowers, the call to prayer rang out overhead. She pulled out her purse to purchase the mat. There was no time for negotiation; the merchant was already sweeping a blanket over his stacks of folded cloth. Up and down the street, shopkeepers did the same. Once again Zahra was struck by this shared prioritizing of divine connection over commerce. These were the people, she thought, described in the Qur'an: "There are men whom neither business nor commerce can divert from remembrance of God, and persistence in prayer, and giving of alms."

She tried but could not imagine a moment when everyone in an American shopping mall might pause together to remember God.

Their second day in Mecca, Kareem and Zahra completed their next pilgrimage ritual, walking seven times between the hilltops of Safa and Marwa, retracing the steps of Hagar, the second wife of Prophet Abraham, after she and her son Ishmael had been left alone by him in the desert. Before Abraham departed, she had asked him, "Did God command this?" He answered "Yes." On his journey home, he stopped to make heartfelt prayers for his wife and son, whom he had left alone in the desert.

Hagar surrendered to this trial. And, after she had depleted her meager supply of dates and water, she knew she needed to take action. Her faith told her that God would support her efforts. Placing her infant son, Ishmael, on the ground, she ran across the valley to the nearest hilltop, Safa, to search for water and for anyone who might help her. Finding nothing, she ran to another hilltop, Marwa, and again found nothing. Seven times in the searing heat she ran back and forth between the two hills desperately seeking some way to survive. On her seventh run, she returned to her child, only to find water springing forth from where he had been scratching the ground. That blessed water source, known as the ZamZam Well, from which millions of pilgrims drink each year in Mecca, has been flowing ever since.

Hagar was the first resident of Mecca. Without her, Zahra wondered, would any of this—the city and the pilgrimage—exist? The desolate place where Hagar once ran back and forth was now a well-lit path paved with marble and covered with an ornate ceiling. Where there was once jagged rock on each hilltop, there were now designated areas where people crowded to pray. Where she was once desperate and alone, hordes of pilgrims jostled to follow in her footsteps.

Zahra heard their bare feet slap against marble as the men jogged past. She was grateful to match her father's slower pace; it suited her reflective mood. She considered how she was facing the challenges of her life. Were they revealing her best qualities—or her worst? What virtues might she cultivate in the face of her difficulties? Patience, gratitude, compassion? Having a good opinion of others? Her daughter, Maryam, came to mind. How harshly she had judged Maryam for her opinions—and in doing so, both of their hearts had closed.

Maryam was right, she thought—horrific things had been done in the name of religion. Then she considered an important prophetic guidance: actions are judged by their intentions. Though Zahra was uncomfortable about some of Maryam's political positions, she knew her daughter's intentions were noble. She was in awe of Maryam's deep commitment to justice, her allegiance to the marginalized and vulnerable, and her determination to speak out against oppression. These were Islamic values that Zahra herself had failed to embody. At her daughter's age, Zahra reflected, she had been silent and self-conscious, more concerned with politeness than persecution. Now she blamed herself for judging her daughter; judgment was God's domain. She made a resolution to celebrate her daughter's strengths more—even if she was a little intimidated by them.

Compassion arose in Zahra as she tried to imagine what it was like for young people to grow up in this time of social media, climate change, corruption, mass violence, and perpetual war. Her childhood had been so much simpler, her innocence and her imagination protected. And yet she had struggled in other ways. In this life there was simply no way to avoid suffering. Islam sees tribulations an essential aspect of being human. The Qur'an says, "We will surely test you with something of fear and hunger, and loss of possessions, persons, or crops. But give good news to the patient, those who say, when calamity afflicts them, 'We belong to God, and to God we return.'" Prophet Muhammad is reported to have said, "Whenever God wills good for someone, God subjects them to adversity." Tribulations are an opportunity to purify sins, develop strengths, and turn toward God, who promises good news for those who remain patient and steadfast in their faith.

And that was how her father faced his cancer, Zahra thought. His faith, like Hagar's, was unwavering, even in the face of a deadly disease. Like Hagar, he continued to invest significant effort; this pilgrimage was proof of it. Their fortitude showed Zahra that one must strive *and* surrender. Islam—often translated as "submission"—should never be confused with passivity. Surrendering to the divine will requires an exquisite alertness, a poised receptivity, a willingness to move with the unpredictable flow of life.

In her daughter's urgency, Zahra sensed a kind of despair. She made a mental note to remind her daughter that Muslims are called to never, ever give up hope. Even as the end draws near, Prophet Muhammad reportedly said, if we have a seedling in our hands, we should plant it. We should remain hopeful until our last breath. Also, worship is not enough; believers must take action to benefit others.

How extraordinary, she thought as she was carried along by the crowd, that Muslims came from every corner of the world to follow in the footsteps of a mother who was left alone with her baby and her reliance on God. Even in this spring season, the Mecca sun was a white-hot flame burning down on gray rock and parched brown land. Each time Zahra emerged from her air-conditioned hotel, the dusty air felt like the blast of a hair dryer in her face; she always carried a bottle of water with her. And yet Hagar—a breastfeeding mother who had nothing to drink—*ran*. Considering Hagar's physicality brought back a vivid memory of Maryam: marching at a university protest, holding aloft her hand-painted sign, her mouth wide open, crying out for justice. Her embodied strength, too, was sacred.

After completing her seventh round, Zahra found a place to pray on what was once the hilltop of Marwa. The first prayer she made, as she knelt on that uneven ground, was for God's mercy for mothers everywhere who find themselves alone, in seemingly hopeless situations, holding onto their faith and chasing down miracles.

KAREEM AND ZAHRA DEVELOPED A ROUTINE in Mecca. Before dawn they would meet in the hallway outside their rooms. They would cross the plaza in the dark and pray *fajr* (dawn prayer) at the Kaaba as the sky turned from black to blue. Then they would go their separate ways, meeting two hours later at the hotel's breakfast buffet.

But on their fourth morning in Mecca, Zahra was jolted from a deep sleep by a phone call from Kareem. He was too exhausted, he said, to go to the Kaaba for *fajr*. She should go without him. He assured her he would be fine with just a little more rest.

Two hours later she found a table at the breakfast buffet and waited for her father. When her stomach began to growl, she made a plate for herself of dates, tahini, fruits, and berries. But when she had finished eating and still hadn't seen him, she took the elevator up to their floor and knocked on his door—quietly at first, and then more urgently.

When he eventually opened the door he was in his pajamas, groggy and disoriented, with his prayer beads swinging from his fingers. He asked her what time it was, then apologized for sleeping through breakfast. She followed him as he shuffled back inside and sank into his bed. There were dark circles under his eyes, his lips were pursed, and his forehead was creased in frustration.

"*Babam*, what are you upset about?" she asked.

"What do you think I'm upset about?" he impatiently replied.

As a girl, Zahra had feared her father's temper. Now she could clearly see that his mood had nothing to do with her; he was frustrated with himself for missing the dawn prayer at the Kaaba. She sat down at the edge of his bed, took his hand, and kissed it.

"*Babam*," she said. "If God is not pleased with you, I don't know my faith." Her words dissolved his darkened mood. He smiled weakly and closed his eyes. "Do you remember," she asked him, "the Imam who used to scatter cat food like birdseed outside the mosque in Istanbul?" Zahra recalled the Imam as a true steward of God's creation, reverential to all forms of life. Plants in his care gleamed greener, flowers bloomed bigger and brighter. "I remember that he was as gentle with stray animals as he was with children," Zahra said.

Her father nodded, smiling at the memory of the Imam who often quoted a prophetic *hadith*: "The Prophet's companions asked, 'O Messenger of God, do we have a reward for taking care of animals?' The Prophet responded, 'There is a reward for any good done to any sentient being.'"

"Once, when I was a child," Zahra continued, "he was teaching me to read the Qur'an in Arabic, and I became frustrated. 'It's too hard!' I whined, pushing the text away. He said he understood, then told me, 'Learning to read Arabic *is* complicated. But Islam is simple. It comes down to this: Love God and serve God's creation.'"

Her father nodded and sighed.

"And that is what you do," Zahra added, lifting his hand to her lips once more.

She asked if she could keep him company in his room while he rested, and he nodded. As he drifted off to sleep, Zahra thought about that gentle Imam in Istanbul: white beard, deep wrinkles, and a perpetual smile. The children gathered around him to hear his stories. One he often told came to mind:

> There once was a very wealthy family that had a simple, illiterate housekeeper named Maymouna. All day long she cleaned,

folded, cooked, swept, mended, and laundered. Her work was never done.

Every day, when they heard the call to prayer, the family members made their lustrations, gathered together, and laid out their mats in the direction of the Kaaba to pray. And Maymouna too set aside what she was doing and turned toward the Kaaba. Raising her hands to her ears, she simply said: "Maymouna knows God and God knows Maymouna." Then she wiped her hands together, as if to say, "That's enough," and got back to work.

The children loved this story. They asked him to tell it again and again, and chimed in when he repeated their favorite line: *"Maymouna knows God and God knows Maymouna."* They nudged one another, called each other Maymouna, and giggled. Maybe they laughed because her form of worship was absurd. Or maybe because they liked her little prayer and they too wanted to believe that they knew God and God knew them.

Kareem began to stir, interrupting her reverie. He slowly sat up and made his way to the shower. He returned looking refreshed and sat down in a chair by the window. Zahra saw her opportunity to convince him to come to the United States for medical care. She mentioned the world-class hospitals near her home and the specialist she had researched who seemed most promising. Her father listened patiently as she outlined the physician's impressive credentials.

"Please come to the U.S. for a second opinion," she said, emotion creeping into her voice. "I think it will be good for you, you can stay with us, there are plenty of specialists around . . . and, well, I just think it will be easier . . . I mean, you're so far away from us . . . ," she trailed off. Then she blurted out, "I will never forgive myself if you don't come and something happens."

"If something happens?" he asked, leaning in and raising an eyebrow. "You mean if I die?" Sighing, he turned his head and looked out the window. He rolled his prayer beads in his hand, one by one, then turned to her and spoke gently and patiently.

"*Canim*, death is not something to fear or sweep under the rug. It's not a flaw for us to fix. It's part of God's plan. We don't control when we die, God does. Why hold yourself responsible for what is written for all of us? 'We belong to God and to God we shall return,'" he said, reciting the Qur'anic verse Muslims recite when someone passes on.

Tears welled up in Zahra's eyes.

"Death is inevitable," he continued. "And yet, somehow, this most obvious fact is the one we most frequently forget. That's why the Qur'an uses different metaphors to remind us again and again of how fleeting this life is, and how quickly it passes."

Kareem reached for the Qur'an on his nightstand, flipped quickly through its translucent pages until he found the verse he was looking for, and then read it aloud: "Present them the simile of the life of the world as like rain. We send down from the sky: the earth's vegetation absorbs it, then it becomes dry stubble, which the winds scatter. And God is the one who prevails over everything."

Then, his tone turning upbeat, he pointed out that death was not the end of our story.

"Think about it: seeds scattered by the wind take root elsewhere. Each spring, all over the earth, nature's lessons of renewal are written in green. Death marks a new beginning: the next stage of our spiritual journey."

Then he found another verse from the Qur'an to read to her: "The enjoyment of the life of the world is but little compared to the hereafter." Now he flipped pages and read yet another verse: "For the friends of God, there is no fear, and they will not sorrow."

He closed the book and placed it back on the nightstand. Then he took a deep breath and exhaled slowly.

The words stirred something deep inside Zahra—something she had once known and trusted. And then she had moved to the United States, where people battled their diseases, and death was a problem to be solved. Like a shameful secret, dying was hidden from view. Elders disappeared into assisted living facilities for their final decline. In all the years she'd lived in America, she realized, she had never seen a person in their last days, let alone their last hours. It was remarkable, considering that death was everywhere.

The knot of fear in Zahra's stomach began to loosen. Still, the ease, even enthusiasm, with which her father spoke of his death made her uncomfortable. He saw death as a blessing, a homecoming, a passage to the next life.

"You make death sound like a great gift," she teased him, smiling weakly.

"And that's precisely what it is!" he said, sitting up taller. "Without it, there could be no eternal life! And if we pay attention, death becomes our greatest teacher. Reflecting on mortality makes us prioritize what matters most. Death becomes our source of hope and humility; it compels us to live fully, love fiercely, give generously. And the constant remembrance of God also keeps us on the straight path, always 'enjoining the good and forbidding the evil,' as the Qur'an tells us."

Zahra nodded and fell silent, letting the truth of his words sink in.

"But I will miss you so much," she mumbled. "Without you, there will be a massive hole in my life."

His face softened with compassion. "And I love you just as much, *Canim*. You will never lose me. Death only kills what is false. When the time comes and you feel that emptiness inside, remember this: It can be filled only by the light of God and knowledge of the hereafter."

Zahra leaned back into the pillows and closed her eyes, thereby ending the conversation. A feeling of emptiness had gnawed at her for most of her adult life. Now, considering all she had tried to fill the void with—degrees, romance, money, children, shopping—she felt exhausted. The world disappeared in an instant. What would she regret when she faced her own death? Her husband's face instantly came to mind as grief arose in her chest. Now she could see she had been locked for too long in a power struggle with her husband.

The greater and most transformational jihad, she recalled hearing about many years ago, was the lifelong jihad against the self. Making peace with her husband, she realized, had to be her priority, and that required restraining her ego.

As if in response to her moment of clarity, the *adhan* rang out. Her father stood motionless by the window. He pointed, and she followed his finger. On the highest floor of an unfinished building, under the open sky, construction workers had paused their labors. Gathering in a row on the floor they were working on, they turned as one in the same direction under the open sky.

ZAHRA DIDN'T MIND PRAYING ALONE. It was something she cherished about her faith: that her five daily prayers brought her into direct intimacy with God, without having to rely on an intermediary. The prayers, structured from dawn to late evening, were a constant respite from worldly matters, a time to remember and worship a living God who is ever present in our affairs. "When My servants ask you about Me," God tells the Prophet in the Qur'an, "I am close indeed—I hearken to the prayer of the supplicant when one calls on Me; so let them hearken to Me, and let them believe in Me, that they may go the right way." She treasured her time alone with God.

In Mecca she rediscovered what a delight it was to pray with other women. This was what called her to the Kaaba for her daily prayers. One morning she found herself praying beside an elderly woman with a broad, gap-toothed smile who stared at her with unapologetic curiosity. "Iraq," the woman said, patting her own chest, and when Zahra patted her own and said, "America," the old woman laughed and said, "OK, America! Hello America!"

On another morning, in prostration during her prayer, she felt someone tugging on the hem of her *abaya*. A woman in the row behind her was trying to cover Zahra's naked ankle. Catching Zahra's gaze, she shook her head sternly. Clearly, she thought it inappropriate for Zahra's ankle to be visible. This made Zahra smile. Her childhood had been full of bossy aunties correcting her about one thing or another. Sometimes their scrutiny had gotten under her skin, but now that she lived in Brooklyn, without extended family and with friends who respected her personal space, she longed for at least one intrusive auntie. Individualism sometimes felt oppressive. For someone to scold her meant they cared. It felt like a liberation from loneliness.

The day before her departure from Mecca, Zahra found a Nigerian woman next to her at prayer who spoke flawless English with a crisp British accent. They compared notes on their pilgrimage. Zahra said that because she had a fear of crowds she had circled the Kaaba at dawn—and she still couldn't get anywhere near the structure. The woman leaned close, as if confiding a secret, and suggested she go at 3:00 a.m.; at that hour, she promised, Zahra would have a much better experience.

When Zahra arrived at the Kaaba around 3:00 a.m. to do the *tawaaf*, countless lights bounced off white marble, making the place bright under the night sky. Pilgrims walked briskly, and Zahra joined that steady current of humanity. With the completion of each circle, she drew closer, and the crowd grew denser. But she persisted, edging her way farther in.

An intoxicating scent filled the air around the Kaaba—musky and sweet, with hints of amber and spice—unlike anything in Zahra's experience. It was a rare incense used to perfume the Kaaba several times a day. Its most precious ingredient, more valuable than gold, was extracted from trees infected with a rare fungus. By the time Zahra was close enough to see each Arabic letter of the intricate gold embroidery on the cloth covering the Kaaba, the scent permeated everything.

As she made her way around one corner, Zahra noticed a tight row of women lined up facing the Kaaba, their backs to the crowd. The next time she passed, one of the women turned and caught Zahra's eye. The stranger raised her hand and beckoned Zahra to join them. As she approached, Zahra realized that these women had formed a protective boundary for another row of women, nearly invisible, who were praying in full prostration at the edge of the shrine. In the eye of the storm, women watched over one another so they could pray in a position of total surrender. The stranger was inviting Zahra to join them.

The moment she stepped in, the wall of women closed behind her. Zahra began to pray, finding pure stillness in the middle of that holy human revolution. Touching her forehead to cold marble felt sobering and sublime. In that tight space the air itself was calming, full of love. She breathed it in with awe; she breathed it out with gratitude. She recalled something a *shaykh* once told her: "This world is designed to break your heart." She felt like her heart was breaking wide open.

"Indeed, relief comes with distress," God promises humanity in the Qur'an. Without her father's cancer diagnosis, she would never have come here. She would never have experienced this depth of surrender in a sisterhood of strangers, under the protection of all the mothers she had never known. Her emptiness inside became fullness and spilled over. Only God's mercy, she realized, could have brought her to this moment.

Like the stranger waving to her from a distance, she saw God's hand in every step of her journey. She had been experiencing her life as a rushing current against which she struggled alone—but God had been with her the entire time, summoning, showing her the way. These days in Mecca, she had been circling closer and closer around her true self. Now she had arrived. She felt a true lightness of being.

Zahra had no idea how long she'd been there. When she rose back up, she turned her tear-stained face to the protective circle of women. Then she faced the crowd, looking for another woman like herself, walking alone—and when she found her, she caught her eye, and invited her in.

ON HER SEVENTH DAY IN MECCA, Zahra stood in the doorway of her hotel room with her packed bag beside her, taking in the view one last time. She felt anxious about leaving this refuge—the starched white sheets, the quiet hum of cooled air, the steaming hot shower—and most of all, the privacy.

Something precious had happened in this small room: in her late-night phone conversations with Raheem, they had begun to talk about what mattered most, to share their hopes and vulnerabilities. The fog between them was beginning to clear. These exchanges would not be possible in the coming days, which she would spend in crowded tents with strangers or under the open sky: first in Mina, then Arafat, then Muzdalifah. And then, after completing her pilgrimage, she would visit Medina.

She recalled something the Prophet reportedly said: "I am in this world like a traveler, seeking shade beneath a tree, then catching his breath and moving on." Zahra wished she could live that way, with such detachment from the material world. Feeling her own compulsion to cling to comfort, Zahra sighed and stepped into the hallway. The heavy door whispered closed behind her. Soon, her father joined her, and they rolled their bags down the hallway.

The crowded bus to Mina inched forward through heavy traffic, finally approaching a landscape of identical white peaked tents that seemed to go on forever. This was Mina, dubbed the City of Tents, with an estimated one hundred thousand tents for pilgrims. In a parking lot the size of several football fields, pilgrims spilled from continuously arriving buses.

As her father disappeared into the crowd on his way to the men's section, Zahra felt a rush of panic at being left alone. Moments later, she found her tent and stepped inside. Every inch of the floor was covered with narrow cushions where women lounged, or napped, or sat quietly. Zahra stepped gingerly among them to reach her own cot. She felt like a refugee—uprooted by fate, far from home, stripped of stature and self-determination. Most of that first night she lay rigidly on her back, listening to the stirring and sighing of sleeping bodies. Just as she was finally nodding off, she was jolted awake by movement around her. It was time to prepare for the dawn prayer. Having learned that pulling the hair or cutting a nail affects one's *ihram* (ritual state of purity), she left her tangled hair unkempt, smoothed her wrinkled clothes, and made her way to the women's bathrooms, where she stood in line for nearly an hour.

That whole long day slipped by in a blur. Before each of her five prayers, she stood in long lines to make her lustrations. Between them she sat on her cot or stood in another long line to receive a modest meal. When the crowd overwhelmed her, she stepped outside, but the sweltering heat soon drove her back in. Hours and hours of waiting, without any privacy, left her exhausted and restless.

The following morning, dawn broke on the Day of Arafat, the pinnacle of hajj. The pilgrim's preparation for death culminates with this foreshadowing of Judgment Day, when all will stand before God to face their fate. And on this day the following Qur'anic verse was revealed: "Today I have completed your religion for you, and have fulfilled My favor for you, and approved Islam as a religion for you."

Pilgrims spend daylight hours standing on the Mount of Mercy—where their Prophet delivered his final sermon—pouring their hearts out to God and seeking forgiveness. Muslims at home around the world also repent on this auspicious day when it is believed that mercy descends from the heavens and God showers believers with more forgiveness than on any other day of the year.

Mercy is meaningless without suffering. Pilgrims arrive at the Mount of Mercy raw and tired from the previous days of pilgrimage and become more disheveled and disoriented as the day goes on. Zahra stumbled onto the bus in a fog of exhaustion. Her body ached. Her limbs felt heavy.

Glimpsing her reflection in the bus window, she barely recognized herself. Her father, too, seemed more fragile: the circles under his eyes darker, his smile tighter.

By the time they reached Mount Arafat, pilgrims swarmed every crag and crevice of the mountain. Partway up the incline, Zahra found a narrow place where she could stand beside a boulder with one smooth side to lean against. There, in one of the harshest climates on earth, the sun beat down with vengeance. Hard rock was her only comfort. On the Mount of Mercy there was nowhere to hide, and there were no formal rituals or prayers—she stood alone before God.

Transfixed, she stared at the pilgrims all around her: some raising their hands in prayer, some turning their faces to the sky and crying out, some bowing their heads to the earth and weeping.

Eventually their pleas penetrated her sense of separation and she realized she was not among them; she *was* them. Her skin stung. Her eyes were blurry. Her legs were weak. Her vitality was draining away. It struck her that she had been so focused on her father's mortality that she had forgotten her own death drawing near. "With life as short as a half-taken breath," Rumi said, "plant nothing but love." All that was left of her life was an exhale. Suddenly she had an embodied realization of Islam: this vanishing world is full of trials and tribulations. The *al-akhira* (next life) is everlasting, and blissful for those who believe, and do good, and seek God's forgiveness while they still can.

Like her daughter who demanded justice in the political realm, she had insisted on justice in her personal life. But now, standing in a crush of humanity yet utterly alone before God, all notions of justice evaporated. All she prayed for was mercy. As the sun sank in the sky, she took refuge in God, and as daylight faded, she felt held in God's embrace.

Her mind became as vast and empty as the desert. All that distracted her from God and herself faded along with the light. She had imagined the discomfort of the previous days as an obstacle to overcome—but now she saw that discomfort *was* her path. *Arafa* in Arabic means "to discover," "to find," or "to know." In her hardship she discovered a continuous flow of love inside, a place where everything melted into mercy, and grief and gratitude flowed together.

She had imagined gaining something from her pilgrimage. Now she saw that the spiritual journey was not about addition. Only in subtraction was she able to find the source and sum of everything. "Whoever knows himself knows his Lord," is a statement commonly attributed to the Prophet. Deep inside she had begun to discover her true self—and in that place within her she also found God.

THE NEXT DAY, Kareem and Zahra departed for Medina, Islam's second holiest city, where they would spend their final two days in Saudi Arabia. Also known as the Enlightened City, Medina is where the Prophet went to escape religious oppression and where most of the first Muslims practiced their nascent religion in peace. Every year millions of Muslims visit Medina to pray at the Prophet's Mosque, which is also his final resting place.

Zahra arrived physically and emotionally exhausted, not only by the pilgrimage but also by the relentless noise and congestion of the streets of Mecca. Stepping down from the bus and onto the street in Medina, she was struck by how different this city was from Mecca. It was fairly quiet, and there were no blaring car horns. A sense of peace washed over her. It is said that the Prophet was always well groomed and that long after he passed by, his fragrance hung in the air. Now it seemed to Zahra as if his mercy lingered in the air in this city he called his sanctuary. She had often heard this about Medina—but never believed it until she experienced it herself.

Muslims believe the two primary sources of Islam are God and God's last messenger, Prophet Muhammad; or the Qur'an and the *sunnah* (Prophetic Way). To believers, the Prophet is both a role model and a lawgiver. "His character was the Qur'an," his wife Aisha said after he passed. He embodied scripture; he was a living, breathing, walking Qur'an. His companions worked diligently to document and preserve his words and actions, and since then countless scholars have worked to verify them. Through these *hadith*, Muslims learn to love and emulate their Prophet who was not above the world, but deeply immersed in it. His example offers guidance for every realm of life—from the personal to the political, the mundane to the exalted. Muslims also nurture their love for him through prayers and poetry. He was known by many titles, including The Best of Creation, The Trustworthy One, and the Beloved of God. A burning love for him makes one's faith complete.

When she was a little girl, Zahra had loved him for his abundant mercy. As she grew older, she also adored his exemplary masculinity: he was kind and full of compassion toward children; he played with them, carried them on his shoulders, and even interrupted his teachings to tend to their needs. He wept often—in mourning, in fear, in awe of revelation. He cleaned the house, patched his own robes, kneaded dough, and helped with other chores. He was so gentle to animals that, as he led an army of ten thousand companions to Mecca, upon being informed that in their path ahead were some puppies being nursed by their mother, he ordered some of his companions to stand guard around the nursing puppies as the large army passed by so that they along with their mother would be shielded from any disturbance or harm.

Just before dawn on her first day in Medina, Zahra hurried to the mosque. She laid her prayer mat down beside a young woman in black who greeted her in broken English and smelled like fresh gardenia blossoms. After the prayer, Zahra complimented her scent. The young woman reached into her purse and pressed a small perfume vial into Zahra's palm. "For you," she said with a shy smile, and disappeared into the crowd.

What is it about this city? Zahra wondered, her hand closing around her gift. Maybe it had to do with the fact that while the Prophet didn't require that Muslims visit his mosque, he recommended it. Only hearts burning with love for the Messenger call believers to his illuminated city, which has become a cherished part of pilgrimage. People come to honor their Prophet, practice their faith, and serve others doing the same. They pray at the mosque—the second largest one after the mosque in Mecca—and offer their blessings to him facing the green dome in a corner of the mosque where he was laid to rest. Centuries of believers, starting with the Prophet and his companions, have created a singular climate of reverence, humility, and generosity.

Zahra and Kareem's last two days together stretched out luxuriously. One afternoon between prayers, when they were passing time in the shade outside the Prophet's Mosque, Kareem asked her what aspect of the Prophet's life moved her most.

"That when he was overcome with fear and doubt, he turned to his wife for strength," Zahra replied without hesitation.

The Prophet always relied on his wife Khadija, a successful businesswoman fifteen years his senior who was his employer before she was his wife. At the age of forty, having been married to Khadija for fifteen years, the Prophet was meditating in a cave when the angel Gabriel appeared to him. This first revelation terrified him, and he hurried home to his wife, seeking solace. Keeping her composure, she acknowledged his state, comforted him, and assured him he was not going insane, as he had feared.

To know that the Prophet once trembled in fear and relied on his wife's courage and strength moved Zahra deeply. She had never known a grown man to be that vulnerable and openly reliant on a woman's strength.

"They are garments for you, and you are garments for them," Kareem replied, nodding as he quoted the Qur'anic verse about husbands and wives. "And what does it mean to be a garment for another?" He squinted up at the green dome against a clear blue sky.

"To cover, protect, comfort, or beautify, I suppose," Zahra replied, her mind racing as she tried to recall the last time she did any of those things for Raheem. Not a single memory came to mind... and yet she wanted him to do all of that for her. She felt a sudden longing to become her husband's refuge.

A PEACEFUL SILENCE SETTLED over Kareem and Zahra on their bus ride from Medina to the airport in Jedda. Once they reached the highway, the desert rushed silently by in a brown blur. Kareem leaned back and closed his eyes, but Zahra sensed he was not sleeping.

Her heart ached, knowing she would soon have to say goodbye. But the heavy anxiety and sense of responsibility she arrived with had dissipated. The tenderness she felt now was her wide-open heart. Freed from her illusions of control, and facing the reality of her father's mortality, she felt nothing but love for him. Such wholehearted cherishing, such awakening to the blessing he was in her life, was newfound and unfamiliar, and almost too much to bear. She stole a glimpse of his upturned face. She sensed he felt it too.

At Jedda airport, she stayed with him until his flight was called. Her father told her he had something to tell her.

"*Canim*," he said. "Do you remember the story of Hannah, mother of Mary, in the Qur'an?"

Zahra shook her head.

"I want to share it with you because it relates to us as well," he said. "Hannah was pregnant and expecting a boy, and she promised God that her child would be raised in the temple to live a life of service and worship. But then she bore a girl. 'The male is not like the female,' the Qur'an states. Presumably, girls were not allowed to take up residence in the temple. Yet each of the priests desired to be her custodian; they cast lots to determine who would have the privilege. And when Zacariah visited her in her temple sanctuary, he found that God had provided her with blessings and abundance.

"Hannah imagined limitations for her daughter that did not exist," Kareem continued. "And Mary's gift to humanity—her son Jesus, peace be upon him—was beyond anyone's ability to imagine."

He dropped his eyes and fell silent. "Perhaps I made similar mistakes with you, not knowing your destiny. I never dreamed of the opportunities you have had in your life. Nor could I have imagined the extraordinary woman you have become.

"I'm sorry for my lack of imagination," he humbly concluded, his eyes filling with tears.

Zahra tried to contain her emotions. Kareem unwound the sandalwood prayer beads from his wrist and placed them in her palm. The small wooden globes were stained different shades by oil they had absorbed over time. "These were a gift from a great scholar," he told her. "The eye may see only shades of brown, but in my heart these beads carry the light of wisdom and understanding. Now they are yours," he concluded, closing her fingers over his gift. Zahra was overcome with gratitude.

His flight number was announced over the loudspeaker. His plane would soon be boarding. Only then did Zahra feel a flash of panic. She wished him a safe journey home. She asked him to take care of himself.

"*Canim*," he said, leaning in close, his voice dropping to a whisper. "When I was a young man, I longed for adventure. I still do. And what journey could possibly compare to the one we take after our final breath?"

He stared intensely at her. He held her face in his hands. His eyes were glassy. "Am I scared? Yes. Also curious. I have lived a full life. This world no longer seduces me. My desires have changed. What I long for now is to meet my Creator."

Here we are, Zahra thought, as she watched him disappear into the crowd: two travelers making their way home. She had no idea when she would arrive—but when she did, she hoped and prayed she would find her father waiting with open arms. Faith must be filling that emptiness inside, she realized. She was beginning to trust in their reunion.

As soon as she cast her gaze contemplatively beyond the window, the scents and sounds of Mecca began to return all at once; suddenly, she started hearing the call to prayer echoing in her ears.

She turned her face to the window. In Mecca, the *adhan* had called her back, five times a day, to worship and belonging. Again and again, it invited her to return to a blossoming devotion. She already missed that melodic reminder of what matters most. She chafed at how this call, and those who answer it, are so gravely misrepresented in the Western world.

Reclining her seat and closing her eyes, Zahra recalled that never-ending human revolution around the Kaaba. Everything in existence was in a constant state of revolution: the electron around the nucleus, the moon around the earth, the earth around the sun. And, she wondered, what did her own life revolve around?

She recalled a story she had heard as a child about Prophet Muhammad's triumphant return to Mecca. Going directly to the Kaaba, he found it cluttered with hundreds of idols. He cleared them all out, restoring the holy site as a symbol of the oneness of God.

From that day on, there would be no more divination with arrows, fetishism, or ritual sacrifice at the Kaaba.

She once imagined idol worship as something primitive people did in the distant past. But now it dawned on her that today's false gods were far more pernicious and pervasive—and her heart was cluttered with them. Like the idol of a better job, which she had imagined was the answer to all her problems. Or a better husband; if only he were more romantic, or a better listener, or more successful, she would finally be content. Her thoughts circled around what would make her home more comfortable: new furniture, better lighting, or living on a quieter street with better neighbors. She spent far too much time online: scrolling through vacation rentals, or images of acquaintances' seemingly perfect lives, or her retirement account to see how much it had grown. In all this she lost sight of a simple and certain truth: life was a brief journey from God back to God. Eventually, only God knew when, she would leave her home, her family, and this world behind. Her only true abode was with her Creator, and the pathway to it was prayer and devotion.

Now she thought about the ways her life revolved around money—earning, spending, saving—believing the lie that it could bring security and comfort and happiness for herself and her loved ones. No matter how generous they were with their daughter, they could not protect her from life's challenges. And no matter how much she and Raheem saved, the numbers on their bank statements never added up to ease.

For the first time in many years, she felt compassion for her hard-working husband. For way too long, she had put pressure on him to provide what only God could give her. She had no idea what would become of her marriage—and now she realized that the pressure she had put on her husband wasn't right. Her work was to tame her ego, to clear from her heart the attachments that could never give her peace. "Detachment," Imam Ali said, "is not that you should own nothing but that nothing should own you." She could still appreciate beauty and desire things of this world—but keeping God at the center would bring those desires into perspective.

She was not the same woman who had arrived in Jedda just ten days earlier—anxious, distraught, and overwhelmed, brooding darkly over the troubles of her life. Stripped of distractions and having turned her attention from her own limitations and frustrations to God's infinite grace, she felt as bright as a candle. Surrender did not mean she would stop striving. She would continue to struggle to become a better mother, wife, human being. But she would no longer delude herself by thinking that she could control the outcome. Her job was to simply accept what God gave her—both hardship and ease—with patience, humility, and gratitude.

Realizing she was not the bestower of blessings, or the one who controlled the future, lifted a massive weight from her shoulders. Would forgetfulness make her slip into the same mistakes, like overlooking her blessings or missing her prayers? Would death disappear from her consciousness, allowing her to imagine she had all the time in the world to get her affairs in order? Only God knew. And she trusted she was in good hands.

She wished she had studied more Islam. She wished she could read the Qur'an in its original Arabic, with its poetry and nuance that could not be captured in any translation. But it wasn't too late. *Read*, was the angel Gabriel's first command to the Prophet. Seeking knowledge was the duty of a believer. She made herself a solemn promise that she would keep learning for the rest of her life. Then she thought: I *am* Maymouna, the housekeeper in the children's story—ignorant of the intricacies of Islam, but wholly devoted to its essence. On good days or bad, Islam was alive in her heart. When life felt complicated and her religious obligations overwhelming, Zahra would remember the sober simplicity of Maymouna's teaching: *I know God and God knows me.*

A Saga of Life and Faith

A RETELLING OF THE JEWISH SACRED STORY

A Saga of Life and Faith

The secret crevasse in the wall was the perfect size for twelve-year-old Ari to slip through. The wall, which surrounded the Warsaw ghetto, had been built by the Germans to cut off the Jewish population from the rest of the city, preventing Jews from moving freely; the result was disease and mass starvation. Ari's light brown hair and green eyes allowed him to pass as just another resident of Warsaw as he made dangerous forays beyond the ghetto's imprisonment to obtain food for his family and, especially, medication for his ailing mother. Kind Mrs. Rodzinska ran the nearby pharmacy and, because she knew the family well, sold Ari the medication for little and kept the secret of his travels. The family had sold everything of value in their home to obtain these essentials, which Ari usually placed inside a small cloth bag. Today he tucked the medication inside the loose fabric of his wool vest and held it close.

He reversed his path and soon found himself safely inside the ghetto again. As he approached the building in which he and his family lived, however, he stopped at the sight of what was unfolding. Horrified, he watched as a group of Nazi soldiers roughly hustled his parents, elder sisters, and other residents of the building into a lorry. His mother, glancing frantically around her, saw him in time; she gave Ari a look that would never in his life forget, and, using an upward nod of her head, told him to flee.

He could not feel the bite of early spring as he ran to the *cheder,* the children's Hebrew school, where his little brother Srulik was studying Torah with the beloved teacher, Reb Boruch. When Ari burst into the *cheder* room, Reb Boruch demanded to know what he was doing. "You know that this is not the way to enter a room, and especially my *cheder*. You knock on the door and wait to be allowed in!" Srulik, seated beside him, looked at his brother with a puzzled expression.

"Oh, Reb Boruch," declared Ari. "There has been another *actzia* (round-up)!'" He did not need to explain the rest. "I have to take Srulik with me."

"How terrible," said Reb Boruch. He glanced down at the boy beside him; Ari and Srulik were dear to him. "But you must come and stay with us."

Ari soberly shook his head. "Thank you so much, Reb Boruch, but Mother and Father told me that if ever this happened, I must go to the place in the trees." He used the coded expression that he knew Reb Boruch would understand.

"Of course," responded Reb Boruch. "First go to my home and ask my wife for a few apples for your way and for one of our water bottles. Please take great care, my dear boy. God protect both of you, and may we hear tidings of goodness, redemption, and comfort."

Ari took Srulik by the hand and saw that his little brother's lower lip was trembling. "Don't worry Srulik," he said, "Mamme and Tatte will be back, but we are going on an adventure into the forest. You must be very brave. Put up your *payos* (sidelocks) under your cap like I do, so we don't appear too obviously Jewish, and try not to say anything until we are out of the city. If you have to say something, say it in Polish, not in Yiddish."

AFTER COLLECTING APPLES and a water bottle from Reb Boruch's wife, they went to the gap in the ghetto wall that Ari knew so well. They looked around to make sure that no one could see them and then climbed through and walked eastward until they the Vistula River. From there on they stayed off the main road and continued southeast for hours, stopping for breaks along the way until they saw the sign to the Macierowe swamp and the wetlands beyond. "We have to go to the bottom of the main lake to the southeast corner," Ari said to Srulik, as they followed an overgrown path.

Another mile walking beneath the branches of pines and maples brought them to a clearing. There they found a simple woodsman's lodge, a large vegetable garden, and chickens in a pen nearby. They hesitated at this extraordinary scene which was so different from the ghetto. "Here we are," Ari heard himself say quietly. They approached the cottage and, with Srulik standing behind him, Ari knocked on the door. The curtain in the front window moved a little before the door opened, and a man came out and welcomed them with the traditional Jewish greeting. "*Sholem alaychem,*" he said to the weary boys who stared up at him. "Who are you?"

"*Aleychem sholem,* Professor Noyek," replied Ari. "We are Ari and Srulik Levine, the sons of Moishe and Rivke." He felt an ache in his chest as he said the names of his parents.

"*Oy vei*, alas, " said Professor Noyek, who instantly understood why the boys were standing before him. He was astonished that they had come so far on their own. "You've done well to find us." He embraced the boys, telling them how sorry he was. The three went into the cottage where Ari and Srulik were greeted by a woman with a generous smile. "This is my wife, Gittel," said the professor.

"Welcome, boys," she said warmly. "Our home is your home."

Thank you so much, Professor and Mrs. Noyek," said Ari. Srulik stood beside him, looking about the room.

"Let's do away with formalities. Please call us 'Uncle' and 'Auntie.' Come, sit down and rest—you must be starving. We don't have a lot here, but it is much more than you have had in the ghetto." Ari felt the depth of emptiness in his stomach; he and Srulik had finished the apples long ago. The professor continued, "We're able to grow some vegetables, like potatoes, and wheat from which Auntie makes bread. Throughout the summer and early autumn there are different kinds of berries around us here in the forest. We dry a lot of them to eat in winter, as well, and of course we also have chickens."

The boys watched as Mrs. Noyek placed some rusks and potato salad on the table and poured cups of water from a kettle. "We use the water from the lake," she explained. "It's actually quite clean, but I boil it just in case. Here it has cooled down. Drink and eat up, boys."

After the meal, which to Ari felt like a dream, Mrs. Noyek asked for their clothes so she could wash them in the lake. "I'll bring you two of my husband's shirts, which will be like caftans on you," she laughed. "And you can wear them until your clothes dry."

She brought the boys to the pantry door. "You can rest and sleep in here. It will be a bit tight for you. I'm afraid we don't have proper beds. We cut and dry grasses and put them in sacks to lie down on. And we have extra sacks that we put together when other people have stayed here with us."

Ari looked around the living room and noticed that there was a set of the *Chumash*, the five books of the *Torah*, as well as a set of the *Talmud*, on a makeshift bookshelf together with a few other books. "I can see you're surprised that I have a copy of the *Talmud* here and other *seforim*, holy books," said Professor Noyek. "I know it seems something of a luxury out here, but I had to bring these *seforim* with me. What is Jewish life if we cannot study God's revelation, the Written *Torah* and the Oral *Torah* that He gave us? *For they are our life and the length of our days, and in them shall we study day and night*, he added in Hebrew, quoting a verse from the daily evening prayers. "Now go and get changed, give Auntie your clothes, and have a little rest. I'm going to study the weekly portion of the *Torah*, which we will all read together at *shacharis,* the morning service on *Shabbos* (Sabbath) morning, and we can discuss it tomorrow evening at dinner."

The days of the week had blurred for Ari. "Of course," he said, realizing that it was Thursday. "It's *Shabbos* tomorrow evening." He was trying to be brave, but his shoulders were heavy as he thought of his parents and sisters.

The professor watched the boy knowing what had to be on his mind. "We will do our best to make up for your family's absence, Ari."

After having rested, the boys went into the living room. Professor Noyek looked up from his study. Ari approached him with a question that he had been mulling. "Uncle, may I ask you why you're living here far away from other Jews?"

"There are a few reasons, Ari," he answered, "and I will explain in due course. But now it's getting close to dusk and we must pray *minchah* and *maariv,*" referring to the afternoon and evening services. He went to the bookshelf and removed two prayer books. "Do you pray three times a day, Ari? You're not thirteen yet, are you, and if you are not *bar-mitzvah* you are not obliged. But you should already be davening three times a day."

"Of course I do, and I know the afternoon and evening prayers by heart," Ari said.

"That's wonderful," replied Professor Noyek. "But even if you do know them all by heart, you should still use a prayer book, a *siddur*, and we have two here. The direction for prayer, toward Jerusalem, is this way," he added, pointing south-eastward.

The boys joined the Noyeks at supper, though they were no longer so hungry after their earlier meal, and then prepared for bed. Once they were lying down, Mrs. Noyek came in to them. "Does your Mamme say *Shema* with you every night, Srulik?"

"Yes, always," replied Srulik, feeling even more homesick for his mother.

"Tonight, I am in her place and we will recite the *Shema*, the declaration of Jewish faith, together." Even though Ari was already used to saying the *Shema* by himself when he went to sleep, he joined in with them: *Shema Yisroel Adonoy Eloihenu Adonoy Echod. Hear O Israel, the Lord Our God, the Lord is One. And you shall love the Lord Your God with all your heart, with all your soul, and with all you might…*"

"You know," added Mrs. Noyek, "this declaration of our faith declares that there is only One God in the world. And everything in the world, in His Creation, is connected. He cares about you and is looking after you. The call to Israel is, of course, a call to the Jewish people to testify to this truth, but Israel is also your name, Srulik, isn't it? Srulik is a diminutive of the name Yisroel, Israel, so you could say that you have a special call."

Srulik felt rather proud. "Yes, my Hebrew name is Yisroel Yacov. I have both names of our forefather the Patriarch Jacob, and when I'm bar-mitzvah I will be called up to the reading of the Torah as Yisroel Yacov ben Moishe Cha'im."

Mrs. Noyek smiled. "Very good. Sleep well, Yisroel Yacov and Ari."

THE NEXT MORNING the boys awoke to the sound of the rooster crowing and looked out the window to see Professor Noyek finishing *shacharit*, the morning prayers, adorned in his *tallit*, the prayer shawl, and *tephillin*, the leather prayer boxes and straps. They walked out to join him as he was taking off his *tephillin.* After greeting them, he acknowledged that ideally he would pray with a congregation, a community, but of course here he had to pray alone. "But when I pray wearing these *tephillin,*" Professor Noyek said, "not only do I feel especially close to God, I feel I'm praying with a whole family community. These were my grandfather's *tephillin* and his father's before him." He thanked God that his children had fled Poland before the Nazis invaded and then added, "but I hope that one day, my grandson or great grandson will wear these *tephillin*, too."

A breeze came through the clearing as Ari and Srulik felt a moment of peacefulness. The professor continued. "And though we're far away from any synagogue here, and even though we are living in such terrible times, for Jews especially, I love praying out here in the forest. We can feel God's holy presence among the trees and meadows, the wild animals and birds, the sky and the stars that are visible outside the city." He added, from Psalm 19, *The heavens announce the glory of God, and the firmament declares the work of His hands.*

After Ari recited the morning *shacharit* service, and Srulik also said the prayers that he knew, they washed their hands while making the appropriate blessing, before joining Uncle at the table. The bread that was offered them was a bit stale but made edible by Mrs. Noyek's excellent blackberry jam, which they ate together with *herbata*—Polish herbal tea. Before partaking of the food, they made the blessing over bread that commences every meal, *Blessed are You O Lord our God, Sovereign of the Universe, who brings forth bread from the ground.*

"*Omain,*" responded the Professor, using the usual Polish Ashkenazi pronunciation for Amen.

As they were eating, Ari was bothered by another concern. "Uncle," he said, "may I ask you a big question?" Srulik looked up from his plate to watch his brother. "Why are we Jews so hated and persecuted?"

The professor thought for a moment and then sat back in his chair. "That is indeed a difficult question, Ari." Before him were two boys who had witnessed and survived something that seemed to defy explanation. "There are some simple reasons and some complicated ones, yet in the end none of them are fully satisfactory. But I will try to answer you." He smoothed the worn fabric of the tablecloth with his hands. "If something bad happens to people, they often look for others to blame. People are also suspicious and even afraid of others who are different from them. Throughout most of history in these lands, Jews have been the only other people that local people have seen, and we have been and continue to be the target of their ignorance, suspicion, fear, and blame. In addition, over the ages, most Christians were taught that Jews were guilty as a people for the crucifixion of Jesus. So, people often said that Jews deserved to suffer. There are other motivations as well, especially for those in power seeking political and economic benefit. For example, when people do not have enough food or security, authorities often seek to pin the blame of their own failures on a convenient, and usually vulnerable, innocent target."

He sighed and looked gently at the boys' faces. "Now, I will share with you a profound idea that comes from the prophet Isaiah, which you might not understand today, but you might remember in the future. Already more than two and a half thousand years ago, the prophet was bothered by the question as to why the Jewish people suffered so disproportionately. By way of explanation, he described the Jewish people as God's suffering servant. Basically, he was telling us that if you have been chosen by God to testify to His Presence in the world, whether you deserve it or not and whether you live up to it or not, everything that hates the Godly and the goodly will hate you. In that sense the Jewish people 'take on' and bear the sins and sicknesses of the world. It is the terrible consequence of the wonderful privilege we enjoy to lead the life of the covenant made between God and the children of Israel at Sinai, thanks to our forefathers having discovered the true One God and His Word and Way."

His expression became more upbeat. "But there are still many good people in the world as well, thank God. Many of them here in Poland are sheltering Jews from the clutches of the Nazis at the peril of their lives and the lives of their dear ones. And many people here are fighting against the Nazis and their collaborators." He realized he could not burden the boys with his secret. He and Gittel had had to leave the ghetto before the Nazis cut it off from the rest of Warsaw for various reasons, but the most important was to aid the resistance against the Nazis. In their seclusion in the forest, the Noyeks could treat members of the resistance who were wounded or sick, as well as pass along information to them. Though the professor and his wife lived in constant danger of discovery, they did their best to prepare for the possibility, including how to survive in the very woods that surrounded them. The professor was determined to teach the boys to do the same.

He leaned toward Ari and said, "I want you to explore the forest around us with me, to learn where to hide and where to go, and to learn to recognize edible berries and plants. So, I am going to take the two of you with me each day into the forest to teach you these things." The boys smiled and nodded.

"But now, come and help me *shecht* a chicken that Auntie can prepare for our *Shabbos* meals. As you know *Shabbos* meals have to be as festive as possible." The Sabbath is considered both a Queen and a Bride. "This day is special and precious to us; so, we must make sure to make it as good and enjoyable an experience as we can, both spiritually and physically, even in these terrible times."

Srulik knitted his brow. "What do you mean *shecht*?"

The professor cleared his throat, sensing some resistance to what he was about to say. "You know, we have to kill it in the proper *kosher* way…" He paused. "Luckily I studied the laws of *shechitah* when I was in *yeshivah*, so I know what to do."

Srulik gasped. "I don't want to help kill a chicken!"

"But you want to eat chicken and drink chicken soup, don't you?"

Srulik slumped a little in his chair. "Yes," he answered quietly. "But I don't want to do the killing. Do you think that one day we can eat without killing, Uncle?"

"Perhaps," replied the Professor. "The first book of the *Torah*, Genesis, tells us that Adam and Eve were vegetarian, and of course the Children of Israel lived on manna during their travels through the wilderness for forty years on their way to the Promised Land. Maybe one day people will be able to get all their nutrients and vitamins without needing to eat animals, but I don't think that is possible here, and surely not in winter. Still, it is good that you care for animals, Srulik. You know our ancient sages tell us that one of the most important psalms that we recite in our daily prayers is Psalm 145, which we recite more often than any of the other psalms; and one of its verses declares *God is good to all, and His mercies are extended to all His creatures.*

"You know that if you have animals, like we have chickens, you must always feed them first before you feed yourself; and it is a grave sin to cause cruelty to animals. That is why even when we need animals for food, we must make sure that we slaughter them in the most painless and respectful manner." Much to Srulik's relief, he added, smiling, "But if you don't want to join us, you can stay here and help Auntie make the bread."

EVERYTHING FOR THE SABBATH had to be cooked or baked in advance, as it is prohibited to do so on the Sabbath itself. The stove fire was now on a low flame that would keep the food warm for a few more hours. The professor and Ari returned with the slaughtered chicken, which they handed to Mrs. Noyek, and then Professor Noyek took the boys out to the forest for their first lesson in exploring the woods. By the time they returned hours later, the cottage was full of Sabbath cooking smells, of bread and cake, of roasted chicken, chicken soup, roasted potatoes and seasoning.

"You can't eat any of this food yet," said Mrs. Noyek, "but there are still some rusks made from the leftover bread from last week, that you can have with jam and some dried berries. Then go down to the lake and wash yourselves well for *Shabbos*. Your clothes are clean and dry, and you must be fed up already of wearing those smocks," she laughed.

By the time dusk was descending, everyone had bathed and dressed for the Sabbath. The table had been laid, and blue and purple wild flowers were arranged next to two gleaming candlesticks waiting to be lit. "Uncle's luxury are his *seforim* and these candlesticks are mine," she said laughing. "But I have no wax candles or olive oil, so I have to make do with chicken fat."

Mrs. Noyek lit a taper from the stove fire, lit the candles, blew out the taper, and then covered her eyes as she made the blessing over the Sabbath candles. *Blessed are you O Lord our God Sovereign of the Universe who has sanctified us with His commandments and commanded us to kindle the Sabbath candle.*

"*Omain*," they responded. She kissed her husband and then embraced the boys.

Suddenly, Srulik said, "*Brochahs*, blessings, are very important. We just learned with Reb Boruch this week that if you don't make a *brochah* before eating or drinking, it is like stealing , because you are not thanking God who has created everything and to whom everything belongs. And he told us that we should try to make a hundred *brochahs* a day."

Mrs. Noyek nodded. "Particularly on *Shabbos*. We must be mindful of God's gifts to us as much of the time as possible and give thanks for any benefit and pleasure, as well as for special occasions. And *Shabbos* is, of course, the special occasion every week, when we are reminded of, and give thanks for, God's creation that reached its culmination on this seventh day of rest."

Srulik's lip lower trembled and he began to cry. "I miss Mamme and Tatte and our sisters so much."

"Of course you do, darling," she said, placing her hand over her heart. "Please God you will be reunited with them in good health soon. But in the meantime, let's give thanks to God that we are here with one another and can celebrate *Shabbos* together."

They all sat down and recited the psalms receiving the Sabbath day, culminating with the hymn, *Come my beloved to greet the Bride, let us welcome the Sabbath Queen,* which they sang with gusto, even the boys; this was followed by the evening service.

When they gathered around the table, they sang the hymn welcoming the Sabbath angels and the thirty-first chapter of the book of Proverbs extolling the woman of valor, seen by the Jewish mystics as a metaphor for the Sabbath. The professor had an expectant look on his face; he called the boys over to him. "Tonight, I am representing your Tatte," he said to them. Ari and Srulik stood before him; what was to happen next was Ari's favorite part of *Shabbos* with his own family. "I will give you the blessing that parents give their children on *Shabbos*."

Ari closed his eyes, feeling the presence of his father and mother as the professor placed his hands on each boy's head in turn. Professor Noyek recited the traditional Sabbath parental blessing using the Biblical priestly benediction. *May God make you like Ephraim and Menasseh. May the Lord bless you and protect you. May the Lord light up his countenance to-*

ward you and be gracious to you. May the Lord lift up his countenance toward you and grant you peace."

Srulik became peaceful and still, and the most settled Ari had ever seen him. Professor Noyek poured a liquid into a cup and then turned to the boys, smiling. "We have no wine here, boys, with which we are supposed to make *kiddush*, the prayer sanctifying the *Shabbos* day. But I have a non-Jewish friend who brings me this homemade schnapps and I make *kiddush* on it. I actually like it very much and so does Auntie, but I think you will find it very strong, so only take a small sip when I pass it round."

Before Uncle made *kiddush*, Mrs. Noyek brought out two plaited loaves to the table, placing them in front of her husband's setting and covering them with a cloth; as she did so, Ari thought of his mother and longed for her.

The professor said, "God sent down manna from Heaven to feed the Children of Israel in the wilderness on their way from Egypt to the Land of Israel, and they would go out of their camp every day to collect it. But on the eve of Sabbaths and festivals, God sent down a double portion so that they would not need to go out and work to collect manna on the holy day itself. These two *challahs* represent that double portion. Our rabbis tell us that the manna tasted like whatever the children of Israel wished it to taste of. But I can tell you that Auntie's *challahs* themselves taste heavenly."

The professor recited the *kiddush* prayer over the schnapps, sanctifying the Sabbath day, recalling above all the Creation story that testifies to God's presence in the world, but also recalling the Exodus from Egypt, and the presence of God in history. He drank from the cup, then gave it to Mrs. Noyek to drink, and she then passed the cup to the boys. Ari took a sip and gasped, tears coming to his eyes, and couldn't help but blurt out that it tasted awful. Srulik said, "I don't think I will drink any of it," which made the Noyeks laugh.

The professor said, "Now, wash your hands with us and say the *brochah* for doing so before I make the *brochah* over the *challah* and we eat this divine bread." He offered a little salt (which a Polish friend had given them) for dipping the bread. They washed their hands, made the blessing, and then sat down. The professor made the blessing over the bread and broke off a plait of the *challah*, taking a piece of it himself and handing out pieces to the others, which they dipped in the salt and ate. Ari blurted out, "A *mechayeh,*" using the Yiddish word for something wonderful.

"When the Temple was destroyed by the Romans thousands of years ago and we were exiled from our land," Professor Noyek declared, "most Jews thought that this would be the end of Judaism. But our rabbis told us all that there are miniature temples that guarantee the future of Jewish life. These are the synagogue, and above all the home."

He looked at Ari. They were seated in a rough and simple cottage, deep in the forest, in hiding, and yet the Noyeks had together forged a warm, traditional home here. "The Jewish home is the most important place of Jewish life. We cannot survive without it, and much, if not most, of our religious life revolves around it. Especially the crown of the week, *Shabbos,* our day of rest. Our rabbis taught us that we should see the table where we eat and give thanks to God as our altar. And just as the offerings in the Temple had salt on them, so do ours; we start off our meal in this fashion, giving thanks to God for all His blessings." Ari could not help but begin to smile at him, even in his sorrow, and the professor smiled back warmly. "Enough talk for now. Let's tuck in."

After months of deprivation in the ghetto, including at times starvation, this relatively modest meal was an amazing banquet for Ari and Srulik; the joy of the Sabbath was so robust that they were able to briefly transcend their sadness. "On *Shabbos* we are especially mindful of God's wonderful Creation," declared the professor, "but we also remember the Exodus from Egypt in the *kiddush* and in our prayers, especially because we were brought as a people to Mount Sinai where God gave us the *Torah.* As you know, the fourth of the Ten Commandments is the instruction to keep the Sabbath day. But the Exodus story also tells us that eventually God redeems us from evil; and just as he redeemed us then, so he will redeem us from the evil that we are suffering currently."

He clapped his hands together. "And now let us sing *zemiros, Shabbos* songs of praise to God. Srulik, what is your favorite one?"

"*Mnuchoh vsimchoh*" replied Srulik, and, surprising Ari, he began to sing. After a few moments, the others joined in.

At the conclusion of the meal, with the air still ringing with their voices, they continued by reciting the grace aftermeals, introduced by the singing of Psalm 126, *A Song of Ascents. When the Lord returned the captivity of Zion we were as dreamers … Return our captivity O Lord, like streams in the desert. Those who sow with tears shall reap with joy.*

When the psalm was over, the professor paused, allowing silence to accumulate. Mrs. Noyek watched him affectionately. Finally, he placed his hands on his knees and, looking momentarily at the ground, said, "Many centuries ago we were expelled from our land, *Eretz Yisroel*, the Land of Israel. We have always kept alive our love for it and the hope of our return to it, as God promised us." He looked up at Ari and Srulik. "That is why we sing this psalm on every Sabbath and festive day before *bensching*, saying grace after meals. Indeed, he added, such dreams of returning to our historic homeland of Zion are heard in many of our prayers and woven into our rituals. That dream is ever a source of hope and comfort for us." He mentioned to the boys that today more Jews than ever before had returned to rebuild Jewish life in *Eretz Yisroel*; it would be a place where Jews would be able to live their lives freely and not be persecuted or dependent on the good will of gentiles. "One day," he said, "we must all try to get there."

"But Uncle" said Ari, "Reb Boruch told us that most of those Jews in *Eretz Yisroel* today are not religious and do not keep the *mitzvot*, commandments. He told us that we should stay here and keep away from them because they will have a bad influence on us—that we must stay here and wait for the *Moshiach*, the messiah, to take us back to Eretz Yisroel."

The professor knew Reb Boruch and admired him, but parted ways with him on this point. "We can see now how much good that kind of advice has done for all of us who stayed here," he said. "You must remember that to be Jewish is not just to be religiously observant. It is to be part of a community, a people of destiny. All Jews are your brothers and sisters, whether they are religious or not. We are responsible for one another, and you must always remember that. But maybe it was necessary for some Jews to rebel in order to have the energetic spirit for a new and confident kind of Jew in the Land of Israel today. Also, things can change; someone who is not religious today might become religious tomorrow. You know that our sages tell us that 'the gates of repentance' are always open."

"God has unlimited compassion and forgiveness for everyone," said Mrs. Noyek, "and it is always possible for people to mend their ways."

The professor nodded. "As for the coming of the *Moshiach*, maybe God precisely does *not* want us to wait here, but to return to the Land of Israel to prepare the way." Ari was satisfied with these responses and felt a warmth moving through him, the power of the day. The professor continued, "Now, let's *bensch* and give thanks to God that we are alive and can enjoy what we can, especially His gift of *Shabbos*."

After grace after meals, Professor Noyek read aloud part of the weekly portion of the *Torah* reading in Hebrew, translating the text and some of the commentaries. The boys listened for a while before their eyes started closing and Mrs. Noyek said, "Off to bed with you, boys." She would come shortly to say *Shema* with them.

"Good *Shabbos* and good night," said the Professor.

AFTER WAKING THE NEXT MORNING, they washed and prayed the Sabbath morning service. Then the professor made the blessing over some schnapps for the daytime *kiddush*, the blessing of sanctification, reciting the passage from the Ten Commandments: *Six days shall you labor and do all your work and the seventh day is a day of rest to the Lord your God. You shall not do any work on it, not you, your son, your daughter, your manservant, and maidservant, and your livestock, and the stranger that is within your gates.*

They ate some refreshment and then went for a walk in the woods. The air was cool and filled with spring birdsong as the professor pointed out various wild herbs and berries, and explained about their uses. He showed the boys different routes that led for many miles through the forest, especially the route eastwards, telling them that if ever they had to make their way out of the forest by themselves, they should go that way. Ari, knowing that he had Srulik in his care, paid particular attention. The branches overhead formed a lush and protective canopy that comforted him.

As they neared the cottage, the boys noticed that there was an open area where a number of young trees had been planted and enquired about them. Srulik raced up to the small orchard.

When the professor arrived at the edge of the plantings, he lightly touched the leaves of an apple tree sapling. "I asked some of my non-Jewish friends to get some fruit trees for us, which I've planted here." The precariousness of time weighed heavily on his mind. "I don't know how long we will be here. Even if we don't get to enjoy their fruits, we are still helping nature extend its wonderful provisions—perhaps to other people; if not, then to the animals and birds." He told them that nature was God's handiwork and the more it could be helped to flourish, the more they honored His holy presence in the world. "You may know that our sages declare that if you are planting a sapling and are told that the Messiah has arrived, you must first finish planting the sapling before you go to welcome the Messiah. This tells us that planting and caring for the natural world is a religious duty and honor of the greatest importance."

They went inside for lunch, which consisted of cold leftovers from dinner the night before, and which they enjoyed after washing hands and breaking bread, making the blessings over both. Once again, there was discussion over the Sabbath *Torah* portion, and they sang Sabbath table hymns and concluded with grace after meals.

The professor brought out a humble but beautiful chess set, which he had resourcefully carved from pieces of wood. Ari was deeply charmed by it, and he and the professor played a game, while Mrs. Noyek told Srulik stories from the Bible. After a rest and another walk by the lake, followed by afternoon prayers, they had a light "third Sabbath meal" and the professor taught them passages from the "Ethics of the Fathers," a book of the *Talmud* filled with pithy moral aphorisms.

Soon dusk was descending, and it was time for evening prayers. Srulik and Ari peered out one of the windows; when three stars could be seen in the darkening sky, they knew they could make *havdalah*, the Sabbath conclusion service, distinguishing between the Sabbath day and the rest of the week.

Sparks flew from the flint that Professor Noyek struck in order to light a taper; this was a living demonstration that fire could be kindled now that the Sabbath was concluded, and brought to mind the light created on the first day of the week. He made a blessing over schnapps, over the wild herbs they had collected, the fragrance of which symbolized a sweet and fragrant week ahead, and over the light of the flame. Then they sang *Shavua tov shavua tov*, "Have a good week, have a good week," followed by a song expressing hope that the prophet Elijah would come quickly as the harbinger of the Messiah and redemption.

"Our day of rest has concluded," said the professor, "and now we have some work to do cleaning up, especially clearing away the ashes from the stove." Ari and Srulik felt a certain satisfaction in this transition and the shift in energy toward doing. "Tomorrow morning you will come with me when I go to chop wood and collect sticks, all to bring back for the fire to keep us warm and for the stove for cooking."

The professor and Mrs. Noyek knew that the boys would receive comfort from helping with these meaningful tasks. And so, life continued in this vein for a few weeks, during which time Ari and Srulik would make educational forays into the woods and help Mrs. Noyek tend the gardens and plant corn. While the boys were engrossed in these tasks, the professor was visited by three Polish resistance fighters who had come to receive medical treatment and to give him information to pass on to others. Serendipitously, the visitors arrived while the boys were in the woods, enabling the professor to protect them from discovery.

SUDDENLY ONE MORNING after breakfast, however, as Ari and Srulik helped Mrs. Noyek with the dishes, they heard the sound of a motor and realized it was a vehicle on the dirt path approaching the house. The professor, who had been seated at the table, glanced at his wife before he rushed to the window. His normally serene demeanor changed to one of great agitation, though he did his best to check himself when he turned to speak. "Boys, you have to listen and do exactly what I say. No questions. Run out the back door as fast as you can, making sure you aren't noticed." Ari and Srulik stared at him in disbelief. "Come now—quickly! Hide in the forest until all is clear." He took the dishcloth from Ari and placed his hand on Srulik's back to nudge him toward the door. "Go! Go!"

Ari grabbed Srulik's hand and they raced toward the back of the house, turning when they reached the door to look at their protectors.

The professor gave them a nod. "May God protect and bless you," he said, and the boys fled through the door.

Ari could feel his heart pounding as he pulled Srulik to the distant shrubs beneath the trees where they could hide. Srulik gave a whimper as his brother shushed him and pushed him into the undergrowth. By this point in his forest education, Ari knew the ivies and plants to avoid. He crouched beside Srulik as they looked through the weave of branches and leaves, and heard the sounds coming from the cottage. They watched with ragged breath as the professor and Mrs. Noyek were led out the door by Nazi soldiers and placed into the running command car. This was followed by shouts, the slamming of the car doors, and the rasping roar of the engine as it pulled away. In a blink, the car with the Noyeks inside it was entirely gone from view and then the sound of the engine diminished until it, too, was gone.

The boys stayed still inside their hiding spot. Ari was in disbelief that he was witness to yet another such calamity. He surmised that the soldiers would return to ransack the cottage and so they had limited time. He nudged Srulik, who appeared to be in shock but was still able to do what his brother instructed. They went back to the cottage for a water flask, gathered whatever food they could find, and took a last look at the humble rooms. Ari saw the chess set, picked up one of the queens and, in honor of the Sabbath and to remember the Noyeks, put it in his pocket. Then the boys set off for the forest path that the Professor had told them to take and began another long walk.

At night they huddled together to keep warm, as it was still early spring and the nights were cold. After two days, their food was finished, they were unable to find enough wild berries to sustain themselves. The the nights became too much for Srulik. With no apparent choice, Ari decided that they had to leave the forest to look for kindness from among the local villagers.

TOWARD DUSK they came upon a little hamlet. They knocked on the door of the first house.

A stout man came to the door. "What do you want?" he asked gruffly.

Ari felt his heart sink. "Please, sir. We are lost and hungry and have nowhere to go." Srulik clung tightly to his brother's hand.

The man looked at them suspiciously. "Lost, eh?" He tilted his head. "You boys are Jews and you ... are running away. Why should I help you? Do you know what I am? I'm a good Christian and you Jews are cursed for the death of Jesus." Ari remembered that Professor Noyek had mentioned that Christians had been taught that Jews were guilty as a people for the crucifixion of Jesus, even though he could not understand how he was guilty for the death of anyone. Maybe I should apologize, he thought. But before he could do so, a woman appeared from inside the house and said to the man.

"Even if they are Jews, Stephan, didn't our Lord care for all people, even criminals and outcasts? Wouldn't he want us to care for these boys, too?"

The man grunted. "Very well, then. But just for one night. You should know, you boys, that we are endangering our lives by taking you in. We can be executed by the Nazis for this."

"Thank you so much, sir and madam." said Ari.

The boys entered the house and the woman pointed to a dining table. "Sit there and I will give you some bread and beef bone soup."

Ari took a deep breath. "Thank you, madam," he said, "but we can't eat the beef soup." The woman turned and looked at him. "We can't eat it because it is not *kosher,* but perhaps we can eat your bread. Do you use animal grease to grease your pans for baking bread?"

"Grease for the pans!" exclaimed the woman. "Who do you think we are, aristocracy? We are simple folk. I make our bread with just flour, water, and yeast."

"In that case," said Ari, "we would be very happy to eat your bread, please."

The woman grunted, much as her husband had, but she gave them bread and prepared for them a place where they could sleep on the floor near the fire. Though it was uncomfortable, the exhausted boys soon fell asleep.

Early the next morning, Stephan woke them up. "You boys can have more bread and tea," he said, "and then I am taking you to a neighbor." Ari and Srulik exchanged worried looks.

The boys followed behind the man as he went to another cottage on the other side of the hamlet. Stephan knocked on the door, and exchanged a few sentences with the man who opened it. The man let the boys in, and Stephan turned to leave. "Thank you, sir," said Ari to Stephan, who waved his hand in the air over his shoulder as he departed. The boys looked anxiously at the new stranger.

"I AM PIOTR," said the man. "I'm going to take you somewhere safer than here in this village." Piotr explained to them that he was a member of the Polish Guard, which had been formed to fight against the German occupation; some of their units worked closely with Jewish partisan fighters. "I'll take you to join them." Ari felt a rush of gratitude. After taking care of some things inside the house, Piotr led them to the side alley where he hitched a cart to a large brown horse and urged them to get in. The boys eagerly climbed aboard, squeezing together on the small seat beside the man. After Piotr snapped the reins and the cart began to roll, he said to the boys, "This is a journey of about a day and a half. Not too bad."

Taking mainly paths through the forests to avoid German soldiers, Piotr stopped the horse every few hours so they could all rest and stretch and have something to eat and drink. He encouraged the boys to tell him about themselves and their family, and in turn he told them about himself and also about the history of Poland. How he and his friends had hoped to build a country of true freedom and dignity for all people. How they could never have envisaged such a tragedy as they were now experiencing in Poland. How he hoped, prayed, and was working for a better future for the country and all its residents, Christians and Jews.

"After all, we are all the children of One God," said Piotr, "and we should treat one another as if we are all brothers and sisters. Surely, that is what God wants of us."

"Oh, how wonderful that would be, if possible," said Ari.

At one point Piotr told them that they would be leaving the forest and traveling for a while on the main road, and that if they heard any traffic approaching, they should hide under the hay. "Unfortunately, not all Polish freedom fighters are kind to Jews," he told them, alluding to those Polish partisans of the Home Army, among whom Jews were unwelcome. "I am taking you to a place close to the border where Polish and Jewish partisans work together and support one another."

After an hour or so, they left the main road again and came to a place where there had evidently been an encampment, though now it stood empty. "We will camp here for the night," said Piotr, as he removed blankets and a tent from the cart.

In the night, although Srulik and Ari could hear the haunting sounds of wolves and jackals, they felt safe and protected lying by Piotr's side. When morning came, they continued on their journey, eventually coming to a much larger and more impressive forest than they had ever been in. Piotr brought the horse to a stop. "This is the Naliboka forest," he said, gesturing about him, "where there is one of the largest partisan encampments, and there are many Jews here as well."

After a little while, a young man with a rifle on his shoulder stepped out from between the trees where he had been keeping guard, and shouted a greeting, "Hello, Piotr, so good to see you!"

Piotr beamed. "Lolek, how are you?" He shook the man's hand. "Boys, this is Karol, but everyone calls him Lolek. Lolek, I'm taking these boys to the Bielski Otriad—the partisan brigade they have gathered."

Lolek smiled approvingly and patted the horse. "Of course. See you around, Piotr. Good luck."

Piotr snapped the reins, and the trio continued through the forest. Ari looked about in wonder as they encountered various groups of people. Some of the groups contained only men, many of whom were doing fitness training. Then they came across family groups of men, women, and children, and a variety of places of work and provisions, similar to any village. After another half mile, they encountered people who were evidently Jewish, some of them in ultra-Orthodox dress with sidelocks and untrimmed beards. They passed by a makeshift hospital, a bathhouse, a laundry, a mill, a bakery, a winery, a kosher abattoir, a sausage factory, a blacksmith, a tannery, a tailor, a cobbler and even a soap factory. "You're amazed, aren't you!" Piotr laughed when he glanced at Ari and Srulik's faces. Ari had no words for his astonishment.

They came to a stable where Piotr stopped the wagon and unharnessed the horse. "Hello, Cha'im," he said to the man who was caring for other horses in the stable. "This mare of mine has worked hard for a day and a half, bringing these boys and me here. She could do with some tender loving care before I take her all the way back with me."

The man stroked the horse's head and replied, "I will look after her."

Piotr then took the boys to a hut nearby where a woman was sitting behind a desk writing in a book of records and lists. "Good day, Mrs. Bialystoker. I have two boys here for you who escaped from the Warsaw ghetto."

The woman looked up from her work and smiled. "Well done, boys. Welcome."

Piotr placed his hands on Ari and Srulik's shoulders and peered into their faces, which were far more relaxed than when he had first encountered them. "Goodbye, boys. You are in safe hands here. May God bless you. I wish you everything of the best."

"Thank you so much, Piotr," said Ari, and he and Srulik shook Piotr's hand and bid him farewell.

MRS. BIALYSTOKER SAT THE BOYS DOWN in two wooden chairs by her desk and began the process of learning about their background, asking them who they were, who their family members were, and what they had been through. With Srulik quiet beside him, Ari relayed what he could in spare terms, hoping to save his brother from reliving their experiences. She understood, and moved on to explaining that while the stores and services of the area were above ground, most of the people lived in *zemlyankas* or bunkers, and that there were some for children who were there without parents. "You will live in a special *zemlyanka* for boys from *frum*, religiously observant homes, like you." Ari didn't really understand what it meant to be a Jew *not* like him, but he decided that now was probably not the appropriate time to raise such questions. Mrs. Bialystoker added, "We will go there now via the storehouse and collect two blankets and a change of clothes for you.

Then you must go to the bathhouse, and I will take the clothes you are wearing to the laundry. You will have assigned times for each of you to go the bath house once a week."

As they approached the "religious orphans *zemlyanka*," a group of about twenty boys of different ages wearing caps and yarmulkes were sitting in a semi-circle under a canvas, listening to a teacher who was giving them a *Torah* study lesson.

"*Sholem Alaychem,* Rabbi Brook," said Mrs Bialystocker. "These boys are Ari and Srulik Levine from Warsaw. I think that Ari is suitable for this class, but I will take Srulik to the younger group."

"*Sholem Alaychem*, boys," said Rabbi Brook. "You are welcome."

After settling in at their *zemklyanka* the boys joined their outdoor religion classes, where they quickly began to make new friends. Studies continued after lunch until the afternoon drew to a close and the time drew near for afternoon and evening prayers. Ari joined the others in a designated area a distance away from the rest of the camp near the tannery where there was a makeshift synagogue. Opposite the entrance against the far wall was a cupboard covered in an embroidered velvet cloth—a "holy ark" housing two Torah scrolls.

"Why did they make the place to *davven*, to pray, here?" he asked another boy.

"Because almost all of the people working at the tannery are *frum*, religiously observant, and this way they can daven and then quickly get back to work, especially in the morning."

"You mean that not all the Jews here *davven*?" asked Ari.

"Of course not," said the boy. "Probably the majority here are not religious."

Ari was perplexed. "But if they are not religious, in what way are they Jewish?"

The boy snorted. "To begin with, the Nazis want to kill all of us, and most of the gentiles don't like us, so that's good enough reason to stick together. We can look after one another and work together to fight against the Nazis. But there are Jews here of all kinds, some who are devout, others who are traditional and keep some religious observances. There are Jews here from non-Orthodox liberal Jewish congregations, and many who describe themselves as secular."

Ari found this all very perplexing.

After the afternoon prayer, and before the evening prayers, someone clapped his hands and shouted "*Rosh Chodesh*," indicating that the evening was the commencement of the new moon, and that they had to insert a special passage into the central prayer of the service. At the end of the service, the man who was now Ari's teacher, Rabbi Brook, addressed the congregation.

"A good *chodesh* to you all. As you know this is the new month of *Nissan*, the month in which we celebrate *Pesach*, Passover, our redemption from suffering and bondage in Egypt thousands of years ago. Our sages teach us that 'just as Israel was redeemed back then in *Nissan*, so their future redemption with the coming of the Messiah, will be in *Nissan*. May the Almighty grant that we be redeemed this *Nissan* from our suffering and our oppressors at this time, and that we be taken back to our land, the Land of Israel, to live in fulfillment of the Divine Covenant given to us through Moses at Sinai."

"*Omain*," the congregation responded. It seemed clear to Ari, however, that most of the people around him were unconvinced that the prayer would be fulfilled, at least not this *Nissan*.

AFTER A NIGHT getting used to their surroundings, the boys went with their new friends for *shaharit*, the morning prayers. Being *Rosh Chodesh*, a special reading from a *Torah* scroll was read and additional passages inserted into the service, especially the *Hallel*, songs of praise taken from the book of Psalms. These were sung by the congregation with great fervor and the boys joined in with the familiar tunes and words that made them feel ambivalent—comforted to be part of the community, yet missing their own family so much.

The boys were also drafted to perform various duties, including helping to bring water from the river near the forest edge, and buckets of milk from the herd of cows, to the communal kitchen.

Their sadness and homesickness, especially at night, was eased by their new friendships, and the daily and weekly cycle of Jewish religious life in the community of which they were a part, as well as the schedule of lessons and duties.

About ten days later, a strong, young man in a tunic with a rifle slung over his shoulder approached them after breakfast. "Ari and

Srulik!" he declared. "It *is* you! I heard that two Levine boys from Warsaw were here and I couldn't believe that maybe it really was you!" Ari looked at him in confusion. "What, don't you recognize me? I'm your cousin, Shmulik!"

Ari felt a surge of emotion when he realized that another member of his family stood before him. He threw his arms around the young man. "Shmulik! I haven't seen you for more than a year." He drew back to look at his cousin. "But you've changed! Where are your *payos* and how come you have no head covering?"

Shmulik grimaced. "Don't you know what happened with me and my family? Where did you think I went and why?"

Ari thought of his parents and sisters. "I don't know. You just disappeared."

"I didn't just disappear. I joined the Communists and this led to a complete rupture with my father and family."

"Communists?" Ari was aghast. "So you do not believe in God? And you don't observe the commandments anymore?"

"No." Shmulik paused and ran a hand reflexively through his short hair. "I've not been religiously observant for almost a year and a half. I certainly don't believe in God the way you and the most of our family still do. But I suppose a Jew is never completely separated from the idea of God. We have believers, doubters...," he smiled, "and rebels like me."

Ari listened as Shmulik continued. "I suppose my relationship with God is a bit like my relationship with my father. I have turned my back on him, and I feel he has turned his back on me, and I am angry with him. But I suppose I think that if God does exist, then like with my father, I hope he will forgive me and always love me."

"But you are still Jewish, Shmulik, aren't you?" piped up Srulik.

"Of course. Even if I'm not religiously observant, all Jews are my brothers and sisters, and I want to help my community defend itself and be free. I also want all people to be free. I consider myself a citizen of the world. But being Jewish is being part of a particular family, a community, a people."

In spite of Ari's belief that it was not right for a Jew to deny God and the religious observances of Judaism, he was elated to see his cousin, and also impressed with his appearance. Clearly, he was a significant soldier in the partisan brigades.

"Moreover," continued Shmulik, "many of us who are not observant still like to participate in certain Jewish religious celebrations with our brothers and sisters. In fact, some friends and I have been given the task of going out now to the hills on the other side of the river to collect dandelion leaves to eat as *maror*." He was referring to the bitter herbs for all those participating in the *Pesach seder* meal the next night and the night after. "Would you like to come with me? It will be for most of the day. I'll give you a piggy back, Srulik. If you want to join us, I will ask your teachers to let you do so."

The boys responded eagerly to Shmulik's invitation. After obtaining the permission of their teachers, Shmulik took them to join his friends, and they went off through the forest to the other side of the river, with Srulik contentedly perched on Shmulik's back. On the way, Shmulik told the boys what he knew about members of their family. Their parents and sisters had been taken to the Treblinka concentration camp, but Shmulik had not heard anything more than that. He did not tell the boys that Treblinka was a death camp and that there was little or no chance that anyone taken there would survive.

THEY RETURNED IN THE LATE AFTERNOON with bundles of dandelion leaves that they delivered to the communal kitchen, where preparations for the *seder* were well under way. They detected the all-pervasive smell from the bakery next door of the preparation of the *matzah*, unleavened bread, eaten on *Pesach*, when all leavened bread and products are prohibited.

Back at their *zemlyanka*, all the boys were going through whatever few belongings they had, to make sure that there was no *chametz*, no leaven remains or crumbs of any kind. After the evening prayers, Rabbi Brook came to their *zemlyanka* to conduct the symbolic *bedikat chametz*, "search for leaven."

The next morning the boys were up early, as they were all given five minutes each in the course of the morning at the bathhouse to prepare themselves for the festival.

After the ceremonial "burning of the *chametz*," all the boys in Ari's group were enlisted for preparations for the *seder* (ritual meal), to be held outside under canvas. A few different *seder* meals would be held according to the level of religious observance, but anyone could join any of them if they requested to do so in advance. The boys washed all the tables and chairs and cleaned the area where the *seder* for the most religiously devout would take place.

They helped spread out sheets as tablecloths and placed posies of wild flowers they had gathered to adorn the rows of festive tables. Pairs of candles were placed every few seats along the tables for the women to light the festival lights. Srulik and the other younger children were sent to have an afternoon nap as the *seder* would go on late into the night.

AS EVENING APPROACHED, everyone gathered around the tables, while the women lit the festival candles, making the appropriate blessing and receiving the "amen" response from the men and children around them before most of them went off to evening prayers. Returning from the Passover evening service, Ari and Srulik stopped in delight to see how beautiful the rows of tables looked. Along with the tablecloths, posies and glowing candles, there were settings of plates, spoons, and cups, together with bottles of wine that would fill four cups for each celebrant; with these, they would toast Divine redemption of the Children of Israel from Egypt. Every few seats along there were piles of *matzah*s to be eaten in memory of the fact that the dough that the Children of Israel had prepared for their journey did not have time to rise before they had to rush out of Egypt to leave for the Promised Land. There were also *seder* plates containing the special symbolic foods for the occasion. These were a burnt chicken's neck and a burnt egg symbolizing the paschal offering and the festival offering that were made in the Temple in Jerusalem before it was destroyed.

A pile of the dandelion leaves served as the bitter herbs that the *Torah* requires the Jewish people to eat to remember the suffering of the Children of Israel in bondage. This was accompanied by a gooey mixture of wine, apple, nuts, and dates, call *haroset*, that served as both a reminder of the mortar used by the Children of Israel in their enforced labor, and as sweetener to take off the edge of the bitter herbs. A pile of celery sticks would serve as an hors d'oeuvre, dipped in salt water, to make the participants feel that they were part of a royal feast.

Together, these items enabled the people gathered to reexperience the foundational event of Jewish history, the Exodus from the pain and suffering of servitude in Egypt, to the jubilation of experiencing Divine deliverance and salvation. Also on the table were *Haggadahs*, pamphlets which, together with the order of the *seder* rituals, contain the recitation of the Exodus narrative and commentaries that they would all read at the meal.

Some families took seats separately, and the children without parents sat together. It was very different from past Passovers in their home, which Ari and Srulik missed, but sitting together with their new friends provided its compensation. Rabbi Brook made an announcement before the proceedings began. "Friends," he said, "tonight we are celebrating the *seder* in a way that reflects our present circumstances. Of course, when we have *seder* in our homes, we spend much time discussing every aspect of the meal and every passage of the *Haggadah*. Tonight, that will not be logistically possible to do, but we will go through the *seder* together, just as it is printed in the *Haggadah*. Those who want to remain after the meal to join me in further study of commentaries and insights and the *Haggadah* are very welcome indeed to do so."

He then invited everyone to pour wine into their neighbors' cups so that each one would be served, like royalty; and he proceeded to recite the *kiddush*, the prayer over the wine sanctifying the holy day of the festival. With its conclusion, everyone sat down and drank from their individual cups of wine reclining to the left, as nobility did in Roman times when the *seder* format was instituted. After washing their hands, the participants ate the hors d'oeuvre of celery dipped in saltwater. Rabbi Brook set aside some of the *matzah* to eat as the *afikoman*, the last taste of the *seder*, before leading the gathering in the recitation of the *Haggadah* starting with the first paragraph, *this is the bread of affliction that our ancestors ate in Egypt*.

He announced to everyone, "As you all know, the format of the *Haggadah* is in keeping with the verse in the Torah, *and you shall tell your son on that day saying [the observance of the commandments regarding the*

Passover is] because of what God did for me when he brought me out of Egypt. That is why we begin with the asking of the four questions by the youngest child of the house. These will be asked here tonight by Srulik Levine of Warsaw."

As his brother looked proudly on, Srulik stood on his chair and chanted, *Why is this night different from all other nights? On all other nights we can eat leavened and unleavened bread, but on this night only matzah? On all other nights we eat all sorts of vegetables, on this night we eat bitter herbs? On all other nights we don't dip [our food] even once, on this night (we do it) twice ? On all other nights we eat seated or reclining, on this night we all recline?*

Rabbi Brook led the gathering in response, *We were slaves to Pharoah in Egypt*, which summarized the biblical narrative of Jewish enslavement and persecution, and of Divine deliverance, recalling the Divine promise to care for and protect the Children of Israel. At the end of the first paragraph, everyone stood and raised their cups of wine. They sang, *[and God's promise] has sustained our fathers and us; for not only one has risen against us to destroy us, but in every generation there are those who arise against us to destroy us; but the Holy One Blessed be He delivers us from their hands.*

Virtually all who sang these words felt an upwelling of sadness and happiness simultaneously—sadness that Jews were being destroyed as never before, and happiness in the knowledge of God's promise ensuring that no matter how terrible the suffering and destruction was and would be, the Jewish People would survive and flourish.

They continued reciting the text of the *Haggadah* with its recalling and embellishment of the story of Divine deliverance from Egyptian bondage. Among the passages recited was a summary of the ten plagues that God brought down on Egypt to get Pharaoh and the Egyptians to let the Children of Israel go. With the mention of each plague, they dipped their fingers in their cups and took out a drop of wine for each one, to signify that even while celebrating the deliverance of the Children of Israel, as the plagues involved the suffering of others, our cups of joy cannot be full. All human beings are created in the Divine image and the messianic hope is for a world of universal peace, free from all persecution and suffering.

The text continued with songs celebrating God's graces and gifts to the Jewish people, followed by a passage declaring that, *in each and every generation each person should see oneself as if they themselves had gone out of Egypt,* emphasizing that the purpose of the *seder* is to re-experience the wonder of Divine redemption. The first part of the *seder* concluded with the singing of psalms of praise. After eating *matzah*, the unleavened bread, and *maror*, the bitter herbs, they ate eggs in salt water, the mourner's food, before starting the festive banquet. Everything emphasized the transition from bondage to freedom, from suffering to deliverance, from sadness to joy. The eggs also symbolized spring and rebirth, as Passover is the spring festival celebrating the renewal of the agricultural cycle.

After a hearty and enjoyable meal, they ate the *afikoman*, so that the last taste of food that evening would be *matzah*, and recited and sang grace after meals. Then everyone stood up for the Cup of Elijah, a large cup of wine that stood in the middle of the table. Rabbi Brook announced, "I know I said before that we will not be able to have discussion during the meal because of the unusual nature of this *seder*, but I would like to make this exception." He paused and looked about at all those who were gathered, their faces softened by candlelight. "There are many reasons for the cup of Elijah, and why, when we celebrate the *seder* in our homes, we open the front door at this time. But hands up: who among you children here can give me a good reason for this Cup of Elijah and why we open our doors?"

Many raised their hands. Rabbi Brook turned to one—a girl with pigtails who was wearing a blue dress. "Yes, Rochel, please tell us."

Rochel replied, "The prophet Elijah prepares the way for the coming of the *Moshiach* who will be a descendant of the house of King David, and will be a just ruler at a time when the Jewish people will live in peace in our land. There will be peace as well for all people in the world. So, we are hoping that Elijah is here now to prepare the way, and we open our doors for him."

Rabbi Brook smiled appreciatively. "Excellent, Rochel. Would anyone like to elaborate a little more? Yes, Nachum," he said to a studious-looking boy with long *payos*.

"*Pesach* has been a dangerous time for Jews," Nachum added. "Gentiles have made the terrible libel against us, saying that on *Pesach*, Jews kill a non-Jewish child to eat his flesh for *matzah* and drink his blood for wine. As a result, Jews have been attacked, beaten, and even killed. So we also open our doors to show that we have nothing to hide, as well as for Elijah's protection and paving the way for the Messianic Age, as Rochel said."

"*Yashar koach*, very well explained. And here you children can all see that we are most honored and protected by Elijah's very presence with us, because you can see he is here drinking from his cup. Look! Can you see, there is already a bit less wine in the cup, so he must have drunk from it!" Rabbi Brook had a twinkle in his eye and a little smile. The adults and older children smiled with him, but Srulik had not noticed and was doubtful. He looked hard and it did not seem to him that the amount of wine in the cup had decreased at all, but he felt it would not be polite for him to say so.

"And now," said Rabbi Brook, "we must bid farewell to Elijah," adding with a quiet laugh, "he has many *seders* to attend, visiting Jewish people all around the world celebrating *Pesach* tonight."

They then completed the *seder* service with additional psalms of thanksgiving and songs of praise to God, prayers for the future, and songs of religious instruction, concluding with the words *May You soon lead us redeemed back to Zion in joyous song. Next year in rebuilt Jerusalem.*

Almost all the children then went to bed, while most of the adults stayed on until after midnight studying and discussing ideas and interpretations of the *Hagaddah*.

The first two days of the Passover festival were *yom tov*, like the Sabbath day of rest when no work was performed, and most of these days were spent in prayer, study, and celebration around meals and socializing, enabling Ari to spend most of the time together with Srulik.

The *seder* was repeated on the second night. "This is wonderful but a bit exhausting," observed one of Ari's new friends. "That's another reason to get back to the Land of Israel," responded another boy. "There, you only have one day of *yom tov* at the beginning of *Pesach* and one at the end of the seven-day festival, so you only have one *seder*!" he laughed.

THE DAY AFTER PASSOVER, one of the older boys asked Ari if he would like to join the Hebrew language class they were organizing to learn how to speak Hebrew as a modern language. "Many of us hope to make our way to Eretz Yisrael, and there they have renewed the Hebrew language," said the boy. "It is no longer just a language of prayer and study as it has been for us for centuries, but now it is a daily spoken language. Would you like to learn how to speak it? It's not now pronounced the way we here use it in our prayers and study, but more the way it has been pronounced by Sephardic Jews, mostly in Arab lands."

Ari eagerly accepted the boy's invitation, enticed by the symbolic power of language, and as he learned how to read Hebrew somewhat differently than the way he had been taught, and to speak it with others, he in turn taught some of this to Srulik.

In the evenings, Shmulik would often visit them, and together they would recall the stories of their family members. One day he arrived in an excited state and, drawing up a chair next to Ari and Srulik, said, "Boys, it has happened." They regarded him expectantly. "An army in exile is being formed under the leadership of General Anders, with the support of the British, to join with the Allies to fight the Nazis. Thousands of Polish soldiers and resistance fighters are following him."

"Are you?" Ari asked. He closed the book he had been reading.

Shmulik grinned. "Some of my friends and I plan to join, although we'll have to travel a long way to do so. Many refugees, including Jews, are going. They are also taking many children with them who are without parents as a result of the war. General Anders is marching to the Caspian Sea, which is where we plan to join him." The boys watched as his hands traced in the air the shape of their potential journey. "We'll travel by horse and cart for four or five days to Moscow," he said. "From there, we take a train to the city of Kazan; then a boat on the Volga, and then another train."

He leaned toward the boys' attentive faces. "My friends have agreed to let me take you with us if I take full responsibility for you and I have the permission of the Otriad leadership in principle. It won't be an easy journey, but what do you say? I might add that it's rumored Anders will be taking his army to and through Eretz Yisroel."

Ari and Srulik looked at each other and smiled knowingly. Even though Shmulik had said it would be a difficult journey, there was the excitement of adventure, and moreover the prospect of getting to Eretz Yisroel. Ari, too, hoped against hope that they would be united with their family once again.

Preparations were made in the course of the week, and the following Sunday the boys set out with Shmulik and four others—Avrohom, Dovid, Shloimeh, and Yanky—with their provisions, in two carts. Keeping away from the main roads, they travelled mainly through forests. Their spirits were high, they sang songs they knew, and they stopped a few times a day for rest and refreshment. On the first evening, after they had set up camp for the night, Dovid went off a little distance away to say the evening prayers, and when the boys saw him do this, they went to join him. Dovid was the only one among the young men who was religiously observant and wore a head covering. After making a fire, they sat around it, eating from their provisions, and the young men debated political ideologies of which Ari couldn't make much sense. But on the second night of their travels after eating around the camp fire, Shmulik said to the others, "The boys here were rather shocked when they learned that I'm no longer *frum*, no longer religiously observant. I told them that being Jewish was not only a matter of religion, but also of identity and belonging, and that I am part of the Jewish family, community, people. What do you guys think? What makes one Jewish?"

"A sense of humor and being musical," said Yanky, smirking.

"That's ridiculous," responded Shloimeh. "What, Jews are the only ones in the world with a sense of humor? I've met gypsies in Warsaw with as good a sense of humor and as musical as any Jew. Your idea is as nonsensical as saying that Jews are Jews because they eat gefilte fish."

"So what's your take, Shloimeh?" said Shmulik.

"Like you said," he replied. "We are a people—a people with a common past, a common fate, a common destiny."

"You guys are missing the crucial component of values," said Avrohom. "The unique contribution of the Jewish people to the world is the values of ethical monotheism. Even if you don't believe in God, to be a Jew means to believe in fundamental ethical values that Judaism teaches—human dignity, freedom, justice, righteousness, compassion, kindness, making the world a better place. The vision of a world living in peace according to those values is the ideal of the Messianic Age, and this vision has been brought to most of the world through Judaism's daughter religions, Christianity and Islam. That by the way, is what Maimonides says," he added with a smile.

Dovid chimed in, "What Shloimeh said and what Avrohom has now added is of course all true, but it is still only part of the picture." The others turned to listen. "Even if Judaism brought those values to the world, living in accordance with those values does not make one Jewish. I agree that to be truly Jewish you have to be a good person, but being a good person does not make one Jewish of course, any more than having a good sense of humor and being musical." He chuckled, making Yanky blush a bit. "It's not just the values themselves, but the *manner* in which they are recalled and cherished that characterizes Judaism. There is a specific Jewish way of celebrating these values that is the fabric of being Jewish. For example, we have just celebrated *Pesach*. *Pesach* expresses a universal value of human freedom and a repudiation of any kind of oppression and enslavement. But for us, freedom is bound up with our own history, the experience of redemption from slavery in Egypt. It would be ridiculous to expect Eskimos in Iceland for example, to have to eat *matzah* and *maror* on the eve of the fifteenth of *Nissan* because someone else's ancestors came out of slavery thousands of years ago at that time. Different cultures and religions express their values in different ways. Of course, I personally think that Judaism as a way of life is fully lived only when it expresses our religious faith. But it is still a way of life, the Jewish way of life, even if you do not believe. The more one expresses the values of Judaism in these traditional Jewish ways—ways that religious Jews call *mitzvos*, commandments—the more Jewish one is."

The others remained silent and thoughtful. Ari didn't completely understand what Dovid was saying, but he somehow felt that it represented him, and he felt appreciative that Dovid was with them.

THEY CONTINUED ON THEIR JOURNEY eastward for a few days, often quite close to main roads where they could hear military traffic. Eventually they came to the dark blue water of the Moskva-Volga canal, and they felt a collective surge of relief knowing that they had passed out of Nazi-controlled territory.

They followed the canal south past Iksha and from there continued southward. After an hour or two, they could see the distant spires of the Kremlin. But while Moscow was the biggest city they had ever seen, it appeared grey and miserable. Most of the people they saw were clothed in rags, and everywhere beggars pleaded for food. Shmulik and his friends had been given the name of a trader at the Izmaylovskiy Bazar to whom they could sell their horses and carts.

Now, with the Russian money they had, they were able to buy train tickets at the Kazansky railway station. Never having seen such a magnificent building, they slowed their pace to gaze at the enormous arches overhead where chandeliers dangled; the scene was in stark contrast to the misery around it. The only train they were able to board was full of troops, exhausted and weak, and many badly wounded. The group had no more food or water with them, and Ari put his arms around his brother in the cramped conditions; Srulik wrinkled his nose at the stench of the train car, but otherwise pretended he didn't mind.

After sixteen hours, they arrived in the city of Kazan, the center of Tartarstan, or what was now called the autonomous Tatar Soviet Socialist Republic. Christianity and Islam (and later Judaism) had coexisted relatively amicably there in the past, and the city's skyline was still dominated by the blue-and-gold domed Annunciation Cathedral and the vast, colorful Kul Sharif Mosque, in addition to the centuries-old Kazan Kremlin-fortified citadel. In recent years the Soviets had built important industrial factories in the city for the manufacture of tanks and planes, making it a major center for the Soviet military, as was evident in the large number of soldiers that filled the city's streets.

Not far from the station was the house of a Jewish merchant by the name of Tarnopolsky, whose address they had obtained through Shmulik's communist friends and who was expecting them. He and his family welcomed them into their spacious home, where they were fed, could wash and refresh themselves, and where they spent the Sabbath.

Around the Sabbath table, Tarnopolsky told them about the fortunes of the local Jewish community. After the Soviets nationalized their beautiful synagogue a decade earlier, making it into a cultural center for teachers, Jewish communal life had come to a halt. However, life in the Tartar region and in the city of Kazan was easier for religious people of different faiths than it was in most other places in the Soviet Union. Even though he was a loyal servant of the Soviet state in charge of a significant shipping import and export operation, he was still able to live an observant Jewish life.

"We have to find a balance between our religious obligations as Jews and our civic responsibilities as citizens," he said, adding, "I think this is the authentic Jewish balance, to preserve our particularity and to affirm our universality. The Divine Presence is found in both and perhaps most fully when we embrace both. Appropriately, this Shabbat's reading from the Bible is the portion of *kdoshim* from the book of Leviticus. And the prophetic lectionary for this Sabbath comes from the ninth chapter of the book of Amos, and opens with the words, *Behold are you not like the children of the Ethiopians to me, O Children of Israel. I took Israel out of Egypt, and also the Philistines out of Caphtor and the Arameans out of Kir*. God cares about all people and peoples and His redemption has been experienced by many nations, not just ours!" Tarnopolsky declared.

EARLY ON SUNDAY MORNING, he took the group down to the port, where the vessels in his charge were moored, and paid a helmsman to take them down the Volga to Saratov in one of his smaller boats. The trip took more than a day, but they almost felt on holiday, relaxing as they sailed down the wide, calm river with spacious views of fascinating architecture arising from rich greenery. Ari noted the contrast to their horrible journey by train. They disembarked in Saratov and walked from the port to the train station where they purchased tickets for Astrakhan. This train journey was a similar length to the one they made from Moscow, yet it was not unpleasant at all. In Astrakhan they found a cargo boat bound for the Caspian seaport of Pahlavi in Persia, which was under British control. The sight that met them on arrival was astounding: scores of thousands of Polish soldiers and refugees filled the area around the port.

Shmulik inquired as to where the Jewish refugees were encamped, and with embraces and promises to meet up again, the boys parted from Avrohom, Dovid, Shloimeh, and Yanky, who went to report to the Anders army registrar. Shmulik took the boys to a tent city where conditions were somewhat precarious; in response to their inquiries, they were directed to an area of the encampment where they encountered hundreds of Jewish children.

The scene before Ari and Srulik seemed to be a hive of activity, which piqued their interest. "What's going on?" asked Shmulik of someone who carried a clipboard; the man replied, "I'm from the Jewish Agency. My colleagues and I are evacuating the Jewish children here without parents to an orphanage in Dustan Tappeh outside Tehran." He raised his eyebrows. "And hopefully the British will enable us to take them all to Eretz Yisrael."

"Then we have arrived just in time," said Shmulik. "These two boys are Ari and Srulik Levine from Warsaw and we have traveled here from Naliboki forest. I'm joining the Anders army, and so depart from them here."

The man's face registered surprise. "From the Naliboki forest? You are having me on! Well, it doesn't matter how tall your story is, the boys are here now. We will take care of them. You boys will now be with us and hundreds of Jewish children as one Jewish family."

Ari and Srulik tearfully hugged Shmulik. "Now don't be upset, boys," Shmulik said. "We've come a long way, but there is still a long way to go." His face grew especially serious. "You must be strong and brave, and hopefully soon we'll all meet again in *Eretz Yisroel.*" With one last hug he parted from them, and they watched him leave until he was absorbed in the crowd of milling people.

THE BOYS WERE PUT on dusty trucks together with many other Jewish youngsters, and after several hours arrived at the camp, which became known as the "Tehran Home for Jewish Children." The camp was situated on an old airfield where light colored tents were spread out under the hot sun. Ari and Srulik climbed down from the back of the truck feeling apprehensive about facing yet another transition, but Ari felt, too—in spite of tiredness from all that had happened—a faint glimmer of adventure. They had come so far, he felt. He understood that he and Srulik would be taken care of with limited resources; still, they would be taken care of. He looked around gratefully at the people around him, many of whom were volunteers from the local Jewish community and from American Jewish charitable organizations, in particular Hadassah Women's Zionist Organization and the American Jewish Joint Distribution Committee.

The people who would spend the most time looking after Ari and Srulik were from the Youth Immigration Department of the Jewish Agency for Palestine. In addition to ensuring that the children were taken care of physically, they organized sports activities and held various classes on subjects such as the geography and history of the Land of Israel, the Hebrew language, and basic agricultural skills they would apply when they reached the Land.

ONE WARM MORNING, as Ari and Srulik were seated in a tented classroom with other students, a young woman entered and greeted them in modern Hebrew, "*Boker tov yladim, shmi Vered.* Good morning children, my name is Vered." She continued in Yiddish, but for Hebrew words she used modern pronunciation.

Vered's eyes sparkled as she looked about the room at the ragged but hopeful children. "I want to ask you this morning to give me examples of the place that Eretz Yisrael has in Judaism," she said.

A girl raised her hand, and Vered asked her to state her name. "I'm Tovah," said the girl. Vered invited her to continue.

"The Hebrew calendar is a calendar of nature," Tovah said, and Ari liked this, remembering his time in the Polish forest; he still carried in his pocket the chess piece carved by the professor, and frequently remembered, and gave thanks for, the Noyeks' loving care.

Tovah continued, "Except for the week and Shabbat, the months and the main festivals are all determined by the moon and the seasons. The pilgrim festivals of *Pesach, Shavuot,* and *Sukkot*, are all festivals of the seasons—of sowing, harvesting and in-gathering—and we celebrate these seasons at the time that they occur in the Land of Israel, even if we're somewhere else in the world, where the seasons might be different at that time."

"Excellent," said Vered. "And why do you think it is important to celebrate the seasons at all?"

"So that we are always mindful of and thankful for God's gifts," answered Tovah.

"Very good. Do you have something to add," Vered asked Ari who had his hand up. What's your name?"

"My name is Ari," he replied, "I would like to add two things. First, in our daily prayers, we pray for rains according to the rainy season in the Land of Israel. Also, there are seven special fruits of Eretz Yisrael, and after eating any of them, there is a special *brochah* of thanksgiving that we recite."

"Wonderful, thank you for those important additions," said Vered. She added, "Living in and on the land makes you aware of God's gifts more than if you live in a city. But if you celebrate nature's cycle in your prayers and festivals, you can also feel close to the Land and be aware of God's gifts and blessings even in the city—and especially when the whole community, and even the whole people, are all celebrating together at the same time."

Vered gestured with her hands in a mode of offering. "You also all know that when the Temple was standing, we would bring offerings of our produce to the Temple in Jerusalem on the seasonal festivals. There were many other laws related to agriculture, such as, at reaping time, leaving the corners of your fields for the poor, and other similar commandments."

She added the comment of the sages of old that the reason that Moses wanted so much to enter the Land of Israel, which he was prevented from doing, was because he wanted to fulfill all the commandments, including those that apply only to the Land of Israel and cannot be fulfilled outside the Land. "However," she said, "there are still *mitzvot*, commandments that relate to nature that we must observe wherever we are, such as *bal tashchit*. Who can tell me what that means?"

A few of the pupils raised their hands. Vered turned to another girl, "Please introduce yourself and let us hear your answer."

"My name is Sarah," said the girl. "*Bal tashchit* is the prohibition against wasting anything, but especially food."

"Excellent, Sarah, and do you know what the basis in the Torah is for this prohibition?"

"Yes, it is the prohibition in the fifth book of the *Torah* against cutting down fruit trees even to make weapons in times of war. Our sages tell us that we must therefore be even more careful not to waste in times of peace."

"What a wonderful reply," said Vered. "I see that some of you are real scholars." She continued, "Here we manage with very little, and even in Eretz Yisrael today life is not easy. But whatever we have, we must always give thanks for and appreciate it, and try to never waste."

AFTER THIS DISCUSSION, all the children in the camp were called to gather in the assembly tent. One of the leaders of the Jewish Agency had an announcement to deliver. The young man waited as the children settled themselves on canvas mats. When they were ready and the air was full of suspense, he said, "Dear boys and girls, we have wonderful news: The British authorities have granted all of you certificates to immigrate to Palestine, to Eretz Yisrael."

This caused a ripple through the gathering of children, as a hot breeze blew through the open walls of the tent. Ari and Srulik looked at each other, trying to absorb the words, and began to smile.

"The journey will not be easy," said the man. "We will be traveling mostly by sea through the Persian Gulf, the Arabian Sea, and the Red Sea." This sparked a welling up of expectation within Ari, who had enjoyed his time on the water. The man continued, beaming, "But this is a moment of great joy and hope for us all."

As the full understanding of this new declaration grew throughout the gathering, a cheer erupted. Many of the children and adults embraced and some of them wept, with gratitude and hope, and for all that they had endured.

"We will be just like the Children of Israel," said Srulik excitedly to Ari, "crossing the Red Sea on the way to the Promised Land."

Aru laughed and said, "Yes, but I hope it doesn't take us forty years to get there!"

Srulik suddenly looked wistful. "Do you think we will meet up with Mamma and Tatte in the Land of Israel?"

"I don't know," said Ari. "But we will have a new life. It will be a wonderful and happy one, and we will put our sorrows behind us."

"*Omain*," said Srulik.

"Not *Omain* anymore," said Ari. "Now we must say it with a modern Hebrew accent, like our Sephardic brothers and sisters from Arab lands—'Amen.'"

"Amen." said Srulik.

The House by the Sea

A RETELLING OF SIKH SACRED WISDOM

The House by the Sea

Learning for life's journey—to embrace this path named Sikhī,
Keep cultivating and contemplating the Guru's radiant wisdom.

Touched by the glance of infinite grace,
The inner self then safely crosses life's turbulent ocean.

—*"Sikhī sikhiyā gur vīchār"*
Sri Guru Granth Sahib, *ang* 465

Here you all come,
To sail with me,
Into the sea.

I hear melodies of wisdom
Like lullabies that once rocked me
Now setting me free

Across the waves, orange petals
Following the trace of me
Into the sea

Dwelling or departing
When the spark finds its true home
It blazes with peace

Give me, friends, just your blessings
With pearls for the journey
I return to time's ocean
Here at the sea.

THE FAMILY

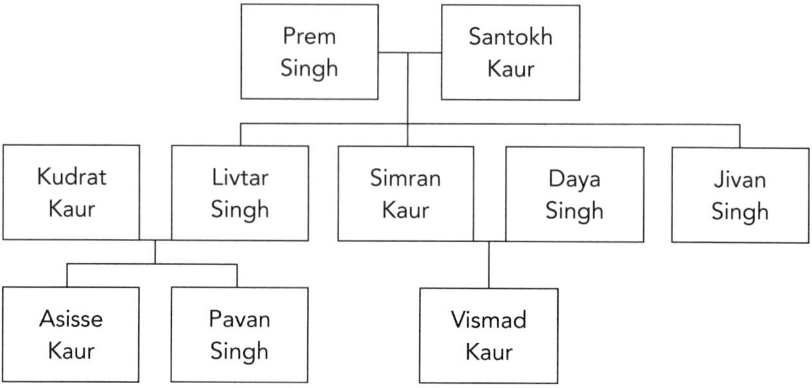

Grandparents:

Prem Singh (72 years old)	Quiet, contemplative grandfather
Santokh Kaur (70 years old)	Engaging, insightful grandmother

Parents:

Livtar Singh (41 years old)	Philosophical, outgoing elder son to Prem and Santokh
Kudrat Kaur (40 years old)	Imaginative, practical wife of Livtar, lover of science and poetry
Simran Kaur (35 years old)	Sister to Livtar, several months pregnant, thoughtful, creative
Daya Singh (35 years old)	Husband to Simran, reserved, kind, troubled

Children:

Asisse Kaur (16 years old)	Daughter to Livtar and Kudrat, reflective, curious, creative
Pavan Singh (10 years old)	Brother to Asisse, playful, inventive, knowledgeable
Vismad Kaur (7 years old)	Daughter to Simran & Daya, dreamy, diligent, love of wonder

Deceased son, brother, uncle to family members:

Jivan Singh (lived to age 30)	Youngest son of Prem and Santokh fun-loving, adventurous, best friend to Daya

PART ONE

The Fragrant Archway

Reaching the realm of the eternal Enlightener,
Cross the threshold to the Guru's abode,
And feel the wisdom deep within you
start to blossom.[1]

One warm spring weekend, a family came to stay at a house by the sea.

It had been a long drive. There were two couples, with three children between them, as well as the grandparents. Despite having packed lightly, the adults felt a heaviness. As the sight of the horizon stretched open before them, that weight began to lighten. They were thinking about their final farewell, out by the coast, to someone they all loved.

"We're here!" The children, excited, ran through the leafy archway above a wooden gate. Its vines were studded with star-shaped jasmine flowers. The two young cousins were followed by their parents. The grandmother, walking arm-in-arm with her teenage granddaughter, murmured, "How beautiful, Asisse."

The girl smiled, watching her grandmother breathe in the delicate, soothing scent of the jasmine petals. She glanced at her grandfather behind them. The engraved wooden box that he carried with great care—that was what had brought them here.

1. "*Gurū duārai hoi sojhī pāeisī*..."—Sri Guru Granth Sahib, *ang* 730. This and all further citations are creative, contextual translations of lyrical verses from Sikh teachings.

His name was Prem Singh. Stepping under the archway, he looked up at the vines. Wasn't it said that their heritage was like a vine planted in the time of the Sikh Gurus? Across the generations and continents, whenever Sikhs gathered to sing sacred wisdom or to serve others, they would water that vine. It had its own special leaves, buds, and flowers, yet reached out to all with its fragrance.[2]

Prem took in the air like a balm. With a quiet nod, he thanked Asisse who had stopped to wait for him at the doorstep.

The house was simple and comfortable. After some refreshments, the children were eager to explore outdoors. Simran, who was several months pregnant, decided to unpack and rest. Her husband, Daya, stayed with her, letting the others find their way to the shoreline.

Following a tree-lined path, they could smell the sweet grass and salty ocean air. Soon they came to the edge of a small cliff. Before them, the sea seemed almost still, yet was in constant motion, glistening under the dome of a clear blue sky.

Prem Singh heard a distant melody. Did it come from the sea or sky, or from somewhere inside him? He could not tell. But it carried familiar words that suddenly felt new to him—three questions that came and went with the breeze:

From where did we emerge?
What are we here to do?
And where do we merge back to in the end?[3]

He glanced at his wife, who was watching the distant waves. Had she heard these words too? He would not say anything for now. Still, the words echoed in his mind, leaving a golden dust—a clue to the treasures they would discover there. This would be no ordinary stay.

---

2. "*Sri Gur Hargobind achārā*. . . "—Sri Gur Pratap Suraj Granth, vol. 5: 44: 18–23.

3. "*Kithhahu upjai keh rahai keh māhi samāvai*". . .'—Sri Guru Granth Sahib, *ang* 1193.

Seashells

Through the Unseen Flow,
Myriad forms take shape.
The Way, the Will,
Miraculously ordering,
Intricately inscribing
Yet ever indescribable
In all its mystery.

Understand the Flow
And you will feel your mind released
From the mutters of the ego.[4]

"Wow!" A girl of seven and a boy of ten marveled at the sunlit sea. The boy's parents led them down to the beach. Asisse, his teenage sister, stayed on the clifftop with her grandparents, watching as the children flung off their shoes and ran barefoot in the sand.

"When I was little, the ocean was on our doorstep," her grandmother told her, remembering her days by the Kenyan coast. Back in Malaysia, her grandfather had made many family trips to the beach. Asisse wondered what he must have looked like as a child, before he had a beard and turban. As they set off back to the house, she headed down the slope. What about her great-grandparents? They came from the Punjab, the famous land of five rivers. No sea there, she mused. But where do rivers lead? Stepping onto the sand, Asisse thought too her of grandparents' unspoken sadness, and of the sea's vastness, waiting.

"Look!" her mother gestured. "Vismad's begun a treasure hunt."

Asisse glanced over at her little cousin, Vismad. She was rapt in collecting shells that the tide had scattered across the shore. Before

4. "*Hukamī hovan ākār hukam na kahiā jāī...*"—Sri Guru Granth Sahib, *ang* 1.

long, Vismad came and emptied her bucket on the towel that her aunt Kudrat—Asisse's mother—had spread on the sand.

"What amazing shapes and patterns!" exclaimed Asisse. Vismad's fingers traced their grooves and contours. Cockle shells and scallops spread out like fans, and periwinkles and top shells spiraled up like turbans and twirled into small cones. They are so elegant, thought Asisse. Like the visible traces of some invisible architect.

"They're like miniature miracles, aren't they?" asked Kudrat. "Did you know, Vismad, that once upon a time, small shells called cowries were used like money?" Asisse had seen them once in an exhibition. Like pennies, they were not worth much at all.

Just an empty shell, thought Asisse. That's how we all start to feel, sometimes. But shells once housed little sparks of life. Asisse remembered that steady melody and drumbeat as they gathered to sing their teachings:

The birth of every human
Is as precious a diamond.
How is it that we let a diamond
Get traded for cowrie shells?[5]

For Vismad, though, those shells had miracle-value, not monetary-value. Their patterns told a different story. Asisse imagined all the patterns of our life, shaped by everything we think and do. And patterns laid by others around us, and long before us. Then came all those ideas, feelings, and forces that come and go, outside us and inside us. Who then writes our story?

Her mind lit up, as more verses came to her. We each have, in our hands, some power to manoeuver where we go.[6] Yet all the while a greater will, the *hukam*, keeps flowing—from the pen of the invisible mystery that made us.[7] As children of that mystery, she figured,

---

5. "*Hīre jaisā janam hai, koudī badale jāi . . .*"—Sri Guru Granth Sahib, *ang* 156.

6. "*Āpan hathhī āpnā āpe hī kāj savārīai*"—Sri Guru Granth Sahib, *ang* 747.

7. "*Āpe pattī kalam āp upar lekh bhi tū(n)*"—Sri Guru Granth Sahib, *ang* 1291.

we too have a will that flows. Our story gets written where both intertwine.

Vismad's eyes were still bright with delight. True to her name, she was wonderstruck. Asisse scanned the vast ocean. She felt like thanking it for its gifts, the little signs it had brought along with the tide.

Song of the Sea

Listening deeply, you start to dive into the ocean of virtue,
Listening deeply, you attain the noble wisdom of sovereigns and saints.
Listening deeply, you discover the path you were unable to see,
Listening deeply, you touch at last what was once unfathomable.[8]

"Look, a present." Kudrat held a conch, much larger than the other shells Vismad had collected. "Put it to your ear and you'll hear the song of the sea." She paused. "Did you know the world is full of hidden songs?"

Vismad nodded, smiling at her little piece of evidence. "Well, everything is vibration, they say. Nothing's really solid." That was Mum, Asisse thought, always fascinated by how the world works. "Can you imagine," Kudrat continued, "behind the shape of everything, there's a hidden music that made it, that still sings inside it? That music is the hum of *Nām* . . ."

"*Nām* is name!" exclaimed Vismad. She knew the word in Punjabi.

"Well done," Kudrat nodded. "You use a name to call someone, to remember them. A name is a word. And every word has a sound that is carried by invisible waves..." Smiling at Vismad, she traced waves in the air. Then she turned to Asisse.

"Here's a word: *ocean*. Say it and you imagine something vast and deep. But it's the motion of the waves that makes you know and feel it's real. Then imagine the air. Totally invisible. You wouldn't even know it's there, until you feel the wind, the breeze. . . .

---

8. "*Sunniai sarā gunā ke gāh* . . .'—Sri Guru Granth Sahib, *ang* 3.

"Well, we imagine the Great Oneness too, with names like God. But greater still is *Nām*[9]— the hidden melody of infinite wisdom, that makes the Oneness real."

How can you feel it, thought Asisse, past all those words and ideas?

She whispered the sound of their sacred symbol and started to draw it in the sand. First came the Punjabi numeral for "1," like a "q" with a soft curve at its tail.

"*Ik*!" Vismad recognized the first shape instantly.

Next, Asisse made a number 3, then curved the line back upwards on the left, leaving an arc on top and a swirl that pointed to infinity.

"*Ik Oang-Kār*!" exclaimed Vismad.

So many meanings to still discover, reflected Asisse. The Oneness, whose living presence is *Nām*. An eternal awareness and vibration, generating, sustaining, and transcending all the spheres and cycles of creation.[10]

"*Nām* is always there," continued Kudrat, "the soundtrack we miss behind the mutters of our ego. Of course, we all need a sense of self, but that ego can stop us feeling connected to others, by forgetting the One who connects us."

Asisse glanced between the swirls of the sacred symbol in the sand and the spirals of the conch shell. Before she could notice it, a whisper came and went with the wind.

Eternal Source of all existence, You created Your own very self.
You Yourself manifested Nām, then gave form to Kudrat–
Nature's infinite realms and cycles of creation.
Sitting amidst the universe, You behold it with delight.[11]

---

9. "*Ūche upar ūchā nāou*" —Sri Guru Granth Sahib, *ang* 5.

10. "*Nām ke dhāre sagale jant...*"—Sri Guru Granth Sahib, *ang* 284.

11. "*Āpīnai āp sājio, āpīnai rachio nāou...*"—Sri Guru Granth Sahib, *ang* 463.

Buried Treasure

Vismad pulled out a small tin box from her backpack. In it were some beaded bracelets and hair bands, a whistle, a toy compass, and mini magnifying glass. Peering at her shells, she placed her favorites in the tin.

"A treasure-box!" exclaimed Kudrat, "Those shells will be your souvenirs."

"Ah, pirate treasure!" Pavan walked up and knelt next to Vismad. Whispering together, the two cousins came up with a plan. They grabbed a bucket and a spade, dug a hole, buried the tin box, then leveled the sand back over it. Pavan marked it with an "X." Pavan's father, Livtar, joined them and said, "I'm looking for buried treasure!" The children laughed as they hid the "X."

"Aha! X marks the spot!" Livtar began digging, and then, with a flourish, he pulled out the hidden box. As Assise looked on, a verse from her morning prayers suddenly came to her:

Our mind forms a mindset, but hidden underneath
Are jewels, gems, emeralds and rubies.
Listen even once to the Guru's wisdom
And you will start to see them glistening.[12]

Those hidden treasures, were they the mind's amazing capabilities? But if the mind can do good and bad, surely the qualities that guide it, like love or wisdom or courage, are the real treasures. She remembered what her grandparents would often say: "We come to this world like merchants. And what's our business here? To trade in precious virtues. To exchange and invest them. To gather and spend them. They cost no money and can't get destroyed. They make the world a better, richer place. Those qualities, Asisse, are the only souvenirs we can take back from our stay."[13]

12. "*Mat vich ratan javāhar mānik* . . ."—Sri Guru Granth Sahib, *ang* 2.

13. "*Khāveh kharcheh ral mil bhāi* . . ."—Sri Guru Granth Sahib, *ang* 186.

"But what if they're hard to find?"

"Make *Nām* your North Star. Hear the Guru's wisdom. Let that be your compass. You'll find your direction."

Those jewels of the soul. Asisse whispered their names. *Dayā*, compassion. *Sat*, true goodness. *Santokh*, contentment. *Nimrata*, humility. And *prem*, love. Where did they come from? She imagined rainbow hues, a spectrum from our inner light. Or perhaps they came from the cleverness of our genes, all the caring impulses that help our species survive.

What was Asisse hearing? A stream of words flowed toward her from the ocean. It startled her, but she felt its music.

Every human virtue, its infinite origin is You,
Not one is my own possession.
Whatever enlightened path we follow,
To live by those virtues is the true meaning of devotion.[14]

Wading into the Mystery

I was a bard adrift
Without use or purpose
Until I entered the service of the unseen Master.

From the realm of sacred mystery
Came the command to sing melodiously
Over all the nights and days of life...

And so, with work assigned, the bard set off
To sing and spread vibrations of the shabad—
The eternal Word that emanates waves of wisdom.[15]

14. "*Sabh gun tere mai nāhī koi...*"—Sri Guru Granth Sahib, *ang* 4.

15. "*Hou dādī vekār kārai lāeiā...*"—Sri Guru Granth Sahib, *ang* 150.

"I dare you to walk into the sea, Mum!" Pavan followed his mother, Kudrat, as she walked barefoot by the rolling waves. "Don't disappear, Mum!" Asisse called. Kudrat was soon knee-deep, the waves lapping around her.

"Didn't Guru Nanak disappear into the water?" Pavan asked Livtar. "He did!" Vismad said before Livtar could respond. "For three days!"

"You're right," Livtar said. "You know the story—when Guru Nanak disappeared into the water and met the Great Source—the *mool*, the root of everything!"

"Tell us the story, Dad," said Asisse, with an odd yearning to hear it again. Livtar retold the familiar tale that took them back to the Punjab, more than five hundred years ago.

"By then, Guru Nanak was a young man working in the imperial storehouses of Sultanpur, distributing grain to the townspeople, who loved and respected him. Even at work, he showed what good can follow, when you remember the True Giver." Livtar then paused. "And where did Guru Nanak go every morning before work?"

"To the riverbank!" answered Vismad.

"Yes, to bathe in the stream, then meditate on its banks. Except one day, he waded in and was nowhere to be found. That was his dive into the Great Mystery."

"When he met God?" asked Vismad. Livtar nodded. "What did he see?"

"From the stream, he was transported to a heavenly *darbār*. That's a royal court, where a king or queen might rule from a throne. Except Guru Nanak couldn't see a human face. He heard a voice and felt an energy."

"An invisible ruler!" exclaimed Pavan.

Asisse pictured Guru Nanak as a deep-sea diver, journeying to the center of life's deepest reality. Then as an astronaut, landing in a cosmic court, to meet the invisible power that governs everything. It now made sense. If there are ruling forces behind all things, like gravity on this earth, or love in a person's heart, what must power them? It was as if Guru Nanak was transported right to the headquarters.

"Back in the ordinary world, what was life ruled by?" continued Livtar. "You had rulers with governments and laws. People's everyday rules, rituals, and habits. Guru Nanak saw the narrow traits that start to reign inside us, like small-mindedness and greed, or selfishness and arrogance. Wherever we come from, we forget we're all living in the realm of life's invisible ruler—and that the laws of that realm are to live with love and wisdom."

"What happened in the *darbār*, Dad?" asked Pavan.

"In that heavenly court," continued Livtar, "Guru Nanak was given a robe of honor and a cup of nectar to sip, and then his life's assignment."

"An assignment?" asked Pavan.

"Yes, an assignment, to help a suffering world."

"How?"

"By helping humans see we are sparks of the Divine at our core. If we make that spark our friend, we start to see it in each other. It moves us to create a better world, as equals who honor their differences."

Kudrat had been quietly listening, her feet still tingling from the icy waves. "That cup of *amrit nām*. With one sip of that sweet nectar, every cell within Guru Ji must have come to know something that no words could ever explain."

"The *a-kath kathā*, the untellable story," said Livtar softly.

The wisdom of the Divine story is so blissfully sweet
Like someone without the power of speech
I taste, but cannot describe it.[16]

16. "*Har har kathā banī at mīthī, jio gūngā gatak samāre...*"—Sri Guru Granth Sahib, *ang* 980.

Meeting the Source

Oh my mind, you are a spark of the Divine flame;
Recognize the true root of your very own being.[17]

"But Guru Nanak did come back with some words. With the Mool Mantar," said Pavan.

Asisse imagined it as a message in a bottle: a parchment with inky calligraphy, coming back with Guru Nanak from the mystical court through the waves of the stream to the everyday world, to where they were today. She had written it in the pages of her notebook. By the original script, she had scribed the words in English, jotting notes around them.

Next to "Mool Mantar" Assise had written "metamorphosis," sketching a seed becoming a tree, and a caterpillar becoming a butterfly.

"So, the Mool Mantar, does it describe God?" she asked.

"It does, but as the *mool*, the root of existence," said Kudrat, "and the root of our very own being. What else did Guru Nanak say, coming back from the stream?"

Asisse answered, "There is no Hindu, there is no Muslim."

"Yes," continued Kudrat, "those words puzzled everyone because Guru Nanak respected all faiths. But he showed that our rituals can become fake and shallow, masking our hypocrisy. We forget we share a truer, deeper identity, as sparks of the One Light."

"Great faiths had worshiped this Oneness," added Livtar, "but viewed it differently. Like a God high up in the desert sky, or a force deep down in the greenery of the forests. Some saw only 'my God' or 'your God', or no God. Guru Nanak saw One Formless Source, expressed in all forms." Asisse touched the rim of her steel *karā*, the sacred bracelet that they all wore, a circle of oneness without beginning or end.

---

17. "*Man tū(n) jot sarūp hai āpnā mūl pachān*..."—Sri Guru Granth Sahib, *ang* 440.

"So the Mool Mantar," her father continued, "is like an introduction. Say you were introduced to someone, Asisse, what would you want to know about them?"

"Well, their name, what they do. I'd wonder about their personality. Maybe where they were born. And how old they are!" She smiled as she looked at the silvery strands in her father's beard.

Kudrat began to chant the Mool Mantar. As everyone joined in, Asisse pulled out her notebook. She added some questions.

(HELLO, WHAT ARE YOU?)	IK OANG-KĀR *One Source, One Light, One Sacred Sound,* *Resonating everywhere infinitely—* *Forming, interconnecting,* *Sustaining and protecting all creation*
(WHAT'S YOUR NAME?)	SAT NĀM *Everlasting vibration of existence,* *Naming the True Reality*
(WHAT DO YOU DO?)	KARTĀ PURAKH *Doer and Creator,* *Working at the heart of everything*
(WHAT QUALITIES DEFINE YOU?)	NIRBHAU, NIRVAIR *Free of fear, free of hatred*

Without fear, without hate, she thought. Why not just say "Love"? Love is beautiful, her mother would say, but it can make us cling too hard. A mind minus fear and hate, now that would give you a sublime love, one that knows that, even in battle, no one is really a stranger or an enemy.[18] That brings you courage to protect, and the power to give and forgive.

---

18. "*Nā ko bairī nahī bigānā . . .*"—Sri Guru Granth Sahib, *ang* 1299.

Asisse then scanned the next words:

(WHAT DO YOU
LOOK LIKE?)

AKĀL MOORAT

The face of eternity,
Undying and timeless

(WHEN WERE
YOU BORN?)

AJOONĪ, SAIBHANG

Not born or formed,
Self-existing, indestructible,
Stable, Self-illumined

(HOW CAN I
KNOW YOU?)

GURPRASĀD

Known through the sweet grace and
Blessing of the Guru, the Enlightener.

What, she wondered, was the blessing? Next came *Jap*. The title too, of their first morning prayer.

(HOW CAN WE
CONNECT?)

JAP

Here is the gift of wisdom,
To chant and contemplate

And then came the couplet that bore Guru Nanak's name, singing to humanity as he sang to his own deepest self.

(YOU WILL ALWAYS
BE THERE...
ACROSS ALL
SEAS OF TIME...)

ĀD SACH, JUGĀD SACH,
HAI BHĪ SACH,
NĀNAK, HOSĪ BHĪ SACH

True before the birth of time,
True when time's ages began,
True now, in every moment,
Says Nanak, true always and forever.

Asisse looked up to the horizon. *Sach:* a reality that stays real and true, she thought, while everything else comes and goes. Right now, so much was changing, inside her and around her, as she swung between childhood and adulthood.

Who is the true me? You can be true to your shifting moods, but hurt or harm people, or not see the bigger picture. What should you be true to, then? What did the Mool Mantar say? You should be true to that true, wise root of you. Not just preaching or pretending to be good, but learning to let goodness steer you. On her wrist, the metal curve of her *karā* sparkled in the sunlight.

Yes, truth is high, but higher still
Is walking the path of truthful living
Of radiating Truth, hands-on in practice.[19]

Landscapes and Mindscapes

Livtar and his children had gone to explore the caves. As they walked along together, he thought about the children. Asisse, she was almost an adult now. Pavan was ten. He reminded Livtar of his younger brother—the same navy-colored cloth covering his topknot. The only Sikh in his class, Jivan had often been misunderstood. But he had this knack of moving past setbacks towards life's next adventure. Now that Jivan was gone, those qualities were the most precious reminders of him. Some months had passed. It still wasn't easy. Soon they'd return his ashes to the elements.

Along the shoreline, the cliff-face was striped by layers of maroon- and khaki-colored rock. A tiny waterfall trickled down, like a signature to all the natural forces at work, carving the coves and caves into the landscape. Asisse talked about the rocks being formed over millions of years and how the wind, waves, and weather gradually shaped their contours. They passed an old washed-up fishing net. Pavan pointed to

19. "*Sachahu orai sabh ko ūpar sach āchār . . .*"—Sri Guru Granth Sahib, *ang* 62.

the strands of entangled plastic waste—signaling faster, human-driven forces that were pushing the planet deeper into crisis. The landscape was wordlessly speaking to them—appealing to them almost, as it shared its ancient and modern-day story.

Walking back, Livtar joined the grown-ups. They sat and chatted about home, health, work. It had been hard for all of them to stay afloat.

"Do you ever feel your mind is like a landscape?" asked Livtar.

"You mean a mindscape?" said Daya.

"Yes. Your thinking can become your mindset, with its own grooves and layers."

"A mindscape. I like the sound of that!" said Kudrat. "The mind isn't just one thing, is it?"

She was right, thought Livtar. First, there was the *mann*, responding to what we experience through our senses. Our moods and tendencies, swaying like the sea waves. In the mind's sky, the intellect, the *budhī*, was its light of reason, helping us to discern. But that sky gets overcast when *haumai*, our ego, clouds it. Reasonable desires grow out of proportion. The intellect becomes arrogant, and the *jyot*—the soulful inner light—gets forgotten.

"You know," said Kudrat, remembering her maternal grandmother, "Nani Ji often told me, that the real learner sits in the mind—it's the *surat*. Whenever she tuned her *dilrubā*, she'd put her ear to the string and explain, if the Guru is the *shabad*, the word, the vibration of eternal wisdom—then the real disciple is the *surat*, our awareness, that absorbs and applies that wisdom.[20] Our mind, she said, is also an instrument. Prayer is our way to tune it, ready for each day."

Surat, thought Livtar. An awareness in our inner landscape. Like a resonance, with magical energy to change our wavering thought-patterns and clear the clouds of the ego. Remembering the tangled-up fishing net, he thought of all the degradation in the world, from poverty and slavery to climate catastrophes and raging wars. You could trace each back to a mindset run by impulses that rob us of our humanity. The ego in cahoots with the five thieves—blind lust, vengeance, greed, possessiveness, and arrogance.

---

20. "*Sabad Gurū surat dhun chelā* . . ."—Sri Guru Granth Sahib, *ang* 943.

Molding that mindset, he reflected, is also the outside world. Habits passed down from bygone generations. Imprints left, across lifetimes, on our travelling soul. Every mindscape tells its own story. Deposits from long embedded memories layer up. Traits disintegrate or persist. Qualities erode or arise to stand majestically.

Daya drew two circles in the sand—a small one and much larger one. "Mind, and world," he said.

"Or maybe," Kudrat suggested, "that small one is *ahan-kār*, the circle of self-importance. Sometimes we seal ourselves in it, not to be mean, but just to feel safe. And the other one is *Ik Oang-kār*, the bigger circle of awesomeness. When we feel connected, and part of a whole. Isn't that why Guru Nanak told the yogis up in the mountains to serve and care for the world?"

Inside the mind, thought Livtar, storms can throw us, gloom can seep in, but such things don't have to last forever. In the sky of his own mind, he heard a melody drifting in:

Entering the sanctuary of the Infinite Creator
My low thoughts shift to a higher vibration
A sinking stone, I have become uplifted
Such is the true greatness of the Divine.
As the mind absorbs the Guru's wisdom
Old toxins transmute into ambrosial nectar
The bitter scent becomes a sublime fragrance
Suffusing, like sandalwood, the space within.[21]

It was now late afternoon. Livtar walked to the shore to collect the litter he had spotted. The others joined him. Then they all put their shoes back on to head back to the house.

---

21. "*Ham nīch se ūtam bhe har kī sarnāī*..."—Sri Guru Granth Sahib, *ang* 565.

The Little Cradle of Ocean

Vismad reached up to the brass lion's head doorknocker. Her mother, Simran, opened the door. "We missed you, Vismad!"

Vismad flung her arms around her mother, patting her hand on Simran's curved belly. She imagined her unseen sibling, wrapped up like a present.

From an earlier loss, Simran knew how fragile life before birth can be. In her mind, she lit two candles, one of hope and the other of acceptance. She thought of the small carved box her father had carried in when they arrived—the last trace they had of her brother. Taking Vismad's hand, she prayed for balance to walk that tightrope through the canyon of her grief, while staying strong for her daughter.

As the others settled, Vismad snuggled with her mother in the glass-roofed sunroom, filled now with the sunset's pink glow. "So, you went to meet the sea?' Did you meet any mermaids or dolphins as well?"

"I forgot to look," sighed Vismad.

"Don't worry. Perhaps next time you'll see them. There's a whole wide world of life hidden deep beneath the sea!"

"The baby's like a sea-creature!"

"Ah, you remember. The baby's being cradled in a sack of water. That's how we start our life, Vismad, like a fish! Then we're born, and then we crawl. Then we walk, run, and jump! So, we should care for all creatures like they're part of us too."

Blinking slowly, Vismad imagined she had the eyes of a fish, a turtle, then a lion. She thought of the baby's eyes blinking open to the world. Simran thought back to the first flutters of a heartbeat with a verse from their daily prayers:

Placing the soul in the cave of the body,
The Creator infused it with the melody of life.
And so, we came alive, like an instrument,
Played by the breath of the Divine.[22]

---

22. "*Har jīou guphā andar rakh kai vājā pavan vajāeia . . .*"—Sri Guru Granth Sahib, *ang* 922.

"Doesn't the baby get bored in there?" asked Vismad.

"Well, it can't be easy, can it, hanging upside down in the dark, inside a bubble!"

Another verse, Simran knew, described our soul's remembrance of the Divine while our tiny body hung cramped and suspended in the womb. Though easily forgotten, that *simran*, that remembrance, was the golden thread that sustained us.[23]

"A bubble?" asked Vismad, trying to picture the scene.

"Yes. Right inside that bubble, where the baby grows, miraculous things are happening. We grow like a seed, packed with amazing powers."

Vismad rested her head on her mother's tummy. "Like our five senses?" she said looking up with a yawn.

"Yes, *puttar*," said Simran, using the soft, caring word for "my child," used as much for daughters as for sons. For the Gurus taught that every child is equally precious.

She patted Vismad's two eyelids and ears, her nose, then her lips. The body's doorways to the world, she thought. Then, an unseen one, that leads us to sense the Divine.

Simran's voice became a whisper: "Did you see the little limpets, like shells stuck on the rocks?" Eyes closed, Vismad nodded. "How mysterious, that even they get all the food they need, as if someone is always caring for them, invisibly. . . ."[24]

Simran could smell the sea-salt on her daughter's skin and hair. With one child visible, and another still invisible, she marveled at our human birth, at the genes that make us—journeying across millions of years, at the story of evolution, from the realms of matter to plants, animals, and humans. And what about the story of the *atma*, the soul? She had learned its journeys too, across lifetimes and life-forms, until it reaches the shores of human life—in the waters of a mother's womb.

---

23. "*Re nar garabh kundal jab āchhat uradh dhiān liv lāgā*. . ."—Sri Guru Granth Sahib, *ang* 93.

24. "*S-ail pathhar meh jant upāe, tā kā rijak*. . ."—Sri Guru Granth Sahib, *ang* 10.

Wasn't the world also like a womb for the soul to flourish? What prayer, then, could she now offer? She began to sing a tune, like a lullaby, to bring a cool sweetness to the little ocean inside her. For water, she had learned, could become sublime.

O my child, this is your mother's asīsse, her blessing—
May you never, for a moment, forget the Divine,
and stay ever-attuned to the wondrous Creator.

Gifted with love for the company of the wise
May you be clothed in dignity, and nourished daily
With melodies of Divine wisdom and praise.

Drinking in the amrit-nectar, may you ever-live
To delight in that sweet connection…

Like the bumble bee, may your mind seek out
The fragrant lotus feet of the Divine…[25]

"Beeline." Simran fondly remembered how her dad put it. "The mind can buzz in all directions. Land in any place, like a fly. Or move, like a bee, straight to the nectar source." She felt nature come alive in their sacred teachings. Like the fish, who feels but can't see the water all around her. Without it, she dies. Then, the musk deer, searching outside for the scent that's really within him. And the legendary swan that chooses only jewels from the lake of existence.

The sun had almost set. Daya came in and helped to put their sleeping daughter to bed.

---

25. "*Pūta mātā ki āsīs…*"—Sri Guru Granth Sahib, *ang* 496.

Swing under the Stars

The house stood under a night sky filled with stars. The children were tucked in bed. Livtar and Kudrat stayed behind in the kitchen to put the last things away. Soon Asisse joined them, looking to get a warm drink before they sat on the long garden swing.

Far away from the city lights the stars were more luminous. The moon was almost full, and clouds stumbled across its face.

"Can you hear the ocean?" murmured Kudrat. She caught the scent of flowers on the evening breeze. She knew that trees could communicate and care for one another across whole forests. With nature, there was always more than meets the eye.

Asisse rested her head on her mother's shoulder. The swing swayed and creaked in the stillness. "It's strange, isn't it," mused Livtar. "The ground feels steady. Night has tucked us in her blanket. But everything's in motion."

"Just like you taught me, Dad," said Asisse, "the moon orbits the earth. The earth orbits the sun. And if you stand at the equator, it's moving at a thousand miles an hour!"

"And what holds up our planet?"

Asisse knew the answer from their morning prayer. "*Dharam*, the invisible order."

"And *dharam* is the child of *dayā,* compassion," added Kudrat, continuing the verse, "and *santokh*, contentment, holds it in balance."[26]

Asisse tried to fathom what all that meant. Behind the mysterious force that keeps the world up and running, there was a quality, a feeling, in the background.

Kudrat was looking up to the sky. "The moon is like a magnet, making tides. Everything is on the move, isn't it? Our blood circulates, pushed by hidden heartbeats, while our lungs pump our breath."

"Nothing's really still," Livtar murmured. "In the background, there's a harmony."

---

26. "*Dhaul dharam deiā kā pūt . . .*"—Sri Guru Granth Sahib, *ang* 3.

Asisse wondered if she could ever still her mind. The more she tried, the more it raced.

"Stillness and motion; both have their beauty," said Kudrat. She recited the night-time verse.

The vast sky is the worship tray,
Studded with luminous stars, like pearls.
The sun and moon are the oil lamps
And the swaying of the breeze is the celestial fan.
Spreading the sandalwood incense of the mountain air.
The lush forests of the world make their flower offerings.
Oh Luminous Creator, what a beautiful ārtī this is![27]

"Back in India," her mother explained, "*ārtī* was an age-old ceremony. You'd arrange oil lamps, incense, and flowers on a decorated tray, then circle it before a deity, singing prayers. It was a way to show devotion and gratitude, to seek blessings or admire the deity's qualities." She paused. "Then Guru Nanak expanded people's horizons, to see nature's own celestial ceremony."

"And he said the whole earth spins," added Livtar "in a universe of countless planets, skies and stars. Did you know it was by eastern coast, in India, when Guru Nanak first sang that *ārtī* prayer? In Europe, that was time of Leonardo da Vinci, of new awakenings, of the Renaissance. . . ."

"Well, Guru Nanak also sparked an awakening," continued Kudrat, "He led the way to an enlightenment that lights up the intellect with the lamp of wisdom—and never forgets the One Light that sparks life in all. "[28]

"Stardust," said Asisse. "That's what we're made of, isn't it? Stuff that came from the stars."

"As in the body, so in the cosmos," said her father.[29]

---

27. "*Gagan mai thhāl rav chand dīpak bane . . .*"—Sri Guru Granth Sahib, *ang* 13.

28. "*Gurā ik deh bujhāī . . .*"—Sri Guru Granth Sahib, *ang* 2.

29. "*Jo brahamande soī pinde . . .*"—Sri Guru Granth Sahib, *ang* 695.

Asisse pictured a whole cosmos inside her body, lit up by luminous living cells and tissues and intricate constellations of neurons. What was that *other* element, that sparked her into being?

The *jyot*, she thought, the Divine flame. Dormant in the diversity of all beings—the 8.4 million lifeforms. Like a game of hide and seek, our life comes with signs, quests, and countdowns—to help us discover and kindle that flame.

"If the universe has a Source," her dad continued, "the Generator of everything, then *Nām* is the energy, the electricity. The unseen light, the unstruck sound. Connecting with the Source, we energize our connection to others. Disconnect, and those bonds get weaker."

Asisse's eyes grew heavier. Her mother continued with the prayer before they went to bed.

In all beings is the Divine jyot,
The Divine light—that is You.
A radiance that dwells in all beings.
Through the Guru's teachings,
The light shines forth within us.
When we learn to live in harmony,
With what is pleasing to the Creator,
Consider that to be life's true ārtī—
The best way we can ever express
Our true wonder and devotion.[30]

30. "*Sabh meh jot jot hai soi* . . ."—Sri Guru Granth Sahib, *ang* 13.

PART TWO

Sunrise

The twinkling of the night stars had faded as the sun spread its rays. The house by the sea was now bathed in daylight.

Asisse was making milky tea spiced with fennel seeds, cardamon, and cinnamon. Its warming fragrance would make everyone feel at home. Her parents would have recited the five cherished prayers by now. As initiated Sikhs, that's how they greeted each morning.

Asisse too had been up early, out again on the garden swing. "Wahe…guru", she had chanted, in the same rhythm she was rocked to as a child. That first sound "Wah-" was a "wow" word. Leaning into a shout out in wonder—"Hey!" Then, "Guru." The center of gravity, that draws us to wisdom. The source of light, that lifts darkness.

To touch and transform us, she had learned, this real and timeless wisdom takes form. That's why the light of Guru Nanak shone through all ten Gurus and the sacred words they left behind. She heard her mother's voice explaining: "You know those states of solid, liquid, and gas? To bring us wisdom, the Guru can be person, word, or spirit.…A different form, but the same light."

Gurdev mātā. Gurdev pitā. "Guru is Mother, Guru is Father."[31] Her mother and father were only human. Lately, she needed more space from them. But if the Guru is a parent for your soul, she knew that they had tried to echo that, raising her to be ready for the world, while helping her to kindle the wisdom inside her. Probably to remind themselves of it too. She thought about this place, and that whispered wisdom, like a gateway to endless time and space.

Asisse strained the boiled tea into a teapot. Except for the children, everyone was up.

---

31. "*Gurdev mātā gurdev pitā*…"—Sri Guru Granth Sahib, *ang* 250.

"Thanks, Asisse." Uncle Daya helped her set out the mugs. Of all of them, he was the most subdued.

"How about we take a walk?" asked Santokh, glancing at her husband. Asisse and Daya offered to take them on a tour across the clifftop, then down to the beach.

"Do you remember, Asisse," asked her grandfather, as they walked along the shoreline. "It was like a sunrise, when Guru Nanak Dev Ji was born."

Asisse sang the familiar verse:

Guru Nanak was born;
a true enlightener had arrived,
To uplift, with illuminating rays,
A world sunk in mist and shadow.
It was as if the sun had risen,
causing the last stars of night to fade,
And the overhanging gloom to dissolve away.[32]

"This gloom," said Prem, "comes from a mind that is poorly lit. When people are phantoms of themselves, losing their harmony with the Divine, getting stuck in arrogance or ignorance, in hopelessness or greed.... You know the verse, Asisse:"

Even if a hundred moons and a thousand suns were to rise,
Without the Guru, the mind would still be lost in utter darkness.[33]

Daya had said nothing. Asisse glimpsed the sorrow behind his silence. In Jivan, he had lost a best friend as well as a brother-in-law. Her grandparents always seemed to have a way of detaching themselves from what troubled them. This time, their pain had left them wordless. But still, they seemed to honor that teaching to live like the

---

32. "*Satgur Nānak pragatiā mitī dhundh jag chānan hoā*"...'—Bhai Gurdas Ji, Var 1, pauri 27.

33. "*Je sou chandā ugveh sūraj charheh hajār*..."—Sri Guru Granth Sahib, *ang* 463.

lotus flower, with its roots in life's muddy waters and its petals blossoming above.[34]

Asisse could see that tender grace in them now, as they walked along the shore on this clear and golden morning.

Traveling Companions

Oh traveling yogi, see all people
as fellow travelers and learners,
Make the highest sect you belong to
the human collective—
If you conquer your mind, and rise above the ego,
You have conquered and won the whole world.[35]

Santokh was glad to hear her husband and their granddaughter in conversation. A walk was sometimes the best way to talk. She gazed out over the horizon. First retirement from her school. And then her loss. A world of less talk now, though she had much to share. She reflected, then spoke.

"Did you know Guru Nanak was one of the most traveled people of his time?" Asisse could hear the teacher in her grandmother's voice. "Europeans found sea routes to India, to America. They called it the Age of Discovery. Landing on new coasts, they made new conquests, new profits—and new maps. Well, Guru Nanak was also map-making."

"Map-making?" asked Asisse.

"Far and wide, he traveled mostly by foot, meeting people from all walks of life. He helped them chart the world inside us—the landmarks and pitfalls, the treasures and dead ends."

Scanning the coastline, Asisse pictured the map of Guru Nanak's four great journeys, to each corner of India, and westward to the Middle

34. "*Braham giānī sadā nirlep, jaise jal meh kamal alep*..."—Sri Guru Granth Sahib, *ang* 272.

35. "*Āī panthī sagal jamātī man jītai jag jīt*..."—Sri Guru Granth Sahib, *ang* 6.

East, for over more than twenty-five years. More years than she had lived. He had crossed farmlands, forests, mountains, deserts, and reached coastlands. He had visited remote villages, bustling towns, and great centers of pilgrimage for different faiths. Each journey was called an *udāsī*. It sounded to her like an "odyssey," but in Punjabi it had a touch of sadness. She felt Guru Nanak's compassionate gaze, aloof yet still hopeful, as he saw humanity's suffering, yet also its promise.

"Wherever he went," continued Santokh, "he'd show how easily we sink into traits that are traitors to our true self. *Amul gun, amul vāpār*—make those priceless virtues your true business and your trusted traveling companions. Make timeless wisdom your Guru and guide. Then your *yātrā*, your pilgrimage to this planet, will be fruitful and fulfilled."[36]

"Traveling in those days wasn't easy," added Prem. "So, Guru Ji prepared for the hardships ahead—sleeping on rocks, eating plants like cactus, and meditating deeply. He wasn't planning an escape or holiday, or to conquer or convert people. It was to help us conquer ego's pull, to see and feel the Oneness, for all the world to flourish."

"*Sarbat dā bhallā*," said Asisse. That phrase sought the well-being of all people, all beings, the whole earth. With it came, *chardī kalā*, to build hope, faith, and courage in yourself and others.

"You see this pebble?" Prem lifted one from the sand. "In time to come it will outlive us. Maybe Guru Nanak was saying that we cannot cling to this single life, but should live to make the world better now and for the future."

Daya glimpsed a boat out on the waves. "Maybe Guru Ji was also reminding us that we're all migrants, really."

Santokh nodded and said, "You're right, Daya. This planet is a *dharamsāl*. A stopover for our soul, to earn the wealth of precious qualities before we depart."

"And the earth is where we are granted our stay," added Prem. "But it comes with a responsibility to look after this sacred planet, with gratitude to the Creator."

Prem looked at their footprints, knowing that they would fade in the sand. He felt an ache. Jivan's soul has traveled onward, he

---

36. "*Amul gun amul vāpār* . . ."—Sri Guru Granth Sahib, *ang* 5.

thought. "Daya, *puttar*, this body is like a ship. On board is the wisdom of the soul, for the mind to grasp and the heart to reveal." Daya listened, wearing his grief like armor, yet touched by Prem's love and care.

Asisse thought about Guru Nanak's lifelong friend and travelling companion, the Muslim bard, Bhai Mardana. Sometimes Mardana would get tired or frustrated, hungry or thirsty, baffled or confused. Yet he was always inspired and reassured by Guru Nanak's grace and wisdom. It made Asisse think that it's never too late for the wavering mind to honor the soul's presence and recognize its greater journey. Even though such ideas still puzzled her, she felt a stirring of understanding.

O breathing being,
If you've ever felt conscious of the Divine
Then be fully conscious now, night and day.
Like water from a cracked pitcher,
At each moment, life slips away.

It is never too late to marvel in praise at the Sacred Mystery
So meditate, says Nanak, and resonate with the Divine,
To reach the sublime and loving state, beyond all fear.[37]

The Breeze's Three Questions

Wanting to spread her wings, Asisse ran on ahead. She slowed down by a volleyball net, with the lines of a court still pinned in. She wondered who had set it up. Spreading her hoodie on the sand, she lay down to look at the clouds.

"What are we doing here?" she heard Daya say, as the others walked up. Was it one of those big questions, or not that deep?

"See this net, this ball, these boundary lines?" Prem gestured at the empty court. "Say you landed here from outer space, wouldn't these look like random objects, unless you knew the game?" He paused and

37. "*Chetanā hai tou chet lai nis din mai prānī...*"—Sri Guru Granth Sahib, *ang* 726.

felt the breeze. "To work that out, the Gurus gave us three questions: Why are we here? Where have we come from? Where are we going?"

"Origin. Purpose. Destination," said Asisse, remembering another way he'd once explained them. She imagined three cards, one for each word, being laid out on a table.

"You remember those Russian matryoshka dolls, Asisse?" asked Santokh. "One doll comes out of another."

"Yes, I felt they could go on forever!"

"Well, that's how I taught you 'origin.' It's funny, isn't it, how we love to trace our biological or cultural origins, the origin of our universe."

Prem pictured the origin of his *dharam*, his faith. Like a film fast-forwarding, he saw all the teachings, symbols, and practices materialize—all signposts to the same goal.

"We land in this life," he continued. "We go to school and work, we follow our interests, the groups we're part of. Each activity is like a game, isn't it, with different goals—to get educated, get a job. But we play them best by keeping life's bigger goal in mind: to kindle the Divine spark, instead of living in the dark with a narrow view of who we are or can be. The Gurus shaped every part of our *dharam*. But ours is not the only path. The Gurus got us to see a greater purpose behind all faiths and paths of wisdom."

Walking up to the abandoned net, Daya listened on. He knew that once a game inspires you, its tools gain an aura of possibility. They are random objects no more.

"If you connect to the root of you, it's like coming home, really," added Asisse, "your origin becomes your destination."

"Quite right, Asisse." Santokh thought about all the teachings on homecoming, about that bliss or *anand* we feel when a long-awaited loved one returns home. With that came a soft pain. Her son Jivan, his name meant life itself. She thought of his brother Livtar, and that state of *liv*, of constant connection to the Source. By nurturing it, you become a *jīvan-mukat*—liberated, not after death, but in this very life. Whatever happens outside you, inside you feel at home.

It was time to get back to the house. There, Kudrat and Livtar had laid the table for a late breakfast of spiced chickpeas and yogurt, with a stack of *paranthā* flatbreads. And, of course, more tea. After that, the children went back down to the beach with their parents.

Of all the chants that are chanted,
Chant the one that sings of the Creator—
That leads you to win the game of life,
And dwell in your soul's true home.[38]

Land of Five Rivers

"Amazing!" Kudrat exclaimed. The children had built an impressive sand construction.

"It's our sandcastle town. And look, Mum, here's our farm!" Pavan pointed at a patch of seaweed.

"A farm?" asked Kudrat, surprised.

"Like the one Guru Nanak made in Kartarpur."

"Ah Kartarpur, where he made a *dharamsāl,* like a school to learn to live out the Sikh way of life. He made it in the Punjab, the land of his birth, where he lived after his travels."

"Panj is five!" exclaimed Vismad.

"Yes, Panj for Punjab—the land of five rivers. Did you know they all flow off the mighty Indus River, that rolls down from the mountains of Tibet, and out into the Arabian Sea? Imagine one of the world's longest rivers, flowing past the world's highest peaks. And its five rivers, branching out across the plains. . . ."

In the sand, Vismad made a handprint.

"Those rivers fed rich soils and farmlands. They brought other wonders too, that got buried and forgotten, like the ruins of cities, lost in the sands of time. . . ."

"From before Guru Nanak's time?" asked Pavan.

"Way back, to the time of the Egyptian pyramids! The technology of those cities would amaze you! Then, over many centuries, from all four directions, traders, saints, and scholars came—Hindus and Buddhists from India; Greeks, Turks, and Persians from lands to the west. It had a famous university too. And from the Punjab came ancient wisdom that spoke of the Great Oneness behind everything. Over time, that Great Wholeness got forgotten. People started to admire just the parts.

---

38. "*Nanak nām japoh tar tārī . . .*"—Sri Guru Granth Sahib, *ang* 1026.

"The Punjab also saw the most terrible destruction. Everyone knew the Mahabharat, the story of the colossal war between royal families. Out of millions of warriors, they say just a dozen survived. Punjab was also a gateway into India, but over time it was unprotected. Waves of invaders came, raiding and demolishing, stealing and killing."

And abducting women and girls, Kudrat thought, as she remembered Guru Nanak's lament. Millions of *pīr*, spiritual leaders, were helpless before the *mīr*, the mighty ruler, when Babur stormed over the hills and plains:

In this age of darkness, rulers have become butchers
True dharam, all that is good and right, has flapped its wings and taken flight
In this long night of falsehood, the moon of truth cannot be seen.[39]

Pavan looked at their sand creation. What must it be like—seeing it trampled into dust, then built all over again, unsure of when another invasion might come.

"Fear and hatred had sunk into the land," continued Kudrat, "There was silent suffering and injustice. People became shallow, fake, and stuck in their ways. Saintly poets brought many glimmers of light, dreams of dignity, freedom, equality, and peace. Then Guru Nanak was born, like a sunrise in dark times."

In 1469, thought Asisse.

"As Babur conquered India, the Guru made him reflect on ruling with wisdom. The early Mughal emperors had respect for the Gurus. Later rulers turned more hostile. They were disturbed to see a strong and hopeful faith growing within their empire, ready to defend even those of other faiths from oppression. Our ninth Guru gave his life for that. Then, the tenth Guru formed the Khalsa, a new order of disciples who had stepped forward to be initiated. They promised to live with the courage of warriors and the loving wisdom of saints. That's why, after our first names, Sikhs have the brave, noble names of Singh and Kaur."

"A Singh is a lion," explained Vismad.

---

39. "*Kal kātī rāje kāsāī, dharam pankh kar udariā*..."—Sri Guru Granth Sahib, *ang* 145.

"Yes, Vismad, a lion or tiger, but in India, Singh was also a special name given to royal leaders. And Kaur would be given to a prince or princess. To someone majestic!"

"So, we all have to find the majesty within us," reflected Asisse.

"And all the good power to lead our lives well," continued Kudrat. "Now, after the Khalsa was born came years of persecution and invasion. But then, after centuries of rule by outside powers, Punjabis of all faiths came to rule themselves in a flourishing, well-protected kingdom, led by a Sikh emperor."

"Maharaja Ranjit Singh," announced Pavan.

"Correct! No kingdom is ever perfect, but his Punjab became a place to feel the dignity and unity of all faiths and people, by remembering a common Creator."

Asisse pictured a timeline. Where had they got to? In the 1800s, the British began their century of rule. Then the Punjab was split in two. One side India, one side Pakistan. A huge and violent partition. Over many decades, Sikhs had also left for new places, to work, to survive or seek their fortune, to fight in the world wars. In all directions, they carried whatever they knew of their teachings and traditions.

"Now, across the world," continued Kudrat, "Sikhs are spread out like a family. Our way of life, it all started in the *dharamsāl* at Kartarpur." She pictured Guru Nanak tending to his farm, to a budding community, and to the seeds of a hopeful vision:

With your mind, work the plough,
To cultivate a life of inner richness.
Let your body be the field, irrigated by the waters
Of your hopeful trepidation.
And in it, plant the seed of the Divine Name.
With contentment, level the soil,
And fence your field with quiet humility.
Through deeds of love, watch the seed grow,
And the home of the self begin to flourish.[40]

40. "*Man hālī kirsānī karnī, saram pānī tan khet*..."—Sri Guru Granth Sahib, *ang* 595.

The Dharamsāl

. . . Wind, water, fire, earth realms underground,
From these, the Creator stationed our planet
In the cosmos, as a dharamsāl.[41]

"Isn't the whole planet also a *dharamsāl*?" asked Asisse.

"Yes, that's what Guru Nanak wanted us to understand. In India, if people were on a pilgrimage, a *dharamsāl* is where you could stop over and stay a while. It could also be any place of worship, to learn the way of *dharam*—to live in harmony with the Great Wisdom."

"Why did he call the town Kartarpur?" asked Pavan.

"*Kartār* is the clue," said Kudrat, "the Great Doer and Creator."

Pavan thought for a moment. "It reminds us that the land is God's gift, so we need to care for it."

"And maybe," Kudrat added, "it reminds us to build a life with those qualities the Creator has gifted us with. If Sikhs are learners, what's the school motto?"

"Pray, Work, Share!" said Vismad instantly.

"Yes!" said Kudrat. "Number one: pray. *Nām Japo*. Remember *Nām*, God's invisible presence. It would be rude to keep taking and not say thank you."

"Number two: *Kirat Karo*," Pavan said, "Work hard. Remembering *Kartār*."

"If we are all little echoes of the Creator, then there's lots for us to create and do! To help ourselves and others. By working hard, we earn good qualities, and not just money. This helps us with number three. . ."

"Share!" exclaimed Vismad. "*Vand ke chhako*."

"So, if God is the Great Giver, then we should be givers too?"

"But didn't people do that anyway? I mean pray and work and share?" Pavan asked.

---

41. '*. . . Pavan pānī aganī pātāl, tis vich dhartī thhāp rakhī dharamsāl. . .*'—Sri Guru Granth Sahib, *ang* 7.

"At that time, some people lived just to pray, cut off from ordinary life. Some weren't allowed to say or even hear certain prayers. Others lived only to work, or beg, or just make others work! People shared by giving to charity, but they kept a wall between rich and poor, high and low. At Guru Nanak's *dharamsāl*, everyone learned to be prayerful, hardworking, and generous, whoever you were and however much you had."

"But what about the other three?" asked Pavan. "*Sevā*, *Simran*, and *sangat*."

"All that happened every day in Kartarpur." Kudrat added. "*Simran* and *sevā*—to remember the Creator and serve creation. This helps you become wise, yet humble. Then came *sadh sangat*, learning in the company of the wise. Then there was *kīrtan*—singing to bring alive and remember the teachings, like a tune that stays with you."

Kudrat thought of that other pattern of three in Guru Nanak's teachings: *Nām, dān, ishnān*. *Nām*, a prayerful life; *dān*, a generous life of giving—and of knowing when to let go, to forgive; *ishnān*, cleansing the mind, body, and soul. Three habits to keep renewing you, for the Divine is never stagnant, but ever fresh and ever new.[42]

"In Kartarpur, in the Guru's *langar* people sat as equals, like never before. A poor person could be served like a noble, and a rich merchant could wash dishes like a servant. Selfless acts which brought rich but invisible blessings."

Pavan pictured each practice like a castle flag, telling him the kind of life the Gurus stood for. The things to keep doing to equip you, like a toolkit, to move through changing times.

Those who work hard for what they eat,
and give from their hands to others
O Nanak, such people know and live the true path.[43]

42. "*Sahib merā nīt navā sadā sadā dātār . . .*"—Sri Guru Granth Sahib, *ang* 660.

43. "*Ghāl khāei kichh hathhoh dei, Nānak rāhu pachhaneh sei . . .*"—Sri Guru Granth Sahib, *ang* 1245.

Script in the Sand

Says Nanak, meeting the True Enlightener,
One discovers the perfect and wholesome way
Amid laughter and play, dressing and eating
One's spirit is liberated, in the heart of the everyday.[44]

Pavan had written three Punjabi letters in the sand, with the sounds "p," "v," and "n." They spelled his name. It meant wind or air. Seeing it written under the sky, he felt a little larger than life. Asisse added the letters for "Guru." The bringer of wisdom, she thought.

"Pavan Guru" they both said the start of a famous couplet.

Their father had often explained how the Guru is like the air, carrying wisdom's message, breathing life into our best qualities—like oxygen for our spirit. Water and Earth were Father and Mother, blending to bring each of us into being. And sustaining us, unconditionally. If we really saw that, we would feel a reverence for nature, and not use it thanklessly. We'd be sure to listen, in the air, for wisdom.

Kudrat loved looking on as her children etched those letters. In that script she saw a face of timeless wisdom.

She pictured Guru Angad, the second Guru, imagining his awe at inheriting the teachings revealed by Guru Nanak, and his passion to keep them visible, long into the future. In those days, when only the learned elite could read or hear ancient wisdom, he devised and taught an alphabet from simple, local scripts. It helped ordinary people access a shareable wisdom. Words uttered by the Guru—that's why he named it Gurmukhi.

A flock of seagulls trumpeted across the sky. Vismad walked over to her cousins, keen to show she too could read.

"Pavan Guru!" It was her cue to sing it, like a nursery rhyme. They all joined in. Kudrat felt the whispers of its meanings in the wind.

---

44. "*Hasandiā khelandiā painandiā khāvandiā viche hovai mukat*…"—Sri Guru Granth Sahib, *ang* 522.

Air is the Guru, Water is Father
And Mother—is the Great Earth.
Day and night are the two care-givers;
Spinning between them,
The whole world plays.

The best and worst, of all we ever did,
Will come to be heard in the cosmic court.
The sum of our deeds will surely lead us—
Some nearer to, some further from, the Divine.

Those who leave this planet, attuned to Nām,
With a life that was rich in dedicated effort—
They will depart, says Nanak, with radiant faces
And liberate many others along the way.[45]

Near and far, thought Kudrat. That's how the Gurus helped us to see our inner growth, so we don't fix labels of good or bad on ourselves or others. And when we learn to uplift those around us, that's when our life becomes truly fruitful.

Tending the Buds

"Could the baby hear you singing, Bhua Ji?" asked Pavan, using the name for "father's sister."

"For sure," replied Simran. "The baby can hear through all the layers!"

"It can?" Pavan looked curious.

"Yes, through the layers of my body and bones, through the water it floats in. Imagine being in there—no light, only sound. And just your mum's breathing and heartbeats. You wouldn't even know if your mum exists, though you might feel her!"

---

45. "*Pavan Gurū pānī pitā mātā dharat mahat*..."—Sri Guru Granth Sahib, *ang* 8.

Maybe that's what *Nām* is, thought Asisse; that mystery you can feel, but not fathom.

Kudrat thought again of Guru Angad. Like a touchstone, that tests metals for the truest gold, Guru Nanak tested and selected him to be his successor. Then, astonishingly, the great master bowed low before his worthy student, transferring to him the light of Guruship. By naming him "Angad." Guru Nanak honored him—as an *ang*, as an extension of his own self.

"It's amazing how our life starts. We're not even a speck, but over a span of nine or ten months, we bud and and start growing from a tiny embryo. Everything starts forming—our heart, brain and skeleton, our organs and limbs—all protected in the fortress of our mother's body." Kudrat paused. "It's like the way our faith took form, over the lives of the ten Gurus, like a seed that budded and flowered, with a fence of quiet strength to protect it. Then it blossomed into the *Guru Panth,* the body of the Guru's disciples, dedicated to the path. And the *Guru Granth*, the body of scripture, that holds the Gurus' timeless message."

"So how did Sikhī grow, under the Gurus?" asked Asisse. She used the name Sikhī for their faith. It meant a way of learning.

"When Guru Nanak appeared, change was already in the air, in the words of the well-known *bhagats*, the wise poet-saints of different faiths, who sang of human unity, of shedding hypocrisy and injustice. Then, to turn dreams of change into change around us, Guru Nanak shaped and showed us simple formulas for living—to tend to daily, like buds. Guru Angad gave the wisdom a written form. Through the grace of his wife, Mata Khivi, the Guru's *langar* became well known. And then came the third Guru . . ."

"Guru Amardas Ji," exclaimed Pavan. Kudrat nodded. "The oldest disciple to become a Guru. He lived into his nineties! You all know that painting of him, in the river." The children pictured his long white beard and strong arms as he walked in the darkness before dawn to fetch a pitcher of water for Guru Angad's daily bath.

"Yes, dear Guru Amardas," Simran said warmly, "who brought us the Song of Bliss—the verses of Anand, brimming with the joy of knowing the Divine with all your senses."

Vismad was cartwheeling now across the sand, silhouetted against the hues of the evening sun.

"Did you know," continued Simran, "the first time Guru Amardas heard the verses of Guru Nanak, they were being sung by his nephew's wife—she was the daughter of the second Guru. And it was Guru Amardas who appointed women as educators in new Sikh centers. He also let widows live in dignity, or remarry, instead of sacrificing their own lives or living as outcastes. No wonder he was named 'the shelter of the shelterless.'"

"Then Guru Ramdas built the *sarovar*." Pavan was recalling the fourth Guru.

"Yes, the *amrit sarovar*, the sacred pool, that gave Amritsar its name." Simran remembered sitting by its waters. "With his own hands, Guru Ramdas had dug out the tank and carried baskets of mud on his head. He grew up as a poor orphan but was destined to be Guru, and to earn the hand of Guru Amardas's own wise daughter."

"Guru Ramdas spread the love of *kār sevā*," said Kudrat. "Of turning up, to give your hands-on help, to build places that serve the common good, and to give at least a tenth of what you have—whether it's time or money or skills—for common causes. So, you don't just rely on others to change things. And he showed us the first step to call yourself a Sikh."

To be called a Sikh, a disciple of the True Guru,
Resolve to rise early, at every new tomorrow,
To wash your body, then bathe your mind
In the inner pool of amrit, the ambrosial nectar
That brims from our sublime union with the Divine.[46]

46. "*Gur satgur kā jo sikh akhāe su bhalke utth har nām dhiāvai* . . ."—Sri Guru Granth Sahib, *ang* 305.

Shrine in the Waters

Of all the places I have visited, none is comparable to you.
Such a feat of construction and beauty;
It can only arise from the unseen touch
Of the Unknowable master architect.[47]

Livtar and Daya were walking back from their stroll. Kudrat looked at Livtar, thinking back to the day they got married. Sometimes, in the thick of things, they only mirrored to each other their own exhaustion and difficulties. Then, in odd moments, there was a patient bond that arose from something greater, resting in the space between them.

She thought again of the fourth Guru, creator of a shimmering space—the sacred pool in which a famous shrine would sit. She now realized that Guru Ramdas had also opened a space in their minds—by composing the sacred wedding verses, the four stanzas sung one by one, as they both walked around the majestic scripture. Enthroned before them as their Guru, it would be their anchor of wisdom for all their years to come. That singing and slow circling, wasn't it different to two people tying the knot? Guiding you to see that life unfolds, in cycles and in stages, the journey of your own very spirit, that you can help each other fulfill.

The melodies came back to her. The first stanza sang of inner focus, of setting your course, to follow the Guru's path of *dharam*, to commit to practicing what will transform you. The second sang of an awakening, of the loving awe that arises from perceiving the Divine, inside and out. The third sang of a yearning, to seek the companionship of those who will lead you to make that sacred connection. And the fourth sang of the soul's bliss at uniting with the Creator, of the sweet peace that enters the body and mind.[48]

"47. "*Ditthe sabhe thāv nahī tudh jehiā* . . ."—Sri Guru Granth Sahib, *ang* 1361.

48. "*Har pehlarhī lāv parvirtī karam* . . ."—Sri Guru Granth Sahib, *ang* 773.

Livtar walked up to the children's sand creation. "A fine construction," he said.

"Not bad at all," Daya agreed as Vismad ran up to hug him. "Did you have a good rest?"

"Vismad has," said Pavan, "Mum was telling us stories about the Gurus. We reached Guru number four. Guru Ramdas."

"Well, next came Guru Arjan Dev, a master of construction," Livtar said. "He completed the shrine in the sacred pool, Sri Harmandir Sahib. Do you remember why it had four entrances?"

"To welcome people from all directions, north, south, east, and west."

"And from all classes. In those days, people were divided, some inferior, some superior. That's how the world was—and still is, in a way. So yes, the Guru welcomed everyone."

"And what about the steps?" asked Simran. "They go down instead of up when you enter."

"It makes you feel humble!" Vismad piped up. Livtar looked pleasantly surprise.

"Yes, *puttar*," said Livtar. "The Gurus made it a place of humility. Whoever comes, of any faith, all are served. Thousands of people are fed each day. While melodies of wisdom remind us to feel a togetherness, and awe at our One Creator."

"What about the shining gold?" asked Pavan.

"Well after the ten Gurus, there were many years of oppression and conflict. When a Sikh emperor brought peace to the land, he had the shrine plated in gold, to remind everyone why it was so precious. When the British came, they called it the Golden Temple."

Simran remembered walking down to stand before the sacred pool. The air was soft with the sounds of *kīrtan*, as the shrine's golden reflection shimmered in the waters. She would often close her eyes and transport herself there, thinking of the baby in its watery cradle.

"The *kīrtan* welcomes everyone," said Simran, "like the voice and mind of the Guru, at the heart of the sacred building." She thought of those hymns, the water carrying the sound waves across the sacred space, like streams from the ocean of the scripture at the heart of the shrine. "Even if people didn't know the script, or couldn't read at all, the singing of its verses would move and touch them."

"That too was thanks to Guru Arjan," pointed out Livtar. "He didn't only build a sacred structure; he compiled a sacred scripture. Sitting with the enlightened scribe, Bhai Gurdas, he organized the verses of the Sikh Gurus, and of Hindu and Muslim *bhagats*—not by topic or author, but by different styles of melody—thirty-one musical *rāgas* in all. That was a clue, I think, that the verses were meant to stir you, and not just fill you with knowledge."

Asisse draped her arm around her brother's shoulders and looked at their sand construction. Those landmarks of their faith, she thought—those sacred places, the traditions, the script and scripture. They were inspired and revealed, but they didn't just appear. They were shaped by the Gurus in their lifetimes and blessed with their seal of approval.

She thought too about the ordinary things we construct as humans, the places or habits we build, the words we think or say. As time goes on, we keep constructing and reconstructing them. What about all the elements of life, like water, like nature, that we can't humanly create? Behind all that non-stop creation are a mind and hands that can never be seen.

Like a shrine in the water, we float in a miracle.

Melodies at Sunset

I am content and fulfilled, savoring the food of Truth,
By meditating on the Name, with my whole body and mind.
And the nourishing wisdom that I taste.[49]

Hearing animated conversation in Punjabi, Livtar stepped into the sitting room. While walking earlier, his parents had met a gentleman named Farid. Together they had joked that wherever you went in the world, you would always bump into a Punjabi. Farid's family were Muslim, and like Santokh's, from East Africa. He remembered joining his school friends to go to the gurudwara Sikhs had built in the town.

---

49. "*Tripat bhei sach bhojan khāia . . .*"—Sri Guru Granth Sahib, *ang* 684.

"The gurudwara," he reflected, switching to English as Asisse walked in "isn't it the *dwār*, the doorway to the Guru? Like the *dargāh*, the heavenly doorway, of Sufi shrines? And like Haridwar, the holy Hindu city, named as a doorway to the Divine?" The others nodded as he made the connections.

"Where there is *sangat*," added Prem, "a gathering where God is remembered, that place becomes holy."

He remembered the jasmine vines under the archway that had greeted them on their arrival, and that brought to mind another jasmine flower. One day, as Guru Nanak reached the gates of Multan, a city famous for its Sufi masters, he was presented with a full bowl of milk—a sign indicating that they had no room for more holy people. In turn, Guru Nanak placed a jasmine petal on the milk's surface as a sign that he was bringing nothing more than wisdom's fragrance. That's what Guru Nanak did, each time he felt the Divine message descending and asked Bhai Mardana to lift his stringed *rabāb* and play.

"Asisse," said Santokh, "call the others for Rehras. Farid Ji, please stay for our evening prayers and *kīrtan*. And, of course, for a meal. Think of it as *langar*."

Farid rested his palm on his heart in thanks.

"I remember my parents explaining how the *langar* was an old Sufi tradition, one that Baba Nanak lifted to new levels to help us see the *noor*, the light of Allah, in all. Hadn't his father sent him to market with some funds to learn how to trade? But he used them to feed a group of hungry *sādhus* along the way. Now, a true *sādhu* is one who has tamed the mind and brought it to a state of peace and wisdom. So, to his very angry father, Guru Nanak explained that those *sādhus* he fed had given him, in turn, a priceless blessing. That was *sachā saudā*, life's true business, an invisible trade that yields unseen inner riches."

"Farid Ji, you remembered that well!" observed Santokh.

"That is how they say the Sikh *langar* started. And then we have *kīrtan*, the musical food for the soul, with nourishing words of the wise," explained Prem.

"Words of the Gurus," added Livtar, "and from the *bhagats*, saintly souls from different faiths and walks of life, like Ravidas and Kabir. All found in the scripture that we bow to as Guru. Like the old Punjabi verses of Sheikh Farid, the great Sufi mystic."

Moving to the sunroom, they discussed the cordial relations between the Gurus and the early Mughals. Times changed after Akbar the Great when Emperor Jehangir arrested Guru Arjan, concerned about the Sikh faith thriving in his empire. Farid had seen the paintings of Guru Arjan's brutal torture. With no malice toward his oppressors, the Guru did not even let his dear friend, a renowned Sufi saint, intercede for his release.

"That's why," Santokh added, "we serve a sweet cooling drink each year—to remember Guru Arjan's steady, sweet acceptance of the Divine will." In the brief silence that followed, Farid too remained quiet. He knew that a family loss was the reason for their visit.

Draping a scarf over her head, Santokh beckoned Simran to begin the evening prayer.

Pain is the awakening cure, and comfort the malady—
When comfort stagnates us, to neglect the Divine…[50]

As the long prayer concluded, Asisse brought out her *dilrubā*, the instrument Sikhs had carried through exile and war, to sing the wisdom that kept them from becoming heartless or hopeless. Pavan stood his two *tablā* drums on their ring-shaped cushions as Asisse lifted up the *dilrubā's* cedarwood neck. That first long sound as the bow pulled the string, it always lifted something in her. She explored the notes of the *rāga*, the melodic style, and began to sing to the cycles of a drumbeat.

Oh birahā—pain of longing, pain of separation—
So many are they, who talk of you.

But when you push the soul to know
Its separation from its Source,
Then, you hold that power to awaken;
Then, birahā, you are king, you are sultān.

50. "*Dukh dārū sukh rog bheiā…*"—Sri Guru Granth Sahib, *ang* 469.

Oh Farid, that body is no more than a cremation ground,
Where the birahā, the pain of the soul, does not arise.[51]

During dinner the conversation drifted to beyond the shores of this life. They all agreed that the Gurus reached out to people of all faiths, with their different visions of an afterlife. In the end, they said, neither our labels, nor calculated moves, can take us closer to the Divine. What counts is the essence of who we become in our lifetime, with the support of infinite grace.

After thanking them for the meal, Farid bid them farewell.

Flames and Embers

Just as a path is found
In the vast wilderness of existence—
In the company of enlightened souls,
One's inner light shines forth.[52]

A flame glowed in the fireside stove. Over the ashes, Daya had piled up and lit small sticks from the tin marked "Kindling." Pavan and Asisse added the larger chopped logs. A fire in the darkness. Flames and sparks, appearing, then disappearing. The mystery of where they came from, and where they went.

In the early days of her grief, watching a flame would steady Santokh as she prayed. She would light a ghee-soaked wick in a *dīvā,* an old earthen lamp. You hardly saw them in the rituals of Sikh life, but those lamps appeared everywhere in the teachings. *"Pour the oil of remembering reality's essence. Light the wick of nām. And keep the inner lamp glowing."*[53] Words that would keep her afloat, in a dark sea of senselessness.

---

51. "*Birahā birahā ākhīai birahā tū sultān . . .*"—Sri Guru Granth Sahib, *ang* 1379.

52. "*Jiou mahā udiān meh mārag pāvai . . .*"—Sri Guru Granth Sahib, *ang* 282.

53. "*Tat tel nām kīā bātī . . .*"—Sri Guru Granth Sahib, *ang* 1350.

"The small twigs burn the fastest," Pavan noted. "That's what Baba Budda Ji said."

"When he met Guru Nanak," added Asisse, "when he was little."

"Yes." Her grandfather watched the flames. "That's what he'd notice, when he saw his mother collect the firewood. "Why do you come each day, a boy so young, to pray and serve here at Kartarpur?" Guru Nanak asked him. Like the small twigs, the boy explained, he feared his life could be short, so he would not waste it, he had to make it count. So, Guru Ji blessed him as 'Baba Budda,' the old, wise elder. He lived a long, long life, right until the time of the sixth Guru."

Jivan, thought Santokh. Like all of us, he didn't know how many days were ahead of him.

They were quiet for a long while. In the amber glow, each of them saw different images playing in the flames—from the history of the Gurus, and the poetry of their teachings.

The peacebuilder Guru Arjan, forgiving his torturers while seated on the hot stove. Next, the sixth Guru, Guru Hargobind. A beacon of hope and solidarity for political prisoners unjustly held inside a deadly, remote fort. With great ingenuity, he met the emperor's condition, to lead all fifty-two local rulers to their freedom. In Amritsar, rows of glittering lamps were lit to welcome the Guru's return, echoing an ancient story of homecoming and triumph over darkness.

More pictures came and went.

Igniting our inner embers—before we turn into shadows and phantoms of our own true self. Burning away all that is shallow and fake for that spark to shine through. Cooling the heat of hatred, even in war, as Bhai Ghanaiya did, by giving water to the wounded, friend or foe.

Daya stoked the fire. Prem saw the vivid scene at the close of their first morning prayer.

Make a space in your mind, a workshop of pure dedication
With patience and perseverance as the goldsmith.
Let wisdom shape the mindset, as the hammer taps the anvil
Let the bellows be your every breath, in total awe of the Divine,
To fuel the furnace of your spiritual discipline and striving.
In the crucible of love, melt and cast the amrit nectar
To forge the wisdom of the sacred word within you,

Like a coin of pure gold, minted in life's true workshop.
This inner work comes to those who are so blessed
Says Nanak, touched by the gaze of Grace, they serenely flourish.[54]

The *suniār*, the goldsmith, that's who we want to be, thought Prem. Without forging a life of truth, we're like counterfeit coins, deceiving ourselves and others, circulating falsehood in the world.[55] And to help transform us, the Guru is like the *pāras*, the fabled philosopher's stone, turning lead into gold. Prem gazed on quietly, watching the sparks.

Kudrat broke the silence. "You know a black lump of coal, Pavan, it's made deep in the underground heat. Nothing in the world can bring it color. Not until the fire embraces it. Then it finds its glow.[56] We are the coal. Lighting up when we touch our Source. That's why we search for the wise, for the Gurus, the saintly ones, who guide us there."

Asisse felt the world was still lost in a Dark Age. With wars raging and forests burning, oceans warming and land turning parched. With species dying, hunger burning, and homelessness rampaging the globe.

Everyone sat with their thoughts. Prem and Santokh, Kudrat and Livtar, Daya and Simran, Assise and Pavan. Vismad had drifted into a deep sleep. The firelight spoke.

The world is ablaze with the flames of selfish vice.
We reach to You, our Creator, to shower it with Your healing grace.
From whichever door, of whichever faith, we approach You,
Save this world from the heat of such destruction.
The True Guru shows the way to peace
by contemplating the message of true wisdom.
Says Nanak, no peace can come without embracing You, our Forgiving Creator.[57]

---

54. "*Jat pāhārā dhīraj suniār . . .*"—Sri Guru Granth Sahib, *ang* 8.

55. "*Sach tā par jānīai jā ridai sachā hoi . . .*"—Sri Guru Granth Sahib, *ang* 468.

56. "Work a piece of coal with soap . . ."—translation from "Parting and Reunion" by Bhai Vir Singh.

57. "*Jagat jalandā rakh lai āpnī kirpā dhār. . .*"—Sri Guru Granth Sahib, *ang* 853.

PART THREE

Morning Twilight

Blessed is the land where You dwell, oh my dear and beloved friend,
I am forever indebted to You, my beloved Guru and friend.[58]

Fresh from his shower, Livtar was in the sunroom. The dark sky was tinged with a luminous glow. It would be dawn soon. He opened the door to the garden and breathed in the cool dewy air. Today, the dust of Jivan's ashes would disappear into the ocean. "Waheguru," he uttered as he exhaled, noticing the birdsong that rose from the trees in the morning twilight.

Amrit velā, he thought, that threshold between night and day, when time felt timeless. *Amrit* and immortal, didn't both mean undying? Yet *amrit* sounded so sweet and alive, like ambrosia, the nectar savored by the immortal gods of ancient India and Greece. How did the Gurus speak of it? As a freshness you could taste, which springs from loving life's Eternal Source. And whatever sublimely transforms one's inner chemistry, is like *amrit* too: an ambrosial pool, an ambrosial hymn, an ambrosial hour.

"Waheguru," Livtar repeated, now comforting his invisible pain. Its ache would squeeze at his heart, then pulse like a lonely star. The Oneness behind all impermanence—that's where he tried to rest his mind. He rested his hand, too, on time's steady arm, telling himself that all things pass. Hadn't poets talked to Time, as a person? Or described Nature nurturing us, and Death visiting us? And we call to the Oneness with words like God, *Kartār*, Creator. As *Akāl*, Timeless, Deathless. Don't we all talk to Someone, in the end?

Combing through his long, washed hair, Livtar gathered his locks into a topknot, tucking into it his small wooden comb. With a length of cotton, he tied a simple turban. Going to get his shawl, he kissed

58. "*Dhan su des jahā tū(n) vasiā . . .*"—Sri Guru Granth Sahib, *ang* 96.

Kudrat and Asisse to wake them. He'd be back soon, for today they'd recite their morning prayers together.

From the clifftop, the huge basin of the sea looked so ethereal, inhaling and exhaling, infinitely. Livtar pictured the rim of a large iron bowl, brimming with *amrit*, the water sanctified for initiation.

He thought back to the tenth Guru, preparing *amrit* to bless the first five legendary disciples. To the water, the Guru's wife had added light airy wafers of sugar. Dissolving them with back-and-forth strokes of a double-edged sword, the Guru infused it with the vibration of five sacred compositions, and blessed it with his benevolent touch and gaze, to stir the depths of kindness, dignity, and courage in every ordinary man and woman.

Sweet. Strong. Sacred. Each drop, thought Livtar, evoked two centuries and more of loving service and sacrifice, from the lifetimes of the ten Gurus. It held the essence of the saintly warrior, ready to defend others, with the heart of a saint and the grit of a solider. Taking that *amrit* elixir, you dedicated your mind, body, and wealth to a Guru-inspired life,[59] enriched through living out the wisdom, to pursuing life's true business, always seeing the bigger horizon as you carried on with the everyday. Your account now open, your focus was committed to spiritual earnings and yields for your journey across this life and beyond it.

Peering down at the lapping waves, Livtar remembered his own initiation, his pledge. Five times he sipped the *amrit* in his cupped hands. Five times he felt its splash in his eyes and hair. Joining the Khalsa, he'd strive to live pure of mind and sovereign in spirit, instead of as ego's captive. *Amrit* was the birth water, from which the Khalsa had risen. He had felt reborn, reset. So too had Kudrat, who sang of it as a gift:

Through Your sweet will, amrit is found,
By your will, we are inspired to drink it.[60]

Livtar pictured Guru Nanak receiving the cup of *amrit nām*, when he was mystically gifted the *mool mantar*. The day Livtar sipped the

---

59. "*Tan man dhan sabh saup Gur kou*..."—Sri Guru Granth Sahib, *ang* 918.

60. "*Tere bhāne vich amrit vasai*..."—Sri Guru Granth Sahib, *ang* 119.

amrit, that same *mool mantar* was gifted to him, along with the *gur-mantar,* the chant of "*Waheguru.*" From then on, those mantras he had grown up with took on a new aura as *Nām*—a chant specially blessed to a disciple, who commits to a spiritual path.

Finding a boulder, Livtar sat down, a small figure in the early morning landscape. From his wrist, he took his *māla*, with its string of metal beads. Pausing on, then pushing back, each silver sphere between his fingers, he quietly chanted. He remembered his brother.

In his mind, before the day ahead of them, he had already released Jivan, painfully, tenderly, peacefully, back to the ocean.

The Cherished Five

By singing, listening,
Enshrining love in your mind,
See suffering shift, and peace come home.[61]

In the conservatory, Kudrat and Asisse spread a sheet on the floor and lit incense. Covering their heads, they brought their *gutkās*, printed collections of sacred compositions, wrapped in fabric. Soon Livtar arrived, then Simran and Daya.

Now, they were five. That special number, thought Kudrat. Like the five rivers, the five beloved of the Khalsa, the five virtues and vices, the five elements and senses. And their five cherished morning prayers. For many Sikhs, those prayers were half-known or half-forgotten.

Kudrat thought of the final parting ahead of them, on the boat they'd take out to sea. Their voices merged, as the *mool mantar* led to the heading of the first prayer, "*Jap.*" Under time's infinite canopy, she pictured them sailing on a quest that quivered in their hearts.

Then came the first question: "*Kiv sachiāra hoī-aī*. . . How can one live truly?"

Questions, she thought. Don't we all base our lives on them? How to be rich and famous, or just survive? How to get a place in heaven,

61. "*Gāvīai sunīai man rakhīai bhāou* . . ."—Sri Guru Granth Sahib, *ang* 2.

or hang on to what we love? But the Guru asked, how to be true, and see past what is fake, what is hollow. "By walking the way of *hukam*," came the answer.[62]

What was *hukam,* that word for a royal command? "God's will," some said. It could sound like the weight of fate, so hard to accept. Kudrat listened on keenly. *Hukam* shapes reality's mysterious flow, with all its joys and sorrows. Nothing is outside it, but we all maneuver with and within it. And when the din of the ego quietens, we discover a "way" for us to be—the *hukam* inscribed within us.

Today, thought Kudrat, she'd simply be there for everyone. Nothing else was in her control.

From verse to verse, she noticed the paradox, of doing and surrendering, of empowering the self, yet bowing to the Power Source. Then came the realms we move through. We follow faithful practice, then start to expand our awareness. And in the realm of humble effort, the mind gets beautifully transformed, to touch the realms of grace and truth. In that sublime state, the mind deludes itself no more. That's how we find true strength and beauty, in the end.[63]

Kudrat beckoned Asisse to lead the second prayer, Jaap Sahib. From the spectacular scenery of the mountains, the tenth Guru had composed it when he too was not yet twenty. A young leader, guiding all to stay resilient. Asisse was always drawn to its steady incantation, like hoofbeats galloping forwards, cascades of praise, bowing with words like "*Namo*" before the Divine without mark or colour, shape or form.

And yet, she contemplated, the whole body of scripture was, for them, a form of the Divine. The tenth Guru had given Sikhs the command, to lovingly follow and obey it, as Guru for all time. She glimpsed at her parents. To obey the Guru, they had also committed to the Guru's path, through the *amrit* initiation. For the first time, she felt the path calling her also.

---

62. "*Kiv sachiārā hoī-ai kiv kurhai tuttai pāl...*"—Sri Guru Granth Sahib, *ang* 1.

63. "*Nā oh mareh na tthāge jāeh*"—Sri Guru Granth Sahib, *ang* 8.

They had now reached halfway, "*Gobinde, mukande, udare, apare. . . .*"

Preserver, Liberator. Benevolent, Boundless.[64]

What an out-of-the-box experience of the Divine, thought Asisse. Its words cut across faiths and broke past all borders and frontiers. "*Sadā ang sangay*"—she loved that closing line. That same awesome Divinity was always part of us too.[65] Today she would return her departed uncle to something vast and magnificent.

Next came the ten stanzas, the Svaiye, of the tenth Guru. Observing people's empty searches for power, in the panorama of humanity, they'd always struck a chord with Daya. Kings amassing armies and riches. Warriors seeking the strength of mountains. Sages pursuing silence or self-denial. People lost in shallow rituals. "*Listen well, everyone,*" he heard the words say:

Only the practitioners of prem, of love,
can truly find the way to the Beloved.[66]

Today's ritual with the ashes, he had bound it tightly with grief. Maybe love was his clue. To expand in love, by expanding his vision, and embracing his pain within it.

Livtar now led Benti Chaupai, a humble plea for strength and protection. It had carried Sikhs through the darkest times of tyranny and persecution.

Finally, came Anand Sahib, that melodious celebration, taking us back to the home of the self, with the sublime awakening of our mind, our body, our senses. "*Oh my mother, I am in bliss. . . .*"[67] How it honored the human bonds that sow the seeds of love within us. Simran thought of the unborn listener inside her, and of someone, maybe, listening on in spirit.

---

64. "*Gobinde, mukande, udāre, apāre . . .*"—Sri Dasam Granth, panna 6.

65. "*Sadā ang sang-e abhangan bibhūte . . .*"—Sri Dasam Granth, panna 10.

66. "*Sāch kahou(n) sun lehu sabhai, jin prem kīo tin hī prabh pāio . . .*"—Sri Dasam Granth, panna 15.

67. "*Anand bheiā merī māe satguru mai pāeiā . . .*"—Sri Guru Granth Sahib, *ang* 917.

They wrapped their *gutkās*, then stood for the *ardās* prayer—offering, for a soul's onward journey, the fruit of their contemplation.

In the end, what is my deepest desire?
Not to seek dominance in this world, nor liberation in the hereafter,
But for the mind to rest lovingly at Your fragrant lotus feet.[68]

The Sky-Blue Crown

"Here's what we promised, Pavan."

Simran held out the fabric of Jivan's *dastār.* That sky-blue turban was his favorite. She could see him now, eyes smiling warmly, yet with a faraway look. And eyebrows that spoke plainly, with a soft touch of humor. What fun they both had as kids, running under their dad's long turban fabric as their parents held each corner to stretch and fold it.

"How do I tie it?" replied Pavan.

"That's what I'm here for," said Daya, unravelling the material as Pavan stood before the mirror. Placing one end diagonally across Pavan's forehead, his uncle began the neat rotation, stopping to check the angles and adjust the cloth. Pavan felt a snugness over his head as he watched the fabric spiraling into formation.

"There's your crown!" said Simran.

Santokh remembered saying those same words, as she would comb through Jivan's long hair, until he learned to tend his locks and crown them himself.

"But a crown is pointy, and made of gold," insisted Vismad, "with jewels stuck on!"

"You can make a crown out of daisies," remarked Asisse, walking in. "Let's do your hair." Asisse lifted a comb, ready to transform Vismad's pony into a braided bun.

"Well, your mind is a jewel. So the turban crowns it!" said Simran. "You know, around the world, in many places, a turban *was* a

68. "*Rāj na chāhou mukat na chāhou man prīt charan kamalāre...*"—Sri Guru Granth Sahib, *ang* 534.

crown, worn by wise prophets, by scholars and nobles, kings and queens. Some of our Sikh sisters wear one too."

"It reminds us to be good rulers," said Santokh. "It makes you think, what crowning qualities should reign inside us? Jivan said that by tying the turban, we should wrap our minds with our best thoughts, our best values, for each day."

"Raveled into the *dastār*" added Prem, "I see the long story of how Sikhī was formed, over the lives of the ten Gurus, and how they transformed Sikhs into saintly warriors."

"When Guru Hargobind wore the two swords of *mīrī* and *pīrī*?" asked Simran.

"Yes, when he became the sixth Guru. And what did that mean," asked her father.

"That we need good leadership, led by virtue and wisdom, so that any power we use comes from a place of oneness and loving devotion. So instead of seeing masters and slaves, friends and enemies, we seek a more equal and peaceful world, where everyone feels honored and connected, and where nature is respected and protected."

Listening on, Asisse pictured their martial emblem, the *khandā*. The circle of Oneness crossed and flanked by noble swords, that spoke of the power to uphold goodness, to feed and protect. Her mind flitted to that famous slogan she had studied at school, "Liberty, Equality, Fraternity." Now those same words echoed in her mind in a different, deeper way.

Santokh then spoke with quiet passion. "For that kind of world, Simran, you need to be lionhearted. To have vision, courage and commitment. To protect goodness, like a fence protects an orchard. When rulers became hostile, the Gurus built forts. They trained armies to defend. Each morning they sang *Āsā Kī Vār*, the heroic ballad about conquering the worst in us and magnifying the best." She remembered the opening lines:

A hundred times a day, I'm filled with indebtedness to my Guru
Who transforms ordinary humans into Divine beings, without delay.[69]

---

69. "*Balihāri gur āpne diouhārhī sad vār, jin mānas te devte kīe*..."—Sri Guru Granth Sahib, *ang* 462.

"What else did the Gurus do?" asked Pavan.

"The seventh Guru," continued Simran, "made medical clinics, gardens, and sanctuaries, to care for people, plants, and animals. Our eighth Guru was the child Guru. In his short life, he showed that wisdom does not always depend on age. And the ninth Guru became a famous peacebuilder, then gave his life so all people could follow their faith without fear of oppression or forced conversion. He taught Sikhs to protect our diverse world, by seeing all faiths as a family. You know what happened to him."

"The emperor had Guru Ji beheaded," said Asisse, "and his disciples cruelly tortured."

"Yes," affirmed Santokh, "he gave his head, but not his conviction. But too many people still lived in fear. Then, the tenth Guru invited Sikhs from far and wide to a gathering, and asked the astonished crowd, 'Who will step up to give their head?' The five who answered the call came from different castes and regions. Passing that test of faith, they gave up their old egos and were brought back to life—to live it more truly, boldly, honorably and humbly. All five appeared before everyone, reborn and adorned with turbans like the Guru."

"And with the *Panj Kakkār*," joined in Vismad. "The Five Ks."

"Ah, yes," said Santokh, "the Guru's five gifts for wise leadership. What were they?" On her fingers, she counted them. "The steel *karā* on our wrist. Our long uncut hair, our *kes*, that we comb with the wooden *kanghā*. The *kachhehrā*, the cotton undershorts that we can tie securely to cover us. And lastly? The *kirpān*, the noble sword. *Kirpā* and *ān*. Loving grace and dignity. That special sash for it crosses our heart."

Santokh paused. "Those five gifts speak to our heads, hearts, and hands. They help us to live with dignity, boldly but not recklessly, as part of nature, as members of society and sparks of God. To be responsible and wise. And to live up to the royal names of Singh and Kaur, as if we've all been given an invisible crown."

Santokh looked at her grandchildren. The tenth Guru had lost his four children and both parents to the Mughals. Yet he moved forward, seeing the Khalsa—and all of humanity—as his family. After him, Mata Sundari, his widow, led the Khalsa for forty years, over brutal decades of persecution. Santokh remembered so many mothers, wives and grandmothers who faced the slaughter of children, the torture of loved ones, then rose to lead others.

With these reflections, Santokh found her strength, gazing at that sky-blue turban she knew so well.

Crossing the Waters

The boat engine murmured through the waves. With an arm over Pavan's shoulder, Livtar watched from the stern, as they passed the cliffs and caves, then viewed the mountains, still shrouded in light cloud. On the deck, Vismad sat between her parents, a basket of rose-orange petals on her lap. Opposite her sat Santokh and Prem, who held the wooden box. To Vismad, they were simply Nani and Nana—her mother's mum and dad.

"Nana Ji will pour out the ashes," Simran explained to Vismad, "so they move with the breeze into the water. Then you can sprinkle on the petals with Nani Ji."

Asisse looked across at her grandparents, at their quiet strength. "Those elements that made Jivan," said Kudrat, sitting by her, "they're returning to their source."

"Earth, water, fire, air…" Asisse searched in her mind for the fifth one.

"*Akāsh*,' said Kudrat. "Some say it's space, or ether. But miraculously, it turns the other four elements into a living being. What could you call it? Spirit. Presence. Spark."

Kudrat gazed at the sea's expanse. Wasn't there an Awareness that always existed, long before we became aware? And a presence that looks out of our eyes, then moves on, when they close for the last time? Here they were now, before water—that liquid state, between solid and gas, like a threshold, between matter and spirit, this place for their final goodbye.

"Let's begin," said Livtar. He led the bedtime prayer, a reminder of life's close, ever-present on the horizon. Asisse heard her own name in the soul's call to its earthly companions: "*Give me, my dear friends, your sweet blessings, that I may merge with the Source of all.*"[70]

---

70. "*Dehu sajan asīsarhīā jiou hovai sāhib siou mel…*"—Sri Guru Granth Sahib, *ang* 12.

Soon came the last verse:

With each passing night and day, our time here is diminishing.
Oh my mind, meet the Guru, to fulfil life's purpose.
So lost, the world becomes, in deception and delusion,
Those knowers of life's True Origin, they cross the ocean safely.
Those who are awakened, who sip the sublime nectar
They know the untellable story…[71]

The boat rocked in the waves. Beneath its sturdy frame, the immense sea was ever-moving. Santokh and Prem remembered past struggles, rocked by events beyond their control, or the currents of their own weaknesses. The same verse would always come to their minds:

As the ocean brims to the full with water,
So is my mind filled with flaws and failings.
I reach out for Your compassion, Your mercy,
Please lift me, this sinking stone,
And help me cross life's waters.[72]

Santokh re-lived the moment, when the ground beneath her turned to liquid and she was lost at sea. Waheguru—that sound became her lifeboat. It resounded with a history that moored her; that showed her suffering could be overcome. It returned to her in the words of the *ardās* prayer, bringing her a rising breath of courage. "…*Sarbat dā bhallā,*" she thought. No matter the suffering, may we always strive to serve the well-being of all. She moved a little closer to that horizon—to a place of peace that knows all its wounds.

Then dust blended with water. Flower petals floated, like final companions, across the waves, and out into the blue.

Kissing his daughter, Daya felt his own mountain of grief was slowly transforming. Vismad got up to sit with her cousins, by the instruments they had laid on a mat on the deck. Asisse lifted her bow, as melody and rhythm began to intertwine.

71. "*Audh ghattai dinas rai-nāre, man gur mil kāj savāre…*"—Sri Guru Granth Sahib, *ang* 13.

72. "*Jeta samund sāgar nīr bhariā tete augun hamāre…*—Sri Guru Granth Sahib, *ang* 156.

Just as sunrays merge with the sun,
And water blends with water,
So too does light blend with Light,
And therein finds its completeness.[73]

Under the dome of the sky, they all felt the sea and the breeze were listening.

The Ever-Present Portal

The message is the Guru,
And the Guru is the message,
Suffused with the amrit nectar.
When the Guru's words are truly embraced,
The Guru becomes manifest and liberates the disciple.[74]

"We all come and go, with our baggage." said Livtar, as they loaded the car to leave.

"You mean invisible baggage?" said Asisse, guessing what he meant.

"Yes, what we carry but can't see. Marks left by the pushes of our ego, and the patterns they create. They all leave their weight."

"Who does the carrying?" asked Asisse. The invisible mind, she supposed.

"It's the *ātmā*, the spirit, that continues its journey." Kudrat added a last bag as she closed the boot. She remembered a statue, with butterfly wings, of the Greek goddess Psyche. It had felt like a clue, that life holds the promise of our own metamorphosis, before the *ātmā* takes flight and moves on.

"Isn't the *ātmā*, part of *Param-ātmā*, of God?" Asisse wondered how that pure spark could be dulled or weighed down.

---

73. "*Sūraj kiran mile jal kā jal hūā Rām...*"—Sri Guru Granth Sahib, *ang* 846.

74. "*Bānī Gurū Gurū hai bānī vich bānī amrit sāre...*"—Sri Guru Granth Sahib, *ang* 982.

"It is," said Livtar. "But it gets wrapped in layers. We grow stagnant, gather moss, get stuck in the cave of our anger and fears, our pain, our selfishness. But we can work through and dissolve those layers. Just as the Gurus taught. Through waves of Divine remembrance, gestures of service, and touches of grace."

To Asisse, that word "grace" had sometimes sounded like grown-up make-believe. But here, in this place, she felt that behind life was an unseen hand, a knowing face, and feet you were drawn to bow at. Inside, the others stood ready to give a final thanks, for the shelter of the house; for the open space by the coast; for the *samā*, the time given to them.

Asisse bolted the wooden gate under the vine and joined her grandparents in the car. Prem remembered their arrival, those three questions, in the breeze up on the clifftop. Santokh remained quiet. As the car wheels turned, she remembered hearing them too.

On the drive closer to home, they decided to stop at a *gurudwārā*.

"It's like a palace," exclaimed Vismad, noticing the dome and turrets.

"It's like a school," explained Simran, "where the Guru is our teacher."

"It's the Guru's home, the Guru's sanctuary," thought Asisse, seeing the familiar *khandā* emblem on the flagpole.

With heads covered, they removed their shoes and washed their hands, then entered the *darbār*. There, the Guru held court, like a sovereign—the scripture enthroned under a canopy and wrapped in beautiful fabrics, like royal robes.

Those words of honor for their sacred text arose in Prem's mind:

The living light of eternal wisdom,
The ever-present, luminous revelation.
The boat across the age of darkness,
The ship of the Divine Name.
Our support in every circumstance,
In this world and the next.
The sovereign of sovereigns.[75]

In this homely, majestic court, he felt at peace.

---

75. "*Jāgdī jot, hāzarā hazūr, jāharā jahūr, kaljug ke bohit . . .*"—element of Sikh *ardās* prayer.

As they all lined up to pay their respects, the air rang with familiar couplets, as a reading of the entire scripture came to a close:

Says Nanak, listen oh mind, a person who finds peace and poise
Beyond the sways of pleasure and pain, or pulls of greed and pride.
Such a human being becomes the very image of the Infinite.[76]

Those were the words, thought Prem, of the ninth Guru, as he faced death by an emperor's command.

Know that this life is like a dream, a wall of sand.
Unreal, without the presence of the One, who is always Real.[77]

Prem felt transported again, to life's outermost coast, with its view on to the mystery that made us, that touches us with its waves and tides.

Vismad placed her golden coin in the box, playing her part to feed all who visited. Around her was the familiar expanse of white sheets. Following Asisse to sit on the floor, she cupped her hands in anticipation. There it came, the hand-scoop of golden, velvety *parshād*, the sweet, warm mixture that signaled the Guru's hospitality and blessing, equally to all.

"Gur-prasād," murmured Asisse, thinking of that word in the Mool Mantar. Then it dawned on her. The Guru's wisdom—*that* was the Guru's sweet blessing: a gift from the Light of life, that we are joyously given, that leaves us with clues, signs, and portals to discover its radiance. She was ready for that blessing of *amrit*. She closed her eyes and heard the scripture's final message:

"Says Nanak, blessed with Nām, may I learn to truly live,
Like the greenery of our world, may body and mind come to flourish."[78]

---

76. "*Sukh dukh jeh parsai nahī lobh moh abhimān . . .*"—Sri Guru Granth Sahib, *ang* 1427.

77. "*Kahu Nānak thir nā rahai, jiou bālū kī bhīt . . .*"—Sri Guru Granth Sahib, *ang* 1429.

78. *"Nanak nām milai tā(n) jīvā(n) tan man thīvai hariā"*—Sri Guru Granth Sahib, *ang* 1429.

EPILOGUE

"Before the awesome Giver of all, nothing is really mine to give.
So, what could I offer - to glimpse that sublime court, the Sovereign's realm?

If all I have to give is love, then what could I even say,
To evoke the Beloved's love and feel connected?

In the ambrosial hours, awaken your awareness to Nām,
Attune to that eternal, all-sustaining resonance.
Contemplate the vibrant greatness of the Infinite."[79]

79. *"Pher ki agai rakhīai jit disai darbār…"*—Sri Guru Granth Sahib, *ang* 2.

ACKNOWLEDGMENTS

On behalf of the Fetzer Institute, Dr. William Vendley, director of the project that produced this book, gratefully acknowledges all the people who contributed to its production.

The Modern Legacy

The human family has lived with ever more rapid and tumultuous change for the last four centuries. Notwithstanding lamentable religious intolerance, colonialism, and violent political upheavals, this has also been a time of ever-expanding religious encounters, dialogs, friendships, and concrete collaborations. For the last couple of centuries, there has been an ever-quickening pace of penetrating historical studies on humanity's sacred stories, symbols, and traditions. Efforts to discern resonances and complementarities across sacred traditions can be found in the work of scholars coming from all traditions, scholars such as Martin Buber, Karl Jaspers, Mircea Eliade, C. G. Jung, Swami Vivekananda, Hossein Nasr, Nishida Kitaro, John Samuel Mbiti, Huston Smith, Tu Weiming, R. C. Zaehner, Eric Voegelin, Hans Küng, Ines M. Talamantez, and many others.

Meanwhile, beginning a little over one hundred years ago, quantum physicists began challenging the reductive materialistic interpretation of science, opening the door to efforts to discern the complementarity of the sacred and scientific modes of inquiry. The present volume is an heir to this rich history, building on and gratefully acknowledging it.

Precursory Studies Related to Science and the Sacred

Three studies related to science were undertaken, including on (1) science and religion focusing on the complementarity of the scientific and spiritual ways of knowing, (2) the rich hemisphere theory linked to the bipartite structure of the brain and its dual modes of attention that can ground in the human brain an exceptionally fertile hypothesis on the complementarity of the scientific and religious modes of understanding, and (3) social science on the impact of Love on human flourishing. These three studies provided essential background for the authors of the stories in this book, especially "Journeys to the Sacred: A Telling of a Shared Sacred Story."

The Science and Religion Work Group

Dr. David Bentley Hart, Senior Research Scholar at the University of Notre Dame, expert in world religions, philosophy of science, consciousness, and a celebrated and highly prolific professional writer

Dr. Iain McGilchrist, Quondam Fellow of All Souls College, University of Oxford, brain researcher, physician, distinguished author, and leading proponent of the two-hemisphere hypothesis

Dr. Celia Deane-Drummond, Director of the *Laudato Si'* Research Institute and Senior Research Fellow in Theology at Camion Hall, University of Oxford; former co-editor of the *International Journal of Philosophy, Theology, and Science*

Dr. Philip Goyal, Associate Professor of Theoretical Physics at the University at Albany (State University of New York), postdoctoral fellow at Perimeter Institute for Theoretical Physics

Dr. Pui Him Ip, Director of Tutorial Programmes at the Faraday Institute for Science and Religion, University of Cambridge

Dr. Nicholas Spencer, Senior Fellow at Theos (part of the British and Foreign Bible Society), Fellow of the International Society for Science and Religion, and celebrated author

The Dual Hemisphere Hypothesis

Dr. Iain McGilchrist, Quondam Fellow of All Souls College, University of Oxford, brain researcher, physician, distinguished author, and leading proponent of the two-hemisphere hypothesis related to the complementarity of two modes of attention exemplified by the scientific and spiritual modes of knowing

A Survey of Social Science and Sacred Flourishing[1]

Dr. Matt Lee, Professor of the Social Sciences and Humanities at the Institute for Studies of Religion at Baylor University and Director of the Human Flourishing Program's Flourishing Network at the Institute for Quantitative Social Science at Harvard University

The Stories

The remarkable scholars gathered in the project are gratefully acknowledged as the authors of the eight Retold Sacred Stories, the Interspiritual Story, and the Shared Sacred Story. They brought their sincere religious convictions, spiritual practices, acute scholarship, creativity, and relational hearts to their work. The scholars are listed below, arranged by authorship of the stories, beginning with the Shared Sacred Story and proceeding through the other stories alphabetically. Also listed are the literary consultants and scholar reviewers of the stories. Their work is warmly acknowledged.

1. See "Love and Human Flourishing: A Converging Synthetic Evidentiary Summary and Directions for Strategic Growth," published by Fetzer and available at www.Fetzer.org.

Journeys to the Sacred: A Telling of a Shared Sacred Story

The Authors

Dr. David Bentley Hart, Senior Research Scholar, University of Notre Dame, professional writer, and producer of the first draft

Dr. Judith Simmer-Brown, Professor Emerita of Contemplative and Religious Studies, Naropa University, Boulder, Colorado

Dr. Anantanand Rambachan, Emeritus Professor of Religion, Saint Olaf College, Northfield, Minnesota

Dr. Anna Sun, Associate Professor of Religious Studies and Sociology, Duke University

Dr. William Vendley, Fetzer Vice President for World Religions and Spirituality

Contributing Authors

Dr. Ruben Habito, Professor Emeritus of World Religions and Spirituality, Perkins School of Theology, Southern Methodist University

Dr. Mark Unno, Department Head of Religious Studies and Professor of Buddhist Studies, University of Oregon

Dr. R. Trent Pomplun, Associate Professor of Theology, University of Notre Dame

Dr. Ruben Rosario Rodriguez, Clarence Louis and Helen Steber Professor of Theological Studies and Director, Master's Programs, Department of Theological Studies, Saint Louis University

Dr. Jessica Joustra, Associate Professor of Religion and Theology, Redeemer University, Ancaster, Ontario

President Hamza Yusuf, President Zaytuna College, Berkeley, California

Dr. Laura Dunn, Managing Editor, Center for Biographical Research, University of Hawaiʻi Mānoa

Dr. Linda Hogan (Chickasaw), award-winning author and poet, Professor Emerita, University of Colorado

Dr. Melissa K. Nelson (Turtle Mountain Anishinaabe), scholar-activist, Professor of Indigenous Sustainability, Arizona State University, Professor Emerita of American Indian Studies, San Francisco State University

Dr. Rory McEntee, Co-president and Executive Director of the Charis Foundation for New Monasticism & Interspirituality

Pir Netanel Miles-Yepez, Co-president of the Charis Foundation for New Monasticism & Interspirituality and Chair of the Department of Wisdom Traditions and the Program in Religious Studies, Naropa University, Boulder, Colorado

Dr. Mohammed Elsanousi, Executive Director of the Network for Religious and Traditional Peacemakers

Zain bin Bayyah, Doctoral Student in Islamic Theology, University of Cambridge

Rabbi David Rosen, KSG, CBE, Special Advisor, Interfaith and Jewish Affairs, Abrahamic Family House, Abu Dhabi; former International Director of Interreligious Affairs, the American Jewish Committee; and former Chief Rabbi of Ireland

Dr. Gopinder Kaur Sagoo, Author and Interdisciplinary Researcher

Munpreet Kaur, Media and Communications Professional

Literary advisors

Maria Mutch

Salley Vickers

Kisa Gotami: A Retelling of the Buddhist Sacred Story

The Authors

Co–Team Leader, Dr. Ruben Habito, Professor Emeritus of World Religions and Spirituality, Perkins School of Theology, Southern Methodist University

Co–Team Leader, Dr. Judith Simmer-Brown, Professor Emerita of Contemplative and Religious Studies, Naropa University, Boulder, Colorado

Co–Team Leader, Dr. Mark Unno, Department Head of Religious Studies and Professor of Buddhist Studies, University of Oregon, Eugene, Oregon

Senior Advisor, Dr. Pamela Yetunde, Pastoral Counselor, Author, Chicago, Illinois

Senior Advisor, Dr. Sarah Shaw, Senior Advisor Fellow of the Oxford Centre for Buddhist Studies and Member of the Faculty of Asian and Middle Eastern Studies, University of Oxford, Oxford, United Kingdom

Literary Advisor

Laura Simms, New York, New York

Scholar Reviewers

Dr. Rima Vesely-Flad, Visiting Professor of Buddhism and Black Studies, Union Theological Seminary, New York, New York

Dr. Zenju Earthlyn Manuel, Soto Zen Priest, Author, Still Breathing Zen Sangha, New Mexico

Ven. Dhammananda Bhikkhuni (Chatsumarn Kabilsingh), Abbess, Songdhammakalyani Monastery, Nakhonpathom, Thailand

Dr. David Loy, Professor, Author, and Sanbo Zen teacher, Rocky Mountain Ecodharma Retreat Center, Colorado

Rev. Lynda Caine-Barrett (Myokei), Bishop of the Nichiren Shu Order of North America, and Guiding Teacher of the Texas Myoken-ji Temple, Houston, Texas

Dr. Carolyn Jones Medine, Professor of Religion and Director of the Institute of African American Studies, University of Georgia, Athens, Georgia, and President, Society of Buddhist-Christian Studies

Dr. Roger Jackson, John W. Nason Professor Emeritus of Asian Studies and Religion, Carleton College, Northfield, Minnesota

Dr. Pyi Phyo Kyaw, Senior Lecturer in Theravada Studies, Shan State Buddhist University, Taunggyi, Myanmar

Ven. Dr. Yifa, Taiwanese Buddhist Nun, Scholar, Asia Center, Harvard University, Cambridge, Massachusetts

Dr. Kenneth K. Tanaka, Professor Emeritus, Musashino University, Tokyo

Dr. Vanessa Sasson, Professor of Religious Studies in the Liberal Arts Department, Marianopolis College, Westmount, Quebec

Ven. Thupten Chodron, Founder and Abbess, Sravasti Abbey, Newport, Washington

Dr. Jimmy Yu, Associate Professor of Chinese Buddhism, Department of Religion, Florida State University, Tallahassee, Florida

Dialogue in a Desert Place: A Retelling of the Christian Sacred Story

The Authors

Co–Team Leader, Dr. David Bentley Hart, Senior Research Scholar, University of Notre Dame, and professional writer

Co–Team Leader, Dr. R. Trent Pomplun, Associate Professor of Theology, University of Notre Dame

Dr. Ruben Rosario Rodriguez, Clarence Louis and Helen Steber Professor of Theological Studies, and Director, Master's Programs, Department of Theological Studies, Saint Louis University

Dr. Jessica Joustra, Associate Professor of Religion and Theology, Redeemer University, Hamilton, Ontario

Research Consultant

Alfred Turnipseed

Literary Advisor

Maria Mutch

Scholar Reviewers

Dr. Alasdair John Milbank, Emeritus Professor, Department of Theology and Religious Studies, University of Nottingham

Dr. John Renner Betz, Associate Professor of Systematic Theology, University of Notre Dame

Dr. Bruce Lindley McCormack, Chair in Modern Theology, University of Aberdeen, and Charles Hodge Professor Emeritus of Systematic Theology at Princeton Theological Seminary

Dr. Judith Wolfe, Professor of Philosophical Theology, School of Divinity, St. Mary's College, University of St. Andrews

Dr. Grant Kaplan, Professor of Historical and Systematic Theology, Saint Louis University

Dr. Susan Miller, Associate Teaching Professor, Rutgers University, New Brunswick, New Jersey

Rev. Dr. Robert Imbelli, Associate Professor Emeritus of Theology, Boston College

Dr. Emmanuel Katangole, Professor of Theology and Peace Studies, University of Notre Dame

Dr. Grace Ji-Sun Kim, Professor of Theology at Earlham School of Religion, Richmond, Indiana

Dr. Amos Yong, Professor of Theology and Mission, Fuller Theological Seminary, Pasadena, California

Dr. Fellipe Do Vale, Department Chair and Assistant Professor of Biblical and Systematic Theology, Trinity Evangelical Divinity School, Deerfield, Illinois

Dr. Natalia Marandiuc, Associate Professor of Systematic Theology at United Lutheran Seminary, Philadelphia, Pennsylvania

Dr. Agnes Chiu, Director of Research and Strategic Initiatives, Director of the Center for Public Theology, and Assistant Professor of Systematic Theology and Christian Ethics, China Evangelical Seminary North America, West Covina, California

Dr. Vince Bacote, Professor of Theology and Director of the Center for Applied Christian Ethics, Wheaton College, Wheaton, Illinois

When the Fire Came: A Retelling of the Confucian Sacred Story

The Authors

Team Leader, Dr. Anna Sun, Associate Professor of Religious Studies and Sociology, Duke University

Senior Advisor, Dr. Pauline Lee, Associate Professor of Theological Studies, Saint Louis University

Senior Advisor, Dr. Bin Song, Associate Professor of Philosophy and Religion, Washington College, Chestertown, Maryland

Literary Advisors

Maria Mutch

Lindsay Hawdon

Scholar Reviewers

Dr. Stephen Angle, Professor of Philosophy, Wesleyan University

Dr. Sebastian Billioud, Professor of East Asian Studies, Université de Paris, France

Dr. Erin Cline, Professor of Theology and Religious Studies, Georgetown University

Dr. Owen Flanagan, Distinguished Professor Emeritus of Philosophy, Duke University

Dr. P. J. Ivanhoe, Professor of East Asian Languages and Cultures, Georgetown University

Dr. Anne Behnke Kinney, Professor of Chinese, University of Virginia

Dr. On-Cho Ng, Professor of History, Asian Studies, and Philosophy, Penn State University

Dr. Bryan van Norden, James Monroe Taylor Professor of Philosophy, Vassar College

Dr. Ann Pang-White, Professor of Philosophy, University of Scranton

Dr. Guoxiang Peng, Distinguished Professor of Chinese Philosophy, Intellectual History, and Religion, Zhejiang University, China

Dr. Sor Hoon Tan, Professor of Philosophy, Singapore Management University

Dr. Frederic Wang, Professor of Chinese Intellectual History, Institut National des Langues et Civilisations Orientales, Paris, France

Maitreyi's Quest: A Retelling of the Hindu Sacred Story

The Authors

Team Leader, Dr. Anantanand Rambachan, Emeritus Professor of Religion, Saint Olaf College, Northfield, Minnesota

Dr. Laura Dunn, Managing Editor, Center for Biographical Research, University of Hawaiʻi Mānoa.

Contributing Authors

Dr. Rita Sherma, Founding Director and Associate Professor, GTU (Graduate Theological Union) Shingal Center for Dharma Studies, Berkeley, California

Dr. Ravi Gupta, Charles Redd Endowed Professor of Religious Studies, Utah State University

Dr. Christopher Fici, Educator and researcher working in K–12, higher ed, and digital learning spaces, focusing on practices of social justice and climate justice

Dr. Jeffery Long, Carl W. Zeigler Professor of Religion, Philosophy, and Asian Studies, School of Arts and Humanities, Elizabethtown College, Elizabethtown, Pennsylvania

Literary Advisor

Maria Mutch

Scholar Reviewers

Swami Medhananda, Senior Research Fellow at Vedanta Society of Southern California and Hindu Chaplain at UCLA/USC

Dr. Kenneth R. Valpey, Research Fellow of the Oxford Centre for Hindu Studies, Oxford, United Kingdom

Dr. Neela Saxsena, Professor of English and Women's Studies at Nassau Community College, Garden City, New York

Dr. Prea Persaud Khanna, Visiting Instructor of Peace, Justice and Human Rights, Haverford College, Haverford, Pennsylvania

Dr. Debashish Banerji, Haridas Chaudhuri Endowed Chair for Indian Philosophies and Culture and Doshi Professor of Asian Art, California Institute of Integral Studies, San Francisco, California

Dr. Neil Dalal, Director of Religious Studies, University of Alberta

Dr. A. Raghuramaraju, Professor, Department of Humanities and Social Sciences, Indian Institute of Technology, Tirupati

Pravrajika Vrajaprana, female monk at the Vedanta Society of Southern California

Kindred Spirits: A Retelling of Indigenous Sacred Stories

The Author

Dr. Linda Hogan (Chickasaw), award-winning author and poet, Professor Emerita, University of Colorado

Contributing Authors

Dr. Melissa K. Nelson (Turtle Mountain Anishinaabe), scholar-activist, Professor of Indigenous Sustainability, Arizona State University, Professor Emerita of American Indian Studies, San Francisco State University

Grandfather Chief Dominique Rankin, Hereditary Chief from the Algonquin First Nation

Grandmother Marie-Josée Rankin-Tardif, Elder of the Algonquin First Nation, President of Kina8at Together

Overall Coordinators

Dr. Melissa K. Nelson, Team Leader and Lead Editor

Taina Diaz-Reyes, M.Div. (Taino/Huichol/Maya), Ph.D. student, School of Sustainability, Arizona State University

Jaune Evans, Indigenous Creative Researcher, Soto Zen Priest, Indigenous advocate, Heart of Compassion Sangha

Scholar Reviewers

James Sa'ke'j Youngblood Henderson, J.D. (Chickasaw), Royal Society of Canada

Rowen White (Mohawk), writer, farmer, seed keeper, Founder and Creative Director of Sierra Seeds

Season of Remembrance: A Telling of the Interspiritual Sacred Story

The Authors

Co–Team Leader, Dr. Rory D. McEntee, Co-president and Executive Director of the Charis Foundation for New Monasticism & Interspirituality

Co–Team Leader, Pir Netanel Miles-Yepez, Co-president of the Charis Foundation for New Monasticism & Interspirituality and Chair of the Department of Wisdom Traditions and the Program in Religious Studies, Naropa University, Boulder, Colorado

Contributing Authors

Alejandra Warden, Author and teacher

Brenda Salgado, Nepantla Consulting and Program Director, Racial Healing Initiative

Rev. Matthew Wright, Pastor St. Gregory's Episcopal Church, Woodstock, New York

Literary Advisor

Maria Mutch

Scholar Reviewers

Dr. Ann Holmes Redding, Teacher, spiritual guide, scholar-practitioner, consultant, writer, and singer

Fr. David Denny, Executive Co-director, The Desert Foundation, Tucson, Arizona

Dr. Edward W. Bastian, President, Spiritual Paths Institute

Rev. Dr. Kurt Johnson, PhD, Evolutionary Biology, and ordained Interfaith Minister

Chris Maddox, Founder, Wild Woman Project and Wild Woman Fest

Dr. Will Keepin, PhD, Founding Director, Gender Equity and Reconciliation International, Satyana Institute

Dr. Ruben Habito, Professor Emeritus of World Religions and Spirituality, Perkins School of Theology, Southern Methodist University

Mirabai Starr, Award-winning author of creative non-fiction and contemporary translations of sacred literature

The authors would also like to thank Duncan Anderson, Maka Black Elk, Rabbi Tirzah Firestone, Alicia Forde, Venerable Pannavati Bhikkuni, Cooper Sims-West, and Bin Song for feedback on early drafts of the story.

Surrendering to the Merciful Will of God: A Retelling of the Sacred Story of Islam

Honorary Chair

His Eminence Mustafa Ceric, Grand Mufti Emeritus of Bosnia-Herzegovina

Team Leader

Dr. Mohammed Elsanousi, Executive Director of the Network for Religious and Traditional Peacemakers

The Co-authors

President Hamza Yusuf, President Zaytuna College, Berkeley, California

Dr. Mohammed Al-Samak, Secretary General of the Islamic Christian National Dialogue Committee, Lebanon

Dr. Amany Lubis, Former Rector of Hidayatullah State Islamic University, Jakarta, Indonesia

Imam Muhammed Nuruddeen Lemu, Director of Research and Training, Islamic Education Trust, Nigeria

Zain bin Bayyah, Researcher in Theology, University of Cambridge

Haleema Oladamade Ahmad, Senior Research Fellow and Chief Editor, Da'wah Institute, Nigeria

Dr. Asad Tarsin, Emergency Medical Doctor and Islamic scholar

Krista Bremer, Writer and Editor, Zaytuna College, Berkeley, California

Chief Writer

Krista Bremer, Writer and Editor, Zaytuna College

Literary Consultant

Safir Ahmed, Director of Publications, Zaytuna College, Berkeley, California

Scholar Reviewers

His Eminence Shaykh Abdalla bin Bayyah, President of the United Arab Emirates Fatwa Council and the Abu Dhabi Forum for Peace

His Eminence Dr. Shawki Ibrahim Abdel-Karim Allam, Former Grand Mufti of Egypt

His Eminence Dr. Raja Naji Makawi, Morocco's Ambassador to the Holy See

Dr. Noor-ul-Haq Qadri, Former Pakistani Minister of Religious Affairs and Interfaith Harmony

A Saga of Life and Faith:
A Retelling of the Jewish Sacred Story

Team Leader

Rabbi David Rosen, KSG, CBE, Special Advisor, Interfaith and Jewish Affairs, Abrahamic Family House, Abu Dhabi; former International Director of Interreligious Affairs, the American Jewish Committee; and former Chief Rabbi of Ireland

Main Author

Rabbi David Rosen

Advisors

Mordechai Beck, Author and artist

Russel Neiss, Educator and technologist

Rabbi Dr. Jeremy Rosen, former Chair and member of the Faculty for Comparative Religion (FVG), Antwerp, Belgium; Former Principal, Carmel College, Oxfordshire UK

Dr. Diana Lipton, Teaching Fellow Tel Aviv University; former Reader (associate professor) in Hebrew Bible and Jewish Studies, King's College London

Literary Advisor

Maria Mutch

Scholar Reviewers

Rabbi Professor Daniel Sperber, former Professor of Talmud, Chairman of the Talmud Department, President of the Jesselson Institute for Advanced Torah Studies, Bar Ilan University, Israel; head of the Bar Ilan University Press; Visiting Professor, Bernard Revel Graduate School, Yeshivah University, New York

Rabbi Shoshana Boyd Gelfand, Director of Leadership and Learning, Pears Foundation, London

Dr. Edward Kessler, MBE, Founder/President of the Woolf Institute, Cambridge, UK; Fellow, St. Edmund's College, University of Cambridge; Principal, Cambridge Theological Federation

Rabbi Jonathan Wittenberg, OBE, Senior Rabbi, Masorti Judaism, UK

The House by the Sea: A Retelling of Sikh Sacred Wisdom

The Authors

Dr. Gopinder Kaur Sagoo, Author and Interdisciplinary Researcher

Munpreet Kaur, Media and Communications Professional

Literary Advisors

Maria Mutch

Michele Rubin

Sikh Sacred Wisdom Advisor

Bhai Sahib (Professor) Mohinder Singh Ahluwalia OBE KSG, Spiritual Leader and Chair, Guru Nanak Nishkam Sewak Jatha

Scholar Reviewers

Dr. Balbinder Singh Bhogal, Professor of Religion, Sardarni Kuljit Kaur Bindra Chair in Sikh Studies, Hofstra University, New York

Guruka Singh Khalsa, retired CEO, Sikhnet

Dr. Inderjit N. Kaur, Assistant Professor of Musicology, University of Michigan, Ann Arbor, Michigan

Inni Kaur, Creative Director, Sikh Research Institute (SikhRI)

Professor Jagbir Jhutti-Johal, Professor of Sikh Studies, University of Birmingham, UK

Dr. Nikky-Guninder Kaur Singh, Crawford Family Professor and Chair of the Department of Religious Studies, Colby College, Waterville, Maine

Professor Pal Singh Ahluwalia, Vice Chancellor and President, University of the South Pacific, Oceania

Professor Eleanor Nesbitt, Professor Emerita, Education Studies, University of Warwick, UK

Dr. Pritpal Kaur Ahluwalia, Faith and Religious Education Lead (Nishkam Schools Multi-Academy Trust, UK) and Co-president, (World Council, Religions for Peace)

The Fetzer Institute

The entire Fetzer Institute supported this project in countless ways that allowed it to go forward.

The Fetzer community read, meditated with, and engaged in group reflections on the early drafts of the story "*Journeys to the Sacred: A Telling of a Shared Sacred Story.*" In addition, Fetzer Board members Rev. Jennifer Baily, Mr. Bob Boisture, Dr. Carolyn Brown, Mr. Dan Cardinali, Dr. Anna Sun, and Ms. Lynne Twist,[2] with the participation of Executive Vice President and Chief Operating Officer Jonathan Lever, engaged in a four-day retreat on the story. The reflections from the entire Fetzer community and the Board retreat were delivered to the writers, who acknowledged the value of this input as they refined the draft.

2. Two distinguished Board Emeriti, Dr. Bruce Carlson and President Emeritus Rob Lehman, are joyfully acknowledged for their active board leadership prior to their emeritus status.

In addition, the Senior Fetzer Management Team led by Executive VP/COO Jonathan Lever, and including Vice Presidents Ms. Sara Critchfield, Rev. Steven Harris, Rev. Rodney McKenzie, Dr. Anne Cullen Puente, Dr. Shakiyla Smith-Sengu, and Dr. William Vendley, provided ongoing support.[3]

Senior Program Officer Dr. Mohammed Mohammed, Executive Assistant Terri Riemland, and Dr. William Vendley served as the core team responsible for the project, and they were greatly assisted by many other Fetzer colleagues, including Mr. Roberto Lara, Ms. Jenny Smith, Ms. Dawn Hitson, and Ms. Sandy Oaks. Former Program Officer Ms. Meghan Cambell and Executive Assistant Ms. Rylee Prach are no longer with the Fetzer Institute, but they helped launch and serve the project with commitment, zeal, and skill.

Initial Consultants

Three outside consultants engaged in helpful discussions with Dr. William Vendley as he prepared a technical guideline[4] for the project before it was launched.

Dr. Claus Dierksmeier, Chair for Global Ethics, University of Tübingen

Dr. David Walsh, Professor of Politics, The Catholic University of America

Dr. Glenn Hughes (deceased), Professor Emeritus of Philosophy, St. Mary's University in Texas

Their rich, creative, and engaging exchanges are warmly acknowledged for the light they provided and the encouragement they offered.

---

3. The former Vice President of Programs, Mr. Kurian Thomas, provided strong support for this project prior to his assuming a professional post in another organization.

4. See "A Shared Sacred Story: An Overview and Technical Guide," available at www.Fetzer.org.